proletarian days

A Hippolyte Havel Reader

edited by Nathan Jun
introduction by Barry Pateman

Proletarian Days: A Hippolyte Havel Reader
© 2018 Nathan Jun, Editor
Introduction © 2018 Barry Pateman

This edition © 2018 AK Press (Chico, Edinburgh)
ISBN: 978-1-84935-328-1
E-ISBN: 978-1-84935-329-8
Library of Congress Control Number: 2018932263

AK Press   AK Press
370 Ryan Ave. #100   33 Tower St.
Chico, CA 95973   Edinburgh EH6 7BN
USA   Scotland
www.akpress.org   www.akuk.com
akpress@akpress.org   ak@akedin.demon.co.uk

The above addresses would be delighted to provide you with the
latest AK Press distribution catalog, which features books, pamphlets,
zines, and stylish apparel published and/or distributed by AK Press.
Alternatively, visit our websites for the complete catalog, latest news,
and secure ordering.

Cover and interior design by Margaret Killjoy | birdsbeforethestorm.net
Printed in the USA on acid-free, recycled paper

CONTENTS

ACKNOWLEDGMENTS

THE EDITOR WISHES TO EXPRESS HIS GRATITUDE TO Charles Weigl, Kate Khatib, and Zach Blue of AK Press for their enthusiastic support of this volume as well as their patience and helpfulness in bringing it to publication; to Jonathan Henderson and John Edgar Shockley for assisting with research during the writing of the initial draft; to Kenyon Zimmer, Tom Goyens, Dominique Miething, Allan Antliff, Jesse Cohn, Patricia Leighten, Fred Notehelfer, Peter Zarrow, John Rapp, Ed Krebs, and Ben Middleton for their assistance in demystifying several of Havel's more obscure references; and most of all to Barry Pateman for carefully reviewing the manuscript, recommending additional selections, filling in and expanding upon the annotations—in short, molding and, in general, easing the volume into its mature form.

EDITOR'S NOTE

TO DESCRIBE HIPPOLYTE HAVEL AS A PROLIFIC WRITER
would be a monumental understatement. From the
1890s until the 1940s he produced hundreds of essays,
reviews, and others writings for a variety of anarchist
publications.[1] In lieu of assembling these writings into
a single, comprehensive collection (a formidable task,
to say the least!), the present volume instead provides
a representative sample of Havel's most important and
influential work. The fact that much, if not most, of this
work appeared in Emma Goldman's *Mother Earth*—a
journal which Havel himself had a hand in creating and
to which he contributed voluminously for more than a
decade—is reflected in the range of selections chosen for
inclusion herein. In an effort to authentically capture the
idiosyncrasies of Havel's writing, the editor has faithfully reproduced these selections from the original texts,
including any errors in spelling, grammar, etc. they happen to have contained. Editorial annotations for each selection appear in numbered footnotes, the first of which
provides bibliographic information about the source

---

1   In addition to writing for *Chicagoer Arbeiter-Zeitung* (1877–
    1931), *Free Society* (1897–1904), *Regeneración* (1910–1918), *The
    Modern School* (1912–1922), *The Anarchist Soviet Bulletin* (1919–
    1920), and *Freedom* (1919), Havel also founded and edited (or
    assisted others with editing) a wide array of anarchist publications
    including *The Revolutionary Almanac* (1914), *Revolt* (1916), *The
    Social War* (1917), *Free Society* (1921–1922), *The Road to Freedom*
    (1924–1932), *Open Vistas* (1925), and *Man!* (1933–1940). His
    work also appeared occasionally in non-anarchist publications
    such as *Bruno's Weekly* (1915–1916) and Alfred Stieglitz's *Camera
    Work* (1903–1917).

material. Havel's original annotations are designated by [Havel's note] in the footnote.

Nathan Jun
Wichita Falls, Texas
October 6, 2017

INTRODUCTION

Barry Pateman

THERE ARE MANY MYTHS AND STORIES ABOUT HIPPOLYTE Havel, a good few he created and shared himself, so we might want to begin by providing a bare bones account of his life and deal with the legends another time. Hippolyte Havel (1869–1950) was born in what was then Bohemia. He was educated in Vienna and became an anarchist there, writing for the anarchist press. He was arrested in 1893 after giving a May Day speech that was considered incendiary and went to prison for eighteen months. On his release he was expelled from the city. He was arrested again in Prague (the charges are a little less certain but had something to do with being involved in a demonstration). He lived in Germany for some time, apparently still involved with the anarchist movement. Havel returned to Vienna and was arrested for ignoring his banishment. He eventually moved to London although there is no evidence, as yet, that he took any active part in the movement there. He did, though, meet Emma Goldman there while she was speaking at the "Autonomie Club" in November/December 1899, and became her companion for a short while. They were both in Paris in September 1900 attempting to attend the banned Revolutionary Congress of the Working People.

Havel accompanied Goldman to America in December 1900 and soon was in Chicago working on the anarchist communist newspaper *Free Society*. Together with other anarchists editing the paper, Havel was arrested on 6 September 1901, immediately after Leon Czolgosz had shot President McKinley. He was still part of the editorial team when they relocated the paper to New York in the Spring of 1904 and in 1906 became a key member of the *Mother Earth* editorial group. He left the group in February 1911 and visited Paris, before returning to New York in the same year. Together with Harry Kelly he went on to form the Syndicalist Educational League, based at the Ferrer Center in New York and, by this time, appears to have adopted his role as a historian of the anarchist movement. During 1910 he wrote the biographical introduction to Emma Goldman's *Anarchism and Other Essays* and in 1914 did the same for Voltairine de Cleyre's *Selected Works*—both books printed by the Mother Earth Publishing Association. The introductions provided a template for future scholars to draw on and, in general, their accuracy is detailed and impressive, even though his biography of Goldman had to be circumspect in places— especially on her involvement with Alexander Berkman's attempt on the life of Henry Clay Frick in 1892 and her part in Berkman's attempted escape from prison in 1900. Also in 1914 Havel produced the pamphlet *Bakunin* (New York: The Centenary Commemoration Committee) and edited the *Revolutionary Almanac* (New York: The Rabelais Press). In 1915 along with others he signed the *International Anarchist Manifesto On The War* which was both a powerful anti war statement urging anarchists to foment insurrection in this time of capital's war as well as a pre-emptive strike against Kropotkin and other anarchists who were calling for support for the Allies. He returned to newspaper production in 1916, editing *Revolt*, which was published in the basement of the Ferrer School in New York.

In 1917 he was one of the editors of *The Social War* and was briefly arrested for his troubles. During World War I he is only occasionally glimpsed, mainly at Stelton in New Jersey where the Modern School was based. From 1923 to 1924 he worked as a cook at the Mohegan Colony before returning to Stelton to help edit the anarchist newspaper

Road To Freedom. He would live in the Kropotkin Library
at Stelton for the next twenty-five years. In 1925 he edited
six issues of *Open Vistas* with Joseph Ishill and went on to
be active in support of Sacco and Vanzetti, visiting both of
them in jail. Havel helped Marcus Graham with his paper
Man! and throughout the twenties and thirties was heavily involved in trying to resurrect the American anarchist
movement. In 1932 he published the disappointing and
heavily plagiarized *What's Anarchism?* (Free Society Group
of Chicago and the International Group of Detroit).
Tired and ill he undertook one last lecture tour through
parts of America in 1934. The last years of his life were
bitter ones. He was physically damaged by his drinking,
probably suffering from Alzheimer's disease and he led an
increasingly fragmented existence, eventually dying in a
psychiatric hospital in New Jersey in 1950.

There is still a lot for us to learn about this man. At the
moment there are two periods of his life when he becomes
somewhat clearer to us: between 1912 and 1916 when he
was involved with the nascent New York art and literary
scene where he was friends with host of artists and writers such as Eugene O'Neill, Theodore Dreiser, and Man
Ray; and, for some time after 1924 when he lived at the
anarchist colony at Stelton where the Modern School was
based. In the first period he appears in memoirs by Mabel
Dodge, Max Eastman, Hutchins Hapgood and other writers. In these narratives Havel comes across as larger than
life, irascible, obscene, often drunk, and a master of the
clever and witty one- liner. To the children at Stelton, in
the second period, he was a small bewhiskered eccentric sit-
ting on the steps of the Kropotkin Library as they wandered
past. He appears as essentially kindly but prone to wild out-
bursts. None of these portrayals allow us to see Havel as the
contemplative and militant propagandist of the anarchist
movement that he, essentially, gave his life to.

There is one rather famous literary portrayal of him.
Eugene O' Neill, his friend from the Greenwich Village

days, portrays him as the character Hugo Kalmar in his play *The Iceman Cometh* (1939). Based on a true story of betrayal in the American anarchist movement in 1914–1915, Havel is presented as an ex-newspaper editor, a drunken sad character prone to shouting slogans and lost in an alcoholic blur. Of course there is a bitter truth there—but one wonders if such a portrayal tells us at least as much about O'Neill and his attitude to his own past radicalism as it does about Havel and the other people portrayed in the play.

How exciting it is then to have in hand a volume that offers us some of the missing Havel—the constant propagandist, the ruthless critic of capitalism, and the recorder of the lives and actions of the anarchist past. What we have here are the writings of an anarchist in his time. Of course, we can cherry pick and extract from his work phrases, or even articles, that appear to be prescient and particularly pertinent to the themes and tactics of today's struggles, but that would surely miss the point. Havel's work, here, isn't an exercise in relevance but a window into what some anarchists understood anarchism to be, both in times of optimism and despair, as well as being a reflection of *their* understanding of its place in the cultural and political forces of their time.

The selections in this volume reflect the two distinct periods that make up Havel's writing. The first period, roughly between 1906 and 1917 highlights the urgency and excitement that was so much a part of the anarchist movement in America during that time. For Havel, Emma Goldman, and others, anarchism was a critical part of the intellectual avant-garde that was breaking down all tradition and creating the structures for a new world of morality and economic fairness based on mutual aid. (Often, Goldman would title her travel reports written when on her US speaking tours, "Light and Shadows In the Life Of An Avant Garde.") There was a sense of being ahead of one's time, of being trail blazers in the journey to the new world and this excitement and sense of possibility is palpable in Havel's writings of this period. Until 1911, Havel wrote in German and Alexander Berkman would translate his writing into English and we might suggest that Berkman occasionally added his own voice to Havel's writings. Gradually, though, Havel found confidence both in his English-language voice as well as the potential of the anarchist movement. In his article "The Faith and Record of an Anarchist" (1912) he writes exuberantly of "the great spread of Anarchist ideas in the last decade." The possibility of a new world seemed almost tangible.

The second period is far less optimistic. From 1917 onwards, anarchism had to contend with the attraction of Bolshevism and the Soviet Union, which offered radicals a supposedly definitive path to a new world for humanity. The idea of state control as an agent of change colonized the consciousness of many of the anarchists and radicals who Havel had known before the outbreak of the War. Along with a few other anarchists, Havel fought an exhausting battle to critique both the power and brutality of state socialism as well as the perceived necessity of a revolutionary party to bring about social change, while still arguing for an anarchist solution to capitalism. Havel's writings reflect both this isolation and his own mental decline. His work during this period remains interesting yet there is an uncomfortable sadness for the reader as we see his intellect and writing slowly disintegrate.

There are clearly observable themes that regularly run through Havel's body of work. Before World War I there is the excitement of blending anarchism and artistic expression—especially through art and literature. Writing from Paris in 1911 Havel states, "I saw what a factor artistic expression could be in the spreading of the Gospel of Anarchy." As well as assessing the works of Dostoevsky and Jack London, his articles often review the work of long forgotten writers, now barely read, whose writing appeared to either spread this gospel or hinder its success. A stringent critic, Havel could be hard on friend or foe if he felt they strayed from the anarchist path.

We can also see in Havel's writings the importance he gave to internationalism seeing it as an essential part of anarchist practice. It is Havel who writes, in *Mother Earth* about the execution of Francisco Ferrer in 1909 as well as the culture of the Modern School that Ferrer had created. It is Havel who relentlessly covered the trial and execution of Kotoku Shusui and the Japanese anarchists in late 1910 and early 1911—the latter case appearing to haunt and bother him for the rest of his life. In both of these cases he was active in the struggle to prevent execution and in spreading the ideas of the victims of the state to the American public. There were regularly other, less vivid, examples, and we sense that this internationalism also impacted on Havel's belief in the importance of anarchist history as a learning tool for contemporary comrades. This sense of history would be even more important in the 1920s where he lamented that some younger anarchists had no idea of anarchism's past. For Havel history was the building block for today's movement and his work throughout his writing career regularly reinforced this idea. The wonderful essay "Proletarian Days" (1906) is a lovely example of how Havel saw the relationship between past and present. As his abilities declined all he had left sometimes was this sense of history that was so much a part of him. His writings (often no more than a paragraph or two) would still attempt to keep the memory of lost comrades alive and relevant.

Havel's own anarchism was, intuitively, a fierce, uncompromising and insurrectionary one but he was no major theorist and his attempt to write a primer on anarchism with the pamphlet *What's Anarchism?* in 1932 was a disaster. Such writing was simply beyond his abilities (the effects of alcohol and memory loss had been apparent to others around him for some time) and he simply plagiarized, without any acknowledgment to his sources—on a scale that is of real concern. Great chunks of the pamphlet were merely copied from the original sources and the result is an awkward hodge-podge of ideas, miles away from the clarity of his earlier pieces. Certainly it reflected his wide reading, but little else. We should remember that at this time in his life he was rather isolated, desperately attempting to keep the ideas of anarchism alive, and sometimes lacking the mental facilities to do so. It would be cruel of us to remember him for that single publication, even if it had some contemporary significance.

Havel was possessed of a rather acerbic wit and he could use it to withering effect. Like many who drank heavily, his character was sometimes defined by his behavior while drinking. All that is well and good, but we should not let any of these characteristics define him. At his best, he was a challenging and powerful writer who took on all types of repression and state cruelty and played no small part in spreading the possibilities of anarchism beyond the circles of its adherents and out into the world at large. Together with a handful of others, Hippolyte Havel helped keep anarchism alive in America during the bleak and fallow years after World War I and the Russian Revolution. Hemmed in by growing fascism on one side and Stalinism on the other, Havel's work helped maintain an anarchist presence by providing reminders of its history and offering anarchist commentary on current affairs. He had done the same in the good times before World War I and never abandoned his beliefs. Through his writings, he kept the movement alive for others to build on in the years to come. All of his life, he had fought fiercely for "the ideal" even though he had to combat his own demons to do so. His final years were harrowing; he had done all he could for the movement and could do no more either for it or for himself. Reacting to the death of Alexander Berkman in 1936 Havel wrote, "To the last hours of his life he worked for the Ideal, to which he had consecrated his life." We would be remiss in describing Havel any differently.

PROLETARIAN DAYS (1908)[1]

MARCH, THE RED MONTH, IS WITH US AGAIN.

The month of rebellion, the awakener of the down-trodden, the harbinger of hope.

The days of past grand deeds are here, their memory rousing the proletariat to a clear consciousness of their world-liberating mission, strengthening them with the fires of noblest aspirations.

And joyfully, hopefully the workers of today honor the memory of the heroes of the past, and prepare to emulate their example.

After the soldiers of liberty of 1848 had suffered defeat, the international bourgeoisie celebrated its orgies in the fond hope that the spirit of rebellion had forever been buried.[2]

Yet but a brief space intervened between 1848 and 1871. During that time the supposedly dead Socialism circled the world, and thousands of hearts beat in joyful tumult as the Commune was proclaimed at Paris.

But once more the reaction triumphed. After a heroic struggle the proletariat was defeated. Again was heard the cry, the Revolution is dead, dead and buried forever! But who can doubt that the rebels have since grown a hundredfold? The Titanic struggle of Russia is giving the lie to bourgeois assertions.

In vain we seek the names of those heroes who—on that memorable March 18, 1871— by their self-sacrifice

---

1   This essay first appeared in *Mother Earth* 3, no.1 (March 1908).

2   Havel is referring to the series of republican-led uprisings against feudalism and monarchy that swept across Europe in 1848. Principal areas included the Italian states, the German states, and France.

ensured the triumph of the proletariat.[3] Obscure were they; nameless men, women, and children of the streets: inspired by the solemn moment, they ushered in the revolutionary tide. It overflowed Paris, arousing an enthusiasm felt far beyond the confines of France. It still lives and bursts into flames whenever the cry is heard, *Vive la Commune!*

The obscure, the nameless! They are the true heroes of history. We know no books they have written. Not authors, nor orators they. Yet how lifelike they tower before our mental eye in all the glory of their self-sacrifice, their noble passion and immortality. We see them, these brave unknown, in the thick of combat, their eyes aflame, their fists clenched. We hear their songs of battle, witness their inspiring devotion. We behold them dying, serenely joyous, the devoted martyrs of a noble cause.

Countless times duped, deprived of the fruits of their triumph, again we see them enter the arena. Restlessly they storm forward, ever forward!

An unbroken thread of red runs through proletarian history, from the ancient slave revolts and peasant wars of feudal days, to the uprisings of the proletariat in 1792, 1830, 1848, 1871, down to the heroic struggle of the Russian people of our own time.[4]

---

3 The Paris Commune was a short-lived revolutionary socialist government that seized power in Paris on 18 March 1871 and ruled for approximately ten days before being violently suppressed by the French army on May 28.

4 Havel is referring, respectively, to the French Revolution (1792), the July Revolution (1830), the Revolutions of 1848, the Paris Commune (1871), and the Russian Revolution (1905). The French Revolution, as is well known, resulted in the abolition of the monarchy and the installation of a democratic republic. This First French Republic lasted until 1799, when it was overthrown in a *coup d'etat* by Napoleon Bonaparte. About thirty years later, the July Revolution resulted in the overthrow of the House of

It is an uninterrupted warfare; and we of this generation shall continue the fight till the victory of the downtrodden is complete.

The men and women of fame are the meteors momentarily lighting up the horizon, then fading away into the night of the past. But the nameless do not vanish. They are like the phoenix, eternally resurrected in the ashes of his fiery death. We know that we do not hope in vain when we rest in them our faith for the future.

* * *

We live in pregnant days. Dark clouds are gathering; all signs portend the coming struggle.

Our bourgeoisie has grown to look upon the workingman as its mere slave, incapable of independent thought or action. How horrified they feel when the masses evidence by demonstrations that they have awakened to self-assertion and refuse to starve.

A labor demonstration serves to remind the rulers of the misery suffered by the disinterested. It clarifies their vision to threatening danger; it points to the terrible chasm yawning before them.

That they may not be continually reminded of their crimes against the proletariat, the exploiters have exiled them into obscure alleys and barrack tenements. There poverty lives apart. It is not suffered to obtrude its misery upon the rich, to the possible detriment of their digestion. There it does not exist for the bourgeois. It is to him a strange land.

Bourbon, which had been restored to the throne in 1814, and the installation of a constitutional monarchy under Louis Phillipe I of the House of Orléans. The Russian Revolution of 1905, which served as a precursor to the Bolshevik Revolution in 1917, implemented a limited constitutional monarchy and the creation of a Russian republic.

But a demonstration brings the proletariat to the palaces. The rulers and exploiters are overcome by fear and horror. They see, like Belshazzar of old, the handwriting on the wall.[5]

History repeats itself. These are our March days.

---

5   Belshazzar was a sixth century BCE Babylonian prince who is described as the King of Babylon in the biblical Book of Daniel. In the story to which Havel refers (Daniel 5:1–31), Belshazzar is hosting a banquet when his guests begin to desecrate various sacred vessels that had been taken during the pillaging of the Temple in Jerusalem. At this point a supernatural message appears on the wall reading "*Mene, mene, tequel, upharsin*"—which Daniel interprets as "you have been weighed in the scales and found wanting." That same night the Persians sack the city and Belshazzar is killed. The idiomatic expression "seeing the writing on the wall" refers to perceiving the imminence of a negative event.

THE CAREER OF A JOURNALIST: A CONFESSION (1908)[1]

OURS IS AN ERA OF DEEP SOCIAL UNREST; THE FINEST minds and souls are filled with it; the social conscience will no longer be silenced.

The much-dreaded class of muckrakers is steadily growing.[2] Their criticism stops short at nothing, not even the most cherished institutions. In fine, we are witnessing the most radical transvaluation of all values.[3]

---

1   "The Career of a Journalist" appeared in *Mother Earth* 3, no. 6 (August 1908). On the surface, "The Career of a Journalist" appears to be little more than a review of a mediocre and long-forgotten book. In fact, it is one of Havel's most important early contributions, as it prefigures later radical critiques of the media such as Sinclair's *The Brass Check* (1919) and Chomsky and Herman's *Manufacturing Consent* (1988).

2   "Muckrakers" are reform-oriented investigative journalists who attempted to expose the abuses of government, business, and other powerful institutions.

3   "Transvaluation of all values"—"*Unwertung aller Werte*," a favorite expression of Havel's which he borrows from Nietzsche. The concept of "transvaluing values" is discussed in section 4 of *Beyond Good and Evil*, sections 1–7 of *The Antichrist*, and the Preface of *On the Genealogy of Morality*. In Havel's usage it refers to a critique or transformation of conventional values. Nietzsche's own account, in contrast, emphasizes positively embracing natural drives and instincts and affirming and celebrating life. For a similar use of the phrase, see Emma Goldman, *Victims of Morality* (New York: Mother Earth Publishing Company, 1913).

One institution, however, our social critics have hitherto spared. Journalism, the disgrace of our age, the most shady profession of civilization, they dared not touch. The press, the supposed harbinger of truth, the bearer of culture, the teacher and moral guide of the people, was ever considered unassailable.

At last one came to the front who would not halt before the "sacred" shrine; one who found the necessary courage to tear the veil from the treacherous face of the press, so that the beguiled public may see, as it has never seen before, journalism at work.

Mr. William Salisbury, with his work, *The Career of a Journalist*,[4] has rendered society a great service by his graphic and able portrayal of the corruption and degradation of the American press. Having worked on the leading papers of New York, Chicago, and Kansas City for more than nine years, he is well equipped with the necessary experience to substantiate his charges.

Radical critics have ever maintained that journalism under the capitalistic regime has degenerated into a trade that condemns its votaries to mental prostitution. It is, therefore, encouraging, indeed, to find these contentions verified by one who speaks from personal experience.

And what are Mr. Salisbury's experiences? Simply this: Every newspaper man today is under the lash of the political shade and business interests of his paper. Personality, intelligence, judgment, conscientiousness, must make room for the holiest of all Trinities, Profit, Sensation, Lies. Indeed, the highest salaried editor, down to the obscurest penny-a-liner, must bend his knee before that divine power. Thus the press represents a swamp that chokes the mental individuality of its writers, while the readers are made to content themselves with the slimy reflex of our decaying social conditions.

But let the author speak:

---

4   [Havel's note] E.W. Dodge & Co., New York.

I engaged in journalism with the belief that I was entering the noblest of professions. I found American journalism mainly a joke—a hideous joke, it is true, but still a joke—and the joke is on me, and on the immense majority of the American public...

Journalism in America is, in nearly every case, but a business to newspaper owners and managers, and a trade to writers and editors...

No journalist has any rights which owners or business managers are bound to respect, except in the almost unknown case of the journalist, being himself the owner...

To engage in American journalism, the first requisite is lack of individuality; and beyond a certain point, the more one knows, and the higher his aims and purposes, the less are his chances of keeping on the payroll—and the less should be his desire to stay on it...

Anybody with enough money can own a great newspaper in America. The men at the head of railroad companies, of oil companies, of steamship lines, and of other large interests, including trade combinations known as trusts, are also owners of newspapers, secretly or openly...

The owners and managers of newspapers are simply businessmen and politicians. Their ideal of success is moneymaking...

Editors, reporters, and correspondents are but puppets on strings the other ends of which are in the hands of these men. The employees with less than one-half dozen exceptions in all America, have no more individuality than have department store workers...

When I became able to do really important work—when, with added ability as a writer, I had acquired opinions and ideas worth expressing, I grew less valuable to my masters. What they wanted from me was what they want, and what they get, from other journalists. And what I was, other American journalists are, and must be, in greater or less degree. I was a Paul Pry, a tattler, a crime-and-scandal-monger, a daily Boswell to anyone and everyone—all to promote the business interests of others. I realize, now, though I could only occasionally, and vaguely, realize it then, that at times I was worse than all this—in politics I was a veritable Hessian of the press, even a hired assassin of the character, striking from the dark, or from behind the mask of journalistic seal for public welfare—all to promote the political interests of others. At other times I was an aid to piracy, helping to hold up commercial enterprises, and firing broadsides of abuse until the booty was won. Often I had to attack men and measures that I secretly longed to champion. On occasions, however, when it was not unprofitable to my masters, I favored good laws and good men.[5]

A horrible picture, indeed; yet one conversant with conditions will not find it overdrawn.

---

5   Salisbury, pp. 518–522.

The Career of a Journalist will prove particularly interesting to those who believe in "Anarchist conspiracies."[6] It will tell them where and how these conspiracies are manufactured and launched upon an unsuspecting public. Thus an "old-timer" to our author:

> This Anarchist business reminds me of the hot times in the old days. I saw the bodies piled up after the Haymarket affair, and it was a fierce sight, all right. There was plenty to write about for weeks then. But after the arrests and trials, excitement died down for a while, and in the spell before the hanging we had to do some thinking to keep the dear public interested. All kinds of rumors were cooked up, and every little gathering of harmless cranks was told about as a breeding place for terrible plots. We had the people believing that Anarchists were on the way from this town to blow up every ruler in Christendom... The best faking in the Anarchist days—the most artistic—was done by Dickson, of the old *Herald*. We were all fakers in those days, I think, but Dickson had the whole bunch of us beaten for a while.

This old recipe seems to be in operation up to the present day.

---

6   In 1908, several crimes occurred in the United States that were attributed by the press to anarchist conspiracies. These included the murder of Catholic priest Leo Heinrichs in Denver (February), the murder of Jewish immigrant Lazarus Averbuch in Chicago (March), and the Union Square bombing in New York (also March). The press frequently insisted that Emma Goldman was the principal instigator of these and other incidents.

The "ideal mission" of journalism is a worn-out myth, believed only by debutantes. Stupidity, ignorance, and dishonesty of newspapers are not only the exception; they are the rule. The cause of this, however, the author failed to grasp. The corruption of the press in its present form is a result of capitalistic development. The age of the journalistic reign of a Bryant, Greeley, Raymond, Storey, Dana, and Medill is no more.[7] The time when Bayard Taylor earned his laurels as correspondent, too, belongs to the past.[8] It is sentimental and impractical to long for the era of heroic American journalism.

Ours is the era of Spreckles, Ochs, Pulitzer, Lawson, Kohlsaat, Hearst, and Rosewater, and the Creelmans and Brandenburgs are the worthy exponents of this modern journalism.[9]

---

7   Havel is referring to William Cullen Bryant (1794–1878), poet and long-time editor of *The New York Evening Post*; Horace Greeley (1811–1872), founder and editor of *The New York Tribune*; Henry Jarvis Raymond (1820–1869), founder of *The New York Times*; Wilbur F. Storey (1819–1884), editor of *The Chicago Times*; Charles Anderson Dana (1819–1897), editor of *The New York Sun*; and Joseph Medill (1823–1899), editor of *The Chicago Tribune*, respectively. Dana's work *Proudhon and His Bank Of The People* had been published by the anarchist Benjamin Tucker in 1896.

8   Bayard Taylor (1825–1878) was a renowned poet, literary critic, and travel writer. His popular dispatches from abroad were published in newspapers such as *The New York Tribune*, *The United States Gazette*, and *The Saturday Evening Post*.

9   Havel is referring to various newspaper magnates. John D. Spreckels (1873–1926) was a transportation and real estate tycoon and owner of *The Union-Tribune* (San Diego); Adolph Ochs (1858–1935) was owner of *The New York Times*; Joseph Pulitzer (1847–1911) was publisher of *The St. Louis Dispatch* and *The New York World*; Victor Lawson (1850–1925) was editor of *The Chicago Daily News*; Herman Henry Kolhsaat (1853–1924) was

When the nineteenth century dawned there were but one hundred and fifty journals of all sorts in the new American Republic. Less than two score were dailies. They were supported mainly subscriptions. Now there are more than two thousand three hundred dailies, over fifteen thousand weeklies, and five hundred semi-weekly newspapers in the country. This exceeds half the total number in the world. All these newspapers are maintained principally by advertising.

The United States census of 1900 showed that almost ninety-six million dollars was the sum spent for advertising- in newspapers and periodicals, principally in newspapers; in that year the subscriptions and sales amounted to seventy-six millions. The disproportion between the receipts for advertising and those for subscription was much more on the side of the former in the case of newspapers than in that of the periodicals, since the latter charge several times as much per copy as the newspapers do.

This gigantic change is thus ably characterized by an independent journalist:

> Our great newspapers were once controlled
> by their editors, who, whatever their faults,
> were moved by journalistic impulses.
> Those were the days of Greeley, Bennett,
> and Raymond.[10] Then came the era of the

---

an entrepreneur and owner of *The Chicago Record Herald*; William Randolph Hearst (1863–1951) was founder of the Hearst media empire, which published dozens of newspapers and periodicals across the United States; Edward Rosewater (1841–1906) was editor of *The Omaha Bee*; and James Creelman (1859–1915) and Earl Broughton Brandenburg (1876–1963) were both notorious "yellow journalists" of the era. See W. Joseph Campbell, *Yellow Journalism* (Westport, CT: Greenwood Press, 2003).

10   James Bennett, Sr. (1795–1872) was the founder, editor, and publisher of *The New York Herald*.

counting room, when the editor had to subordinate the interests of his readers to the demands of the advertising patrons. Yet the impulse was journalistic—at least to this extent, that the interest of the paper as a whole was the governing consideration. But now we have come upon a time when the interest of the paper is treated as second to other interests in which its more or less anonymous owners are concerned So long as those interests are prospered by the misuse of the paper, the interests of the paper as an independent enterprise are ignored. As the counting room dethroned the editor, so collateral interests of owners have dethroned both.... And as this process has gone on, a radical change has taken place in journalistic ideals. In the editorial era, partisanship gave color to editorials, but they were the honest expressions of their writers—except under Bennett, who taught his editorial writers to be automatons; and the news reports in all papers were, by journalistic ethics, required to be truthful. In the counting room era, the editorials were deceptive, but the ideal that the news should he true still had vogue. The natural effect upon the public mind was a popular aversion to editorials, but a childlike acceptance of news reports. Editorials are now intended to be deceptive, but they count for little, and it is on the news reports that the owner relies for deceiving his readers.[11]

11 Louis Post, "Degraded Newspapers," *The Public* 10 (November 2, 1907), p. 724.

Faith in, and reliance upon, the authenticity of even the news reports are, happily, on the decline. *The Career of a Journalist* will surely contribute to the demolition of that false and vicious idol.

Mr. William Marion Reedy, the able editor of the *St. Louis Mirror*, is quite right when he says: "The independence of the press is a fake... I am inclined to believe that the time is about here when we shall have to return to the day of the pamphlet, if we are to have any such thing as free utterance of heretical opinion."[12]

---

12 William Marion Reedy (1862–1920), "The Myth of a Free Press," reprinted in *The Fra* (August 1909), pp. 122–128:127. Reedy would go on to write a very positive appreciation of Emma Goldman in "Emma Goldman: The Daughter of the Dream," *St. Louis Mirror* (November 5, 1908).

RUSSIA'S MESSAGE (1908)[1]

THE RUSSIAN REVOLUTION IS BUT IN THE MAKING. A complete and thorough estimate of its world-import is reserved for the future chroniclers of history. Meanwhile we must content ourselves with gathering loosely strewn material, to sift the fragments and documents.

The influence which this stupendous drama has exerted upon the Russian people, the revolutionary movement of the world, and especially upon the Oriental nations is already apparent. Its far-reaching power, however, will make itself felt later. At present we are still in the midst of the battle, our finger upon the pulse of the movement,

The numerous works on Russian affairs that have recently flooded the market are naught but impressionistic sketches superficially drawn by journalistic authors. Some are, no doubt, quite interesting and instructive; not, however, of lasting import. A book of exceptional value is Mr. William English Walling's work, *Russia's Message: The True World Import of the Revolution*, published by Doubleday, Page & Co.[2]

---

1   This essay first appeared in *Mother Earth* 3, no. 7 (September 1908). Like many anarchists, Havel was very enthusiastic about the Russian Revolution of 1905. As the text makes clear, however, he was deeply suspicious of and hostile to the Russian Marxists from the beginning—a view that only sharpened in the aftermath of the October Revolution in 1917.

2   William English Walling (1877–1936) was an American trade unionist and socialist and co-founder of the American Civil Liberties Union. Walling's account is based on his experiences of living in Russia between 1905 and 1907. After the racist violence in Springfield, Illinois in August 1908, Walling published an article entitled "Race War In The North" that was instrumental in

Thorough understanding of a great struggle, full knowledge of its underlying principles, and deep sympathy with Russia's heroic champions make Mr. Walling's effort a standard work on the Russian Revolution.

Two striking features of this book deserve special mention: the brilliant characterization of the Russian peasant, hitherto so cruelly misrepresented and misunderstood, and the emphasis of the influence of the Russian Revolution upon the entire civilized world.

The author shows in a most convincing manner that Russia conveys to the world a vital message, an attempt to solve an all-absorbing problem: the reorganization of human society.

The Revolution embodies not merely Russian issues; its force is also directed against the financial powers of the world. A speedy victory is therefore not so easily achieved, much as all justice-loving people may desire it.

Indeed, we stand before a long and desperate battle, a battle of greater dimensions than the French Revolution, one that will truly justify the significant remark of Carlyle, "the account day of a thousand years."[3]

The spirit of Tsarism is rampant in all countries, but more than anywhere in our own Republic. Mr. Walling must have realized that when he dedicated his work to the men and women who in all walks of life are contending against the forces that are trying to introduce into America the despotism and class-rule of eastern Europe; to all those who, in the traditional revolutionary American spirit, are leading our country against all the reactionary tendencies

---

the founding of the National Association for the Advancement of Colored People (NAACP).

3   "All this (for be sure no falsehood perishes, but is as seed sown out to grow) has been storing itself for thousands of years; and now the account-day has come." Thomas Carlyle (1795–1881), *The French Revolution*, ed. T. Dwight, et al. (New York: Colonial Press, 1899 [1837]), pp. 51–52.

prevailing in politics, morality, education, literature, and science, to its great, democratic and social world-destiny,

The Russian Revolution has filled the proletariat of the world with new hope. The opportunistic coolie-tactics of the Neo-Marxists had extinguished the revolutionary fire of a large portion of the working class.[4] Revolutionists have been ridiculed as Utopians, or scorned as ignoramuses. The idea of armed insurrections has been discarded as out of date, and the General Strike declared to be general nonsense.

The events in Russia have proved the absurdity of our Marxian pseudo-scientists.[5]

In October, 1905, the workers of Russia gave to the world an example of the General Strike upon a national basis which resulted in the renowned Manifesto,[6] the first guarantee of liberty ever wrenched from the Tsars. When the bloody Nicholas betrayed the trust of his people, an armed insurrection resulted. And in one week, justly says Mr. Walling, were belied the theories of a whole generation of revolutionary but timid European Socialists, and a century of military dogmas on the hopelessness of insurrection.

A great lesson remains fixed in the minds of all the revolutionists, especially of the workingmen—the possible success of guerilla tactics in a modern city.

---

4   Havel is referring to social-democratic and revisionist Marxists such as Eduard Bernstein (1850–1932) and Jean Jaurès (1859–1914). By "coolie-tactics," he means manipulating the working classes for gains in elections and party politics more generally.

5   Presumably Havel has in mind the historical-materialist notion that full capitalist development is a necessary condition for communist revolution.

6   "The Manifesto on the Improvement of State Order" was issued by Tsar Nicholas II on October 17, 1905 in response to the Revolution. The Manifesto granted a broad range of civil rights and liberties, including freedom of speech, association, assembly, religion, and the press.

In Moscow the revolutionaries succeeded with a little body of armed men, far inferior numerically to the army to which they were opposed, in holding several days large portions of the city. Their success was due to the enthusiastic support of the population.

Both friends and foes have painted the Russian *moujik*,[7] representing by far the largest proportion of the Russian people, in a highly prejudiced manner. It is, therefore, refreshing indeed to find a non-Russian who has shown us the unfortunate victim of terrible abuse as he really is.

That alone marks the true and earnest champion of a people.

Thanks to Mr. Walling, the English-reading public will see at last that the Russian peasant is neither a saint-worshipping cretin brutalized by drink, nor a Jew-baiter adoring the "Little Father,"[8] nor even an incurable sectarian. On the contrary, he is a good-natured being, with a deep social spirit, a character we have learned to love through the portraitures of Turgenev and Tolstoy.[9] The myth of his dull submission, too, has been dispelled. We know now that the *moujik* is an untiring rebel whose wonderful heroism in the battle against his vampires is

---

7   *Moujik* (also *muzhik*)—Russian peasant.

8   "Little Father"—i.e., the Tsar.

9   Ivan Turgenev (1818–1883) was a Russian novelist and playwright. Leo Nikolayevich Tolstoy (1828–1920), was a Russian novelist and essayist who espoused Christian anarchism, pacifism, nonviolence, and voluntary simplicity. Both writers tend to romanticize the Russian *muzhik* in their works (Tolstoy even took to dressing like a peasant in old age.) See, for example, Turgenev's short story collection *A Sportsman's Sketches* (1852) and Tolstoy's *The Cossacks* (1863) and *Anna Karenina* (1877). Turgenev was a friend of Kropotkin's who rated his work very highly. The main character in Turgenev's first novel (*Rudin*, published in 1856) was based on Mikhail Bakunin.

of centuries' duration. That he is absolutely essential to a free Russia has been recognized by all Revolutionists, excepting such political wiseacres as Lenin and Plekhanov.[10] Because of that, the party of the Revolutionary Socialists, as well as the Anarchists, have directed their main energies to the awakening of the peasant.

The Russian peasantry has always been an eminently rebellious people, and the tradition of rebellion has been revered and kept alive for hundreds of years. Over two centuries ago, almost immediately after the institution of serfdom, occurred the revolt of Stenka Razin, in which millions of peasants took part.[11]

---

10 During the Revolution the Russian Social Democratic Labour Party split into two factions—the hard-line Bolsheviks ("majority") and the moderate Mensheviks ("minority"). Vladimir Ilyich Lenin (1870–1924) was the leader of the former, while Georgi Plekhanov (1856–1918), who had helped found the RSDLP, sided with the latter. Havel's claim is somewhat misleading here. Plekhanov did, in fact, argue that "[t]he proletariat and the 'muzhik' are political antipodes. The historic role of the proletariat is as revolutionary as the historic role of the 'muzhik' is conservative. The muzhiks have been the support of oriental despotism for thousands of years. In a comparatively short space of time, the proletariat has shaken the 'foundations' of West European society" ("The Tasks of Social Democrats in the Famine, 1891, *Works*, vol. 3, Moscow: Progress Publishers, 1976, pp. 382–383). Unlike Plekhanov, who favored an alliance between the proletariat and the bourgeoisie against the autocracy, Lenin believed in the revolutionary potential of the peasants in association with the industrial proletariat. See Lenin, "Two Tactics of Social Democracy in the Democratic Revolution" [1905], *Works*, vol. 9 (Moscow: Progress Publishing, 1977), p. 112; "Social-Democracy's Attitude Towards the Peasant Movement" [1905], *op. cit.*, pp. 230–239; and "Socialism and the Peasantry" [1905], *op. cit.*, pp. 307–315.

11 Stenka Razin (1630–1671) was a Cossack rebel who led a peasant uprising in southern Russia in 1670.

More than a hundred years ago half of peasant Russia was infected with the rebellion of the serfs against their masters, under the leadership of Pougatchev.[12] In this rebellion hundreds of thousands of peasants died, apparently in vain, for freedom. But neither the authorities nor the peasants have ever forgotten the event. Stenka Razin and Pougatchev are still the most popular heroes.

The great emancipation of the serfs was accomplished neither from philanthropic motives nor from economic considerations, but from a highly justified fear of immediate revolution.[13]

The first Duma[14] was dissolved, not on account of the revolutionary political measures or the radical social reforms of the constitutional majority, but because the peasant deputies were making ominous preparations for social revolution. All government changes since the fall of 1905, along with innumerable false promises of changes, have been aimed at the growing peasant discontent. All real concessions were made during or after the time of hundreds of armed peasant revolts.

And what is the outcome? The peasants feel that they have forced the government to terms. They are not grateful as they would have been had the changes been freely granted. They arc only crying for more. Nothing short of full social and economic freedom will satisfy them.

The Russian upheaval is a conscious social movement, and this is why it may develop into the most portentous

---

12 Yemelyan Pugachev (1742–1775) was the leader of the Cossack rebellion of 1774–1775. Both he and Razin had a profound influence on anarchists and other radicals. Berkman, for example, gives high praise to Razin in his *Prison Memoirs of An Anarchist* (New York: Mother Earth Publishing Association, 1912), pp. 38, 490.

13 The serfs were liberated in 1861 by Tsar Alexander II. Havel's explanation of this event, as well as the others that follow it, tends to hyperbolize the power of the peasants' revolutionary fervor.

14 The Russian parliament.

historic event. Like former revolutions and civil wars in Europe and America, it claims for the citizens the political rights of men. But unlike any preceding national cataclysm, it insists on social as well as political rights, on economic equality, the right of every man to as much land as he can till, and of no man to more, and on the right of all the people to all the land for all time.

This evolutionary process is in the direction of Anarchist Communism, as can easily be gathered from the interviews the author of *Russia's Message* has had with many distinguished Russian thinkers.[15] It is therefore to be regretted that Mr. Walling uses, in a certain passage, the term Anarchy in the popular sense, that of chaos. A litterateur of his caliber, one who is undoubtedly conversant with the philosophy of Anarchism, should never stoop to such misrepresentation.

Three giant names, Bakunin, Kropotkin, and Tolstoy, point the way to liberation: Bakunin as organizer, Kropotkin as the scientific expounder, and Tolstoy as the awakener of the social consciousness.[16]

---

15   Walling's interviewees include Tolstoy, Gorky, and Lenin.

16   Mikhail Alexandrovich Bakunin (1814–1876) was a Russian revolutionary and philosopher. Never a systematic thinker, Bakunin's principal contributions to the nineteenth-century anarchist movement were made as a militant and an activist rather than as a theoretician (although his book *God and the State*, published in 1882, did have a seminal impact on the development of anarchism in Europe and the United States). For example, Bakunin was an important figure in the early days of the First International and had a hand in organizing several (ultimately abortive) armed uprisings in France, Italy, and elsewhere. Peter Alexeyevich Kropotkin (1842–1921) was a Russian zoologist, evolutionary biologist, geographer, philosopher, and revolutionary who wrote extensively on anarchist-communism. Compared to Bakunin, Kropotkin's contributions to the movement were mostly—though by no means exclusively—intellectual in nature.

Russia's Message will render important service to the revolutionary movement of Russia, as well as that of the entire world. It is to be hoped that this work may receive the recognition it merits so well.

In his writings, he frequently draws upon the insights of the empirical sciences to make the case for anarchism. See, for example, his article on anarchism in the eleventh edition of *Encyclopedia Brittanica* (1911).

LITERATURE: ITS INFLUENCE UPON SOCIAL LIFE (1908)[1]

IMPORTANT CHANGES IN THE LIFE OF A PEOPLE FIND THEIR most decisive expression in contemporary art. The work of the artist, the composer, the painter, the sculptor, or the writer mirrors the reflex of the various struggles, hopes, and aspirations of our social life.

The creative artist has the deepest appreciation of the tendencies of his time. He is therefore the fittest exponent of new ideals, the true herald of the coming reconstruction; indeed, he is the prophet of the future social order.

The fiercer the combat between the old and the new worlds, the more intensely will their ideals find expression in the literature of the time.

We, too, the children of the twentieth century, have our problem—probably the greatest problem mankind has ever been confronted with. To find a similar yearning in all social ranks for the change of things one must turn to the time of the Reformation, and with the most valiant rebel of that period, Ulrich von Hutten, we may joyously proclaim: "Ours is the most glorious era to live in!"[2]

---

1   This essay first appeared in *Mother Earth* 3, no. 8 (October 1908). Despite his self-described working class sympathies, Havel was a bibliophile, an art aficionado, and a self-styled bohemian who associated with creative people for most of his adult life. "Literature: Its Influence Upon Social Life" is one of the first of many instances in which Havel declares a natural affinity between art and revolutionary politics; this becomes a recurrent theme in his writing. The first two or three paragraphs appear to be indebted to Kropotkin's "Appeal to the Young" (1880).

2   Ulrich von Hutten (1488–1523) was a German scholar and poet.

As in previous times of social reconstruction, it is the discontented intellectuals who are the leading spirits in the struggle. Old ideals no longer satisfy them. The existing injustice arouses their indignation. Thus the literary rebel is the most pronounced type. True, he is still denounced and attacked by the philistine pillars of society. Nevertheless he has achieved the greatest success. Read by everybody, he becomes the admonisher and the awakener. The growing number of rebels among modern writers of this country is certainly a good omen for the progress of the American people. The considerable output of radical books is unquestionable proof of the great social unrest and leavening.

* * *

Together, a social critique of considerable merit by Robert Herrick[3] (Macmillan Co., New York), treats of a vital problem—modern marriage. The background of the theme is to be found in the recent crisis which has acted like a cloudburst upon our industrial and financial world. Mr. Herrick shows how middle-class marriage, largely based upon monetary considerations, inevitably proves a failure and ends in the courts, while the

---

He is regarded as a "rebel" for his pursuit of knowledge in the face of Church-sponsored repression as well as his militant advocacy of the Protestant Reformation. The actual quotation is "*O saeculum! O litterae! Juvat vivere, etsi quiescere nondum juvat*" ("O era! O learning! It is a joy to live, though not yet to rest"); Letter to Willibald Perckheimer (*Ad Bilib. Perckheimer Epistola*), 1518, in *Opera quae extant omnia*, vol. 3, ed. Ernst Münch (Sumtibus J.G. Reimer, 1823), p. 100.

3   Robert Herrick (1868–1938) was an American novelist and literature professor at the University of Chicago. Herrick published several works in a social realist vein that call attention to the miseries and depredation of the working classes in industrial society.

offspring of these unions grow into heartless and soulless parasites.

The few solitary souls of independent mind in this social stratum, attempting to live their own lives, are soon pushed to the wall, made impossible by their stifling philistine surroundings.

Together is a fine psychological study of the pressing problem of the sexes; but the solution proposed therein is in no way satisfactory.

Mr. Herrick's ideal of the strong, self-reliant man, as personified in Dr. Ranault, would soon suffer shipwreck and fall back into the fangs of our insatiable social monster. The author's conception of a free union entered into by free men and women, a union that is to replace modern marriage with all its degrading influences, one that is to bring joy and fellowship, is very beautiful; but under our present social and economic inequality such unions must forever remain the privilege of the very few.

The problem of the sexes is too closely related to other social problems; its solution lies in entire social regeneration.[4] Men and women of a free society will indeed be able to lead their own lives, to be truly free and find one another without hindrance.

However, that does not detract from the value of Mr. Herrick's effort. Both for its able and bold criticism, as well as on account of the author's social position, it cannot but act as a potent influence in stirring mental inertia and moral laziness.

* * *

---

4   Havel's position here—i.e., that single-issue approaches to "the problem of the sexes" are short-sighted and counterproductive—is echoed by other anarchist writers of the period. Emma Goldman, for example, adopts a similar perspective in her essays on suffrage and women's emancipation, *inter alia*, in *Anarchism and Other Essays* (New York: Mother Earth Publishing Association, 1910).

Moneychangers, Upton Sinclair's second volume of his Trilogy[5] (B. W. Dodge & Co., New York), is by no means an artistic success. One seeks in vain for a single character that awakens the sympathy or even the interest of the reader. He will find nothing but stilted figures without life or psychological definiteness. The author was probably seized by the maddening whirlwind of our capitalist world and therefore feels in duty bound to turn out a new book every three months. Naturally one cannot expect thoroughness from hasty work. Maybe Mr. Sinclair doesn't care for artistic quality; he prefers the role of the agitator, his motto being, *J'accuse*. A very commendable role, indeed. But, if it is to strike deep, it ought not to lack form, still less exclude logic.

Moneychangers depicts the manipulations of Messrs. Harriman, Belmont, Rockefeller, Frick, and consorts, the savage attack of these financial hyenas upon the lesser members in the family of beasts.[6] It treats of the collapse of our alleged prosperity, built upon swindle, fraud, and fictitious values; a prosperity that fattened upon the blood and sweat of the masses. All this the author pictures in bold lines; but the effect is completely lost because of the improbable cause of this industrial debacle, which Mr. Sinclair tells us is the passion for a woman on the part of one of the trustocrats. No doubt these worthy gentlemen are willing to go to any extent which their money can purchase. Still, our financial arrangements are a trifle too complicated to be brought to a crisis by such a flimsy cause.

---

5   Upton Sinclair (1878–1968) was a political activist and a leading figure in the social realist movement in literature. The first volume of the trilogy, *Metropolis*, was published in 1908. The third, a play entitled *The Machine*, was published in 1912.

6   E.H. Harriman (1848–1909), August Belmont, Jr. (1853–1924), John D. Rockefeller (1839–1937), and Henry Clay Frick (1849–1919) were powerful industrialists and financiers of the era.

The Jungle was not merely a great agitative stroke; it was equally so literary.[7] It is to be regretted that Mr. Sinclair's succeeding works show evident signs of deterioration.

---

7   *The Jungle*, which is arguably Sinclair's most famous and important work, was published in 1906. It concerns the plight of Lithuanian meatpackers working in the Chicago stockyards.

A REMINISCENCE (1908)[1]

> But the President has paid dear for his White
> Home. It has commonly cost him all his
> peace, and the best of his manly attributes.
> To preserve for a short time so conspicuous
> an appearance before the world, he is content
> to eat dust, before the real masters who stand
> erect behind the throne.
> —Ralph Waldo Emerson[2]

It was a glorious time. The twentieth century was ushered in under the most favorable auspices. The era of prosperity reached its highest zenith, and the sons of the Plymouth Fathers reveled in ecstasy and superfluity.

Uncle Mark Hanna, the great Alonzo, was at the helm of the American commonwealth.[3] He had splendidly organized the machinery of government. Calmly and quietly he now attended to the business affairs of plutocracy.

The parts were well distributed. Aldrich, Quay, Spooner, Foraker, Platt, and Dryden were in the inner

---

1 This essay was published in *Mother Earth* 3, no. 8 (October 1908) as an acknowledgment of the seventh anniversary of the execution of Leon Czolgosz, which took place on October 29, 1901.

2 "Compensation," in *Works of Ralph Waldo Emerson*, vol. 2 (London: Macmillan & Co., 1883), p. 80.

3 Mark Alonzo Hanna (1837–1904) was a businessman and politician who managed William McKinley's president campaigns in 1896 and 1900. He was widely accused of manipulating McKinley from behind the scenes—a charge which Havel alludes to by calling him "Uncle Mark Hanna."

circle.[4] The Honorable Henry Cabot Lodge represented the dignity of the statesmen.[5] Old Senator Hoar played the incorruptible tribune of the people.[6] And the irrepressible rogue, Chauncey M. Depew, acted as drummer at public functions, while Elkins, Pettus, Morgan, Bailey, and consorts formed the chorus.[7]

The presidential chair was occupied by puritanical sanctimony—his Excellency William McKinley. To preserve for a short time so conspicuous an appearance before the world, he was content to eat the dust before the real masters who stood erect behind the throne.[8]

In the background the heir presumptive was a-hunting. And someone was busy fishing in muddy waters—Abner McKinley, the worthy brother of William. He had charge of affairs that could not be reconciled with the dignity of the President.[9]

---

4   Havel is referring, respectively, to Nelson Aldrich (1841–1915); Matthew Quay (1833–1904); John Coit Spooner (1843–1919); Joseph Foraker (1846–1917); Thomas Collier Platt (1833–1910); and John Dryden (1839–1911)—all of whom were prominent Republican "bosses" in the U.S. Congress.

5   Henry Cabot Lodge (1850–1924) was a senator from Massachusetts and leading congressional Republican.

6   George Frisbie Hoar (1826–1904) was a Republican senator from Massachusetts. Hoar earned a reputation for fighting political corruption.

7   In addition to Depew (1834–1928), a Republican senator and one-time governor of New York, Havel is referring, respectively, to Stephen Benton Elkins (1841–1911); John Tyler Morgan (1824–1907); Edmund Pettus (1821–1907); and Joseph Bailey (1862–1929)—all southern congressmen and, with the exception of Elkins, all Democrats. Havel is calling attention to their shared reputation as orators and speechmakers.

8   Havel is alluding to McKinley's reputation as a puppet of big business.

9   Abner Osborne McKinley (1847–1904) was allegedly a con man

Everything was in perfect order. Dignity had to be maintained at all costs. Mud-raking vocabulary was not tolerated. Terms like mollycoddle, milksop, fourflusher, liar, and rascal were not in vogue. Hanna liked patriarchal ways.

Like the *Rattenfänger von Hameln*,[10] the full dinner pail lured the disinherited children of Europe to the golden shores of limitless possibilities. Bankrupt aristocrats were doing a flourishing business. The daughters of Columbia joyfully exchanged the millions, coined from the flesh and blood of their wage slaves, for titles of nobility.

All had signed their souls to his Majesty, Satan Get-Rich-Quick.

The little victims of the cotton mills in the South cried to deaf ears; no one heard the groans of the haggard workers in the sweatshops; in vain, too, the curses of the men in the bowels of the earth; in vain the cry of despair of the disinherited. No one heard; all were deaf.

The air was heavily charged with the odor of hypocritical respectability. It was a glorious time.

Suddenly the lightning struck. Avenging justice made its mighty voice heard.

"Nearer my God to Thee."[11]

What a change since the tragedy at Buffalo![12] The cancer of social corruption has since burst. The highly respectable representatives of the system are unmasked as thieves, swindlers, and robbers. The pillars of society stand in the public, pillory. What a sight for the Gods!

---

who perpetrated several fraudulent schemes including the selling of phony telegraph and railway bonds.

10 That is, the Pied Piper of Hamlin.

11 Havel is referring to McKinley's (alleged) last words, which were said to have been the first few lines from the well-known Christian hymn.

12 The phrase "tragedy at Buffalo" echoes the title of an essay by Emma Goldman ("Tragedy at Buffalo") that was published in the October 6, 1901 edition of *Free Society*.

* * *

Our Redeemer, as a child, played in
Nazareth with the cross on which He saved
the world, O Polish Mother! In thy place I
would give to thy son the toys of his future
to play with, Give him early chains on his
hands, accustom him to push the convict's
dirty wheelbarrow, so that he shall not grow
pale before the executioner's axe, nor blush
at the sight of the halter. . . an unknown spy
will accuse him; he must, defend himself
before a perjured court; his battlefield will
be a dungeon underground, and an all-
powerful enemy his judge. The blasted wood
of the gallows will be the monument on his
grave; a few women's tears, soon dried, and
the long talks of his comrades in the night-
time, will be his sole honor and memorial
after death.
  —Adam Mickiewicz[13]

Who was the youth chosen by destiny to shatter the
bulwarks of the ruling class?

July 12th, 1901, a young man came to see me at the office of *Free Society*, an Anarchist weekly, then published at
Chicago.[14] As I was not in, he was requested to call again.

---

13 Adam Mickiewicz (1798–1855) was a Polish Romantic poet. The
    quotation is from "To a Polish Mother" (*Do Matki Polki*). See
    Polish Romantic Literature: An Anthology, ed. and trans. Michael
    Mikloś (Bloomington, IN: Slavica Publishers, 2002), pp. 42–43.

14 *Free Society* began as *The Firebrand*, which was published in
    Portland, Oregon by Russian-born anarchists Abraham (1856–
    1937) and Mary Isaak (1861–1934) from 1895 to 1897. *Free
    Society* was published in San Francisco from 1897 to 1901,
    Chicago from 1901 to 1904, and New York in 1904.

He returned towards dusk the same day, and I invited him to my room.

My visitor began the conversation in Polish, saying that his name was Niemann, that he had come from Cleveland, and that he desired to inform himself about the Anarchists and their activity.[15] He had seen my name in the Anarchist papers and decided to look me up on his arrival in Chicago.

I remember vividly the change in his face when I told him that my knowledge of the Polish language was too limited to converse in it. The Slavonian sound was soft and melodious, but his voice displayed a hard ring when he began to speak English. His entire demeanor became more rigid.

His features were fine and sympathetic, and his eyes, of a beautiful blue, rested with a shy and melancholy gaze on the things about him. Though born and reared in America, his Slavic descent was apparent. He spoke of his longings and experiences. It was the story of the typical proletarian.

Born in Detroit, the child of poor parents, Niemann was compelled at a very early age to take up the struggle for existence. Oh, for the bitter cup of that struggle, which he had to drink to the very last drop. Nothing but wretchedness, want, misery, and dull despair all his life. His spirit rebelled against the gloom and oppression of his surroundings. He sought for some relief, some deliverance from our social slavery. His fellow workers in the shop and union, however, had very little understanding for his longings. Later he joined a local of the Socialist Labor Party[16] in Cleveland. But there, too, disappointment

---

15   As Havel explains below, "Niemann" (literally, "no man") is Leon Czolgosz (1873–1901), an American of Polish descent who worked for a time as a steelworker in Cleveland. "No man" is apparently a reference to Czolgosz's perception of himself as an anonymous defender of "the people."

16   Marxist political party founded in 1876.

awaited him. He had hoped to find ideals, enthusiasm, and earnest endeavor for human liberation; instead he found nothing but indifference, political compromise, and efforts directed toward vote catching. Disgusted and dissatisfied, he now turned to the Anarchists. He was anxious to learn their aims and how they proposed to bring about the downfall of the capitalist system.

He had but a vague idea of Anarchism; his questions as to Anarchist organization were naive. All this became clear to me only later. At the time of Niemann's visit I was preoccupied with other matters. I regret with all my soul not to have had the chance to know him better, to become more intimate.

I was obliged to discontinue the conversation. Comrade Emma Goldman, on her way East from a lecture tour, was leaving Chicago that day, and I had arranged to accompany her to the station. I invited the young man to come with us that he might meet Comrade Goldman. On our way downtown we exchanged but few words. Having to meet another engagement I left him with some friends at the station.

Two weeks later a letter arrived from Cleveland, denouncing my visitor as a police spy.[17] A terrible blunder of blockheads! I know not whether he ever became cognizant of this denunciation. If he did, it must have gripped him terribly. Again he had sought for understanding and kindred souls in vain.

On September 6th the Associated Press reported the attempt on the life of President McKinley, the assailant's name being given as Niemann. An hour later the office of *Free Society* was raided by the police, and every one present,

17   Emil Schilling, a Cleveland-based anarchist, wrote to *Free Society* suggesting that Czolgosz was a provocateur and police spy. The newspaper published Schilling's accusation on September 1, 1901. See Marshall Everett, *Complete Life of William McKinley and Story of His Assassination* (Chicago: C.W. Stanton, 1901), p. 87.

including myself, arrested.[18] The same evening we learned that the name of the young man at Buffalo was—Leon Czolgosz.

Those were exciting days. The capitalist press raved madly and demanded victims. Plutocracy was deeply wounded. One life did not satisfy its bloodthirsty clamor. Emma Goldman was chosen as a special target.[19] In her person plutocracy hoped to stifle the revolutionary movement in this country.

The pistol shot at Buffalo has demonstrated the lie of the contentment of the American people. It has unveiled the terrible contrast of classes. The shrill voice of the oppressed and the exploited re-echoed all over the world.

The apologists for capitalism made frantic efforts to stamp Leon Czolgosz' act as that of a foreigner. But in vain. He was a true type of the native American workingman.

The patriots of this Republic gladly accepted the aid of Kosciuszko and Pulaski in their fight for American independence.[20] Why should their descendants protest against

---

18 Other arrestees included Abraham and Mary Isaak and their children (Abraham, Jr. and Mary), Enrico Travaglio, Clemens Pfeutzner, Julia Mechanic, and Alfred Schneider. See "Chicago Anarchists Raided," *New York Times*, September 8, 1901, p. 4.

19 On September 6, Czolgosz indicated in a statement that the last public speaker he had heard was Emma Goldman. Although he made it clear, then and subsequently, that Goldman had never spoken nor communicated with him personally in any way, the Secret Service began a search for Goldman and other anarchists presumed to be involved in the assassination. After several days of hiding, Goldman was apprehended on September 10 in Chicago. She was arraigned on September 11 and subsequently released on September 24 owing to a lack of evidence that she had played a role in planning or carrying out McKinley's murder. See Emma Goldman, *Living My Life*, vol. 1 (New York: Knopf, 1931), pp. 296–310.

20 Tadeusz Kosciuszko (1746–1817) and Kazimierz Pułaski (1745–1779) were Polish military commanders and heroes of the American Revolutionary War.

a native American with Polish blood his veins? He, too, gave his life in the name of independence—the independence of the American proletariat

Leon Czolgosz presents a unique figure in the annals of revolutionary history. Never before did a fighter for freedom go to his death so absolutely alone and forsaken. What he suffered before the act, the horrors he endured in Auburn prison—these remain untold.

He met his executioners with haughty contempt; he walked to the death chamber with quiet dignity and simple grandeur.

October 29th, 1901, Leon Czolgosz's heart, so full of human sympathy, was brought to a standstill. His last words were: "I did it for the people, for the good of the workers of America."

But for his act pious corruption were still enthroned unmasked.

THE COALITION AGAINST
ANARCHISTS (1909)[1]

THE WARFARE AGAINST ANARCHISM HAS ENTERED A NEW
phase.[2] Theodore Roosevelt's most passionate wish is at
last realized.[3] The municipal and State pillars have joined
hands with the federal authorities to give the death blow
to the hated enemy.[4] In this laudable effort they are

---

1   This essay appeared in *Mother Earth* 3, no. 12 (February 1909).

2   Havel is responding to the anti-anarchist hysteria which swept
the United States in 1908–1909 following the murder of Father
Leo Heinrichs and other events mentioned on page 18 above. For
a detailed analysis, see Robert Goldstein, "The Anarchist Scare
of 1908: A Sign of Tensions in the Progressive Era," *American
Studies* 15, no. 2 (1974), pp. 55–78.

3   Roosevelt's fear and hatred of anarchists was evident from the moment he took office following McKinley's assassination. (See, for
example, his first message to congress, where he claims that anarchists are the worst kind of criminals and that anarchism is "essentially seditious and treasonable," U.S. Congress, *President Roosevelt's
Message to the Senate and the House of Representatives*, December 3,
1901, 57th Cong., 1st Sess., *Congressional Record*, vol. 35, p. 82).
Arguably his most egregious anti-anarchist endeavor was his attempt, in 1908, to persuade Congress to pass legislation prohib-
iting the circulation of "any paper published here or abroad… if
it propagates anarchistic opinions" (U.S. Congress, *Senate Journal,
A Message from the The President of the United States Transmitting
a Communication from the Attorney-General Relative to the
Transmission Through the Mails of Certain Anarchistic Publications*,
April 9, 1908, 60th Cong., 1st Sess., S. Doc. 426, pp. 32–23).

4   Shortly after the assassination of William McKinley, the State of
New York passed the Criminal Anarchy Act of 1902, which made

cheerfully aided by Socialist speakers and writers. The failure to achieve, single-handed, the desired end is now to be remedied by joint action.

So far, every policeman in and out of uniform felt himself justified to misrepresent and maltreat us. This method indeed called forth many victims from our midst, yet it proved a complete failure. Instead of annihilating the Anarchist movement—the chief aim of our persecutors—these tactics resulted but in inspiring our efforts with greater energy and intensity.

Blind as the Bourbons,[5] who neither learned nor forgot, our rulers now endeavor to conduct their warfare against Anarchism along more concentrated, i.e., imperialistic, lines.

Let us consider for a moment to what extent our enemies are permitting themselves to go.

Our press is hourly threatened by the Postal censorship.[6] Thus *Nihil*, at San Francisco, *Freiheit*, *Volné Listy*,

---

it a felony to advocate "the doctrine that organized government should be overthrown by force or violence, or by assassination … or by any unlawful means" (*NY Consol. Laws* 1909, c.40, §§ 160, 161; 1918 Penal Law §§ 160, 161). By the time Havel is writing, similar laws had been passed in several states and municipalities, including New Jersey in 1902 (*NJ Laws*, c. 33, §1); Wisconsin in 1903 (*Wis. Stat.* §347.14); and Washington in 1909 (*Wash. Laws* c. 249, §312).

5 The Bourbons were the ruling French dynasty at the time of the Revolution, which took them largely unawares (hence their "blindness"—i.e., shortsightedness and naivete).

6 For a history see Linda Cobb-Reiley, "Aliens and Alien Ideas: The Suppression of Anarchists and the Anarchist Press in America, 1901–1914," *Journalism History* 15 (1988), pp. 50–59. As Cobb-Reiley notes, "After McKinley's assassination… restrictive laws aimed at [anarchists] and their activities were passed by the federal government and the states," some of which made it a felony to "advocate anarchist doctrine or opposition to all government,

and *Sorgiamo*, published at New York, are every now and then confiscated by the Postal Department, that is to say, refused transmission through the mails.[7] *La Questione Sociale*, the Paterson, N.J., publication, was entirely suppressed by order of the President.[8]

Freedom of speech and assembly have long since ceased to exist *for us*. Proprietors of halls refuse us their

---

or to join a group or meeting or circulate printed matter for such purposes" (p. 53). Because these laws "expressly prohibited certain forms of communication," they were frequently invoked by the authorities—most notably the U.S. Postal Service—to justify the censorship and suppression of anarchist periodicals (p. 55).

7   The newspapers Havel cites are a representative cross-section of the American anarchist press that attests to the wide and diverse range of perspectives that existed in the movement in 1909. *Nihil* ("Nothing") was an Italian-language individualist newspaper published in San Francisco from 1908 to 1909 (on its suppression, see Goldstein, p. 70). *Freiheit* ("Freedom") was a German-language newspaper published in New York from 1882 to 1910. *Freiheit* was well known its day as an insurrectionist organ reflecting the revolutionary views of its editor, Johann Most. Most was imprisoned at least once for writings he published therein [see, for example, *People v. Most*, 171 N.Y. 423, 64 N.E. 174 (1902)]. *Volné Listy* ("The Flyleaf") was a Czech-language newspaper published in New York from 1890 to 1917. It was suppressed several times by the authorities [see, for example, Emma Goldman, "Suppression of *Volné Listy*," *Mother Earth* 11 (1916), pp. 532–533]. *Sorgiamo!* ("Rise!") was an Italian-language newspaper published in New York from 1908 to 1909.

8   *La Questione Sociale* ("The Social Question") was an Italian-language anarchist newspaper published in Paterson, New Jersey from 1895 to 1908. The principal organ of the Italian-American anarchist movement for many years, it was suppressed several times—most notably, as Havel points out, through the direct intervention of President Theodore Roosevelt, who described the newspaper as "immoral."

meetings rooms, fearing to disobey police orders on the pain of losing their licenses or other privileges. If an occasional hall manager dares to assert his rights and ignores the police ukase,[9] then the audiences are almost invariably clubbed out of the hall with night sticks, as has happened in New York, Philadelphia, Chicago, and now in San Francisco.[10] And when an Anarchist meeting is, once in a while, suffered to take place, the police ruffians endeavor their utmost to provoke a riot. On such occasions young men and women are brutally treated and insulted in every conceivable way. I have even seen these guardians of the peace hold lighted matches to newspapers, trying to create a panic in the crowded hall.

It were difficult to conceive what thoughts and emotions are roused by such police methods in the young revolutionists, recent arrivals from Russia, many of whom have fought heroic battles in their native land and stood perchance behind the barricades. What must such men think of this glorious land of Liberty?[11] Can it be

9   Technically an edict of the Tsar, but more generally any kind of arbitrary government directive.

10   As Goldstein notes, "On at least eight occasions in 1906 and 1907… police in Philadelphia and New York barred anarchist meetings or meetings called to discuss anarchism, sometimes arresting speakers and clubbing protesters in the process" (p. 58). In 1908, anarchist meetings and demonstrations were violently suppressed by the police on several occasions. These included a rent strike in New York on January 5 and unemployment demonstrations in Chicago and Philadelphia on January 23 and February 20, respectively (p. 60).

11   "When staff members of *La Questione Sociale* sought to rent a hall to protest the paper's exclusion from the mails, city officials pressured a hall owner into refusing to rent to them; the group then tried to hold a meeting inside their own offices, but club-swinging police broke it up. The paper's editor protested, '*This is worse than Russia or Italy*. There the officers attend the anarchist meetings

wondered at that such brutality of the representatives of the law incites men to deeds of desperation?

No tactics are too despicable to use against Anarchists. Thus, the trial of two comrades is about to take place at Trenton, N. J., charged by a notoriety-seeking New York detective with attempted robbery.[12] The comrades referred to were passing along the street, in search of work, when they were suddenly pounced upon by detectives and accused of the alleged intention to rob an old woman. The detective responsible for these arbitrary arrests is a member of the "Anarchist Squad," whose sole ambition is to win promotion, no matter at what cost.[13] And what better way than by preying upon Anarchists?

A new form of persecution is now being added to the former well-known methods; its source is at Washington, and it consists in the attempt to deprive the most prominent Anarchists of their citizenship in order ultimately to deport them from the country.[14] We are aware of several such attempts, the latest being the case of Alexander Horr,

---

and if the speaker uses language they think is improper they speak to him and make him change his tone, but they don't prevent peaceful assemblies. *And yet you call this a free country*'" (Goldstein, p. 70, emphasis mine).

12 Havel is referring to John Schreiber and John Adams, who were convicted for conspiracy to commit robbery in June 1909. Schreiber was implicated in an anonymous letter sent to the detective Havel mentions. The conviction was subsequently overturned in February 1910 owing to insufficient evidence. See *State of New Jersey v. Schreiber and Adams*, 79 N.J. L. 447 (1910). I am grateful to Tom Goyens for helping me identify this case.

13 The "Anarchist Squad" was a unit of the New York Police Department that was founded in 1906 for purposes of harassing, incriminating, and arresting anarchists. It was later re-constituted as the NYPD Bomb Squad.

14 See "To Drive Anarchists Out of the Country," *New York Times*, March 4, 1908, p. 1.

of San Francisco.[15] This comrade was arrested by the police of that city for addressing a street audience. Subsequently outrageously maltreated, he was delivered into the hands of the Federal authorities, who are now endeavoring to deprive Horr of his citizenship on the trumped-up charge of having procured his papers by fraud.

Various other arrests of comrades were recently made in San Francisco, culminating in the suppression of all Anarchist meetings to be addressed by Comrade Emma Goldman. At the moment when the Victory Theatre was filled with a large audience, awaiting the arrival of the speaker, the police invaded the hall and mercilessly clubbed the assembled men and women out into the streets. At the same time, Emma Goldman and Dr. Reitman, about to enter the theatre, were arrested, as well as Wm. Buwalda, the latter for courageously protesting against the police outrage.[16]

---

15 Alexander Horr (1871–1947) was a Hungarian-Jewish anarchist and a close friend of Emma Goldman. Horr was a member and outspoken supporter of the Freeland League, which advocated the creation of a utopian society on the model of Theodor Herzka's novel "Freeland: A Social Anticipation" (1891). Horr lived for a time in the utopian Equality Colony in Washington state and eventually settled in San Francisco, where he helped book Emma Goldman's lectures. As Havel notes, Horr was arrested there in December 1908 for inciting to riot. The government's subsequent attempt to deport him was unsuccessful. See Cassius V. Cook, "San Francisco Echoes," *Mother Earth* 4, no. 1 (1909), pp. 29–30.

16 The arrest in question took place on January 14, 1909. William Buwalda (1869–1946) was initially a United States soldier (private first-class). As Havel notes in his introduction to *Anarchism and Other Essays*, Buwalda was court-martialed the previous year (April 26, 1908) for shaking Goldman's hand after a lecture at Walton's Pavilion in San Francisco. He was sentenced to three years' hard labor at Alcatraz but was released early, at which time he returned his medals and became an anarchist.

The guardians of San Francisco have combined with the State and Federal authorities to "exterminate Anarchism." The first battle has been fought. But—*horribile dicta*—the holy alliance has suffered a miserable defeat. They have failed to railroad our friends to prison. The idiotic charge of "conspiracy to riot" proved too much even for the patriotic jury, which returned a verdict of acquittal.[17] It was, indeed, fortunate that our comrades succeeded in taking the case out of the hands of a magistrate and bringing it before a jury. It served to expose the real conspirators: the alleged guardians of law and order.

It is not to be expected that the authorities will remain content with this result. They will continue to "exterminate Anarchism." History might enlighten them as to the probability of success. As to ourselves, we will continue the fight for Anarchism with renewed energy and vigor.

True, we by no means deceive ourselves as to the real situation. We know but too well that in this great struggle we stand almost alone. There is, indeed, a considerable number of men and women in this country who are willing to champion free speech and press, among these lately even Mr. Pulitzer.[18] But these elements mean nothing

---

17 Goldman and Reitman were arrested on the charge of "conspiracy to commit riot" on January 14 (Buwalda was charged with disturbing the peace), arraigned the following day, and released on bail on January 18. On January 28, they were acquitted without trial. See Emma Goldman, "On Trial," *Mother Earth* 3, no. 12 (1909), p. 411.

18 Havel is referring to the newspaper magnate Joseph Pulitzer (previously cited). During this period the Roosevelt administration routinely attacked Pulitzer for criticizing its policies in the pages of *The New York World* and other newspapers. Although he repeatedly defended himself from such attacks on "free speech" grounds, Pulitzer refused to apply the same reasoning on behalf of anarchists and other radicals.

more than the freedom of speech and press for themselves—never for Anarchists.

Our intellectuals, if such there be in this country, are too cautiously respectable and fear to compromise their social position by public protest against discrimination and persecution of Anarchists. They admire the courage of an Anatole France for bravely taking the stand on the side of even persecuted Anarchists.[19] Indeed, they admire him—at a safe distance. But the wings of their admiration are too badly crippled to permit their soaring to the height of following the noble example. They remind one of the Missouri schoolma'am going into ecstasies over the freedom of Parisian life, but who, on returning to her native land, is dutifully shocked by things smacking of that freedom.

Our publicists are sold body and soul to Mammon.

But few exceptions among them, like Wm. Marion Reedy and Louis F. Post,[20] still have the courage to say that Anarchists are not to be regarded as every man's prey.

Least of all can we expect support in the battle for free speech and press from the Socialist side. Indeed, our stepbrothers are often even worse than the masters. While the latter content themselves with persecuting us, the former never lose the opportunity to heap slander upon our heads.

---

19 Anatole France (1844–1924) was a French poet, journalist, and novelist. For example, France defended the anarchist Aristide Delannoy (1874–1911) when he was imprisoned for publishing anti-imperialist cartoons. See Robert Goldstein, *Censorship of Political Caricature in Nineteenth Century France* (Kent, OH: Kent State University Press, 1989), p. 256.

20 Louis Post (1849–1928) was a journalist, reformer, and one-time Assistant Secretary of Labor under Woodrow Wilson. As editor of *The Public*, Post was renowned for his staunch advocacy of free speech. Ironically, Post signed Goldman's deportation order while briefly working for the Bureau of Immigration.

To illustrate:

While our comrades were waging their difficult fight at San Francisco, there took place in New York a Socialist free speech meeting to protest against the decisions in the cases of Pouren, Gompers, etc.[21]

Chairman James G. Kanely, in formally opening the meeting, said that the audience had come, "not only to protest against the actions of the official Anarchists who occupied public positions, but also to warn them that the working class was awakening."[22]

The practice of identifying the exploiting masters with Anarchists has of late grown very popular with Socialists. Their evident purpose is to discredit Anarchists in the eyes of the public. The mantle of ignorance cannot cover their slanders; the Socialists do it against their better knowledge. But they think it good policy to misrepresent us. What would be the astonishment of their dupes, however, were they to learn of the friendly terms on which European Socialists often co-operate with Anarchists, especially in similar cases, where free speech is at stake.

---

21 Jan Pouren was a Lithuanian revolutionary whose extradition was requested by the Russian government on several criminal charges in 1908. See United States Department of State, *Foreign Relations of the United States* (1909), p. 513. Samuel Gompers (1850–1924) was an English-born American labor leader and the founder of the American Federation of Labor. Presumably Havel is referring to *Buck's Stove & Range Company v. The American Federation of Labor* (1908), 36 *Washington Law Reporter* 822, in which Gompers and others were found guilty of contempt for violating a court-ordered injunction.

22 See "Editorial Comment," *The Square Deal* 4, no. 41 (December 1908), pp. 88–96: 95. James G. Kanely (birth and death date unknown) was a trade unionist and a prominent member of the Socialist Party who ran for office several times as a Socialist candidate.

Thus Robert Hunter generously eulogizes his French comrade, Gustave Hervé,[23] apparently quite oblivious to the fact that Hervé fights shoulder to shoulder with the French Anarchists. Another party man, who supplies the Socialist press with you-stand-up-to-pay-for-sitting-down articles (thus competing, in a highly unprofessional manner, with the Johnsons and Dunnes), recently felt his spirit moved to besmirch the character of the late Justus Schwab, whom he characterized as an unkempt, dirty bravado-Anarchist.[24] Just think of a Socialist thus writing of Justus Schwab, one of the founders of the Socialist Party in America, and whose memory such men

---

23 Robert Hunter (1874–1942) was an American sociologist and socialist. Gustave Hervé (1871–1844) was a French politician, initially a socialist and later (from 1919) a right-wing ultranationalist. It is not entirely clear what Havel is referring to here. Hunter generally speaks of Hervé in very flattering language, as, e.g., when he refers to him as "the great apostle of anti-militarism" in his *Socialists at Work* (New York: Macmillan & Co., 1908), p. 80. On Hervé's cooperation with anarchists and revolutionary syndicalists, see Christopher Ansell, *Schism and Solidarity in Social Movements* (Cambridge: Cambridge University Press, 2001), p. 190.

24 Olive Johnson (1872–1952) was an American socialist writer, newspaper editor, and prominent member of the Socialist Labor Party. William Dunne (1887–1953) was an American socialist and trade unionist. Justus Schwab (1847–1900) was a German-American anarchist and a close friend of Emma Goldman. Schwab served for a time (c. 1882) as editor of *Freiheit* and managed a saloon on East First Street which Goldman described as "the most famous radical center in New York" (*Living My Life*, p. 119). The identity of the "party man" to whom Havel refers is unclear, although Daniel De Leon (see note 26 on next page) attacked Schwab in more or less this way in a 1901 lecture entitled "Socialism vs. Anarchism." See D. DeLeon, *Socialism vs. Anarchism* (New York: Socialist Party, 1921), p. 33.

as Alexander Jonas and John Swinton honored with the highest eulogies.[25]

Of course, the Socialist Left, these exclusive Knights of the Holy Marxian Grail, do not lag in the procession of calumny. At critical moments their leader, Daniel De Leon, never fails, as in the present San Francisco case to deal out a few asinine kicks.[26] Daniel is angry. He fears Emma Goldman might get too much free advertising. Of course, no such danger threatens our Daniel, for he is a modest man.

Thus all these great men, however bitter their personal differences, always strike the same chord, "Down with the Anarchists!"

Yet it is just possible, however, that the alliance of the Roosevelts, Socialists, and other cockroaches will not disturb the even tenor of our ways.

---

25 See "Justus Schwab Mourned," *New York Times*, December 21, 1900, p. 2. Alexander Jonas (1834–1912) was a German-American Socialist leader and John Swinton (1829–1901) was a Scottish-American radical journalist and trade unionist. Both offered eulogies at Schwab's funeral.

26 Daniel De Leon (1852–1914) was an American Marxist journalist and politician. De Leon was a prominent figure in the Socialist Labor Party and played a role in the founding of the Industrial Workers of the World in 1905—an organization with which he frequently butted heads and from which he was eventually expelled. It is not entirely clear what Havel is referring to specifically. As suggested in note 24 above, however, De Leon was often extremely critical of anarchists and the anarchist movement.

THE CONFESSION OF AN AUTHOR (1909)[1]

AMONG THE MODERN WRITERS WHO ARE NOT SATISFIED to give merely artistic expression of their creative work, but strive to actively participate in the social and political life of the times, stands in the foremost ranks H. G. Wells. Like Leo Tolstoy, Anatole France, G. B. Shaw, Maxim Gorki, Jack London, Gabrielle D 'Annunzio, Octave Mirbeau, Jose Echegarey—to name only those best known—Wells also enters the arena of social battle to voice his political faith and to defend his *Weltanschauung*.[2]

H. G. Wells is a prolific writer. So far he has published short stories (three volumes), romances (eleven volumes), novels (two volumes), sociological and Socialist essays (five volumes). To the last series also belongs the work recently issued by Putnam & Sons, "First and Last Things." The author calls his book a frank confession of the early twentieth-century man—a confession just as frank as the limitations of his character permit; it is his metaphysics, his religion, his moral standards, his uncertainties, and the expedients with which he has met them. Autobiographies and confessions have ever been a favorite mode of

---

1   This essay appeared in *Mother Earth* 4, no. 2 (April 1909).

2   Of these authors, Tolstoy and Mirbeau (1848–1917) were anarchists—the latter a leading figure in the French avant-garde of the *fin de siècle*. Wells (1866–1946), Shaw (1856–1950), London (1876–1916), and Gorky (1868–1936) were socialists who frequently incorporated radical ideas into their artistic productions. Though they were not socialists, D'Annunzio (1863–1938) and Echegaray y Eizaguirre (1832–1916) were held in great esteem by leftists of this era.

expression of the thinker, the artist, and the social trans-valuator. A confession is the most characteristic *document humain*; a veritable treasure for the psychologue and lit-erary epicure. More true wisdom can be learned from the confessions of a St. Augustine, Benvenuto Cellini, Jacob Bohme, Wolfgang von Goethe, Jean Jacques Rousseau, Soren Kierkegaard, Oscar Wilde, Leo Tolstoy, Peter Kropotkin, or of a Maria Bashkirtseff[3] than from scores of philosophic and historic volumes.

Every pathfinder in the realm of thought is urged by inner necessity to reveal his soul, his inmost being, his doubts, and struggles, to bear witness to the integrity of his faith, and to offer his martyrdom on the altar of hu-manity. Confessions may differ in form of expression and contents, but their aims are always similar. H. G. Wells deals less with his own personality than with his attitude toward the *Zeitgeist* and its problems. As in his former sociological works, "Anticipations," "Mankind in the Making," "Modern Utopia," and "New Worlds for Old," we also find in "First and Last Things" the attempt to solve the riddle of life.

The conscious impulse to solve this enigma was, in-deed, never so strong as in our epoch. We, the children of the twentieth century, lack conviction—a positive *Weltanschauung*. Rudderless we drift upon the ocean of life. We are tormented by the consciousness that in spite of all mechanical progress and our increased cognition of natural laws, in spite of all our knowledge, systematized into sciences, we have approached no nearer the adequate

---

3   Of the thinkers and memoirists mention here, readers might be unfamiliar with Jakob Böhme (1575–1624) and Maria Konstantinovna Bashkirtseva (1858–1884). The former was a German Lutheran theologian whose writings are marked by a deeply personal, almost mystical character. The latter was a Ukrainian artist and diarist. Her diary was published in six-teen volumes.

solution of life's enigma than our forefathers. We strive to find terra firma in the chaos of the innumerable hypotheses and creeds. All the subtle, yet necessary and unavoidable, problems, which occupied the philosophic minds of the ancients, still press for solution. Great unrest characterizes, more than, ever before, contemporary thought. It oppresses alike the philosopher, the man of science, the artist, and the social student. Wearied by the vain efforts and broken in spirit, many are driven into the arms of mysticism: a Verlaine, a Huysmans, a Strindberg, a Laura Marholm, believe to have found the solution of life's problem in the lap of Catholicism.[4] But the strong and vigorous seek new leaders and new values. Ibsen, Nietzsche, Tolstoy, Rodin, and Wagner discover to them new worlds.

What manner of world is offered to us by H. G. Wells? What is his faith? He believes that the time has arrived to revive metaphysical discussion for a satisfactory solution of the modern problems of life. The subject of metaphysics is thoroughly treated in the first part of his "First and Last Things." The author takes the exact sciences severely to account and proves, with a fine touch of skepticism, the delusive character of our senses. By many an apt example we are made to see the ease with which the eye, the ear, and other human organs can be deceived. The fallacy of considering language a satisfactory means of expressing thoughts and feelings is also pointed out with convincing clearness; an observation reminding one of the excellent work of Fritz Mauthner, *Versuch zur Kritik der Sprache*, discussing this theme in an ingenuous and able manner.[5]

4　Laura Marholm (Laura Mohr Hansson, 1854–1928) was a German pacifist and feminist. Marholm and her husband, the Swedish writer Ola Hansson, converted to Catholicism c. 1898.

5　Fritz Mauthner (1849–1923) was German journalist and philosopher. His *Versuch zur Kritik der Sprache* ("Toward a Critique of Language," 1901–1902) is a work in philosophy of language

What, however, are the practical conclusions from these observations, according to H. G. Wells? All the great and important beliefs—he holds—by which life is guided and determined are less of the nature of fact than of artistic expressions. Therefore the right solution of life's problems is, in the estimation of our author, the abandonment of infinite assumptions, the extension of the experimental spirit to all human interests—Pragmatism.

The second part of Wells's book deals with Belief; the third, with General Conduct; and the fourth, with General Things. Under the composite head of General Conduct the author elucidates the problems involved in the social question, and strives to explain his personal attitude toward Socialism. He criticizes both revolutionary Marxian Socialism and the administrative State Socialism, as well as the Cunctator tactics of the Fabians.[6] To him, Socialism is the collective consciousness in humanity ... a common step we are all taking in the great synthesis of human purpose. It is the organization, in regard to a great mass of common and fundamental interests, that have hitherto been dispersedly served, of a collective purpose. He holds that Socialism is, and must be, a battle against human stupidity and egotism and disorder, a battle fought all through the forests and jungles of the soul of man. As we get intellectual and moral light and the realization of brotherhood, so social and economic organization will develop. He considers poverty merely one of the symptoms of a profounder evil never to be cured by mere attacks against itself, which disregard the intellectual and moral factors that necessitate it. And therefore the Socialism which fights poverty and its concomitants alone must inevitably result in failure.

It is rather peculiar that one holding such sound Anarchist views should so near-sightedly fail to draw the

---

which had a profound influence on Wittgenstein, among others.

6   *Cunctator*—Latin, literally "one who delays." Havel is referring to the Fabians' preference for gradual reforms over revolution.

logical conclusions from his premises. The author proves an opportunist of deepest dye the moment he turns from general theoretic questions to practical means and tactics. He is opposed to all individual initiative, even considering the latter anti-social. His views as to marriage, the family, State, war, and especially with regard to militarism, are contradictory and untenable. It is nothing short of ridiculous to consider militarism as "a step to a higher social plane," when compared with the activity of the producer. It is also incomprehensible that the author has failed to emancipate himself from the spook of State—the more so, since he builds his hopes for the future on the co-operation of voluntary associations and brotherhoods, the Samurai, or "new republicans."

However, according to Wells's own confession, he has freed himself in "First and Last Things" from many fallacies he championed in his former sociological works. It may, therefore, not be out of place to express the hope that his next earnest attempt will finally land him on the shores of a Stateless humanity. But even if we cannot give our unqualified assent to the conclusions of H. G. Wells, we can conscientiously recommend his book as a valuable contribution to modern thought.

THE FRENCH REVOLUTION (1909)[1]

THE FRENCH REVOLUTION FORMS THE MOST MOMENTOUS turning point in the newer history of civilization. No event has had greater influence upon the social, economic, religious, scientific, and artistic life of France and other European countries than this tremendous upheaval. It is indeed the source of all modern social ideas, the fountainhead of all the problems we are striving to solve.

One would suppose that an event of such epoch-making import, transvaluing, as it did, all social values, would have been investigated by the social historian along all its phases, and all mooted points cleared, to help us form an adequate picture of those remarkable days. Yet that is not the case. True, we have brilliant portrayals of the heroic side of that Revolution and its leading personalities; nor are splendid descriptions of its ideal phases wanting; but so far we entirely lacked a competent exposition of the economic side of the Revolution, its most important moment, and consequently the most difficult to analyze and describe. The bourgeois historians, whether of the progressive or reactionary camp, entirely ignore this phase of the Revolution. They generally content themselves with picturing the heroic attitude, the differences and controversies of leaders and parties, the political importance of the Revolution. Few, however, attempt to treat its socioeconomic significance. Only recently have certain investigators begun to turn their attention to this important phase.

Among the social thinkers of our day probably none has realized this gap as clearly as Peter Kropotkin. But

---

1   This essay appeared in *Mother Earth* 4, no. 4 (June 1909).

few contemporaries have felt themselves drawn with such strong bonds of sympathy toward the French people as did our comrade. To fill this gap he passed many years in the study of the French Revolution. The result of his prolonged investigations is now before the world in two large volumes.[2]

The work will fill a niche of honor in the literature of the French Revolution. No former work on the subject can compare with Kropotkin's in the lucidity of treatment of this great popular drama, its economic causes and effects. The people, defamed alike by friend and foe, the hated revolutionists of that magnificent period, have at last found in Peter Kropotkin an eloquent advocate. He has thoroughly swept away the accumulated cobwebs of myth, presenting to our view an almost entirely new picture of the great upheaval. It would require more than our limited space to do justice to this remarkable work. Suffice here merely to indicate the importance of the same.

The author elucidates the two great currents which have prepared, brought about, and carried through the Revolution. The one current, the idealistic—the wave of new political, ideas submerging old State forms—originated with the bourgeoisie. The other, that of action, issued from the masses—the peasant and urban proletariat, seeking the immediate and radical improvement of their daily economic life. The juncture of these two powerful currents in a common aim, their temporary mutual aid, was the Revolution.

Without the previous hunger uprisings of the proletariat of the cities and fields, the Revolution would have been impossible. All the idealism and radicalism of the Third Estate would have failed to achieve a similar result. The masses, driven to desperation, sounded the key of the

2   [Havel's note] *The French Revolution, 1789–1793*. By Peter Kropotkin. German Edition of Gustav Landauer. Published by Theo. Thomas, Leipzig.

great drama; and when the Revolution was triumphantly marching through the land it was they, the French proletariat, who forced the bourgeois radicals onward, thus repeatedly saving the oft endangered situation. No sooner, however, were the aspirations of the bourgeoisie achieved than the inherent antagonism between them and the people became apparent. Kropotkin annihilates the legend of the bourgeois historians concerning the alleged voluntary abdication of the feudal nobility. He convincingly proves that the National Convention but sanctioned in principle that which the people had already themselves put into action.[3] The Convention had no choice but to recognize the established fact. And, indeed, it never went further than that. It even attempted, later on, to put reactionary limits on the conquered rights.

One of the most interesting chapters of the work is the one describing the contrast between the Girondists and the by them so bitterly antagonized "Anarchists." The renegade Brissot was the spokesman of the Girondists. He who in his younger days proclaimed "Property is robbery" suddenly became so inspired by reverence for private possession that he even censured the Convention—the day following the historic Fourth of August—for "the inconsiderate rashness" of its decrees against the feudal system.[4] He published a number of brochures venomous-

---

3   The National Convention was the constitutional and legislative assembly that governed France from September 1792 to October 1795, and the first French assembly elected by universal (male) suffrage. The Convention was characterized in its early stages by the conflict between the Girondins, a moderate faction that tried to slow the momentum of the Revolution, and the more radical Montagnards (i.e., members of *Le Montagne*—literally, "the mountain"). The Girondins eventually lost this battle, and many of them were executed during the Terror.

4   Jacques Pierre Brissot (1754–1793) was a lawyer and writer, a leader of the Girondists. The quote Havel cites is in reference to

ly attacking the "Anarchists." Louis Blanc appropriately characterized Brissot as one of those who today are premature republicans, tomorrow lagging revolutionists—men lacking the strength to keep step with the century, having exhausted themselves in marching in its advance guard.[5]

Not only Hébert, Marat, Roux, Varlet, Chaumette, L'Ange, and other members of the *Montagne*,[6] but even Danton and Robespierre were labeled Anarchists by the respectable Girondists.

The communistic movements reared in the lap of the Revolution are described by Kropotkin with interesting detail, forming a valuable contribution to a better under standing of these currents during the Revolution. He clearly points out the origin of modern Communist Anarchist and Socialist views in the great French Revolution.

Similarly to the previous works of Peter Kropotkin, *The French Revolution* is characterized by the creative power of the scientific investigator and independent thinker, coupled with the idealism of the social agitator. Our beloved comrade has placed in our hands a new intellectual weapon of great effect.

Brissot's book *Recherches philosophiques sur le droit de propriété et le vol*, ed. L. Massenet de Marancour (Bruxelles: Rozey, 1872). The original French is « *La propriété exclusive est un vol.* » Feudalism was abolished by the Constituent Assembly on August 4, 1789.

5   L. Blanc, *History of the French Revolution* (Philadelphia: Lea and Branchard, 1848).

6   The term initially referred to the Jacobins in general. However, Havel is referring to the most ultra-radical faction of *Montagnards* which split from other Jacobins in the wake of The Terror. His surprise at the mention of Robespierre and Danton alongside the likes of Marat and Varlet stems from the former's well-documented predilection toward authoritarian policies and tactics.

THE SOCIAL STRUGGLE IN SPAIN (1909)[1]

IN HIS IMMORTAL *CAPRICHOS*[2] THE CELEBRATED GOYA HAS left us an unsurpassed characterization of the Spanish rulers. Bold attacks against the whole political and social order, especially against royalty; severe arraignment of the ruling clericalism, hypocritical religion and its dogmas; merciless critique of the Inquisition, priestcraft, and superstition; biting satire of the court, nobility, and ministry characterize the great work—an ethical panorama of powerful irony alternating with phantastic dreams. In this work the artist is submerged by the free thinker and critical observer of his social and religious surroundings.

A century has passed since Goya has given *Caprichos* to the world. Yet the character of Spanish rule has not changed. Its spirit is today as brutal, bloodthirsty, and destructive as a hundred years ago. The modern descendants of Torquemada rule not only Spain, but the whole Catholic world; one of them, Merry del Val, is carrying out, as the Pope's secretary, the policies of the Holy See.[3]

---

1   This article appeared in *Mother Earth* 4, no. 10 (December 1909). In it, Havel discusses the revolutionary uprisings of 1909, most notably the *Setmana Tràgica* ("Tragic Week"), a left-wing and worker uprising in Barcelona that was ruthlessly crushed by government troops. Anarchists played central roles in these uprisings.

2   *Los Caprichos*—literally, "the caprices," a set of aquatint prints created by Francisco Goya between 1797 and 1798.

3   Tomás de Torquemada (1420–1498) was a Spanish Dominican friar and the first Grand Inquisitor of the infamous Spanish Inquisition. Rafael Merry del Val (1865–1930) was, as Havel suggests, Torquemada's contemporary counterpart, a Spanish

The proverb *y desde Roma por todo* (to Rome for every-thing) still applies in its full significance.

Notwithstanding, the world moves. While clerical do-minion did not change, the life of the Spanish people has undergone a tremendous transformation, a great spiritual evolution, so much indeed, that today we are witnessing a social struggle for emancipation which for determina-tion finds nowhere its equal save in Russia. Russia and Spain—the farthest North and South. What contrast, and yet what striking similarity in the political and social aspi-rations of the two nations. At the same time, what igno-rance abroad in regard to both countries.

To the superficial observer modern Spain is, like New Russia, *terra incognita*. The average man of today knows Spain only as the land of Inquisition and bullfights; a country which once indeed had mastered the world, pro-duced great artists like Velasquez and Murillo, dramatists like Calderon and Lope de Vega, and the immortal author of Don Quixote de la Mancha—yet a land which today is on the road to complete decay. Such works as George Borrow's "Bible in Spain"—a pitiful translation of a drama by Jose Echegaray—or the exhibition of Ignazio Zuloaga, more French than Spanish, and perhaps the latest novel of Maurice Hewlett are about the sole sources of informa-tion of the ordinary man.[4] He is entirely unaware of the

---

cardinal who later served as the Cardinal Secretary of State and was known for his battles against the proliferation of modern ideas among the clergy.

4 George Borrow (1803–1881) was a British novelist and trav-el writer. *The Bible in Spain* (1843) is a travelogue comprised of letters that Borrow wrote while working as a missionary in Spain—not, as Havel seems to suggest, a "translation of a drama" by Echegaray. (Evidently Echegaray's play *El Hijo de Don Juan* [1892] includes certain descriptions that appear to be influenced by, or drawn from, *The Bible in Spain*.) Ignacio Zeluoga (1870–1945) was a Spanish painter whose works frequently involve

tremendous struggle carried on in the Iberian peninsula, during the last half century, between the feudal powers and the legions of modernity; that the struggle has given birth to great thinkers, brilliant writers, and powerful organizers; that in the last decades thousands of revolutionists have bravely held aloft the banner of progress; that innumerable martyrs have laid down their lives on the altar of humanity; and that, finally, Catalonia is the center of the most intelligent and revolutionary proletariat of Europe—all this is quite unknown this side of the Pyrenees.

If we acquaint ourselves, however, with the views on modern Spain expressed by well-known investigators, litterateurs, and revolutionists like Havelock Ellis,[5] Tarrida del Marmol, Bart Kennedy, Enrico Malatesta, Charles Malato, and others who have personally studied the life and customs of the Spanish people, we shall behold a picture that must fill one with respect and admiration for the intellectual and revolutionary aspirations of the men and women of that underestimated nation.[6]

---

sentimental portrays of the ordinary lives of Spanish villagers and peasants. Maurice Hewlett (1861–1923) was a British historical novelist and poet. Havel is presumably referring to Hewlett's 1908 travelogue *The Spanish Jade* which, like Zeluoga's paintings, tends to romanticize Spanish commoners.

5   Havelock Ellis (1859–1939) was a famous British physician and psychologist and a friend of Emma Goldman and Margaret Sanger. Ellis offers sympathetic but unflinchingly honest reflections on the political and social situation of the Spanish underclasses in his travelogue *The Soul of Spain* (1909).

6   The anarchists Errico Malatesta (1853–1932), Charles Malato (1857–1938), and Tarrida del Mármol (1861–1915), travelled to (or, in Mármol's case, lived in) Spain and based their assessments on meetings with comrades and ordinary workers. Bart Kennedy (1861–1930), a British radical novelist and journalist, wrote a series of first-person accounts of Spanish peasant life in his *A Tramp in Spain* (1904).

* * *

No previous economic system has understood so
well as capitalism to identify itself with the existing political form of a given country. In republican America
it allies itself with corrupt politics; in autocratic Russia
with Tsarism; in militaristic Germany with the aristocracy; in Spain with clericalism. The Socialist movement in
Spain, in its essential modern form, dates from the time
of the old International.[7] Yet even prior to that period
Spain possessed a Socialist movement. The workingmen
of Catalonia had already in the 50's of the last century
an organization numbering ninety thousand members.
At the forcible dissolution of the organization by General
Zapatero, in 1855, about fifty thousand workmen quit
their factories, thus initiating the first General Strike in
Europe.[8] In no country did the International gain a

---

7   The International Workingmen's Association, which existed
from 1864 to 1876. As Havel notes below, the Spanish section
of the International was explicitly anarchist in orientation from
the start owing in large part to the influence of Bakunin and the
Italian anarchist Giuseppe Fanelli (1827–1877). Fanelli travelled
to Spain in 1868 at Bakunin's behest and was very successful in
winning Spanish workers to the cause of anarchism. For more
information see G. Esenwein, *Anarchist Ideology and the Working-
class Movement in Spain: 1868–1898* (Berkeley, CA: University of
California Press, 1989), pp. 35–44.

8   Following the Revolution of 1854—a brief military coup led
by General Leopoldo O'Donnell (1807–1867) against the government of Queen Isabel II—conditions in Spain became more
favorable to workers, particularly as concerns their ability to organize. In 1855 Juan Zapatero y Navas (1810–1881), a Spanish
military leader and governor, initiated a strong backlash against
these developments in Catalonia which led, among other things,
to the suppression of labor unions in the region. Catalunyan
workers responded by launching what is widely regarded as the

firmer foothold than in Spain, where all the members of this revolutionary body held Anarchist views. The social uprisings of the 70's, in which Michael Bakunin played such a prominent part, are a matter of history.

With the spread of the revolutionary labor movement, repression on the part of the masters grew ever more inhumane and tyrannous in proportion to the greater energy displayed in the war against the capitalist regime. The names of Mano Negra,[9] Alcala del Valle,[10] and Montjuich are written in letters of fire in the martyrology of the Spanish proletariat.[11] Now, what happened last summer in Barcelona? The international stock gamblers were preparing for new pillage, namely in the Riff district, situated in the Spanish sphere of influence in Morocco. The natives resisted, rising in the defense of their fatherland.[12]

---

first general strike in the history of Spain. (Havel is wrong to suggest that it was the first general strike in Europe; there were general strikes prior to 1855, including a Chartist-led strike in Britain in 1842.)

9   *La Mano Negra* ("The Black Hand"), a secret anarchist organization which allegedly existed in Andalusia in the late nineteenth century. The Spanish government attributed several crimes to *La Mano Negra* in 1882–1883, leading to severe anti-anarchist repression and public executions.

10 Alcalá del Valle—a town in southern Spain, the site of an unsuccessful strike in 1903 during which several workers were killed.

11 Havel is referring to three faces of the repression of anarchism in Spain. *Montjuich* is a hill in Barcelona, the location of a prison fortress where numerous anarchists were executed in 1897. It was also the site of Francesco Ferrer's execution in 1909.

12 *The Rif* is a region in northern Morocco that was subject to severe exploitation at the hands of opportunistic colonial speculators in the early twentieth century. This exploitation contributed to the eruption of violent and ultimately abortive anti-colonial uprisings between 1901 and 1910, including the Second Rif War (1909–1910), to which Havel alludes here. See M. Madariaga, *España y*

The *camarilla* in Madrid, participant in the intended capitalist robbery, arranged a campaign against the rebellious natives. Mobilization orders called out the reservists, consisting exclusively of workingmen and poor peasants unable to buy their freedom from active military service, as do the sons of the rich. Not satisfied merely to exploit the people at home, the rulers of Spain were planning to use them as cannon fodder. Heartbreaking scenes were witnessed when the Catalonian reservists gathered in the port of Barcelona preparing to be shipped to Africa. Old parents sobbed for their luckless children about to be sent to certain death; women cried over the loss of their husbands, and poor children faced the miserable fate of poor orphans. Many reservists refused to go aboard, and numerous riots followed.

Witnessing these terrible scenes, the organized workmen of Barcelona became aroused. They decided to do what the so-called friends of peace de la Carnegie failed to do, too mindful of their financial interests.[13] The *Solidaridad Obrera*, the revolutionary federation of the trade unions of Barcelona, called a special meeting of its delegates to consider the situation, with a view of organizing national protest against the war.[14] The Governor of Barcelona prohibited the meeting. That happened on the 1st of July. Three days later a spontaneous General Strike broke out in Barcelona and other Catalonian cities. The

---

el Rif: crónica de una historia casi olvidada (Málaga, La Biblioteca de Melilla, 1999).

13 Havel is referring to various international "peace conferences" which were financially supported by wealthy tycoons like Andrew Carnegie. With their ostensive goal of ending wars and preventing imminent conflicts, international peace conferences became increasingly common in the decades of mounting international tension leading up to the First World War.

14 *Solidaridad Obrera* ("Workers Solidarity") was a revolutionary Spanish trade federation founded in Barcelona in 1907.

industrial life of that large province suddenly came to a standstill. The railroads ceased operations, and the postal and telegraph service was suspended.

Had the Catalonian uprising received sufficient aid from the workers of the other provinces, the result would have been different. Unfortunately, however, the labor bodies of those districts are under the influence of parliamentary Socialists, who lacked the courage to advise their followers to join the General Strike. Still, the real purpose of that revolt was achieved. The government was paralyzed, and the embarkation of the troops could not take place at Barcelona.

The rage of the authorities transcended all description. They bent all their energies to master the situation, employing toward that end the usual governmental methods of slaughter. The result is well known. But though the popular uprising was thus mercilessly strangled, the General Strike had achieved its aim: the mobilization of reservists had to cease. The *camarilla* at Madrid could not forgive the Catalonians this significant defeat. It thirsted for revenge. The terrible scenes that followed the Paris Commune were now to be repeated in Spain. About fifteen thousand persons—men, women, and children— were arrested in Barcelona, Mataro, Manresa, Sabadell, Gerone, and Angles; among the prisoners were the most prominent labor leaders and many veterans of the revolutionary movement, like Anselmo Lorenzo, Christoval Litran, as well as Francisco Ferrer, the founder of *Escuelas Modernas*.[15]

---

15 Anselmo Lorenzo (1842–1914), Cristóbal Litrán (1861–1926), and Francesc Ferrer i Guardìa (1859–1909) were Spanish anarchists. Lorenzo was an important figure in the early Spanish anarchist movement. He was a disciple of Bakunin and collaborated with Fanelli. Litrán and Ferrer were educators as well as revolutionaries. The latter founded the *Escuela Moderna* ("the Modern School"), a system of anarchist schooling, in 1901. Ferrer Schools

* * *

No other country, except possibly Russia, possesses a greater percentage of illiteracy than Spain. Among its seventeen million inhabitants only five million are able to read or write. In most of the government schools priests and nuns are the instructors; the lay teachers are sworn to defend and support the Catholic Church. The first attempt to broaden the scope of popular education was made in the 70's of the last century by the freethinkers and republicans. They organized a number of secular schools in various parts of Spain—chiefly in Catalonia—financing them in spite of their poverty and in the face of great opposition and persecution. In 1883 these schools became federated into one organization, under the general supervision of Bartolomeo Gabarro, a former priest.[16]

But the new body failed to surmount the difficulties of the situation, with the result that it soon became disintegrated, owing to governmental persecution on the one hand, lack of means and proper methods of instruction, on the other. The factor which brought new life into the educational movement of Spain was Francisco Ferrer. Born in Avella, Catalonia, in 1859, he early joined the republican party and participated in various uprisings, among them

---

were subsequently launched in several countries, including the United States. (Havel himself had a hand in the creation of the New York Modern School—commonly known as the Ferrer Center—in 1911.)

16 Bartolomé Gabarró y Borrás (1846–c.1925) was a Spanish anticlerical journalist, writer, and educator. The organization Havel mentions was the *Confederación Española de la Enseñanza Laica* ("Spanish Confederation of Lay Education") and initially included approximately 38 schools, mostly in Catalonia. Within five years that number had grown to about 200.

the one led by General Villacampa.[17] Subsequently Ferrer became the secretary to Ruy Zorilla, the leader of the Republicans, following him, in 1886, to exile in Paris.[18] There Ferrer came in contact with Elisée Reclus and other radical thinkers, gradually developing into a consistent antiauthoritarian. Like most of his contemporaries Ferrer soon became convinced that education must be the path of the people's emancipation. He therefore determined to devote his life to the enlightenment of the rising generation along rational lines.

With this object in view Ferrer returned to his native country and began the organization of the Modern School. The text-books used in these rational schools were prepared by Ferrer himself, with the cooperation of Elisée Reclus, Professor Letourneau, Dr. Martinez Vargas, Odon de Buen, Anselmo Lorenzo, and other radical scientists.[19] The aim of the school is thus summarized in its program:

---

17 Manuel Villacampa del Castillo (1827–1889) was a Spanish Republican military leader. Villacampa led an unsuccessful coup against the Bourbon Restoration in 1886.

18 Manuel Ruiz Zorilla (1833–1895) was a Spanish Republican politician.

19 Textbooks used by the Modern School in 1905 included *Man and the Earth* by Élisée Reclus (1830–1905), a French geographer, writer, and anarchist; *Ethnic Psychology* by Charles Letourneau (1831–1902), a French Darwinian anthropologist; a *botiquín escolar* (roughly, "school kit") by Andrés Martínez-Vargas (1861–1948), a Spanish physician and one of the founders of modern pediatric practice in Spain; and series of scientific primers by Odón de Buen y del Cos (1863–1945), a Spanish scientist and writer. Lorenzo apparently helped translate various works (for example, by Letourneau) into Spanish. Martinez-Vargas delivered the first lecture to the Modern School's "People's University," and he and de Buen both wrote for the school's bulletin.

"To stimulate the mental development of
the child and to check the rise of reactionary atavistic instincts. Racial hatred, the
spirit of caste, jingoism, and revenge, so
detrimental to all social improvement, are
to be combatted. Our instruction knows
neither dogmas nor traditions, for the latter are mere formulas stifling all life, individual and social."

The remarkable personality of Ferrer and his wonderful energy and ability as organizer succeeded in a
comparatively short time to establish, in Barcelona and
other industrial centers, 53 schools, prior to his first arrest in 1906. The working population of those cities en-
thusiastically took advantage of the opportunity to free
their children from the baneful influence of the clerical schools.

The instruction of the Modern School, freed from all
religious, patriotic, and social prejudices inevitably influenced the children along the lines of liberty and social
equality. This education of the children reacted upon their
parents, in turn inspiring them with humanitarian ideas.
Moreover, the literature published by Ferrer in connection
with the Modern School circulated throughout Spain and
was to be found in every workingman's library.

Ferrer's activity was thus an open challenge to the
clerical, militaristic-capitalistic reaction, which could
conceive of no greater crime than the rational education of children. It felt its very existence threatened. The
name of Francisco Ferrer became the personification of
the struggle between the Old and the New. The reaction
eagerly sought an opportunity to destroy its hated enemy and his work.

This opportunity presented itself in May, 1906, on the
occasion of Mateo Morral's attempt upon the life of the

King.[20] Morral, a former collaborator of Ferrer, threw a bomb at Alfonso's carriage to avenge the terrible atrocities committed upon the striking farm-laborers of Andalusia.[21] Though no indication pointed at Ferrer as the accessory of Morral, the authorities arrested him on the charge of conspiracy. His schools were closed and his property confiscated. But in spite of all efforts to convict Ferrer, even by resorting to forged letters, the government failed in its purpose. The international protest of the scientific world resulted in Ferrer's liberation.

The uprising in Barcelona, three years later, offered the enemies of Ferrer and his work the longed-for opportunity for his final extermination. The unexpected happened. Before a new tremendous protest could be voiced, Ferrer was assassinated. The reaction was determined not to lose its prey again.[22]

---

20 Mateo Morral Roca (1880–1906) was a Spanish anarchist who made a failed assassination attempt on King Alfonso XIII (1885–1941) on the monarch's wedding day (May 31, 1906). Morral collaborated with Ferrer and worked in the library of the Modern School. The primary cause of Morral's actions appears to have been hatred of the monarchy and its history of cruelty and oppression.

21 Uprisings by impoverished Andalusian peasants—often anarchist-inspired—began in the 1890s and continued sporadically for at least the next two decades. It was in this context that the *Confederacíon Nacional de Trabajo* (CNT) was founded in Seville in 1910.

22 As noted previously, Havel is referring to the *Setmana Tràgica* ("Tragic Week"), a left-wing (largely anarchist-inspired) revolution which took place in Barcelona between July 25 and August 2, 1909. The uprising was triggered by Prime Minister Antonio Maura's decision to call up and deploy reserve troops in the Second Rif War (see above). *Solidaridad Obrera* called a general strike on July 26 which quickly escalated into riots, vandalism, and arson—much of it anti-clerical in nature. In the following

The noble educator is dead, and his schools suppressed. But has the cabal of clerical and civil authority achieved its purpose? Can the spirit of a Ferrer be really exterminated? No eulogy could more correctly characterize the modest grandeur of Francisco Ferrer than the introductory remarks to his will, written by him on the threshold of death. In this truly *document humain* he says:

> "Above all, I protest with all possible energy against the unexpected circumstance of the punishment inflicted upon me, expressing my conviction that before very long my innocence will be publicly recognized. I desire that on no occasion, either in the near or the far future, or for any motive whatever, shall any manifestation of a political or religious character be made over my remains, considering that the time spent in connection with the dead would be better employed in improving the condition of the living, the majority of whom have great need of it."[23]

"I desire also," this document goes on,

---

days the government retaliated swiftly and ruthlessly, declaring martial law and opening fire on demonstrators. As many as 150 people were reportedly killed and over 1,700 were indicted by military tribunals for "armed rebellion." Ferrer was arrested on September 1 and accused of leading the insurrection even though he had not been in Barcelona at the time. Following trial he was sentenced to death on October 9 and executed by firing squad at Montjuich on October 13.

23 Ferrer composed his will in the chapel of Montjuich the night before his execution. It is reproduced in full in *Francisco Ferrer: His Life, Work, and Martyrdom*, ed. Leonard Abbott (New York: Francisco Ferrer Association, 1910), p. 87.

"that my friends speak little or not at all
of me, because when men are exalted idols
are created, which is a great harm for the
future of mankind. Deeds alone, from
whomsoever they emanate, should be
studied, exalted, or branded. Let them be
praised in order that they may be imitated
when they seem to make for the common
good; let them be criticized so that they be
not repeated when they are considered injurious to the general well-being."

The assassination of such a man must prove the doom
of any government. Already Ferrer proved that he had not
died in vain. His martyrdom saved the lives of thousands
now imprisoned in Spain. As the General Strike of the
Barcelona workingmen checked the campaign of the further conquest of Morocco, so has Ferrer's death prevented
the planned massacre of the incarcerated revolutionists.[24]

Never since the memorable days of the Paris
Commune, when Elisée Reclus had been condemned
to death by the Versailles reaction,[25] has the intellectual
world made such a tremendous demonstration as in the

---

24 Ferrer's trial and execution spawned international outrage that
    played a significant role in the mass resignation of the Prime
    Minister's cabinet nine days after Ferrer's death. In the end, the
    government spared the lives of the vast majority of individuals
    who had been implicated in and imprisoned for the uprising—
    presumably because they feared retaliation at home and alienation
    from abroad.

25 Owing to his revolutionary activities during the Commune,
    Reclus was initially given a life sentence at the penal colony in
    New Caledonia. The following year, in 1872, his sentence was
    commuted to lifetime banishment from France, thanks to an in-
    ternational outcry led by several prestigious intellectuals, includ-
    ing Charles Darwin.

case of Francisco Ferrer. Nor has any similar event ever before aroused such extraordinary protest on the part of the international proletariat. No one would have believed such unity and spontaneity possible. Within a very few days we witnessed tremendous demonstrations in Paris, London, Rome, Triest, Milan, Amsterdam, Brussels, Rio de Janeiro, Buenos Ayres, Chicago, New York, and many other centers; we saw the embassies and consulates of Spain repeatedly attacked, and Spanish goods boycotted in various countries. Thus the proletariat of the world proved that international solidarity is no mere theory.

We heard the intellectuals of the world voicing their protest in no uncertain manner. Anatole France, Gerhardt Hauptmann, Walter Crane, Ernest Haeckel, Giuseppe Sergi, H. G. Wells, Wm. D. Howells, Maxim Gorky, Maurice Maeterlinck, and many others expressed their indignation at the atrocious assassination of the torch-bearer of a new gospel.[26] The whole world seemed to utter, as one man, a cry of pain and anger. The social conscience was aroused to its very depths. Our comrade fell in the struggle, but the Revolution marches on.

---

26   In addition to the previously cited individuals, Havel is referring, respectively, to Gerhard Hauptmann (1862–1946), a German playwright and novelist; Walter Crane (1845–1915), an English artist and illustrator; Ernst Haeckel (1834–1919), a German scientist, philosopher, and academic; Giuseppe Sergi (1841–1936), an Italian anthropologist; William Dean Howells (1837–1920), an America novelist and playwright; and Maurice Materlinck (1862–1949), a Belgian poet, playwright, and essayist.

THE SUFFRAGETTES (1910)[1]

The line now being taken by the militant
suffragettes heads straight to Anarchy.
—*Daily Chronicle*

The rule of "no physical violence" must now,
writes Mrs. Pethick Lawrence, be abandoned,
the militant tactics are to be pursued, writes
Miss Christabel Pankhurst, "no matter
though social order and harmony be for
a time destroyed." This is the language of
Anarchy.
—*Daily News*

We think we may say that these tactics are
unexampled in British politics.
—*The Nation*

---

1   This essay appeared in *Mother Earth* 4, no. 12 (February 1910).
As Havel makes clear in his description of events, 1910 was a year
marked by increasing militancy in the English women's suffrage
movement—a development of which he obviously approves.
At the same time, it is worth noting that Havel, like Goldman,
tended to be critical of suffrage as a political aim (see, for example, Goldman's essay "The Woman Suffrage Chameleon,"
Mother Earth 12, no. 3, 1917). In its place, he preferred to situate the emancipation of women in the broader context of social
revolution.

NONE MORE LOVED THAN THE LUKEWARM ONES WHO never say yes or no. None more admired than the tolerant ones who never hurt. How they are caressed, those platonic enthusiasts who rapturously bow right and left. How they are respected, those theoretic champions who, with sweeping gestures, demonstrate the truth of the matter. How they are loved, these weak-kneed mollycoddles. But woe to the fiery, the inspired ones! Woe to those in whose veins flows red blood. Woe to the energetic, the conscious, who consecrate their whole life to their ideal—those to whom the struggle is the very personification of life itself. Above all, woe to the *franctireurs*![2] They who forever compromise the good cause of the philistines in the eyes of decent men; who, by their impulsiveness, paralyze the carefully planned moves of diplomacy; to whom the most sancto-sacred is not sacred.

These are the terror of the cautious, of the hesitating, lagging, deferring ones—they are the *bête noire*. Yet, in spite of it all, can history point to a single revolutionary movement—whether political, scientific, or artistic—that has been carried to victory by the lukewarm, the impartial, platonic, and theoretic elements?

The suffragettes of Great Britain are the latter-day *enfant terrible* of all mollusks. The most heinous indictment is brought against them by respectability: they are on the road to Anarchy. What honor for the suffragettes! In truth, the good people are not far amiss. The suffragettes began the fight for votes, and—Oh, Irony—they have ended by destroying the ballot boxes. The most fanatical opponent of the ballot could not act more consistently. This spectacle is to us Anarchists—who have grown out of the ballot superstition—a source of almost diabolic joy. No wonder, then, that the State worshippers—be they

2   "*Francs-tireurs*"—literally "free shooters,"—was a term for irregular militias in the Franco-Prussian War (i.e., guerillas). It has the general meaning of mavericks, rebels, or non-conformists.

named Asquith, Belfort Bax, or Quelch—are horrified at such blasphemous tactics.[3]

The destruction of ballot boxes is, however, not the only spice of humor in the struggle for woman suffrage. We witness disciples of Schopenhauer, Nietzsche, and Weininger champion the cause of the women,[4] while good liberals and even some Socialists, theoretically in favor of sex equality, unmask themselves as the most bitter opponents of women's political rights.

'Tis a transvaluation of all values.

O, man! Stupidity is thy name. Could anything be more stupid than to withhold such an innocent toy from woman, and then to drive her to desperation by utmost brutality, baseness, and vileness?

Yet let us be grateful to these dull-witted blockheads. But for their fiendish persecution mania we would be the poorer in this wonderful revolutionary movement—a movement that has far outgrown its original aims. Mrs. Pethick Lawrence, one of the ablest leaders of the Women's Social and Political Union, explains in *Votes for Women*:[5]

---

3   Herbert Henry Asquith (1852–1928) was Liberal Prime Minister of the United Kingdom from 1908–1916. He is notable for introducing various domestic reforms including social insurance and progressive taxation. Ernest Belfort Bax (1854–1926) was a British Social Democratic journalist, philosopher, and historian. Henry Quelch (1858–1913) was a British Marxist and a member of the Social Democratic Federation. Havel's point here is that all three men were either opposed to the suffragettes on principle (see, for example, Bax's 1916 essay "Legal Subjugation of Men") or else to their use of violent direct action.

4   The philosophers Schopenhauer (1788–1860), Nietzsche (1844–1900), and Weininger (1880–1903) all had reputations as misogynists.

5   Emmeline Pethick-Lawrence (1867–1954) was a British socialist and feminist. As Havel notes, she was a prominent leader of the Women's Social and Political Union, a militant women's

No protest now could find its way into the public meetings except by stones. If the battle was to be continued at all, it must be by the abandonment of the rule hitherto observed, No destruction of any kind! No physical violence !! . . . This is a revolution. This is a war. But this revolution was forced upon us. It is a war which we are called upon to wage in the name of liberty and justice.

For half a century the women of Great Britain have struggled, peacefully and orderly, for their mess of pottage. Like all reformers, they were first ridiculed, then ignored. Silently they suffered abuse and contempt. But when the government began to persecute them with brutal violence, they unfurled the banner of rebellion. Suffragists were transformed into suffragettes. In wonderment we witnessed the heroism and self-sacrifice developed by these women in their unequal fight with man's stupidity and the brutality of his government. Even the opponents of woman suffrage are forced to admit the truth of this. To quote but one opinion out of a multitude. The *Bristol Mercury* thus expresses itself:

> None can question their courage and their willingness to make sacrifices for the cause they have taken up. There was a good deal of rioting and window breaking before men got the vote by the Reform Bill

---

suffrage organization founded in the United Kingdom in 1903 by Emmeline Pankhurst (1858–1928) and her daughters Christabel (1880–1958), Sylvia (1882–1960), and Adela (1885–1961). Pethick- Lawrence edited the Women's Social and Political Union organ (*Votes For Women*, published from 1907 to 1918) with her husband, Frederick.

of 1832, but neither in that agitation nor in any other political movement have men endured so much for their convictions as have the suffragists in Holloway Prison. Whatever one may think of the Votes for Women agitation, men have never made in any political movement of the past such self-sacrifices for their opinions as these women have done.

Never before have such outrages been committed in Great Britain against political prisoners as against these women.[6] What about the celebrated chivalry of Englishmen? Where the boasted Anglo-Saxon respect for the sex? Had the men of England but a spark of shame, a storm of protest should have swept the land. And why this bestial treatment in the prisons? Why the hunger strikes? Merely because the suffragettes demand the rights of political prisoners.

The latter receive worse treatment in England than the common criminal. John Most, Vladimir Bourtseff, David Nicoll, and the Walsall Anarchists could bear witness to this.[7] When the suffragettes demanded the rights of

---

6 Except, of course, in the cases of Irish revolutionaries of the sort Havel describes below.

7 All of the individuals mentioned here were imprisoned at various times, often in deplorable and inhumane conditions, by the British government. Johann Most (1846–1906) was a German-American anarchist who was sentenced to 18 months in 1881 for an article in which he celebrated the assassination of Tsar Alexander II. Vladimir Burtzev (1862–1942) was a Russian socialist revolutionary who was sentenced to 18 months in 1892 for advocating the assassination of Tsar Nicholas II. David Nicoll (1859–1919) was a British anarchist who was imprisoned in 1892 for writing an article which appeared to threaten the British Home Secretary. The "Walsall anarchists" (Joe Deakin, Victor

political prisoners, Home Secretary Herbert Gladstone[8] declared in the House of Commons:

> Political offences are not in any way recognized by the common law of England, nor can political motive be pleaded in justification of an offence or as in itself en- titling the offender to special treatment in prison. Persons guilty of certain offences specified by statute, such as sedition and seditious libel, must by statute be placed in the first division, but it is not, and never has been, the law or practice in this country to accord special treatment to prisoners who, like the suffragists, have offended against the ordinary law in the course of a political agitation or from political motives, and the introduction of such a practice would be likely to have dangerous consequences... If our government differs from all other civilized governments in connection with the treatment of political prisoners, it is about time other governments imitated us.

Herbert Gladstone thus proved himself a veritable political bastard. Let us hear what his illustrious father, William Ewart Gladstone, had to say on this subject in 1889, on the occasion of the Parliamentary discussion of the case of the Irish Nationalist, William O'Brien, who

---

Cails, Jean Battola, William Ditchfield, John Westley, and Fred Charles) were a British-based group arrested in 1892 for manufacturing explosive devices. Subsequent evidence revealed that the group was framed by an agent provocateur.

8   Herbert Gladstone (1854–1954) was a British Liberal statesman who served as Home Secretary from 1905 to 1910.

refused to be treated as a common criminal.[9] After mentioning the cases of Cobbett, Sir John Hobhouse, Feargus O'Connor, Smith O'Brien, Mitchell, and O'Connel[10]—all of whom had enjoyed the rights of political prisoners—the great father of the little son said:

> I am not going to be entangled in arguments as to what are and are not political offences. I know very well you cannot attempt to frame a legislative definition of political offences, but what you can do, and what always has been done, is this: You can say that in certain classes of cases the imprisoned person ought not to be treated as if he had been guilty of base and degrading crime. What does the ordinary

---

9   William Ewart Gladstone (1809–1898) was a British Liberal statesman who served as Prime Minister four times (1868–1874, 1880–1885, February–July 1886, and 1892–1894). William O'Brien (1852–1928) was an Irish nationalist, journalist, and politician.

10 William Cobbett (1763–1835) was an English reformer and journalist who was imprisoned by the British government from 1810 to 1812 for "treasonous libel." Sir John Cam Hobhouse (1786–1869) was a liberal British politican who was imprisoned by the British government in 1819 for authoring a "radical" pamphlet. Feargus O'Connor (1794–1855) was a radical Irish Chartist who was imprisoned by the British government in 1840 for "seditious libel." William Smith O'Brien (1803–1864) was an Irish nationalist and leader of the Young Ireland movement who was convicted of sedition for his role in the Young Irelander Rebellion of 1848. John Mitchel (1815–1875) was an Irish Nationalist who was convicted of "treason felony" in 1848. Daniel O'Connell (1775–1847) was an Irish political leader and advocate for Catholic emancipation who was charged with sedition in 1841 for supporting the Repeal of the Union.

sentence of imprisonment import? The deprivation of literature and visitors, the plank bed, the prison dress, the odious, the disgraceful incidence of the company of felons. . . . But, Sir, I say that though sensitiveness to indignities of this kind may be a matter on which men will differ according to their temperament and their ideas, yet such sensitiveness is a sensitiveness rather to be encouraged than to be repressed, for it appertains to that lofty sentiment—that spirit which was described by Burke in immortal language when he said, 'The spirit which feels a stain like a wound. 'We protest against this prison treatment as being condemned by the country, and as being in itself unwise, inhuman, and brutal. I have not sought to multiply epithets of this kind, but I cannot altogether withhold them. Finally, I say, it is entirely contrary to the usage of other governments.

Can anyone claim that the agitation of the suffragettes springs from base motives, or that its character is not political? Why, then, the discrimination against these women? Is it because of their sex? Not at all. They are persecuted so cruelly because they are the first political party in Great Britain who have resorted to the most powerful and effective weapon in the whole arsenal of life: direct action. No other political group has ever used such tactics, except the Anarchists. And with what ingenuity and effect the suffragettes have employed this method! This the politicians and diplomats will never forget nor forgive.

Since the suffragettes have initiated direct action tactics, they have defeated their opponents at every point. They have created the strongest organization in England, collected a fund of £50,000, organized demonstrations which in point of numbers, enthusiasm, and beauty have never been equaled in the history of the country. What artistic joy, not to speak of the revolutionary spirit, the tremendous Hyde Park demonstration would have afforded William Morris.[11] Since the fifth of July of last year till the dissolution of the Parliament the latter was besieged day and night, without intermission, by the epical watch. Hundreds of meetings, to be addressed by Cabinet Ministers, were broken up; banquets, private and official receptions disturbed, and life made a nightmare for officialdom.

What a spectacle! Never before had England witnessed such a humiliating sight. The dissolution of Parliament and the following elections form a turning point. Such propaganda cannot possibly stop at mere suffrage. Already there are among the suffragettes certain elements whose demands go much further. They are awakening to the realization that the fight for the feminine mess of pottage is but the prelude to a greater and more tremendous struggle of social proportions. They will gradually join that movement, and the experiences they have thus far gathered will prove of great value for the general emancipation of mankind. Their self- sacrifice and heroism can serve as an example deserving the respect and sympathy of every revolutionist. The seed they have sown will not fail of a rich harvest. The words of Mary Neal, one of the participants in the hunger strike, will come true:

> Nearer to the Earth Mother than man,
> wiser in the wisdom learnt at the gates
> of death, through which enters each
> new-born life, in the depths of her being

---

11 William Morris (1834–1896) was a British Socialist and leader of the English Arts and Crafts Movement. Havel is alluding to Morris' twin passions for art, on the one hand, and radical politics, on the other.

untouched by the sophistries of a masculine interpretation of her place in life, woman has committed the seed of her liberty to the earth. Ploughed in by suffering as it has been, ruthlessly cut down again and again, condemned to death by the Kings of Prejudice, Tyranny, and Lust, it has risen triumphant, and the harvest is near at hand.[12]

---

12 Mary Neal (1860–1944) was a British socialist, feminist, and folklorist. The quote is taken from "The Wisdom of the Folk," *Votes for Women* (May 7, 1909).

INTRODUCTION TO ANARCHISM AND OTHER ESSAYS (1910)[1]

Propagandism is not, as some suppose, a "trade," because nobody will follow a "trade" at which you may work with the industry of a slave and die with the reputation- of a mendicant. The motives of any persons to pursue such a profession must be different

---

1   Emma Goldman's *Anarchism and Other Essays* was published by the Mother Earth Publishing Association in 1910 at a time when Goldman was incessantly harassed by the authorities and vilified by the press. As Goldman herself notes in her autobiography *Living My Life*, "Some of the lectures in the volume had been repeatedly suppressed by the police. Even when I had been able to deliver them, it had never been without anxiety and travail" (p. 494). Havel's introduction, which represents the first authorized and comprehensive biography of Goldman, is obviously intended to defend her reputation. As a result, it makes no pretense toward objectivity, and many of the details of her life and character are incomplete or presented in a one-sided manner. These details are clarified by Goldman in *Living My Life*, as well as in subsequent biographies such as Richard Drinnon's *Rebel in Paradise: A Biography of Emma Goldman* (Chicago: University of Chicago Press, 1981); Candace Falk's *Emma Goldman: A Documentary History Of The American Years*, 3 vols. (Berkeley, CA: University of California Press, 2003, 2004, 2012) and *Love, Anarchy, and Emma Goldman: A Biography* (New Brunswick, NJ: Rutgers University Press, 1990); and Alice Wexler's *Emma Goldman: An Intimate Life* (New York: Pantheon , 1984).

from those of trade, deeper than pride, and
stronger than interest.[2]
—George Jacob Holyoake

AMONG THE MEN AND WOMEN PROMINENT IN THE PUBLIC
life of America there are but few whose names are mentioned as often as that of Emma Goldman. Yet the real
Emma Goldman is almost quite unknown. The sensational press has surrounded her name with so much misrepresentation and slander, it would seem almost a miracle that,
in spite of this web of calumny, the truth breaks through
and a better appreciation of this much maligned idealist
begins to manifest itself. There is but little consolation in
the fact that almost every representative of a new idea has
had to struggle and suffer under similar difficulties. Is it of
any avail that a former president of a republic pays homage at Osawatomie to the memory of John Brown?[3] Or
that the president of another republic participates in the
unveiling of a statue in honor of Pierre Proudhon, and
holds up his life to the French nation as a model worthy of
enthusiastic emulation?[4] Of what avail is all this when,
at the same time, the *living* John Browns and Proudhons
are being crucified? The honor and glory of a Mary
Wollstonecraft or of a Louise Michel are not enhanced

---

2   *Sixty Years of an Agitator's Life* (London: T.F. Unwin, 1900), p.
    162. Holyoake (1817–1906) was an English secularist.

3   John Brown (1800–1859), American radical abolitionist.
    Osawatomie, Kansas, was the site of an 1856 battle between
    anti-slavery forces, led by Brown, and pro-slavery forces from
    Missouri.

4   Havel is presumably referring to a statue of Proudhon that was
    erected in 1909 in Besançon (Proudhon's birthplace) to com-
    memorate the centenary of Proudhon's birth. The ceremonial un-
    veiling of the statue was attended by President Armand Fallières.

by the City Fathers of London or Paris naming a street after them—the living generation should be concerned with doing justice to the *living* Mary Wollstonecrafts and Louise Michels.[5] Posterity assigns to men like Wendell Phillips and Lloyd Garrison the proper niche of honor in the temple of human emancipation; but it is the duty of their contemporaries to bring them due recognition and appreciation while they live.[6]

The path of the propagandist of social justice is strewn with thorns. The powers of darkness and injustice exert all their might lest a ray of sunshine enter his cheerless life. Nay, even his comrades in the struggle—indeed, too often his most intimate friends—show but little understanding for the personality of the pioneer. Envy, sometimes growing to hatred, vanity and jealousy, obstruct his

5   Mary Wollstonecraft (1759–1797) was an English feminist, writer, and philosopher. Her book *A Vindication of the Rights of Women* (1792), written as a response to the French Revolution, represents an early articulation and defense of feminism and is widely regarded as a landmark text in the history of the women's movement. Wollstonecraft's husband, the political philosopher William Godwin (1756–1836), is recognized as an important precursor to modern anarchism. Louise Michel (1830–1905) was a French anarchist revolutionary who was active in the French Commune in 1871. Like Wollstonecraft, Michel sought in her life and work to emphasize the connections between revolutionary political activity and the struggle for women's emancipation. Here, Havel is attempting to situate Goldman within the august lineage of these and other female revolutionaries.

6   Wendell Phillips (1811–1884) and William Lloyd Garrison (1805–1879) were important American abolitionists. As crusading opponents of slavery, they were deeply admired in anarchist circles. Indeed, Goldman herself quotes Phillips approvingly in *Anarchism and Other Essays* (p. 79) and cites Garrison and Phillips, alongside Margaret Fuller, Theodore Parker, and John Brown, as "patron saints" in the "American struggle for liberty" (p. 82).

way and fill his heart with sadness. It requires an inflexible will and tremendous enthusiasm not to lose, under such conditions, all faith in the Cause. The representative of a revolutionizing idea stands between two fires: on the one hand, the persecution of the existing powers which hold him responsible for all acts resulting from social conditions; and, on the other, the lack of understanding on the part of his own followers who often judge all his activity from a narrow standpoint. Thus it happens that the agitator stands quite alone in the midst of the multitude surrounding him. Even his most intimate friends rarely understand how solitary and deserted he feels. That is the tragedy of the person prominent in the public eye.

The mist in which the name of Emma Goldman has so long been enveloped is gradually beginning to dissipate. Her energy in the furtherance of such an unpopular idea as Anarchism, her deep earnestness, her courage and abilities, find growing understanding and admiration.

The debt American intellectual growth owes to the revolutionary exiles has never been fully appreciated. The seed disseminated by them, though so little understood at the time, has brought a rich harvest. They have at all times held aloft the banner of liberty, thus impregnating the social vitality of the Nation. But very few have succeeded in preserving their European education and culture while at the same time assimilating themselves with American life. It is difficult for the average man to form an adequate conception what strength, energy, and perseverance are necessary to absorb the unfamiliar language, habits, and customs of a new country, without the loss of one's own personality.

Emma Goldman is one of the few who, while thoroughly preserving their individuality, have become an important factor in the social and intellectual atmosphere of America. The life she leads is rich in color, full of change and variety. She has risen to the topmost heights, and she has also tasted the bitter dregs of life.

Emma Goldman was born of Jewish parentage on the 27th day of June, 1869, in the Russian province of Kovno.[7] Surely these parents never dreamed what unique position their child would someday occupy. Like all conservative parents they, too, were quite convinced that their daughter would marry a respectable citizen, bear him children, and round out her allotted years surrounded by a flock of grandchildren, a good, religious woman. As most parents, they had no inkling what a strange, impassioned spirit would take hold of the soul of their child, and carry it to the heights which separate generations in eternal struggle. They lived in a land and at a time when antagonism between parent and offspring was fated to find its most acute expression, irreconcilable hostility. In this tremendous struggle between fathers and sons—and especially between parents and daughters—there was no compromise, no weak yielding, no truce. The spirit of liberty, of progress—an idealism which knew no considerations and recognized no obstacles—drove the young generation out of the parental house and away from the hearth of the home. Just as this same spirit once drove out the revolutionary breeder of discontent, Jesus, and alienated him from his native traditions.

What role the Jewish race—notwithstanding all anti-semitic calumnies the race of transcendental idealism—played in the struggle of the Old and the New will probably never be appreciated with complete impartiality and clarity. Only now we are beginning to perceive the tremendous debt we owe to Jewish idealists in the realm of science, art, and literature. But very little is still known of the important part the sons and daughters of Israel have played in the revolutionary movement and, especially, in that of modern times.

The first years of her childhood Emma Goldman passed in a small, idyllic place in the German-Russian

---

7   Kovno (Lithuanian: *Kaunas*) is a city—not a province—located in present-day Lithuania.

province of Kurland, where her father had charge of the government stage.[8] At that time Kurland was thoroughly German; even the Russian bureaucracy of that Baltic province was recruited mostly from German *junkers*.[9] German fairy tales and stories, rich in the miraculous deeds of the heroic knights of Kurland, wove their spell over the youthful mind. But the beautiful idyll was of short duration. Soon the soul of the growing child was overcast by the dark shadows of life. Already in her tenderest youth the seeds of rebellion and unrelenting hatred of oppression were to be planted in the heart of Emma Goldman. Early she learned to know the beauty of the State: she saw her father harassed by the Christian *chinovniks* and doubly persecuted as petty official and hated Jew.[10] The brutality of forced conscription ever stood before her eyes: she beheld the young men, often the sole support of a large family, brutally dragged to the barracks to lead the miserable life of a soldier. She heard the weeping of the poor peasant women, and witnessed the shameful scenes of official venality which relieved the rich from military service at the expense of the poor. She was outraged by the terrible treatment to which the female servants were subjected: maltreated and exploited by their *barinyas*,[11] they fell to the tender mercies of the regimental officers, who regarded them as their natural sexual prey. These girls, made pregnant by respectable gentlemen and driven out by their mistresses, often found refuge in the Goldman home. And the little girl, her heart palpitating with sympathy, would abstract coins from the parental drawer to clandestinely press the money into the hands of the unfortunate women. Thus Emma Goldman's most striking

---

8   Kurland is located in present-day Latvia.

9   Members of the Prussian landed nobility.

10   Minor officials in Czarist Russia who often instigated pogroms against the Jews.

11   Mistresses.

characteristic, her sympathy with the underdog, already became manifest in these early years.

At the age of seven little Emma was sent by her parents to her grandmother at Konigsberg, the city of Emanuel Kant, in Eastern Prussia. Save for occasional interruptions, she remained there till her 13th birthday. The first years in these surroundings do not exactly belong to her happiest recollections. The grandmother, indeed, was very amiable, but the numerous aunts of the household were concerned more with the spirit of practical rather than pure reason, and the categoric imperative was applied all too frequently. The situation was changed when her parents migrated to Konigsberg, and little Emma was relieved from her role of Cinderella.[12] She now regularly attended public school and also enjoyed the advantages of private instruction, customary in middle class life; French and music lessons played an important part in the curriculum. The future interpreter of Ibsen and Shaw was then a little German Gretchen, quite at home in the German atmosphere. Her special predilections in literature were the sentimental romances of Marlitt;[13] she was a great admirer of the good Queen Louise, whom the bad Napoleon Buonaparte treated with so marked a lack of knightly chivalry. What might have been her future development had she remained in this milieu? Fate—or was it economic necessity?—willed it otherwise. Her parents decided to settle in St. Petersburg, the capital of the Almighty Tsar, and there to embark in business. It was here that a great change took place in the life of the young dreamer.[14]

---

12 This may not be quite accurate. In *Living My Life*, Goldman claims that her father worked as an innkeeper in Konigsberg (p. 15) and that her family was very poor (p. 23).

13 Eugenie Marlitt (1825–1887) was the pseudonym of Eugenie John, a German writer of popular novels.

14 According to *Living My Life*, Goldman's father moved to St. Petersburg first to serve as a manager at a cousin's dry goods store.

It was an eventful period—the year of 1882— in which Emma Goldman, then in her 13th year, arrived in St. Petersburg. A struggle for life and death between the autocracy and the Russian intellectuals swept the country. Alexander II had fallen the previous year. Sophia Perovskaia, Zheliabov, Grinevitzky, Rissakov, Kibalchitch, Michailov,[15] the heroic executors of the death sentence upon the tyrant, had then entered the Walhalla of immortality. Jessie Helfman, the only regicide whose life the government had reluctantly spared because of pregnancy, followed the unnumbered Russian martyrs to the steppes of Siberia.[16] It was the most heroic period in the great battle of emancipation, a battle for freedom such as the world had never witnessed before. The names of the Nihilist martyrs were on all lips, and thousands were enthusiastic to follow their example.[17] The whole *intelligenzia* of

---

By the time she and the rest of the family arrived in 1882, the business had failed. Goldman's parents subsequently invested in a grocery store, but this venture was not successful and Goldman was compelled to take up employment in a glove factory. While Havel portrays 1882 as a kind of *annus mirabilis* for Goldman, replete with intellectual and political discovery, she herself is more inclined to emphasize the struggle and hardship she endured during this period.

15 Sophia Perovskaya (1853–1881), Andrei Zhelyabov (1851–1881), Ignacy Hryniewiecki (1856–1881), Nikolai Rysakov (1861–1881), Nikolai Kybalchych (1853–1881), and Timofei Mikhaylov (1885–1884) were Russian revolutionaries associated with the group *Narodnya Volya* ("People's Will"), which orchestrated the assassination of Czar Alexander II.

16 Gesya Gelfman (c. 1852–1882) was another member of *Narodnya Volya* implicated in Alexander II's assassination.

17 Nihilism was a Russian revolutionary movement that began in the 1860s, famously depicted in Ivan Turgenev's *Fathers and Sons*. The Russian nihilists were ardent anti-authoritarians and militant opponents of Tsarism who eventually became notorious for their

Russia was filled with the *illegal* spirit: revolutionary sentiments penetrated into every home, from mansion to hovel, impregnating the military, the *chinovniks*, factory workers, and peasants. The atmosphere pierced the very casemates of the royal palace. New ideas germinated in the youth. The difference of sex was forgotten. Shoulder to shoulder fought the men and the women. The Russian woman! "Who shall ever do justice or adequately-portray her heroism and self-sacrifice, her loyalty and devotion?" Holy, Turgeniev calls her in his great prose poem, *On the Threshold.*[18]

It was inevitable that the young dreamer from Konigsberg should be drawn into the maelstrom. To remain outside of the circle of free ideas meant a life of vegetation, of death. One need not wonder at the youthful age. Young enthusiasts were not then—and, fortunately, are not now—a rare phenomenon in Russia. The study of the Russian language soon brought young Emma Goldman in touch with revolutionary students and new ideas. The place of Marlitt was taken by Nekrassov and Tchernishevsky.[19] The quondam admirer of the good

---

open endorsement of the use of violence in pursuit of political ends. They are to be distinguished from philosophical nihilists, such as Nietzsche, who questioned the possibility of objective truth and absolute moral judgments.

18 Published in 1882, the poem, "Threshold" was widely believed by Russian revolutionaries to have been inspired by the execution of Perovskaya in 1881. Turgenev, however, dated it 1878 and the poem was more likely to be referring to Vera Zasulich who attempted to assassinate Trepov, the Governor of St. Petersburg, in 1878.

19 Havel's point here is to call attention to Goldman's radicalization, as evidenced by a shift in her reading habits. Nikolai Nekrasov (1821–1878) was a Russian writer, publisher, and critic. A prominent member of the liberal *intelligentsia*, Nekrasov wrote sympathetically on behalf of the Russian peasantry in poems such as

Queen Louise became a glowing enthusiast of liberty, resolving, like thousands of others, to devote her life to the emancipation of the people.

The struggle of generations now took place in the Goldman family. The parents could not comprehend what interest their daughter could find in the new ideas, which they themselves considered fantastic Utopias. They strove to persuade the young girl out of these chimeras, and daily repetition of soul-racking disputes was the result. Only in one member of the family did the young idealist find understanding—in her elder sister, Helene, with whom she later emigrated to America, and whose love and sympathy have never failed her. Even in the darkest hours of later persecution Emma Goldman always found a haven of refuge in the home of this loyal sister.

Emma Goldman finally resolved to achieve her independence. She saw hundreds of men and women sacrificing brilliant careers to go *v narod*, to the people. She followed their example. She became a factory worker; at first employed as a corset maker, and later in the manufacture of gloves. She was now 17 years of age and proud to earn her own living. Had she remained in Russia, she would have probably sooner or later shared the fate of thousands buried in the snows of Siberia. But a new chapter of life was to begin for her. Sister Helene decided to emigrate to

---

"Peasant Children" (1861) and "The Railway" (1864). Nikolai Chernyshevsky (1828–1889) was a revolutionary socialist whose 1863 novel *What Is To Be Done?* was hugely influential among Russian populists and radicals. (Lenin, for example, recycled the novel's title in his famous 1902 pamphlet.) Goldman and Berkman, too, were huge fans of the novel. Berkman adopted the name "Rakhmetov" (the model revolutionist in *What Is To Be Done?*) when signing in to his hotel in Pittsburgh immediately before he attempted to assassinate Henry Clay Frick. Around the same time Goldman described herself as "Vera Pavlovna," another character in the novel.

America, where another sister had already made her home. Emma prevailed upon Helene to be allowed to join her, and together they departed for America, filled with the joyous hope of a great, free land, the glorious Republic.[20]

America! What magic word. The yearning of the enslaved, the promised land of the oppressed, the goal of all longing for progress. Here man's ideals had found their fulfillment: no Tsar, no Cossack, no *chinovnik*. The Republic! Glorious synonym of equality, freedom, brotherhood.

Thus thought the two girls as they travelled, in the year 1886, from New York to Rochester. Soon, all too soon, disillusionment awaited them. The ideal conception of America was punctured already at Castle Garden,[21] and soon burst like a soap bubble. Here Emma Goldman witnessed sights which reminded her of the terrible scenes of her childhood in Kurland. The brutality and humiliation the future citizens of the great Republic were subjected to on board ship, were repeated at Castle Garden by the officials of the democracy in a more savage and aggravating manner. And what bitter disappointment followed as the young idealist began to familiarize herself with the conditions in the new land! Instead of one Tsar, she found scores of them; the Cossack was replaced by the policeman with the heavy club, and instead of the Russian *chinovnik* there was the far more inhuman slave driver of the factory.

Emma Goldman soon obtained work in the clothing establishment of the Garson Co.[22] The wages amounted to two and a half dollars a week. At that time the factories

---

20 In fact, Goldman prevailed upon her father to allow her to join Helene.

21 Later known as Castle (or Fort) Clinton, a fort on the southern tip of Manhattan Island which served as the point of arrival for immigrants prior to Ellis Island.

22 Garson, Meyer & Company was a garment manufacturing firm founded in Rochester by Moses Garson (1836–1903) and Theobald Meyer (1847–1880) in 1871.

were not provided with motor power, and the poor sewing girls had to drive the wheels by foot, from early morning till late at night. A terribly exhausting toil it was, without a ray of light, the drudgery of the long day passed in complete silence—the Russian custom of friendly conversation at work was not permissible in the free country. But the exploitation of the girls was not only economic; the poor wage workers were looked upon by their foremen and bosses as sexual commodities. If a girl resented the advances of her "superiors," she would speedily find herself on the street as an undesirable element in the factory. There was never a lack of willing victims: the supply always exceeded the demand.

The horrible conditions were made still more unbearable by the fearful dreariness of life in the small American city. The Puritan spirit suppresses the slightest manifestation of joy; a deadly dullness beclouds the soul; no intellectual inspiration, no thought exchange between congenial spirits is possible. Emma Goldman almost suffocated in this atmosphere. She, above all others, longed for ideal surroundings, for friendship and understanding, for the companionship of kindred minds. Mentally she still lived in Russia. Unfamiliar with the language and life of the country, she dwelt more in the past than in the present. It was at this period that she met a young man[23] who spoke Russian. With great joy the acquaintance was cultivated. At last a person with whom she could converse, one who could help her bridge the dullness of the narrow existence. The friendship gradually ripened and finally culminated in marriage.

Emma Goldman, too, had to walk the sorrowful road of married life; she, too, had to learn from bitter experience that legal statutes signify dependence and self-effacement, especially for the woman. The marriage was no liberation from the Puritan dreariness of American life;

---

23   Jacob Kershner, whom Goldman married in 1887.

indeed, it was rather aggravated by the loss of self-ownership. The characters of the young people differed too widely. A separation soon followed, and Emma Goldman went to New Haven, Conn. There she found employment in a factory, and her husband disappeared from her horizon. Two decades later she was fated to be unexpectedly reminded of him by the Federal authorities.[24]

The revolutionists who were active in the Russian movement of the 80's were but little familiar with the social ideas then agitating Western Europe and America. Their sole activity consisted in educating the people, their final goal the destruction of the autocracy. Socialism and Anarchism were terms hardly known even by name. Emma Goldman, too, was entirely unfamiliar with the significance of those ideals.

She arrived in America, as four years previously in Russia, at a period of great social and political unrest. The working people were in revolt against the terrible labor conditions; the eight-hour movement of the Knights of Labor was at its height, and throughout the country echoed the din of sanguine strife between strikers and police.[25] The struggle culminated in the great strike against the Harvester Company of Chicago, the massacre of the strikers, and the judicial murder of the labor leaders, which followed upon the historic

---

24 The federal government revoked Kershner's citizenship in April 1908 as part of an attempt to challenge Goldman's claim to citizenship through him as the two had not officially divorced.

25 As Havel notes, the Knights were instrumental in organizing for an eight-hour working day in the United States, which by the 1870s had become a central demand of the American labor movement. In 1884, the Federation of Organized Trades and Labor Unions resolved that the eight-hour day would be legally recognized effective May 1, 1886. On that day, a general strike was called in which upwards of 300,000 workers participated nationwide, including employees of the McCormick Harvesting Machine Company of Chicago.

Haymarket bomb explosion. The Anarchists stood the martyr test of blood baptism. The apologists of capitalism vainly seek to justify the killing of Parsons, Spies, Lingg, Fischer, and Engel. Since the publication of Governor Altgeld's reasons for his liberation of the three incarcerated Haymarket Anarchists, no doubt is left that a fivefold legal murder had been committed in Chicago, in 1887.[26]

Very few have grasped the significance of the Chicago martyrdom; least of all the ruling classes. By the destruction of a number of labor leaders they thought to stem the tide of a world-inspiring idea, They failed to consider that from the blood of the martyrs grows the new seed, and that the frightful injustice will win new converts to the Cause.

The two most prominent representatives of the Anarchist idea in America, Voltairine de Cleyre[27] and

---

26   On May 3, 1886, police fired upon strikers and locked-out workers from the McCormick plant, resulting in at least two deaths. In response, local anarchists organized a rally to take place the next day at Haymarket Square. At about 10:30 PM, several hours into the rally, the police arrived and ordered the assembled crowd to disperse, at which point an unknown party detonated a home-made bomb. Several officers were mortally wounded in the explosion. Over the course of the following two months, George Engel (1836–1887), Samuel Fielden (1847–1922), Adolph Fischer (1858–1887), Louis Lingg (1864–1887), Oscar Neebe (1850–1916), Albert Parsons (1848–1887), Michael Schwab (1853–1898), and August Spies (1855–1887) were arrested and charged with orchestrating the attack. Of these, the anarchists Engel, Fischer, Parsons, and Spies were executed on 11 November 1887. (Lingg committed suicide in prison the night before the execution.) Fielden, Neebe, and Schwab received prison sentences. They were pardoned in 1893 by Illinois Governor John Peter Altgeld (1847–1902). For a detailed history of the Haymarket Affair, see P. Avrich, *The Haymarket Tragedy* (Princeton, NJ: Princeton University Press, 1986).

27   Goldman maintained a warm if occasionally uneasy relationship with de Cleyre (1866–1912) throughout most of the latter's brief

Emma Goldman—the one a native American, the other a Russian—have been converted, like numerous others, to the ideas of Anarchism by the judicial murder. Two women who had not known each other before, and who had received a widely different education, were through that murder united in one idea.

Like most working men and women of America, Emma Goldman followed the Chicago trial with great anxiety and excitement. She, too, could not believe that the leaders of the proletariat would be killed. The 11th of November, 1887, taught her differently.[28] She realized that no mercy could be expected from the ruling class, that between the Tsarism of Russia and the plutocracy of America there was no difference save in name. Her whole being rebelled against the crime, and she vowed to herself a solemn vow to join the ranks of the revolutionary proletariat and to devote all her energy and strength to their emancipation from wage slavery. With the glowing enthusiasm so characteristic of her nature, she now began to familiarize herself with the literature of Socialism and Anarchism. She attended public meetings and became acquainted with socialistically and anarchistically inclined workingmen. Johanna Greie, the well-known German lecturer, was the first Socialist speaker heard by Emma Goldman.[29] In New Haven, Conn., where she was employed in a corset factory, she met Anarchists actively participating in the movement. Here she read the

---

life. Although the two women were openly supportive of one another (Goldman praised her as "the most gifted and brilliant anarchist woman American ever produced," for example), they often disagreed on matters of substance as well as style.

28 As noted above, Parsons, Spies, Fischer, and Engel were executed on this day.

29 Johanna Grie-Cramer (b. 1864) was a German immigrant active in the Socialist Labor Party.

Freiheit, edited by John Most.[30] The Haymarket trag-
edy developed her inherent Anarchist tendencies: the
reading of the *Freiheit* made her a conscious Anarchist.
Subsequently she was to learn that the idea of Anarchism
found its highest expression through the best intellects of
America: theoretically by Josiah Warren, Stephen Pearl
Andrews, Lysander Spooner; philosophically by Emerson,
Thoreau, and Walt Whitman.[31]

Made ill by the excessive strain of factory work, Emma
Goldman returned to Rochester where she remained till
August, 1889, at which time she removed to New York,
the scene of the most important phase of her life. She was
now twenty years old. Features pallid with suffering, eyes
large and full of compassion, greet one in her pictured
likeness of those days. Her hair is, as customary with
Russian student girls, worn short, giving free play to the
strong forehead.

It is the heroic epoch of militant Anarchism. By leaps
and bounds the movement had grown in every country.
In spite of the most severe governmental persecution new
converts swell the ranks. The propaganda is almost exclusively of a secret character. The repressive measures of
the government drive the disciples of the new philosophy
to conspirative methods. Thousands of victims fall into

---

30 *Freiheit* ("Freedom") was an anarchist newspaper established
    by Johann Most and published in the United States between
    1882 and 1910.

31 Warren (1798–1874), Andrews (1812–1886), and Spooner
    (1808–1887) were American individualist anarchists who, in con-
    trast with the later anarcho-communist tendency, emphasized the
    sovereignty of the individual and her interests over the will of the
    collective. The writers Emerson (1803–1882), Thoreau (1816–
    1862), and Whitman (1819–1892) had long been embraced by
    American anarchists for their unflinching emphasis on individu-
    ality, independence, and self-reliance. In fact, August Spies even
    cited Emerson at his trial as an inspiration for his own beliefs.

the hands of the authorities and languish in prisons. But nothing can stem the rising tide of enthusiasm, of self-sacrifice and devotion to the Cause. The efforts of teachers like Peter Kropotkin, Louise Michel, Élisée Reclus, and others, inspire the devotees with ever greater energy.

Disruption is imminent with the Socialists, who have sacrificed the idea of liberty and embraced the State and politics. The struggle is bitter, the factions irreconcilable. This struggle is not merely between Anarchists and Socialists; it also finds its echo within the Anarchist groups. Theoretic differences and personal controversies lead to strife and acrimonious enmities. The anti-Socialist legislation of Germany and Austria had driven thousands of Socialists and Anarchists across the seas to seek refuge in America. John Most, having lost his seat in the Reichstag, finally had to flee his native land, and went to London. There, having advanced toward Anarchism, he entirely withdrew from the Social Democratic Party. Later, coming to America, he continued the publication of the *Freiheit* in New York, and developed great activity among the German workingmen.

When Emma Goldman arrived in New York in 1889, she experienced little difficulty in associating herself with active Anarchists. Anarchist meetings were an almost daily occurrence. The first lecturer she heard on the Anarchist platform was Dr. A. Solotaroff.[32] Of great importance to her future development was her acquaintance with John Most, who exerted a tremendous influence over the younger elements. His impassioned eloquence, untiring energy, and the persecution he had endured for the Cause, all combined to enthuse the comrades. It was also at this period that she met Alexander Berkman,[33] whose

---

32 Havel probably means Hillel Solotaroff (1862–1921), a Russian-born physician and anarchist whom Goldman heard lecture in New Haven in 1886.

33 Berkman (1870–1936) was Goldman's lifelong friend,

friendship played an important part throughout her life. Her talents as a speaker could not long remain in obscurity. The fire of enthusiasm swept her toward the public platform. Encouraged by her friends, she began to participate as a German and Yiddish speaker at Anarchist meetings. Soon followed a brief tour of agitation taking her as far as Cleveland. With the whole strength and earnestness of her soul she now threw herself into the propaganda of Anarchist ideas. The passionate period of her life had begun. Though constantly toiling in sweat shops, the fiery young orator was at the same time very active as an agitator and participated in various labor struggles, notably in the great cloakmakers' strike, in 1889, led by Professor Garsyde and Joseph Barondess.[34]

---

collaborator, and confidante. Like Goldman, Berkman was a Russian Jew who was exposed to anarchist ideas upon emigrating to the United States in 1888. As Havel explains below, Berkman made an unsuccessful attempt to assassinate Henry Clay Frick (1849–1919), an American industrialist, on July 23, 1892. He spent the next fourteen years in prison—an experience later recounted in his *Prison Memoirs of an Anarchist* (Mother Earth Publishing Association, 1912). Upon his release in 1906, Berkman resumed his place alongside Goldman and other comrades, ardently devoting himself to the anarchist movement until his deportation to Russia in 1919. During this time Berkman served as editor of *Mother Earth* (1907 to 1914) and founded the short-lived but highly influential anarchist newspaper *The Blast* (1916–1917). Berkman fled Russia in 1921 and settled in France, where he remained active in the movement despite ill health and poverty. He died from a self-inflicted gunshot wound on June 28, 1936.

34 The strike took place in New York between May 16 and August 23, 1890 (not 1889). Thomas Garside (1855–1927) was an Englishman of Scottish descent who worked as a professor of mathematics in Sweden before emigrating to the United States in 1881, where he joined the Knights of Labor and subsequently rose

A year later Emma Goldman was a delegate to an Anarchist conference in New York.[35] She was elected to the Executive Committee, but later withdrew because of differences of opinion regarding tactical matters.[36] The ideas of the German-speaking Anarchists had at that time not yet become clarified. Some still believed in parliamentary methods, the great majority being adherents of strong centralism. These differences of opinion in regard to tactics led in 1891 to a breach with John Most. Emma Goldman, Alexander Berkman, and other comrades joined the group *Autonomy*, in which Joseph Peukert, Otto Rinke, and Claus Timmermann played an active part.[37] The bitter

---

to prominence within the labor movement. (Ironically, he married a woman from Berks County, Pennsylvania, named "Emma Goldman.") During the cloakmaker's strike, he served as the strikers' representative to the Consolidated Board of Contractors, Cutters, and Operatives (i.e., the cloakmaker's union). Joseph Barondess (1867–1928) was a Russian-Jewish trade unionist who later dabbled in politics as a member of the Socialist Party. At the time of the strike, Barondess served as leader of the cloakmaker's union. See Hadassa Kosak, *Cultures of Opposition: Jewish Immigrant Workers, New York City, 1881–1905* (Albany, NY: SUNY Press, 2000), pp. 120–123.

35 There were two such conferences which occurred within a year of each other. The first, which took place in December 1890, involved Jewish anarchists and resulted in the establishment of the Yiddish-language newspaper *Frei Arbeiter Stimme*. It was at the second, which took place in December 1891 at the Clarendon Hall in New York, that Alexander Berkman openly challenged Johann Most, an act which precipitated his and Goldman's subsequent break with Most and his group. Havel is most likely referring to the second meeting.

36 This detail cannot be confirmed.

37 *Gruppe Autonomie* (Autonomy Group) was an anarchist organization founded in London in February 1886 by Josef Peukert (1855–1910), a German Bohemian anarchist. With Ernst Otto

controversies which followed this secession terminated only with the death of Most, in 1906.

A great source of inspiration to Emma Goldman proved the Russian revolutionists who were associated in the group *Znamya*. Goldenberg; Solotaroff; Zametkin; Miller; Cahan; the poet Edelstadt; Ivan von Schewitsch, husband of Helene von Racowitza and editor of the *Volkszeitung*; and numerous other Russian exiles, some of whom are still living, were members of the group.[38] It

---

Rinke (1853–1899), a German anarchist, Peukert began publishing the London-based newspaper *Die Autonomie* in November 1886. Claus Timmermann (1866–1941), also a German anarchist, edited various American newspapers [including *Der Anarchist* (The Anarchist), 1889–1895; *Die Brandfackel* (*The Torch*), 1893–1895; and *Der Sturmvogel* (*The Storm Bird*), 1897–1899] and took part in the conspiracy to assassinate Henry Clay Frick. Contrary to what Havel suggests, the autonomists' feud with Johann Most was not just concerned with tactics. At this time Most was essentially a collectivist, whereas the autonomists were communists. The disagreement was therefore deeply ideological in nature as well as personal.

38 Specific information on the group *Znamya* ("The Banner"), which published a paper of the same name, is difficult to come by. Of the individuals Havel lists, Lazar Goldenberg (1846–1916), Michael Zametkin (1859–1935), Louis Miller (Efrim Samuilovich Bandes, 1866–1927), Abraham Cahan (1860–1951), Sergius Schewitsch (1847–1912), and Helene von Racowitza (1846–1911) were socialists, most of them labor organizers. Interestingly Goldman does not refer to the group in *Living My Life* (although Berkman does in *Prison Memoirs of An Anarchist*). Racowitza, a Bavarian, was a princess, as her first marriage was to a Wallachian prince named Boyar Janko von Racowitza. Prior to marrying Prince von Racowitza she was courted by the German socialist Ferdinand Lasalle (1825–1864), who was shot to death in a duel with the prince in 1864. She married her third husband, Sergius Schewitsch, in 1873. Shevitch was an important leader of the

was also at this time that Emma Goldman met Robert Reitzel,[39] the German-American Heine, who exerted a great influence on her development. Through him she became acquainted with the best writers of modern literature, and the friendship thus begun lasted till Reitzel's death, in 1898.

The labor movement of America had not been drowned in the Chicago massacre; the murder of the Anarchists had failed to bring peace to the profit-greedy capitalist. The struggle for the eight-hour day continued. In 1892 broke out the great strike in Pittsburgh.[40] The Homestead fight,

---

Socialist Labor Party and, as Havel notes, edited the *New Yorker Volkszeitung* (The New York Peoples' Newspaper), a German-language labor newspaper published in New York between 1878 and 1932. Solotaroff and the Russian-born poet David Edelstadt (1866–1892) were anarchists. Edelstadt edited the *Freie Arbeiter Stimme* in 1891 until he was forced into retirement by illness.

39 Robert Reitzel (1849–1898) was a German poet, writer, and journalist who edited *Der arme Teufel* ("The Poor Devil"), a German-American anarchist magazine published in Detroit from 1884 to 1898. Reitzel was a great admirer of Heine (1797–1856), a leading German Romantic poet whom Reitzel describes as a political revolutionary in an 1895 essay (see *Robert Reitzel*, ed. A. Zucker, Philadelphia: America Germanica Press, 1917, p. 60). According to J.H. Greusel, Reitzel's life, "like Heine's, consisted of a long struggle against hypocrisy; his defiance of the conventions of life was similar to Heine's; his joy in greeting friends, in drinking wine, his love of life in its merriest phases, was equal to that of the great Heine; and, finally, Reitzel's death was similar to that of the German poet, even in its very form." (*"The Poor Devil": A Memory of Robert Reitzel*, Detroit: The Labadie Shop, 1909).

40 The Homestead Strike was an industrial lockout and strike that took place at the Carnegie steel mill in Homestead, Pittsburgh, Pennsylvania between 30 June and 6 July 1892. Between 1881 and 1892, the Amalgamated Association of Iron and Steelworkers initiated a series of successful strike actions and won considerable

the defeat of the Pinkertons, the appearance of the militia, the suppression of the strikers, and the complete triumph of the reaction are matters of comparatively recent history. Stirred to the very depths by the terrible events at the seat of war, Alexander Berkman resolved to sacrifice his life to the Cause and thus give an object lesson to the wage slaves of America of active Anarchist solidarity with labor. His attack upon Frick, the Gessler of Pittsburgh, failed, and the twenty-two year-old youth was doomed to a living death of twenty-two years in the penitentiary.[41] The bourgeoisie, which for decades had exalted and eulogized tyrannicide, now was filled with terrible rage. The capitalist press organized a systematic campaign of calumny and misrepresentation against Anarchists. The police

----

gains for steelworkers at the Homestead Steel Works. Frick, who had been hired by Andrew Carnegie with the express purpose of breaking the union, entered into negotiations with the steelworkers in February 1892. Having failed to reach an agreement, Frick locked the union out of the plant on June 29. The following day, the steelworkers declared a strike in an effort to keep scabs out of the closed plant. Frick responded by hiring several hundred armed Pinkerton detectives who attempted to enter the property from boats on the Monongahela River the evening of July 5, 1892. By early morning on July 6, a protracted violent skirmish had broken out between the Pinkertons and the workers during which several individuals on both sides were killed or wounded. Although the Pinkertons eventually surrendered, the strike was broken by the intervention of the Pennsylvania State Militia.

41   Albrecht Gessler is the tyrant of the William Tell legend. As mentioned previously, Berkman made an unsuccessful attempt to assassinate Frick in his Pittsburgh office on July 23, 1892 in retaliation for the killing of striking workers. He was quickly apprehended and, as Havel notes, sentenced to twenty-two years in prison, of which he served fourteen. Berkman recounts his time in prison in *Prison Memoirs of an Anarchist* (New York: Mother Earth Publishing Association, 1912).

exerted every effort to involve Emma Goldman in the act of Alexander Berkman.[42] The feared agitator was to be silenced by all means. It was only due to the circumstance of her presence in New York that she escaped the clutches of the law. It was a similar circumstance which, nine years later, during the McKinley incident, was instrumental in preserving her liberty. It is almost incredible with what amount of stupidity, baseness, and vileness the journalists of the period sought to overwhelm the Anarchist. One must peruse the newspaper files to realize the enormity of incrimination and slander. It would be difficult to portray the agony of soul Emma Goldman experienced in those days. The persecutions of the capitalist press were to be borne by an Anarchist with comparative equanimity; but the attacks from one's own ranks were far more painful and unbearable. The act of Berkman was severely criticized by Most and some of his followers among the German and Jewish Anarchists.[43] Bitter accusations and recriminations at public meetings and private gatherings followed. Persecuted on all sides, both because she championed Berkman and his act, and on account of her revolutionary activity, Emma Goldman was harassed even to the extent of inability to secure shelter. Too proud to seek safety in the denial of her identity, she chose to pass the nights in the public parks rather than expose her friends to danger or vexation by her visits. The already

---

42 Goldman did have a hand in planning the assassination attempt, but Havel is obviously not in a position to say so.

43 In the aftermath of the failed assassination attempt, Most subjected Berkman to sustained, vicious ridicule in person and in *Freheit*. In the August issue of the newspaper, Most argued that Berkman's action epitomized the shortcomings and failures of "propaganda by the deed." However, he also described the attentat as an expression of "great heroism." See Paul Avrich, *Sasha and Emma: The Anarchist Odyssey of Alexander Berkman and Emma Goldman* (Cambridge, MA: Harvard University Press, 2012), pp. 87–90.

bitter cup was filled to overflowing by the attempted suicide of a young comrade who had shared living quarters
with Emma Goldman, Alexander Berkman, and a mutual
artist friend.[44]

Many changes have since taken place. Alexander
Berkman has survived the Pennsylvania Inferno, and is
back again in the ranks of the militant Anarchists, his
spirit unbroken, his soul full of enthusiasm for the ideals
of his youth. The artist comrade is now among the well-
known illustrators of New York. The suicide candidate
left America shortly after his unfortunate attempt to die,
and was subsequently arrested and condemned to eight
years of hard labor for smuggling Anarchist literature into
Germany. He, too, has withstood the terrors of prison life,
and has returned to the revolutionary movement, since
earning the well deserved reputation of a talented writer
in Germany.

To avoid indefinite camping in the parks Emma
Goldman finally was forced to move into a house on
Third Street,[45] occupied exclusively by prostitutes. There,
among the outcasts of our good Christian society, she
could at least rent a bit of a room, and find rest and work
at her sewing machine. The women of the street showed
more refinement of feeling and sincere sympathy than the
priests of the Church. But human endurance had been

---

44 The "young comrade" is Josef "Sepp" Oerter (1870–1928), who
     later became involved in the social democratic movement and,
     eventually, German fascism. The "artist" was Berkman's cousin
     Modest Stein (1871–1958), whom Berkman and Goldman re-
     fer to as Fedya in *Prison Memoirs of an Anarchist* and *Living My
     Life*, respectively, in order to conceal his identity. Stein travelled
     to Pittsburgh after Berkman's arrest in order to finish Frick off.
     Upon his arrival he came to believe that his plan had been be-
     trayed. He dropped out of the movement not longer thereafter.

45 According to Paul Avrich, the brothel was located on East Fourth
     Street. See *Sasha and Emma,* p. 112.

exhausted by overmuch suffering and privation. There was a complete physical breakdown, and the renowned agitator was removed to the "Bohemian Republic"—a large tenement house which derived its euphonious appellation from the fact that its occupants were mostly Bohemian Anarchists. Here Emma Goldman found friends ready to aid her. Justus Schwab, one of the finest representatives of the German revolutionary period of that time, and Dr. Solotaroff were indefatigable in the care of the patient. Here, too, she met Edward Brady, the new friendship subsequently ripening into close intimacy. Brady had been an active participant in the revolutionary movement of Austria and had, at the time of his acquaintance with Emma Goldman, lately been released from an Austrian prison after an incarceration of ten years.[46]

Physicians diagnosed the illness as consumption, and the patient was advised to leave New York.[47] She went to Rochester, in the hope that the home circle would help to restore her to health. Her parents had several years previously emigrated to America, settling in that city. Among the leading traits of the Jewish race is the strong attachment between the members of the family, and, especially, between parents and children. Though her conservative parents could not sympathize with the idealist aspirations

---

46   Ed Brady (1852–1903) was an Austrian anarchist whom Goldman met at an Autonomist meeting in December 1892. Brady emigrated to the United States after serving eight years of a 12-year sentence in Vienna for anarchist activities. That Brady and Goldman cultivated a "close intimacy" is an understatement; they became lovers within weeks of meeting and maintained this relationship for about seven years. Brady was married and had a child not long thereafter but he and Goldman remained cordial. He died unexpectedly a few years later. For more information, see Avrich, *Sasha and Emma*, Chapter 9.

47   There is no reference to this illness in *Living My Life* or any of Goldman's letters.

of Emma Goldman and did not approve of her mode of life, they now received their sick daughter with open arms. The rest and care enjoyed in the parental home, and the cheering presence of the beloved sister Helene, proved so beneficial that within a short time she was sufficiently restored to resume her energetic activity. Such a possibility was to be prevented at all costs. The Chief of Police of New York, Byrnes, procured a court order for the arrest of Emma Goldman.[48] She was detained by the Philadelphia authorities and incarcerated for several days in the Moyamensing prison, awaiting the extradition papers which Byrnes entrusted to Detective Jacobs. This man Jacobs (whom Emma Goldman again met several years later under very unpleasant circumstances) proposed to her, while she was returning a prisoner to New York, to betray the cause of labor. In the name of his superior, Chief Byrnes, he offered lucrative reward. How stupid men sometimes are! What poverty of psychologic observation to imagine the possibility of betrayal on the part of a young Russian idealist, who had willingly sacrificed all personal considerations to help in labor's emancipation.

There is no rest in the life of Emma Goldman. Ceaseless effort and continuous striving toward the conceived goal are the essentials of her nature. Too much precious time had already been wasted. It was imperative to resume her labors immediately. The country was in the throes of a crisis, and thousands of unemployed crowded the streets of the large industrial centers. Cold and hungry they tramped through the land in the vain search for work and bread. The Anarchists developed a strenuous propaganda among the unemployed and the strikers. A monster demonstration of striking cloakmakers and of the unemployed took place at Union Square, New York.[49] Emma Goldman was

---

48 As Havel explains below, Goldman was arrested following her Union Square speech and charged with "inciting to riot."

49 The demonstration took place on August 21, 1893.

one of the invited speakers. She delivered an impassioned speech, picturing in fiery words the misery of the wage slave's life, and quoted the famous maxim of Cardinal Manning: "Necessity knows no law, and the starving man has a natural right to a share of his neighbor's bread."[50] She concluded her exhortation with the words: "Ask for work. If they do not give you work, ask for bread. If they do not give you work or bread, then take bread."

The following day she left for Philadelphia, where she was to address a public meeting. The capitalist press again raised the alarm. If Socialists and Anarchists were to be permitted to continue agitating, there was imminent danger that the workingmen would soon learn to understand the manner in which they are robbed of the joy and happiness of life.

In October, 1893, Emma Goldman was tried in the criminal courts of New York on the charge of inciting to riot. The "intelligent" jury ignored the testimony of the twelve witnesses for the defense in favor of the evidence given by one single man, Detective Jacobs. She was found guilty and sentenced to serve one year in the penitentiary at Blackwell's Island. Since the foundation of the Republic she was the first woman—Mrs. Surratt excepted[51]—to be imprisoned for a political offense. Respectable society had long before stamped upon her the Scarlet Letter. Emma Goldman passed her time in the penitentiary in the capacity of nurse in the prison hospital Here she found opportunity to shed some rays of kindness into the dark lives of the unfortunates whose sisters of the street did not disdain two years previously to share with her the same

---

50   Cardinal Henry Edward Manning (1808–1892) was an English Roman Catholic bishop of Westminster. The quote is from "Distress in London: A Note on Outdoor Relief," *Fortnightly Review* 49 (1888).

51   Mary Surratt (1823–1865) was a co-conspirator in the assassination of Abraham Lincoln.

house. She also found in prison opportunity to study English and its literature, and to familiarize herself with the great American writers. In Bret Harte, Mark Twain, Walt Whitman, Thoreau, and Emerson she found great treasures.

She left Blackwell's Island in the month of August, 1894, a woman of twenty-five, developed and matured, and intellectually transformed. Back into the arena, richer in experience, purified by suffering, she did not feel herself deserted and alone any more. Many hands were stretched out to welcome her. There were at the time numerous intellectual oases in New York. The saloon of Justus Schwab, at Number Fifty, First Street, was the center where gathered Anarchists, litterateurs, and bohemians. Among others she also met at this time a number of American Anarchists, and formed the friendship of Voltairine de Cleyre, Wm. C. Owen, Miss Van Etton, and Dyer D. Lum, former editor of the *Alarm* and executor of the last wishes of the Chicago martyrs.[52] In John Swinton, the noble old fighter for liberty, she found one of her staunchest friends. [53] Other intellectual centers there were: *Solidarity*, published by John Edelman; *Liberty*, by the Individualist Anarchist, Benjamin R. Tucker; the *Rebel*,

---

52 William Charles Owen (1854–1929) was a British-American anarchist. Ida Van Etten (1868–1894) was an American labor journalist and activist. Dyer Daniel Lum (1839–1893) was an American anarchist labor activist (however, Goldman could not have met him in 1894 as he had died the previous year). *The Alarm* was an anarchist newspaper published in Chicago from 1884 to 1887 and then in New York from 1888–1889. Lum edited the paper from late 1887 to 1889

53 John Swinton (1829–1901) was a Scottish-American radical journalist and trade unionist. Goldman credits Swinton with convincing her to carry out her propaganda in English rather than German (which she had been using prior to her imprisonment in 1893–1894).

by Harry Kelly; *Der Sturmvogel*, a German Anarchist publication, edited by Claus Timmermann; *Der Arme Teufel*, whose presiding genius was the inimitable Robert Reitzel.[54] Through Arthur Brisbane, now chief lieutenant of William Randolph Hearst, she became acquainted with the writings of Fourier. Brisbane then was not yet submerged in the swamp of political corruption. He sent Emma Goldman an amiable letter to Blackwell's Island, together with the biography of his father, the enthusiastic American disciple of Fourier.[55]

Emma Goldman became, upon her release from the penitentiary, a factor in the public life of New York. She was appreciated in radical ranks for her devotion, her idealism, and earnestness. Various persons sought her friendship, and some tried to persuade her to aid in the furtherance of their special side issues. Thus Rev. Parkhurst,

---

54 All of these publications were anarchist newspapers. *Solidarity* was published in New York from c. 1892 to c. 1895 (with a brief resurgence in 1898) by John H. Edelmann (1852–1900), an American anarchist and architect. *Liberty* was published in Boston from 1881 to 1892 and then New York from 1892 to 1908 by Benjamin Ricketson Tucker (1854–1939), a prominent American individualist anarchist. *The Rebel* was published in Boston from 1895 to 1896. Among its many editors were Harry Kelly (1891–1953), an American anarchist, labor organizer, and Modern School activist, and Charles Mowbray (1857–1910), an English anarchist who emigrated to the United States in 1894. *Der Sturmvogel* ("The Storm Bird") was a German-language newspaper published in New York from 1897 to 1899.

55 Arthur Brisbane (1864–1936) was an American newspaper editor and columnist. As Havel notes, Brisbane's father Albert (1808–1890) was a follower of the French utopian socialist Charles Fourier (1772–1837). Brisbane, accordingly, initially identified as a socialist but eventually "drifted into the profit system" (W.A. Swanberg, *Citizen Hearst*, New York: Galahad, 1961, pp. 390–391).

during the Lexow investigation, did his utmost to induce her to join the Vigilance Committee in order to fight Tammany Hall. Maria Louise, the moving spirit of a social center, acted as Parkhurst's go-between.[56] It is hardly necessary to mention what reply the latter received from Emma Goldman. Incidentally, Maria Louise subsequently became a Mahatma. During the free silver campaign, ex-Burgess McLuckie, one of the most genuine personalities in the Homestead strike, visited New York in an endeavor to enthuse the local radicals for free silver. He also attempted to interest Emma Goldman, but with no greater success than Mahatma Maria Louise of Parkhurst-Lexow fame.[57]

In 1894 the struggle of the Anarchists in France reached its highest expression.[58] The white terror on the

56 Havel is referring to the Lexow Committee, which was a major investigation of the notorious Tammany Hall (a political organization and, later, Democratic political machine founded in New York City in 1789) undertaken by the New York State Senate from 1894 to 1895. Charles Henry Parkhurst (1842–1933), an American clergyman and social reformer, was instrumental in exposing corruption in the organization.

57 Advocates of "free silver" in the late nineteenth century favored inflationary monetary policy, advocating the issuing of bimetal currency (featuring a 16 to 1 ratio of silver to gold), rather than the less inflationary gold standard. John McLuckie (b. 1851, d. unknown) was an American trade unionist who served as the burgess (mayor) of Homestead, Pennsylvania at the time of the Homestead Strike. Marie-Louise (b. 1842, d. unknown) was a French-American suffragist, social reformer, and Hindu mystic. She was the first female Westerner to become a swami monk, taking the name "Swami Abhayananda."

58 Havel is referring to the series of high-profile acts of violence perpetrated by anarchists during this year, including the bombings of Émile Henry (1872–1894) and August Vaillant (1861–1893) in 1894 and 1893, respectively.

part of the Republican upstarts was answered by the red terror of our French comrades. With feverish anxiety the Anarchists throughout the world followed this social struggle. Propaganda by deed found its reverberating echo in almost all countries. In order to better familiarize herself with conditions in the old world, Emma Goldman left for Europe, in the year 1895. After a lecture tour in England and Scotland, she went to Vienna where she entered the *Allgemeine Krankenhaus*[59] to prepare herself as midwife and nurse, and where at the same time she studied social conditions. She also found opportunity to acquaint herself with the newest literature of Europe: Hauptmann, Nietzsche, Ibsen, Zola, Thomas Hardy, and other artist rebels were read with great enthusiasm.

In the autumn of 1896 she returned to New York by way of Zurich and Paris. The project of Alexander Berkman's liberation was on hand. The barbaric sentence of twenty-two years had roused tremendous indignation among the radical elements. It was known that the Pardon Board of Pennsylvania would look to Carnegie and Frick for advice in the case of Alexander Berkman. It was therefore suggested that these Sultans of Pennsylvania be approached—not with a view of obtaining their grace, but with the request that they do not attempt to influence the Board. Ernest Crosby offered to see Carnegie, on condition that Alexander Berkman repudiate his act.[60] That, however, was absolutely out of the question. He would

---

59   The Vienna General Hospital.

60   Ernest Crosby (1856–1907) was an American lawyer, social reformer, follower of Tolstoy, and outspoken advocate of the single tax—a system popularized by the American political economist Henry George (1839–1897) in which tax revenue is based solely on land and resources. Crosby was known to be sympathetic to anarchists and had a reputation for taking up the defense of political dissidents. Evidently Goldman (with the help of Justus Schwab) appealed directly to Crosby for assistance in Berkman's case.

never be guilty of such forswearing of his own personality and self-respect. These efforts led to friendly relations between Emma Goldman and the circle of Ernest Crosby, Bolton Hall, and Leonard Abbott.[61] In the year 1897 she undertook her first great lecture tour, which extended as far as California. This tour popularized her name as the representative of the oppressed, her eloquence ringing from coast to coast. In California Emma Goldman became friendly with the members of the Isaak family, and learned to appreciate their efforts for the Cause. Under tremendous obstacles the Isaaks first published the *Firebrand* and, upon its suppression by the Postal Department, the *Free Society*.[62] It was also during this tour that Emma Goldman met that grand old rebel of sexual freedom, Moses Harman.[63]

---

61 Bolton Hall (1856–1938) was an American lawyer, writer, and activist. Like Crosby, Hall was a single-taxer and a well-known legal advocate for progressive and radical causes. Leonard Dalton Abbott (1878–1953) was an English-born American publicist, politician, and freethinker. Originally a socialist, Abbott turned to anarchism in the first decade of the twentieth century. He is best remembered as one of the driving forces of the Modern School movement. It was in this capacity that he became especially close to Havel, who, like Abbott, played a significant role in the founding of the Stelton Modern School in 1914.

62 Abraham (1856–1937) and Mary (1861–1934) Isaak were Russian-born anarchists who founded the Aurora Colony near Lincoln, California circa 1909. The Isaaks published *The Firebrand* in Portland from 1895 to 1897. *Free Society* was published in San Francisco from 1897 to 1901, Chicago from 1901 to 1904, and New York in 1904. Both of the papers edited by the Isaaks and others were instrumental in developing the ideas of anarchist communism amongst their English speaking readers.

63 Moses Harman (1830–1910) was an American educator, social reformer, and feminist who described himself (and was described by others) as a "sex radical." He edited the anarchist newspaper

During the Spanish-American War the spirit of chauvinism was at its highest tide. To check this dangerous situation, and at the same time collect funds for the revolutionary Cubans, Emma Goldman became affiliated with the Latin comrades, among others with Gori, Esteve, Palaviccini, Merlino, Petruccini, and Ferrara.[64] In the year 1899 followed another protracted tour of agitation, terminating on the Pacific Coast. Repeated arrests and accusations, though without ultimate bad results, marked every propaganda tour.

In November of the same year the untiring agitator went on a second lecture tour to England and Scotland, closing her journey with the first International Anarchist Congress at Paris.[65] It was at the time of the Boer War, and

---

Lucifer the Lightbearer, which was published in Valley Falls, Kansas from 1883 to 1896 and in Chicago from 1896 to 1907.

64   Pietro Gori (1865–1911), was an Italian anarchist lawyer, poet, and writer. He was in the United States and Canada from 1895 to 1896 on a lecture tour. Pedro Esteve (1865–1925) was an Catalan anarchist printer and journalist who emigrated to the United States in 1892. He edited *El Despertar* ("The Awakening"), which was published in New York from 1892 to 1902. Francesco Saverio Merlino (1856–1930) was an Italian anarchist lawyer and activist who went into exile in London in 1884 and spent some time in the United States before returning to Italy in 1894. During this time he edited *Solidarity* with John Edelmann, which was published in New York from 1892 to 1898 (though Merlino only had a hand in the first fifteen issues or so). Orestes Ferrara (1876–1972) was an Italian-Cuban revolutionary; it is unclear whether he was in the United States in the late 1890s. Salvatore Pallavicini (1851–1901) was an Italian anarchist and printer who lived in Barre, Vermont. He edited a newspaper, *Lo Scalpellino* ("The Stonecutter") and published Gori's play *Primo Maggio* ("The First of May") in 1896. It is unclear who "Petruccini" was.

65   Havel is referring to the International Anti-Parliamentary Congress, also known as the International Revolutionary Workers

again jingoism was at its height, as two years previously it had celebrated its orgies during the Spanish-American war. Various meetings, both in England and Scotland, were disturbed and broken up by patriotic mobs. Emma Goldman found on this occasion the opportunity of again meeting various English comrades and interesting personalities like Tom Mann and the sisters Rossetti, the gifted daughters of Dante Gabriel Rossetti, then publishers of the Anarchist review, *The Torch*.[66] One of her lifelong hopes found here its fulfillment: she came in close and friendly touch with Peter Kropotkin, Enrico Malatesta, Nicholas Tchaikovsky, W. Tcherkessov, and Louise Michel.[67] Old

---

Congress, which was planned to take place in Paris in the few days between a CGT (Confédération générale du travail, General Confederation of Labor) conference (13–17 September 1900) and the Fifth International Socialist Congress (23–27 September 1900). The aim in doing so, according to Maurizio Antonioli, was to "involve the delegates of the first Congress and to boycott the second" (*The International Anarchist Congress, Amsterdam, 1907*, ed. Maurizio Antonioli, trans. Nestor McNabb, Edmonton, AB: Black Cat Press, 2009, p. 7). As it turns out, the Congress never technically took place as it was suppressed by the French government, although some delegates met elsewhere (*ibid.*). Note that Havel accompanied Goldman on her trip to Paris, after having recently met her in London.

66 Tom Mann (1856–1941) was a British trade unionist and early syndicalist. Olivia Rossetti Agresti (1875–1960) and Helen Rossetti Angeli (1879–1969) were daughters of the English poet and painter Dante Gabriel Rossetti (1828–1882). They edited the anarchist journal *The Torch*, which was published in London from 1891 to 1896. Havel may be slightly confused on this point, as Goldman had met the Rossetti sisters in 1895.

67 In addition to the three famous anarchists listed, Nikolai Tchaikovsky (1851–1926) and Prince Varlam Cherkezishvli (1846–1925), also known as Warlaam Tchekesoff, were revolutionaries who had been active in Russia in the 1860s and 1870s.

warriors in the cause of humanity, whose deeds have enthused thousands of followers throughout the world, and
whose life and work have inspired other thousands with
noble idealism and self-sacrifice. Old warriors they, yet
ever young with the courage of earlier days, unbroken in
spirit and filled with the firm hope of the final triumph
of Anarchy.

The chasm in the revolutionary labor movement,
which resulted from the disruption of the *Internationale*,[68]
could not be bridged any more. Two social philoso-
phies were engaged in bitter combat. The International
Congress in 1889, at Paris; in 1892, at Zurich, and in
1896, at London, produced irreconcilable differences.[69]
The majority of Social Democrats, forswearing their libertarian past and becoming politicians, succeeded in excluding the revolutionary and Anarchist delegates. The
latter decided thenceforth to hold separate congresses.
Their first congress was to take place in 1900, at Paris.
The Socialist renegade, Millerand, who had climbed into
the Ministry of the Interior, here played a Judas role.[70]
The congress of the revolutionists was suppressed, and the
delegates dispersed two days prior to the scheduled opening. But Millerand had no objections against the Social

---

Both were members of the *Freedom Group* in London. Along with
Alexander Berkman's uncle, Mark Natanson, Tchaikovsky founded a famous underground circle of Russian radicals (known as the
"Tchaikovsky Circle") which eventually boasted Peter Kropotkin
as a member. It was in Tchaikovsky's London home that Goldman
and Kropotkin first met.

68 Havel is referring to the split between anarchists and Marxists
    in the First International, which culminated in the expulsion of
    Bakunin and his followers at the Hague Congress of 1872.

69 Havel is referring to various meetings of the Second International.
    Anarchists were expelled from the London conference in 1896.

70 Alexandre Millerand (1859–1943) was a French Socialist politi-
    cian who served as Prime Minister from 1920 to 1924.

Democratic Congress, which was afterwards opened with all the trumpets of the advertiser's art.

However, the renegade did not accomplish his object. A number of delegates succeeded in holding a secret conference in the house of a comrade outside of Paris, where various points of theory and tactics were discussed. Emma Goldman took considerable part in these proceedings, and on that occasion came in contact with numerous representatives of the Anarchist movement of Europe.

Owing to the suppression of the congress, the delegates were in danger of being expelled from France. At this time also came the bad news from America regarding another unsuccessful attempt to liberate Alexander Berkman, proving a great shock to Emma Goldman.[71] In November, 1900, she returned to America to devote herself to her profession of nurse, at the same time taking an active part in the American propaganda. Among other activities she organized monster meetings of protest against the terrible outrages of the Spanish government, perpetrated upon the political prisoners tortured in Montjuich.[72]

In her vocation as nurse Emma Goldman enjoyed many opportunities of meeting the most unusual and peculiar characters. Few would have identified the "notorious Anarchist" in the small blonde woman, simply attired in the uniform of a nurse. Soon after her return from Europe she became acquainted with a patient by the name of Mrs. Stander, a morphine fiend, suffering excruciating agonies. She required careful attention to enable

---

71   In the summer of 1900 Berkman and other inmates made an unsuccessful attempt to escape from prison via an underground tunnel (see Avrich, *Sasha and Emma*, pp. 129–133). Contrary to Havel's suggestion, Goldman had been closely involved in the escape plan from the beginning.

72   This most likely happened earlier, as the torturing of political prisoners at Montjuich occurred in 1896 and 1897.

her to supervise a very important business she conducted—that of Mrs. Warren. In Third Street, near Third Avenue, was situated her private residence, and near it, connected by a separate entrance, was her place of business. One evening, the nurse, upon entering the room of her patient, suddenly came face to face with a male visitor, bullnecked and of brutal appearance. The man was no other than Mr. Jacobs, the detective who seven years previously had brought Emma Goldman a prisoner from Philadelphia and who had attempted to persuade her, on their way to New York, to betray the cause of the workingmen. It would be difficult to describe the expression of bewilderment on the countenance of the man as he so unexpectedly faced Emma Goldman, the nurse of his mistress. The brute was suddenly transformed into a gentleman, exerting himself to excuse his shameful behavior on the previous occasion. Jacobs was the "protector" of Mrs. Stander, and go-between for the house and the police. Several years later, as one of the detective staff of District Attorney Jerome, he committed perjury, was convicted, and sent to Sing Sing for a year.[73] He is now probably employed by some private detective agency, a desirable pillar of respectable society.

In 1901 Peter Kropotkin was invited by the Lowell Institute of Massachusetts to deliver a series of lectures on Russian literature. It was his second American tour, and naturally the comrades were anxious to use his presence for the benefit of the movement.[74] Emma Goldman entered into correspondence with Kropotkin and succeeded in securing his consent to arrange for him a series of lectures. She also devoted her energies to organizing the tours of other well known Anarchists, principally those of Charles W. Mowbray and John

73 William Travers Jerome (1859–1934) was New York County District Attorney from 1902 to 1909.

74 Kropotkin had previously visited the United States in 1897.

Turner.[75] Similarly she always took part in all the activities of the movement, ever ready to give her time, ability, and energy to the Cause.

On the sixth of September, 1901, President McKinley was shot by Leon Czolgosz at Buffalo.[76] Immediately an unprecedented campaign of persecution was set in motion against Emma Goldman as the best known Anarchist in the country. Although there was absolutely no foundation for the accusation, she, together with other prominent Anarchists, was arrested in Chicago, kept in confinement for several weeks, and subjected to severest cross-examination.[77] Never before in the history of the country had such a terrible man-hunt taken place against a person in public life. But the efforts of police and press to connect Emma Goldman with Czolgosz proved futile. Yet the episode left her wounded to the heart. The physical suffering, the humiliation and brutality at the hands of the police she could bear. The depression of soul was far worse. She was overwhelmed by the realization of the stupidity, lack of understanding, and vileness which characterized the events of those terrible days. The attitude of misunderstanding on the part of the majority of her own comrades toward Czolgosz almost drove her to desperation. Stirred to the very inmost of her soul, she published an article on Czolgosz in which she tried to explain the deed in its social and individual aspects.[78] As once before, after Berkman's act, she now also was unable to find quarters; like a veritable wild animal she was driven from place to place. This terrible persecution and, especially, the

---

75 John Turner (1865–1934) was an English anarchist and trade unionist. He embarked on a seven-month lecture tour of the United States in March 1896.

76 For more on Goldman and Czolgosz, see "A Reminiscence" above.

77 In fact, Goldman was incarcerated for two weeks.

78 The article in question ("The Tragedy at Buffalo") was published in the October 7, 1901 edition of *Free Society*.

attitude of her comrades made it impossible for her to continue propaganda. The soreness of body and soul had first to heal. During 1901-1903 she did not resume the platform.[79] As "Miss Smith" she lived a quiet life, practicing her profession and devoting her leisure to the study of literature and, particularly, to the modern drama, which she considers one of the greatest disseminators of radical ideas and enlightened feeling.

Yet one thing the persecution of Emma Goldman accomplished. Her name was brought before the public with greater frequency and emphasis than ever before, the malicious harassing of the much maligned agitator arousing strong sympathy in many circles. Persons in various walks of life began to get interested in her struggle and her ideas. A better understanding and appreciation were now beginning to manifest themselves.

The arrival in America of the English Anarchist, John Turner, induced Emma Goldman to leave her retirement.[80] Again she threw herself into her public activities, organizing an energetic movement for the defense of Turner, whom the immigration authorities condemned to deportation on account of the Anarchist Exclusion Law, passed after the death of McKinley.[81]

When Paul Orleneff and Mme. Nazimova arrived in New York to acquaint the American public with Russian dramatic art, Emma Goldman became the manager of

---

79 The story of Goldman's "retirement" is repeated in *Living My Life*. In actuality, Goldman spoke until the end of 1901 and throughout 1902 and 1903.

80 Turner returned to the United States in 1903.

81 The Anarchist Exclusion Act, or the Immigration Act of 1903, was a law which codified previous immigration statutes and added four new classes of inadmissible immigrants including anarchists. Turner's cause was taken up by the Free Speech League, a progressive organization founded in 1902. Goldman was a prominent advocate of the organization.

the undertaking.[82] By much patience and perseverance she succeeded in raising the necessary funds to introduce the Russian artists to the theater-goers of New York and Chicago. Though financially not a success, the venture proved of great artistic value. As manager of the Russian theater Emma Goldman enjoyed some unique experiences. M. Orleneff could converse only in Russian, and "Miss Smith" was forced to act as his interpreter at various polite functions. Most of the aristocratic ladies of Fifth Avenue had not the least inkling that the amiable manager who so entertainingly discussed philosophy, drama, and literature at their five o'clock teas, was the "notorious" Emma Goldman. If the latter should someday write her autobiography, she will no doubt have many interesting anecdotes to relate in connection with these experiences.

The weekly Anarchist publication, *Free Society*, issued by the Isaak family, was forced to suspend in consequence of the nationwide fury that swept the country after the death of McKinley. To fill out the gap Emma Goldman, in cooperation with Max Baginski and other comrades, decided to publish a monthly magazine devoted to the furtherance of Anarchist ideas in life and literature. The first issue of *Mother Earth* appeared in the month of March, 1906, the initial expenses of the periodical partly covered by the proceeds of a theater benefit given by Orleneff, Mme. Nazimova, and their company, in favor of the Anarchist magazine. Under tremendous difficulties and obstacles the tireless propagandist has succeeded in continuing *Mother Earth* uninterruptedly since

---

82   Paul Orleneff (1870–1932) was a Russian actor. He was married to Alla Nazimova (1879–1945), a Russian film and theater actress, from 1904 to 1912. See Florence Brooks, "The Russian Players in New York," *The Century Magazine* 71 (1906), pp. 301–306. Emma Goldman served as the tour manager of Orleneff's troupe from July 1905 to early 1906.

1906—an achievement rarely equaled in the annals of radical publications.

In May, 1906, Alexander Berkman at last left the hell of Pennsylvania, where he had passed the best fourteen years of his life. No one had believed in the possibility of his survival. His liberation terminated a nightmare of fourteen years for Emma Goldman, and an important chapter of her career was thus concluded.

Nowhere had the birth of the Russian revolution aroused such vital and active response as among the Russians living in America. The heroes of the revolutionary movement in Russia, Tchaikovsky, Mme. Breshkovskaia, Gershuni, and others visited these shores to waken the sympathies of the American people toward the struggle for liberty, and to collect aid for its continuance and support. [83] The success of these efforts was to a considerable extent due to the exertions, eloquence, and the talent for organization on the part of Emma Goldman. This opportunity enabled her to give valuable services to the struggle for liberty in her native land. It is not generally known that it is the Anarchists who are mainly instrumental in insuring the success, moral as well as financial, of most of the radical undertakings. The Anarchist is indifferent to acknowledged appreciation; the needs of the Cause absorb his whole interest, and to these he devotes his energy and abilities. Yet it may be mentioned that some otherwise decent folks, though at all times anxious for Anarchist support and cooperation, are ever willing to monopolize all the credit for the work done. During the last several decades it was chiefly the Anarchists who had organized all the great revolutionary efforts, and aided in every struggle

---

83 Katerina Breshkovskaya (1844–1934) was a Russian revolutionary and, for a time, a close friend of Goldman's. She founded the Socialist Revolutionary Party with Grigory Gershuni (1879–1908) in the winter of 1901–1902. Goldman was a member of the New York branch of the Party but resigned in 1905.

for liberty. But for fear of shocking the respectable mob, who looks upon the Anarchists as the apostles of Satan, and because of their social position in bourgeois society, the would-be radicals ignore the activity of the Anarchists.

In 1907 Emma Goldman participated as delegate to the second Anarchist Congress, at Amsterdam.[84] She was intensely active in all its proceedings and supported the organization of the Anarchist *Internationale.* Together with the other American delegate, Max Baginski, she submitted to the congress an exhaustive report of American conditions, closing with the following characteristic remarks:

> "The charge that Anarchism is destructive, rather than constructive, and that, therefore, Anarchism is opposed to organization, is one of the many falsehoods spread by our opponents. They confound our present social institutions with organization; hence they fail to understand how we can oppose the former, and yet favor the latter. The fact, however, is that the two are not identical.
>
> The State is commonly regarded as the highest form of organization. But is it in reality a true organization? Is it not rather an arbitrary institution, cunningly imposed upon the masses?
>
> Industry, too, is called an organization; yet nothing is farther from the truth. Industry is the ceaseless piracy of the rich against the poor.
>
> We are asked to believe that the Army is an organization, but a close investigation will show that it is nothing else than a cruel instrument of blind force.

---

84 The congress took place from 27–31 August 1907.

.

The Public School! The colleges and other institutions of learning, are they not models of organization, offering the people fine opportunities for instruction? Far from it. The school, more than any other institution, is a veritable barrack, where the human mind is drilled and manipulated into submission to various social and moral spooks, and thus fitted to continue our system of exploitation and oppression.

Organization, as *we* understand it, however, is a different thing. It is based, primarily, on freedom. It is a natural and voluntary grouping of energies to secure results beneficial to humanity.

It is the harmony of organic growth which produces variety of color and form, the complete whole we admire in the flower. Analogously will the organized activity of free human beings, imbued with the spirit of solidarity, result in the perfection of social harmony, which we call Anarchism. In fact, Anarchism alone makes non-authoritarian organization of common interests possible, since it abolishes the existing antagonism between individuals and classes.

Under present conditions the antagonism of economic and social interests results in relentless war among the social units, and creates an insurmountable obstacle in the way of a cooperative commonwealth.

There is a mistaken notion that organization does not foster individual freedom; that, on the contrary, it means the decay of individuality. In reality, however, the true function of organization is to aid the development and growth of personality.

Just as the animal cells, by mutual co-operation, express their latent powers in formation of the complete organism, so does the individual, by cooperative effort with other individuals, attain his highest form of development.

An organization, in the true sense, cannot result from the combination of mere nonentities. It must be composed of self-conscious, intelligent individualities. Indeed, the total of the possibilities and activities of an organization is represented in the expression of individual energies.

It therefore logically follows that the greater the number of strong, self-conscious personalities in an organization, the less danger of stagnation, and the more intense its life element.

Anarchism asserts the possibility of an organization without discipline, fear, or punishment, and without the pressure of poverty: a new social organism which will make an end to the terrible struggle for the means of existence—the savage struggle which undermines the finest qualities in man, and ever widens the social abyss. In short, Anarchism strives towards a social organization which will establish well-being for all.

The germ of such an organization can be found in that form of trades unionism which has done away with centralization, bureaucracy, and discipline, and which favors independent and direct action on the part of its members."

The very considerable progress of Anarchist ideas in America can best be gauged by the remarkable success of the three extensive lecture tours of Emma Goldman since the Amsterdam Congress of 1907. Each tour extended over new territory, including localities where Anarchism had never before received a hearing. But the most gratifying aspect of her untiring efforts is the tremendous sale of Anarchist literature, whose propagandistic effect cannot be estimated. It was during one of these tours that a remarkable incident happened, strikingly demonstrating the inspiring potentialities of the Anarchist idea. In San Francisco, in 1908, Emma Goldman's lecture attracted a soldier of the United States Army, William Buwalda.[85] For daring to attend an Anarchist meeting, the free Republic court-martialed Buwalda and imprisoned him for one year. Thanks to the regenerating power of the new philosophy, the government lost a soldier, but the cause of liberty gained a man.

A propagandist of Emma Goldman's importance is necessarily a sharp thorn to the reaction. She is looked upon as a danger to the continued existence of authoritarian usurpation. No wonder, then, that the enemy resorts to any and all means to make her impossible. A systematic attempt to suppress her activities was organized a year ago by the united police force of the country. But like all previous similar attempts, it failed in a most brilliant manner. Energetic protests on the part of the intellectual element of America succeeded in overthrowing the dastardly

---

85 See "The Coalition Against Anarchists" above. William Buwalda (1869–1946) was a United States soldier (private first-class). The meeting Havel describes took place at Walton's Pavilion in San Francisco on April 26, 1908. At the end of Goldman's speech Buwalda shook her hand, an act for which he was court-martialed in violation of the 62nd Article of War. Buwalda was sentenced to five years' hard labor (later reduced to three years) at Alcatraz. Upon his release, he returned his medals and became an anarchist.

conspiracy against free speech. Another attempt to make Emma Goldman impossible was assayed by the Federal authorities at Washington. In order to deprive her of the rights of citizenship, the government revoked the citizenship papers of her husband, whom she had married at the youthful age of eighteen, and whose whereabouts, if he be alive, could not be determined for the last two decades. The great government of the glorious United States did not hesitate to stoop to the most despicable methods to accomplish that achievement. But as her citizenship had never proved of use to Emma Goldman, she can bear the loss with a light heart.

There are personalities who possess such a powerful individuality that by its very force they exert the most potent influence over the best representatives of their time. Michael Bakunin was such a personality. But for him, Richard Wagner had never written *Die Kunst und die Revolution*.[86] Emma Goldman is a similar personality. She is a strong factor in the socio-political life of America. By virtue of her eloquence, energy, and brilliant mentality, she moulds the minds and hearts of thousands of her auditors.

Deep sympathy and compassion for suffering humanity, and an inexorable honesty toward herself, are the leading traits of Emma Goldman. No person, whether friend or foe, shall presume to control her goal or dictate her mode of life. She would perish rather than sacrifice her convictions, or the right of self-ownership of soul and body. Respectability could easily forgive the teaching of theoretic Anarchism; but Emma Goldman does not merely preach the new philosophy; she also persists in living

---

86 *Die Kunst und die Revolution* ("Art and Revolution") was a long essay published by the famous German composer in 1849. Bakunin played a prominent role in the May Uprising in Dresden in 1849 alongside Wagner—an experience which proved extremely influential on Wagner's political development at the time.

it—and that is the one supreme, unforgivable crime. Were she, like so many radicals, to consider her ideal as merely an intellectual ornament; were she to make concessions to existing society and compromise with old prejudices—then even the most radical views could be pardoned in her. But that she takes her radicalism seriously; that it has permeated her blood and marrow to the extent where she not merely teaches but also practices her convictions—this shocks even the radical Mrs. Grundy.[87] Emma Goldman lives her own life; she associates with publicans—hence the indignation of the Pharisees and Sadducees.

It is no mere coincidence that such divergent writers as Pietro Gori and William Marion Reedy find similar traits in their characterization of Emma Goldman. In a contribution to *La Questione Sociale*, Pietro Gori calls her a "moral power, a woman who, with the vision of a sibyl, prophesies the coming of a new kingdom for the oppressed; a woman who, with logic and deep earnestness, analyses the ills of society, and portrays, with artist touch, the coming dawn of humanity, founded on equality, brotherhood, and liberty."[88]

William Reedy sees in Emma Goldman the "daughter of the dream, her gospel a vision which is the vision of every truly great-souled man and woman who has ever lived."[89]

Cowards who fear the consequences of their deeds have coined the word of philosophic Anarchism. Emma Goldman is too sincere, too defiant, to seek safety behind such paltry pleas. She is an Anarchist, pure and simple. She represents the idea of Anarchism as framed by Josiah

---

87   *Mrs. Grundy*, a character in Thomas Morton's play "Speed the Plough" (1798), became an idiomatic expression denoting any extremely conventional person.

88   Date unknown.

89   William Marion Reedy, "Emma Goldman: The Daughter of the Dream," *St. Louis Mirror* (November 5, 1908).

Warren, Proudhon, Bakunin, Kropotkin, Tolstoy.[90] Yet she also understands the psychologic causes which induce a Caserio, a Vaillant, a Bresci, a Berkman, or a Czolgosz to commit deeds of violence.[91] To the soldier in the social struggle it is a point of honor to come in conflict with the powers of darkness and tyranny, and Emma Goldman is proud to count among her best friends and comrades men and women who bear the wounds and scars received in battle.

In the words of Voltairine de Cleyre, characterizing Emma Goldman after the latter's imprisonment in 1893: The spirit that animates Emma Goldman is the only one which will emancipate the slave from his slavery, the tyrant from his tyranny—the spirit which is willing to dare and suffer.[92]

---

90 Pierre-Joseph Proudhon (1809–1865) was a French anarchist philosopher and economist.

91 Sante Geronimo Caserio (1873–1894) and Gaetano Bresci (1869–1901) were Italian anarchists. The former assassinated President Sadi Carnot of France on June 24, 1894, and the latter assassinated King Umberto I of Italy on July 29, 1900. Goldman sympathetically discusses the psychology of political violence in a speech to the 1907 International Anarchist Congress and in her essay "The Psychology of Political Violence," first published in *Anarchism and Other Essays*.

92 The quote comes from Voltairine de Cleyre's pamphlet *In Defense of Emma Goldmann* [sic] *and the Right of Expropriation* (Philadelphia, 1894).

DEEDS OF VIOLENCE (1910)[1]

MAYOR GAYNOR'S OPINION THAT THE ATTACK UPON HIS life was the result of the accusations against him by an inimical press demonstrates the peculiar naivety of our reformers.[2] Blind leaders of the blind! They see results but fail to understand the causes. One may be quite sincere and quote Epictetus,[3] yet understand nothing of the psychology of violence.

Indeed, William Randolph Hearst is the *enfant terrible* in the political muck flood of our times; but he is no worse than the Spreckels, Ochses, Reids, Kohlsaats, and Rosewaters, except that he has secured an unenviable prominence in capitalist journalism.[4] The editorials of

---

1   This essay originally appeared in *Mother Earth* 5, no. 8 (October 1910).

2   William Jay Gaynor (1849–1913) was mayor of New York City from 1910 to 1913. He was the victim of an assassination attempt on August 9, 1910. The would-be assassin was James Gallagher, a former city employee.

3   Epictetus (A.D. 55–A.D.135) was a Greek Stoic philosopher. Havel is presumably referring to the 88th saying from *The Golden Sayings of Epictetus*: "Which of us does not admire what Lycurgus the Spartan did? A young citizen had put out his eye, and been handed over to him by the people to be punished at his own discretion. Lycurgus abstained from all vengeance, but on the contrary instructed and made a good man of him. Producing him in public in the theatre, he said to the astonished Spartans:—'I received this young man at your hands full of violence and wanton insolence; I restore him to you in his right mind and fit to serve his country.'"

4   Here and in the preceding paragraph, Havel is referring to Hearst's politically-motivated attacks on Tammany Hall, with which Gaynor was associated. As noted previously, Hearst (1863–1951)

his hirelings, Arthur Brisbane and John Temple Graves, will surely induce no one to commit violence. At the worst, the choice morsels of Reverend Parkhurst might cause some readers acute indigestion.[5]

Deep social causes must underlie the commission of desperate anti-social acts. To be sure, there is a tremendous difference between an idealist like Leon Czolgosz,[6] one who considers himself the executor of the social conscience, and a James Gallagher, the enraged avenger of personal wrongs. It is the difference of intellectual growth: the one awakened to complete social consciousness, the other instinctively striking out in blind, helpless fury.

The act of Czolgosz expressed the dull, tortured soul of mute millions, rebelling against social conditions based on murder and exploitation. The assassination of the chief representative of the plutocratic republic was the deed of a conscious social rebel—not specifically that of an Anarchist. His last words, on the threshold of death, were: "I did it for the working people of America."

His act was not understood. But some day labor, freed from its slavery, will honor his memory.

The act of Gallagher indicates the bankruptcy of the reform politicians. The best among them, like Brand

---

was founder of a media empire which published dozens of newspapers and periodicals across the United States. All of the other individuals Havel lists were newspaper magnates as well. With the exception of Whitelaw Reid (1837–1912), who was editor of *The New York Tribune*, they have been discussed in previous notes.

5 John Temple Graves (1856–1925) was editor of *The New York American* and, along with Arthur Brisbane, an outspoken critic of Tammany Hall. In effect, Havel is suggesting that Graves and Brisbane were acting at Hearst's behest. Parkhurst (who, along with Brisbane, has been discussed in a previous note) was also extremely critical of the Tammany machine in his capacity as a crusading social reformer.

6 See "A Reminiscence" above.

Whitlock, are convinced of the uselessness of their efforts, and are withdrawing from the swamp of political corruption.[7] The history of reformative attempts is forever the same: a number of the smaller fry are deprived of their subsistence and driven into the ranks of the wage slaves, thus still further intensifying the struggle for daily existence. On the other hand, the inherent failure of these efforts dispirits and disheartens the people at large, and makes them the easier victims of reaction.

James Gallagher was a staunch follower of his political party. As a common member of the great machine of corruption he gave conscientious yeoman service. He would have gladdened the heart of Pope Pius as one of the faithful.[8] He was a true Catholic, untouched by modernism or sillonism, and always ready to pay homage to the holy fathers.[9] He was a true patriot, ever prepared to rally under the flag of his country.

He could not help seeing that his party friends, because of their social connections and especially because of the almighty dollar, continually rose on the ladder of fortune. But as long as he felt secure in his little political berth, he was satisfied.

One can easily imagine his horror when the reformers took possession of City Hall, and he, together with

---

7   Brand Whitlock (1869–1934) was an American journalist and Progressive politician. It is unclear what Havel means when he describes Whitlock as "withdrawing from the swamp of political corruption." Whitlock was mayor of Toledo, Ohio, in 1910 and remained active in politics for at least another decade. He also served as vice president of the Free Speech League, an organization with which Emma Goldman worked since 1902.

8   Pope Pius X (1835–1914), who was Pope from 1903 to 1914. He is especially well-known for his total opposition to efforts to liberalize the Church.

9   *Sillonism* was a liberal-left Catholic movement which existed in France from 1894 to 1910.

hundreds of others, found himself on the street, out of a job. In fear and anxiety, he thought of his gray hairs, as he faced the dread specter of starvation. Daily thousands of wage slaves silently suffer this fate, but in Gallagher there lived a different spirit—he would not die of hunger without a cry.

In blind rage he fell upon the person he thought responsible for his undeserved misfortune. It was the fear of starvation which prompted his deed.

As long as human society rests upon injustice, just so long will there be rebels like Czolgosz—conscious enemies of oppression and wrong, or men like Gallagher, desperate in their unenlightened protest.

The defenders and apologists of existing conditions find it sufficient to place the responsibility for such acts upon the teachings of Anarchism. They dupe themselves into the belief that they are able to perpetuate their parasitism by palliatives and the persecution of the pioneers of a new social order based on liberty and economic independence. Yet now and then their peace is rudely disturbed—the *mene tekel* of the Czolgoszes and Gallaghers sounds a terrible warning.

Though absolutely no connection existed between the Anarchists and the act of Czolgosz, the enemy organized a nation-wide persecution against our movement. The campaign of terrorism inaugurated by the capitalist press and the police, in which all the big and little scoundrels and grafters participated, still vibrates in our memory.

Too bad they could not lay Gallagher at the Anarchist door. He is the very type of the desirable citizen. Nothing was heard after the attack upon the Mayor, about the arrest of Gallagher's comrades, religious or political. No patrol wagon was seen in front of the Times office, ready to drive Mr. Ochs and his editors to the police station, and there subject them, for days, to the third degree. Nor has Mr. Murphy, the Tammany chief, been disturbed in his peaceful wigwam; nor John Farley dragged from his episcopal palace to the Tombs; neither Mrs. Belmont, nor Miss Morgan was subjected to physical violence by uniformed ruffians, as happened to Comrade Goldman nine years ago in a police station at Chicago.[10]

Most peculiar of all, no special laws have been framed against Democrats and Catholics.

Such is the even justice of the bourgeoisie.

---

10   Havel is referring, respectively, to Charles Francis Murphy (1858–1924), the head of Tammany Hall from 1902 to 1924; John Murphy Farley (1842–1918), the Archbishop of New York from 1902 to 1918; Alva Belmont (1853–1933), an American socialite and millionaire; and Anne Morgan (1873–1952), an American philanthropist. Taken together, these individuals represent the powerful political, religious, and economic institutions which dominate New York City. Havel's point, of course, is that the attempt on Gaynor's life did nothing to fundamentally challenge or threaten these institutions.

AN IMMORAL WRITER (1910)[1]

GENIUS WITHOUT END HAS BEEN DISCOVERED OF LATE BY our critics and art connoisseurs, and quickly transplanted to our shores. True, it takes several decades for our discoverers to find really great talent. Still, what can one expect: all good things require time. A work of art must first be stamped with the approval of European connoisseurs before it can hope to receive tardy artistic appreciation and commercial value in America. We are modest—the rehashed fully satisfies us. Was not Frank Wedekind discovered for us but lately, and—wonderful to say—Przybyszewski, the German-Polish genius, now also celebrates here his resurrection.[2] The good Stanislaus

---

1   This essay originally appeared in *Mother Earth* 5, no. 6 (August 1910). Written in 1904 on the brink of the Russian Revolution, Mikhail Artsybashev's (1878–1927) novel *Sanin* tells the story of a young man who returns home to confront his family after a long absence. It is notable for its unabashed critique of traditional values and its candid discussion of sexuality. For these and other reasons it did not appear in print until 1907 (an English translation by P. Pinkerton was published by Martin Secker in London seven years later). As Havel suggests, Artsybashev was highly influenced by the anarchist individualism of Max Stirner. This fact, coupled with Artsybashev's unconventional style and provocative subject matter, accounts for Havel's occasionally hyperbolic enthusiasm for the author.

2   Frank Wedekind (1864–1918) was a German playwright and Stanisław Przybyszewski (1868–1927) was a Polish novelist, poet, and playwright. Both were highly controversial writers whose frank discussions of taboo subjects shocked and outraged bourgeois sensibilities. Goldman discusses Wedekind in her book *The Social Significance of Modern Drama* (1914). At the time Havel

would certainly never have dreamed of it. After he had given up German as the vehicle of his artistic expression and passed through repeated accouchements in Polish, his original German offspring are suddenly discovered by our critics and translated into English. If our discoveries continue at the same rate, the American public may within a decade or two become acquainted with a truly great artist, one whose works are being read and passionately discussed in Russia, Germany, France, Italy, and Japan—M. Artzibashev.

At present, however, there is slender hope of such a contingency. Do not our successful translators consider Artzibashev immoral? As patriotism is the last resort of the scoundrel, so the final argument of the impotent critic against a disliked author is an appeal to morality. He is conclusively annihilated by such critics with the charge of demoralizing the youth, and is damned vicious. No eminent artist ever escaped this charge; it would almost seem as if it were the ultimate crown of genius.

But Artzibashev is not an ordinary sinner. He is not merely a demoralizer of youth, morally; nay, even worse: he is the enemy of governmentally ordered life; in fact, an Anarchist. This the partisans of State find impossible to forgive him.

Next to Andreiev and Gorki, Artzibashev is the most prominent personality in modern Russian literature. Since the appearance of his novel *Sanin*, he must be classed with those whose names are inseparably connected with the annals of their time. In the history of Russian literature *Sanin* will find its deserved place among the masterpieces of Gogol, Gontcharov,

---

is writing, English translations of Wedekind and Przybyszewski were just starting to appear. (A translation of Wedekind's extremely influential play *Spring Awakening*, for example, was published one year earlier in 1909.) Contrary to Havel's hopeful prognostications, most of their works remained untranslated for decades.

Dostoyevski, Turgeniev, and Tolstoy. Its socio-historical significance cannot be doubted. Intellectual Europe is agreed upon it.[3]

M. Artzibashev was born in 1878 in a small city of Southern Russia. By descent he is a Tartar, yet with a considerable mixture of other blood; his great-grandfather on the maternal side was no less a man than Kosciusko, the famous Polish patriot. His father was a small landowner, living in straightened circumstances. His mother died when he was but three years old, bequeathing to him tuberculosis as his sole inheritance. After a course in a provincial gymnasium, Artzibashev, at the age of sixteen, entered an art school. Like Goethe, he was enthused with art, believing to possess the talent of a painter. He fared badly: he lived in squalid quarters, often suffering hunger; but worse than all, he even lacked money for colors. To earn a living he drew caricatures and wrote sketches for obscure papers. Some of his writings, especially "Pasha Tumanov"—dealing with the then suicide epidemic among the college youth—attracted the attention of Miroliubov, the publisher of a magazine of liberal tendencies.[4] Among the collaborators on the latter were Maxim Gorki, Leonid Andreiev, A. Kuprin, and other modern writers. Miroliubov, recognizing the talent of

---

3   Havel's claims here are for the most part wildly disproportionate. Artsybashev scarcely received this level of acclaim during his lifetime. In fact, he was driven into exile after the Bolshevik Revolution and remained for many years an extremely obscure figure.

4   The magazine in question was *Zhurnal dlia vsekh* ("Journal for Everyone), which Mirolyubov (1860–1939) published from 1898 to 1906. "Pasha Tumanov" was originally accepted for publication in *Russkoye Bogatsvo* ("Russian Wealth"), the principal literary outlet of the Nihilists, but was rejected at the request of the censor. It subsequently appeared in Artsybashev's first collection of stories in 1905.

young Artzibashev, offered him to join the editorial staff and thus paved the way for his future literary career.

It was during this period, seven years ago, that Artzibashev wrote his famous work, *Sanin*. The manuscript was declined by several publishers, who feared to offend against the censorship. The revolution came. The emotional life of the people underwent a tremendous change. All classes manifested a ravenous hunger for literature. The editors of *Sovremenni Mir*, which had previously declined *Sanin*, now remembered the work and hastened to publish it.[5]

This circumstance is not generally known. The public was led to believe by the Russian critics that *Sanin* was the product of reaction, and that Artzibashev followed the modernist tendencies of the decadent school, manifesting themselves in Russian literature with the downfall of the Revolution. In reality, however, the *Sanin* manuscript had already been perused by prominent writers in 1903, two years before the great upheaval.

Following *Sanin*, Artzibashev wrote a collection of splendid sketches, among them "Millions" and "The Death of Ivan Lande."[6] The latter assured his fame in Russian letters. Various works, written during this period by Artzibashev for propaganda purposes, came under the ban of the censor, and only the timely success of the Revolution saved the author from prison.

Artzibashev is now living in Crimea, undergoing—according to a letter to his translator—treatment for consumption, "without special hope of cure."

Sanin has caused an almost unprecedented division in

---

5   *Sovremenny Mir* ("The Contemporary World") was a literary, scientific, and political monthly published in St. Petersburg from 1906 to 1918.

6   These works were published in 1908 and 1904, respectively. They were both translated by P. Pinkerton and published in London in 1915 by Martin Secker.

the ranks of intellectual Russia. Its effect can be compared only with that produced by such works as *Yevgeni Oniegin*, *Fathers and Sons*, *What's To Be Done*, and *Kreutzer Sonata*.[7] Even if its purely artistic qualities had not stamped *Sanin* as one of the most important literary events, socio-historic reasons would have impressed upon the work lasting significance. Its social effects alone characterize *Sanin* above the class of merely literary effort.

Similarly to Turgeniev's *Fathers and Sons*, *Sanin* was understood neither by the reactionists nor revolutionists. At the same time that the government confiscated the romance, the revolutionists stigmatized Artzibashev as the ally of the reaction. But most of all *Sanin* was misinterpreted by "the youngest youth." A wild sexual intoxication followed upon the publication of the book. The college youth formed themselves into associations for the unhindered practice of eroticism. They called themselves Saninists, claiming to live the views of Artzibashev's hero.

These excesses are easily explained psychologically. The Revolution was suppressed; the intellectuals withdrew; the revolutionary parties became disintegrated. General weariness took the place of activity. But the stimulated energies would not be so easily stemmed: the wakened emotions demanded satisfaction. Such feelings dissolve themselves most readily in sexual passion. Because of its erotic suggestiveness, *Sanin* became the program of the young generation. A misinterpretation, from which almost all extraordinary works have in their day suffered.

In his *Reminiscences* Goethe says in regard to *Werther's Leiden*:[8]

---

7   Havel is referring, respectively, to *Yevgeniy Onegin*, a 1833 novel by Alexander Pushkin); *Fathers and Sons*, an 1862 by Ivan Turgenev; *What's To Be Done*, an 1863 novel by Nikolai Chernyshevsky; and *Kreutzer Sonata*, an 1889 novella by Leo Tolstoy.

8   *Werther's Leiden*—i.e., *Die Leiden des jungen Werthers* ("The Sorrows of Young Werther")—was an autobiographical novel

The influence of this book was so great and unusual because it appeared at exactly the right moment. As it requires but a small fuse to explode a tremendous mine, so the explosion which thereupon followed among the public was so strong because the young generation had already undermined itself, and the shock so terrific, because everyone, being filled with exaggerated demands, unsatisfied passions, and imaginary sufferings, was about to explode. The public cannot be expected to receive a spiritual work in a spiritual manner. In reality only the contents, the material, were considered; to it was added the old prejudice concerning the printed word: namely, that its purpose must be didactic. But true art has none: it neither praises nor condemns; it merely presents the emotions and actions in their sequence, and thus it enlightens and teaches.

These splendid words apply precisely to *Sanin*. Artzibashev wrote neither a defense nor a slander of the Russian youth. He pictured in Sanin a new type of Russian life, a type whose spirit lives in the strongest and most daring representatives of new Russia. Sanin is an individuality which has broken with all the views dominant in modern life, an individuality which has withdrawn from all political parties, however revolutionary—a man who stands alone.

The book is an apotheosis of individualism. Were a classification attempted, Sanin would have to be characterized as a Stirnerian,[9] an Individualist Anarchist. He

---

published by Goethe in 1774.

9   *Stirnerian*—i.e., a follower of Max Stirner (1806–1856), German egoist philosopher.

represents the reaction against the old type of revolutionist, who did not consider his own individuality, and who devoted his whole life to the "cause," to the people. But Artzibashev did not content himself with portraying merely the ordinary, self-satisfied Stirnerian. In "The Workman Shevyriov," from the *Stories of the Revolution*, he pictures the complement of Sanin in the active revolutionary Individualist.[10] Sanin and Shevyriov give a complete view of Artzibashev's social and political beliefs. Either total aloofness from the problems of the day, and the free development of one's individuality—that is Sanin; or Shevyriov's intense participation in the struggle with every fiber of his being, perishing in active resistance.

The post-revolutionary period, beginning with the October manifesto of 1905, followed within two years by the downfall of the great social expectations, serves as the background of the *Stories of the Revolution*.

The original unity of the Revolution is broken, its tremendous energy paralyzed. In place of the great Socialist parties, side-tracked by parliamentarism, we find the actions of separate organizations of Anarchists, partly loosely connected with each other, but mostly operating independently. In their midst are the solitary figures, those who believe in nothing except themselves, and who, protesting by deed, perish.

In this milieu live the types described in the *Stories of the Revolution*. They contain powerful characterizations of great psychologic depth. These stories are a part of Artzibashev's Weltanschauung. They are, as he himself states, the sermon of his dearest ideas, his political faith: Anarchism. "My development"—Artzibashev writes in a short autobiography—"has been strongly influenced by Tolstoy, although I have never shared his opinion regarding 'resist not evil.' He overwhelmed me only as an artist,

---

10   This work was published in 1909. It was translated by P. Pinkerton and published in London by Martin Secker in 1917.

and it has been difficult for me to free my style from his influence. Almost a similar role Dostoyevsky and partly Tchechov played in my life. Victor Hugo and Goethe also stood before me. These five names are those of my teachers and literary masters. Much has been written about Nietzsche's influence on me. The assertion always seemed to me peculiar, for the simple reason that I am not familiar with Nietzsche. I am better acquainted with Max Stirner, whose views I share."[11]

11   M. Artsybashev, *Revolutionsgeschicte* ("Tales of the Revolution"), trans. S. Bugow and A. Villard (München, 1909), xxi–xxii.

MARTIN EDEN (1910)[1]

OUR AGE IS SYMBOLIZED BY THE PRINTED WORD. A veritable deluge of printed paper overwhelms us daily. The veriest witch sabbath celebrates its orgies on the book mart, and we are in danger of being suffocated by this literary high tide. The mind of the conscientious critic simply staggers beneath this oppressive burden. Where is the intellectual able to keep abreast of all this output in five or six modern languages? It fills one with weariness and disgust—disgust at the thousand and one papers, magazines, brochures, and books, at the interminable printed rubbish, the famous and infamous dime literature of literary vanity and commercialism.

Notwithstanding, one must read. Reading has become a part of our life, and I feel a certain mistrust towards people who do not read, a mistrust of their intellect, their depth and love. Books aid us to draw closer the lines separating man and man; they bring us nearer to the suffering, the disappointments and disillusions of our fellow beings; they are the bridges of human souls. There are days when one's heart just cries out for a book; a book that moves one to his depths, one in which the melodies of the heart find an answering echo, a book to live over again life's experiences; a book, in short, standing out from the literary rubbish heap, filling us with deep joy and forming new values.

---

1   This article originally appeared in *Mother Earth* 5, no. 4 (June 1910). In addition to being an author of considerable repute, Jack London (1876–1916) was also an avowed socialist. He belonged to many of the same early twentieth-century bohemian circles as Havel, with whom he shared several friends and associates including Sadakichi Hartmann and Alfred Stieglitz. *Martin Eden* was published in 1909.

Such a book Jack London has given us in *Martin Eden* (Macmillan Co., New York), a book of affecting tragedy and power.

Most men are inexpressibly distant and strange to each other. The soul, mirrored so clearly in the child's eyes, is soon hidden by fear, shame, and pride, and remains buried beneath the weight of its armor. Occasionally emboldened to show itself, it quickly shrinks back in affright, terrified by the suffocating air of conventionality, brutality, indifference, and lack of understanding.

The whole process of man's evolution consists in the struggle against this very conventionality and brutality, which in truth are synonymous. Conventionality and respectability are the means society employs to disguise the soul's differentiations and particular needs, endeavoring to cast them into moulds of uniformity, that is, to level them to the insignificance of ciphers, for only thus similarity is possible. In this manner society paralyzes all upward striving, energy, and independence, robbing individuality of its best elements.

Yet, all these efforts are not entirely successful. At all times there have been souls who prized their independence so highly as to suffer everything for its sake. Such a nature London portrays in Martin Eden.

Martin Eden is an individuality which stands outside its environment, yet continually and ineffectually striving to touch the soul strings of that environment. A stranger to everyone about him, Eden is known only to himself. The flight of his soul is on intimate heights, his language vibrates particular tones, his sympathies are full of distinctive nuances, and these mask him from those about him in spite of the candidness of his motives. The lack of understanding is the rock on which Martin Eden's soul is, must be, wrecked.

Eden is a personality which feels itself superior to formulated life, a nature affirming all that is wholesome, strong, and virile, seeking to free its creative artistic genius from all obstacles; a personality which sees in social manifestations merely the symbol of its unconscious powers. In a world of superficiality and inane incoherence such a personality must inevitably perish.

Jack London has undoubtedly portrayed much of his own life in this book. I am convinced that there is not another work in our autobiographic literature which in point of power and sincerity can compare with *Martin Eden*. It is a masterwork of psychologic perception. The characters are so vital and convincing that one almost feels himself in their actual presence, discussing the problems of life.

Martin Eden himself is a personality of tragic grandeur. The development of this character, his intellectual rise above his environment, finds no parallel in contemporary American literature. But this intimate delineation is not limited only to the central character; it is equally true of all the other characters in the work. With what a depth of appreciation and tenderness is Brissenden portrayed, the ingenious writer; Lizzie Connolly, the heart-genuine proletarian; and how clearly and pointedly Ruth Morse is drawn, the polished product of conventionality, and her bourgeois environment.

Some critics accuse Jack London of painting life in too brutal colors. What superficial criticism! London is not a writer for the matinee girl. His so-called brutality is in reality the virility of the great artist who portrays life as it actually is—too virile for a generation vitiated by a literature of mawkish sentimentality. All the works of London, true artist that he is, are characterized by a background symbolic of the New Life. His description of pity, for instance, as in the case of Gertrude Higginbotham, is not the superficial, passing, coldhearted conventional philanthropy touched with pleasurable egotism; it is the sadness of deep-felt helplessness to lighten the heavy burden of a human soul. To some, pity is a kind of spiritual balm for their own little souls, gladdened by such expression of their high-minded generosity. I mistrust writers like Maeterlinck whose beautiful words of pity sound so profound and appear so deeply felt. They know nothing of the terrible soul anguish which such as Multatuli and Nietzsche experience.[2]

London is by far the most virile writer in contemporary American literature. He personifies the wild beauty of the cruel, merciless, and yet magnificent life of our time, with all its disappointments, its rebellious iconoclasm, its uprising against the slavery and debasement of our existence. At a time when shrewd mediocrity gives the keynote to life, Jack London has struck a new chord, touched our innermost, and set in motion new vibrations. His distinctive quality is nobility of spirit.

---

2 *Multatuli* (essentially Latin for "I have suffered much") was the pen name of Eduard Douwes Dekker (1820–1887), a Dutch writer well-known as a critic of colonialism. His most prominent work is *Max Havelaar* (1860).

AMONG BOOKS (1910)

THE PROBLEM WHETHER THE UNITED STATES POSSESSES
an original literature comparable to that of other civilized nations is again vexing some English minds. Messrs.
Verdad and Williams are conducting a heated discussion
over the matter in the London *New Age*.[1] Mister Verdad
is the self-chosen pope in the world of diplomacy—om-
niscient and infallible in international politics, a prophet
intimately familiar with all coming events. He knows all
the designs of the chiefs of foreign affairs; he is conversant
with the plans of the various financial circles; he is fully
cognizant of all the conspiracies hatched by the numerous
pretenders to European thrones. He knows that the Finns
are conspiring the subjection of Russia, the Egyptians
scheming to overrun Great Britain, the Bohemians de-
signing to conquer Austria.

In the age of the Metternichs, Wellingtons,
Montalemberts, and Nesselrodes he would have played the
role of a diplomatic stool pigeon like Friedrich von Gentz.[2]

---

1   "S. Verdad" was the pseudonym of John McFarland Kennedy, an
English writer and translator (birth and death unknown). In the
article Havel cites ("S. Verdad and America," *The New Age* 7, no.
21 [1910], p. 501), Verdad is taken to task by the English writer Michael Williams (1878–1950) for suggesting that American
literature is "entirely devoid of imagination." *The New Age* was a
prominent radical journal published from 1907 to 1922.

2   All of the individuals Havel cites (i.e., Prince Klemens Wenzel
von Metternich, 1773–1859; Arthur Wellesley, First Duke of
Wellington, 1769–1852; Charles René de Montalembert, 1810–
1870; and Karl Nesselrode, 1780–1862) were great statesmen of
the nineteenth century. Havel compares Verdad to Friedrich von
Gentz (1764–1832), a German statesman who, in his capacity as

But in the twentieth century he cuts a rather pitiful figure in the otherwise splendidly edited *New Age*. Verdad collaborating with the Chestertons, with Shaw, Wells, Belfort Bax, and Ashley Dukes—ye gods, what a combination![3] Only a good dose of humor enables one to stomach Verdad so long as he busies himself with high diplomacy; but, the Lord have mercy when he begins to tap his superior wisdom in matters literary. Especially does he make his reactionist tendencies offensively apparent when he approaches the literature of the "Unistaters,"[4] an epithet Verdad thinks significant because it's his own invention. The "Unistaters" have, according to Verdad, not produced a single poet of importance. Poe was a "sporting plant," Whitman "an Anarchist who found life chaotic and made the chaos more chaotic still." His ecstasy over the literature of Latin America gives one the impression that the North American writers are mere barbarians compared with the geniuses of Paraguay, Uruguay, and British Guiana.

But most deliciously unique is Verdad in his final verdict that the "Unistaters" have no creative imagination, since they have failed to produce a Fichte, Hegel, Schelling, Kant, Schopenhauer, or Nietzsche. The explanation is of course evident to Verdad, and characteristically logical: the American mind is Teutonic, and the Teutonic intellect—of the Fichtes, Kants, Schopenhauers, and Nietzsches—is "slow, stupid, and muddy."

Metternich's toady, essentially functioned as a mouthpiece for the reaction in Europe.

3   In addition to George Bernard Shaw, H. G. Wells, and Ernest Belfort Bax (noted previously), Havel is referring to the English writers Gilbert Keith "G.K." (1874–1936) and Cecil Charles (1879–1918) Chesterton and to the English playwright and critic Ashley Dukes (1885–1959). Havel's point is that Verdad is a lightweight compared to these men, all of whom are intellectual and literary luminaries.

4   "Unistaters"—i.e., citizens of the United States.

The American intellect Teutonic! What more convincing testimonial of gross ignorance could this wonderful critic submit to us? Anyone possessing the least acquaintance with the literature and art of America cannot fail to trace the most pronounced Latin tendencies. To be sure, if critics like Verdad conceive by the Latin spirit the literary craftsmanship of a de Heredia or of a D'nnunzio, in that case the art and literature of the "Unistaters" lacks the Latin spirit.[5] But if the Latin spirit represents the social consciousness and the power of expression of a Meunier, Zola, Mirabeau, or an Ada Negri, then the creative work of America bears strong kinship to the intellectual culture of Latin peoples.[6]

This the Verdads subtly feel because of their very reactionism: indeed one of their capital indictments against modern American literature is that it is pregnant with the spirit of Anarchy, of rebellion against accepted tradition. They commit the fatal mistake of confusing the primeval, natural—often primitively wild—spirit with brutality, inability, and inferiority. People who live in the past are incapable of understanding the spiritual tendencies of modern nations or of appreciating the creative art in which they seek expression. There are but few countries the literature of which expresses life so adequately—in its spiritual, political, and social aspects—as the literature of America. The insurgent spirit which is manifesting itself with ever growing force—not merely in the political, but

5   José-Maria de Heredia (1842–1905) was a Cuban-born French poet.

6   Havel is referring to Constantin Meunier (1831–1905), a Belgian painter and sculptor, and Ada Negri (1870–1945), an Italian poet and writer. Negri was reputed to be the teacher of Sante Caserio, the anarchist who assassinated Sadi Carnot in 1894. Emma Goldman discusses this in *The Psychology of Political Violence*, published as a pamphlet by the Mother Earth Publishing Company in 1911.

also in the social and ethical life of the American people—
is the work of this literature. Not a mere *belles-lettres* literature for the privileged few, but one pulsating with the
life of the people. The great majority of modern American
writers are undisguised social rebels.

Several books now before me clearly express this ten-
dency; among them: *Types from City Streets*, by Hutchins
Hapgood; *The House of Bondage*, by Reginald Wright
Kauffman; and *Burning Daylight*, by Jack London.[7]

Hutchins Hapgood occupies a peculiar position in
the world of American letters.[8] His works cannot be as-
signed to a particular class. He belongs to a school of his
own, one of journalistic impressionism. Our daily press
absorbs unnumbered talents; but few succeed in saving
themselves from the killing drudgery, to win a name in literature. These benefit by the experience gained in the pre-
paratory work on the daily press. The works of Hapgood
bear the stamp of the practical, experienced observer; but
they are something more than mere photographic like-
nesses. A deep, almost mystical, philosophy underlies
them. They are sociological treatises in artistic form. We
see in them the intensive participation of the author in all

---

7   These works were all published in 1910.

8   Hutchins Hapgood (1869–1944) was an American author and
     journalist. Sympathetic to anarchism, Hapgood was an important
     figure in the American radical milieu of the early twentieth-cen-
     tury and a good friend of Havel's and Goldman's, among many
     others. In *The Modern School Movement* (AK Press, 2005), Paul
     Avrich recounts an amusing anecdote in which "[Havel] uri-
     nated in broad daylight on lower Fifth Avenue and was hailed
     into court for disorderly conduct. 'Why did you do it publicly
     on Fifth Avenue?' asked the judge. 'Why didn't you go on a side
     street?' Havel angrily replied: 'You mean, I should do it where
     the poor people live? No, no, I refuse to do it there. I protest!'
     Hutchins Hapgood, over Havel's objections, paid the five-dollar
     fine" (p. 122).

the characters of his sketches. We feel the pulsation of his own life, we sense in the portrayal of their soul the reality of his own passions, ideals, and philosophy. That the types characterized by Hapgood are living contemporaries tends but to enhance the interest of the reader; but the problem of the author is the more difficult therefore. We stand too near these personalities; often we fail to find the qualities which the author perceives in them, their weaknesses or strength. Hence the misconceptions regarding such studies as *The Spirit of Labor* and *An Anarchist Woman*—books which have called forth endless discussion in Anarchist circles. Their titles are misleading. *The Spirit of Labor* portrays only the actual spirit of a small minority, of a certain labor group; but the spirit of labor at large is not evident therein, though its spiritual potentialities are foreshadowed. Nor does *An Anarchist Woman* portray a typical Anarchist woman, though some Anarchist individuals are pictured with realistic touch. Better understanding and more general appreciation fell to the lot of *Life in the Ghetto* and *The Autobiography of a Thief*.[9]

In the last book of Hutchins Hapgood, *Types from City Streets* (Funk & Wagnalls, New York), the whole panorama of the underworld passes before us in review. Not the underworld despised by the self-satisfied bourgeois, nor the philanthropized victims of the would-be humanitarian; rather the strong, independent, self-reliant characters.

---

9   The works Havel lists were published, respectively, in 1907, 1909, 1902, and 1903. (The actual title of "Life in the Ghetto" is *The Spirit of the Ghetto*.) *The Spirit of Labor* (featuring Anton Johannsen, an acquaintance of Havel's) and *An Anarchist Woman* (featuring Terry Carlin—Havel's friend and drinking companion—as one of the main characters) are literary treatments of Hapgood's personal experiences with the radical movement. As Havel notes, both of these books were controversial among anarchists, many of whom regarded them as inaccurate, oversimplified, or sensationalistic in their portrayals of anarchist life.

Types too individualized, too unique, to be assimilated by a society of philistines and pharisees. They represent the world of instinctive rebellion and natural revolt against a social order based on the morality of hypocrisy—a world embracing a considerable percentage of our contemporaries, unfortunately almost entirely ignored by Socialist and Anarchist propaganda. Therefore we owe a debt of gratitude to a writer who with such artistic skill discovers to us this world of instinctive, even if unconscious, rebels. We perceive how much power, beauty, independence, and latent energy here remain unused; we realize how such types would develop in a free society, and what incalculable good they could accomplish.

Hapgood is gifted with the rare instinct of finding behind the common, often rough, exterior the inherent good qualities and especially spiritual and artistic grace. He is an analytical psychologist, a *connoisseur* who everywhere discovers beauty and depth; everywhere except in the ranks of the respectably dull bourgeoisie.

The sudden moral spasm over the so-called white slave traffic has produced a mountain of printed trash. Every spinster of male and female gender felt himself called upon to add his dutiful offering to the dunghill. The busiest of them all proved the soul savers—people who properly should ignore the sinful flesh. In a book called *The White Slave Trade* they retail their supreme panacea at a dollar per copy.[10] The offered solution resolves itself in the demand for increased suppression, the cultivation of chastity, and an extra dose of lemonade. Another book dealing with the same problem is called *The Underworld Sewer*, by Josie Washburn, a woman who was formerly the "Madam" of an assignation house in Omaha, her business affording her exceptional opportunities for intimate

---

10   The National Vigilance Association, *The White Slave Trade: Transactions of the International Congress on the White Slave Trade* (London: Wertheimer, Lea & Co., 1899).

study of the corruption of press, police, and politicians.[11] The book is a rather crude description of conditions with which every student of American city life is quite familiar.

Far superior to these publications, both in point of sociologic insight and artistic expression, is the work of Elizabeth Goodnow, entitled *The Market for Souls*.[12] It contains some exceptionally fine sketches, full of sympathetic observation of the life of prostitutes, sketches which clarify to the reader his human kinship with these social victims.

Of still greater importance is a book by Reginald Wright Kauffman, *The House of Bondage* (Moffat, Yard & Co., New York), a work depicting in a masterly manner the economic causes of prostitution.[13] It is a picture of actual life, palpitating with intense reality; a life the pressure of which no one can escape. The protracted vice investigation by the Rockefeller grand jury sinks into utter insignificance by comparison with the socially complete description in *The House of Bondage*. The author does not hesitate to expose this terrible cancer of civilized life. We behold the pillars of society, the philanthropic lords of department stores, the professional politicians, police, and judges at work, their common purpose aided by procurers, cadets, and pimps; we witness in vivid light the daughters of the poor falling into the clutches of the

11 Josie Washburn (born 1853, death unknown), a Nebraska prostitute who later became a social reformer, self-published *The Underworld Sewer* in Omaha in 1909.

12 Elizabeth Goodnow (birth and death unknown) was an American journalist and social reformer. *The Market for Souls* was published in New York in 1910 by Mitchell Kennerley.

13 *The House of Bondage* was published in 1910. Reginald Wright Kauffman (1877–1959) was an American novelist and screenwriter. A socialist with anarchist sympathies, Kauffman's work was favorably cited by Goldman in "The Traffic in Women." See *Anarchism and Other Essays*, pp. 184–185.

economic Minotaur. The conventional prudery of charitable institutions, social centers, and settlements is analyzed with convincing power. The book is a terrific indictment against capitalistic society.

This work, however, is not above criticism from the standpoint of art. The German Marxian Hermann Hoffmann, eternally singing the patriotic *Wacht am Rhein*,[14] is an impossible figure; also, the psychologic interpretation of some other characters in the book is rather weak. The author was more successful in portraying Mary Denbigh, the heroine of the story. The recital of her destruction in the maelstrom of prostitution is of consummate tragic force. Especially fine is the chapter describing her revenge upon her seducer by designedly inoculating him with syphilis.

Jack London's last work, *Burning Daylight* (The Macmillan Co., New York), has just been issued in book form. This book, too, is a powerful arraignment of the capitalistic regime. London's description of our industrial system is the most vigorous to be found in any contemporary novel. One of the characters in the book thus describes existing society:

> "Society, as organized, was a bunco game. There were many hereditary inefficients— men and women who were not weak enough to be confined in feeble-minded homes, but who were not strong enough to be aught else than hewers of wood and drawers of water. Then there were the fools who took the organized bunco game seriously, honoring and respecting it. They were easy game for the others, who saw clearly and knew the bunco game for

---

14 *Wacht am Rhein* ("The Guard on the Rhine")—a German patriotic anthem made popular during the Franco-Prussian War.

what it was. Work, legitimate work, was the source of all wealth. That was to say, whether it was a sack of potatoes, a grand piano, or a seven-passenger touring car, it came into being only by the performance of work. Where the bunco came in was in the distribution of these things after labor had created them. He failed to see the horny-handed sons of toil enjoying grand pianos or riding in automobiles. How this came about was explained by the bunco. By tens of thousands and hundreds of thousands men sat up nights and schemed how they could get between the workers and the things the workers produced. These schemers were the business men. When they got between the worker and his product, they took a whack out of it for themselves. The size of the whack was determined by no rule of equity, but by their own strength and swinishness."

Yet *Burning Daylight* is not a pessimistic book. Like Zola's *Travail* and *Fecondite*, this novel by London also closes with the splendid perspective of free labor.[15] Back to nature is the keynote of the work. Those weary of the mad haste and rush of our insane life will find here a soothing idyl. Above all, London is a wonderful painter of nature; his description of Alaska and California is of surpassing strength and beauty. And what a portrayer of the New Woman! In Dede he has immortalized her.

---

15   Published in 1901 and 1899, respectively. Zola's novels are renowned for their sympathetic but unflinchingly realistic portrayals of working class life.

THE KOTOKU CASE (1910)[1]

No other country has made such a sudden leap from patriarchic feudalism into modern capitalist industrialism, as Japan. This unprecedented transformation has taken place within a very few decades. When, in 1804, the Russian ship *Nadejda* entered the port of Nagasaki to establish friendly relations with the legendary Empire of Nippon, the offered friendship was unceremoniously rejected. Japan would have nothing to do with the barbarians of the West. Since the massacre of the Portuguese missionaries only a small band of Dutch merchants was tolerated in the land of the Shogun.[2] Such extreme exclusiveness, however, could not be maintained in the face of the nineteenth century. Admiral Perry succeeded in opening the country to Western trade, and within a century, after the appearance of the *Nadejda*, Japan stands in the forefront of "civilization"— in point of armament and ordnance her army and navy proving superior to those of Russia.

---

1   This essay originally appeared in *Mother Earth* 5, no. 10 (December 1910). Of all Havel's writings, his coverage of the persecution of anarchists in Japan attests most forcefully to his deep familiarity with and involvement in the international anarchist movement of the early twentieth century. For more on Kōtoku, see F.G. Notehelfer, *Kōtoku Shūsui: Portrait of a Japanese Radical* (Cambridge: Cambridge University Press, 1971).

2   Christianity was brought to Japan by Portuguese missionaries in the middle of the sixteenth century and were subject to a number of sporadic persecutions over the course of the next two hundred years. By the end of the seventeenth century, the Dutch were the only Europeans still maintaining a trading relationship with Japan—a situation that persisted through the nineteenth century.

But the transformation in the industrial life of Japan has brought no blessing to her people. Here too, as everywhere, capitalism called into life the most horrible conditions. A system of exploitation, such as can hardly be paralleled in any other civilized country, is now sapping the life of the sons and daughters of the land that had once been the paradise of a happy people.

The modern globetrotter who knows of Paris only the Boulevards and is quite ignorant of the existence of the proletarian quarters, sees in his travels through Japan merely the beautiful exterior, and returns home without an inkling of the real life of the exploited masses. Artistic enthusiasts like Lafcadio Hearn, Pierre Loti, and Mme. Judith Gautier, have drawn a veil of poetry over the misery of the Japanese proletariat.[3] But the pitiful sight of frail, delicate women and girls, whose poverty forces them to carry heavy loads of coal to the large steamers in the ports, soon dispels the poetic fancies that scintillate in the works of such writers.

Dr. Kuwada, a member of the House of Peers, describing the condition of the Japanese working men and women in the Tokyo review, *Shin Koran*, says that the treatment of the factory girls in Japan is enough to shock humanity.[4]

---

3   Havel is referring, respectively, to Lafcadio Hearn (1850–1904), an international writer known for his books on Japan; Julien Viaud (1850–1923), known by the pseudonym "Pierre Loti," a French novelist; and Judith Gautier (1845–1917), a French poet and historical novelist. All three authors wrote about Japan in a sensationalistic or romantic fashion.

4   Presumably Havel is referring to Kuwada Kumazo (1869–1932), a professor of law at the Tokyo Imperial University and an outspoken critic of industrialization. The article in question was entitled "The Pitiful Environment of Factory Girls" and appeared in the September 1910 issue of *Shin Koron* ("New Review")—a Tokyo-based general interest magazine.

There are in Japan about ten thousand factories and workshops, employing about a million laborers. Of this total about seven hundred thousand are females. As there is no law limiting the age of factory hands, almost ten percent of the female laborers are under fourteen years. Twenty percent of the girls employed in the match factories, and one percent, of those in the glass and tobacco factories, are even under ten years. In many factories the girls are not even allowed time for meals, but are required to eat while working. Almost all cotton-spinning factories keep their looms in operation day and night. Night work, in which both male and female operatives are engaged together, is found most demoralizing. The methods of punishment are equally inhumane. The lash is employed without stint; sometimes girls are imprisoned in dark rooms, or required to work with reduced rations; in many cases their wages are so diminished by "fines" that they leave the factory penniless at the end of their contract terms. The condition of male workers is just as inhumane; that of miners beyond description.

It is but natural that such a state of affairs should have roused the conscience of the best and ablest men and women of Japan. They are raising their voice in protest against these economic horrors. Thanks to their zeal, modern revolutionary ideas, expressed through Socialism and Anarchism, are now spreading the message of international brotherhood among the oppressed and exploited masses. The very government, which during the late war permitted revolutionary literature to be distributed among the Russian captives, now finds itself face to face with the growing spirit of revolt at home.

As in most countries, there are also in Japan several tendencies of Socialist thought: Marxists, represented by the able Mr. Katayama,[5] and the Anarchists or

---

5   Sen Katayama (1859–1933) was a Japanese socialist who
     co-founded the Japanese Communist Party in 1922. Katayama

"Kropotkinists," also known as the "Allied Socialists," whose ablest exponent is Denjiro Kotoku. The movement as a whole is naturally still very weak. It was the war with Russia which furnished the proper leaven for its growth, speedily, however, drawing down upon itself the persecution of the government.

The reaction has reached its strongest expression under the regime of the present Premier, Baron Katsura. A man reared in the *junker* spirit of militarist Prussia, he is employing the most rigid methods in dealing with radical elements. The persecution has now reached its culminating point in the arrest and conviction of Denjiro Kotoku, his wife, and twenty-four other comrades, for "plotting against the imperial family."[6]

The recent appeal of Mr. Katayama to the International Socialist Bureau in behalf of the persecuted Japanese radicals does not seem to have produced much effect. The

---

wrote *The Labor Movement In Japan* (Chicago: Charles H. Kerr and Company Co-operative, 1918) and was an occasional contributor to the *International Socialist Review* in 1910 and 1911.

6   The High Treason Incident (*Taigyaku Jiken*) was an alleged socialist/anarchist conspiracy to assassinate the Emperor Meiji. In late May of 1910, police arrested Kōtoku and five alleged accomplices on suspicion of plotting to murder the Emperor with explosives. Eventually a total of 26 individuals were indicted for their alleged role in the plot and charged with treason for violating Article 73 of the Japanese Criminal Code (causing or threatening harm to the Emperor or his family). The evidence against the vast majority of the defendants was circumstantial at best. Kōtoku's wife, Chiyoko, was not actually arrested at this time. The person Havel is most likely referring to here is Sugako Kanno, an anarchist-feminist journalist and lover of Kōtoku's. Kanno is now believed to have been planning the assassination without Kōtoku's knowledge. See Takeda Yoshitaka, "Hidden for 100 Years: Kanno's Secret Message from Prison," *The Mainichi Shimbun*, January 29, 2010.

Katsura Cabinet therefore considers its prey secure and is about to murder Kotoku and his comrades, hoping thus to exterminate the movement of discontent. It is now up to the liberty-loving people of the civilized world as to whether the ruling classes of Japan shall succeed in the attempt to kill modern ideas in the persons of Kotoku and friends.

Denjiro Kotoku is a very able writer who has popularized Socialist, Anarchist, and anti-militarist ideas in Japan. He has translated many works of Karl Marx, Leo Tolstoy, and Peter Kropotkin, and has devoted a number of years to propagating the doctrines of these radical thinkers. For this he has been imprisoned many times, resulting in the loss of his health. Imprisonment did not kill him, however, and the government, fearing so able a man, has now decided to do the work itself.

Before the Russo-Japanese War Kotoku was one of the brilliant editorial writers on the influential Tokyo daily, *Yorozu cho-ho.*[7] His anti-militarist convictions, and the fearless expression of his sentiments regarding war, caused him to give up his position. He founded a radical monthly review, *Tatsu Kwa.*[8] This paper, advocating revolutionary ideas, was soon suppressed by the authorities. Other radical magazines suffered the same fate, among them *Heimin Shimbun, Kunamato Hyo-ron, ShinShiho,* and *Nippon Heimin.*[9] In the last review were published the resolutions passed at the International Anarchist Congress in Amsterdam, 1905.

---

7   *Yorozu Choho* ("Universal Morning News") was a Japanese newspaper published from 1892 to 1940.

8   *Tetsu Kawa* ("Iron and Steel") was a Japanese radical newspaper, publication dates unknown.

9   *Heimin Shinbun* ("Commoners Magazine") was published from 1903 to 1905, *Kunamoto Hyoron* ("Radical Review") was published from 1907 to 1908, and *Nippon Heimin* ("The Japanese Commoner") was published from 1909 to 1910. The publication dates of *Shin Shiho* ("New Will") are unknown.

Kotoku did not confine himself to the workers alone. In co-operation with Mme. Ho Chin and Comrade Lien Sun Soh he preached the ideas of Anarchism in the University of Tokyo, among the Japanese as well as the Chinese students.[10] The propaganda among the Chinese has been carried on through the columns of *Chien Yee* and the *Chinese Anarchist News*.[11]

November tenth the following cable reached New York by way of the Associated Press:

> The finding of the special court organized to try the plotters against the life of the Emperor was announced today. Twenty six persons were found guilty, including the ringleader, Kotoku, and one woman, the wife of Kotoku. The court recommends "the severest penalty under Clause 73," which provides capital punishment for plotters against the imperial family.[12]

Similar news came to England via Reuter's Agency. The information was first published by the Tokyo daily, *Hochi Shinbun*.[13] When the news appeared there was no ques-

---

10 Havel is referring to He Zhen (c. 1884–c. 1920), a Chinese anarchist, socialist, and feminist. She was married to the anarchist scholar Liu Shipei (1884–1919). See Lydia Liu, et al., *The Birth of Chinese Feminism* (New York: Columbia University Press, 2013). "Lien Sun Soh" is most likely Liu Shipei.

11 Havel is most likely referring to *Tianyi* ("Heavenly Righteousness") a Chinese-language anarchist journal published in Tokyo from 1907 to 1908. *Chinese Anarchist News* may be *Hengbao* ("Equity"), a newspaper published in Tokyo in 1908.

12 See "Plotters Against the Mikado To Die," *New York Times* (10 November 1910). Sugako Kanno (see note below) was not, in fact, Kōtoku's wife.

13 *Hochi Shinbun* ("Daily Newspaper") was a Tokyo-based

tion of its accuracy, for no paper in the Japanese Empire would have dared to circulate such a report without the consent of the authorities. Indeed, a most rigorous censorship had previously prevented the publication of the news, and when the *Hochi Shinbun* at last printed it, the paper said it assumed full responsibility for its statements.

Immediately after the news reached New York, a protest movement was inaugurated. The representatives of the Japanese government were interviewed, and these, while not denying the authenticity of the cable information, were diplomatically reticent on the matter. Now that the protest is assuming national proportions—hundreds of letters and telegrams of protest having been sent to the Japanese Ambassador at Washington—the Consul General at New York, Mr. K. Midzuno,[14] deigned to send the following letter in reply to the inquiry of a person prominent in public life.

> "Regarding the enclosed manuscript, I have to refer you to Mr. M. Honda, of the Oriental Information Agency, 35 Nassau Street, City, who is better informed in this matter than I am. I beg, however, to say, that it is not correct that I have informed the local Anarchist people that the death penalty against Kotoku and his associates has been recommended by the Special Trial Court. In this respect Mr. Honda will be able to give you full quotations of the constitution and laws relating to the construction of the courts. Judicial courts of Japan are too independent to admit of

newspaper published from 1894 to 1942.

14 Kokichi Midzuno (1873–1914) was a Japanese diplomat who served as Consul General in several imperial embassies during his career.

any political influence or pressure from outside, as well as the public opinion or as agitation of the irresponsible people."

Mr. Midzuno is not very accurate. It was not the local Anarchists, but Mr. Leonard D. Abbott, President of the Free Speech League, and of the Francisco Ferrer Association, and Prof. Bayard Boyesen, Secretary of the latter, who paid their respects to the gentleman.[15]

The prospect of a great American protest is evidently not at all to the liking of this servant of the Mikado.[16] Else it is difficult to explain why he exerted his persuasive powers to induce his callers to desist from the protest.

Mr. Motosada Zumoto, Chief of the Oriental Information Agency, has also endeavored, in a recent interview with the present writer, to pour oil on the troubled waters.[17] This gentleman has now suddenly disappeared and his representative, Prof. M. Honda,[18] in answer to the letter referred to above, sent the following reply:

---

15 Bayard Boyesen (1882–1944) was an American academic, writer, and political activist. A prominent figure in the New York anarchist milieu, Boyesen was among other things a contributor to *Mother Earth* and a driving force in the American Modern School movement who lost his teaching position at Columbia as a result of political activities carried out in response to Ferrer's execution. With Leonard Abbott, he tried unsuccessfully to intercede on Kōtoku's behalf at the Japanese consulate in November 1910.

16 The Emperor of Japan.

17 Motosada Zumoto (1862–1943) was a Japanese publisher and director of the Oriental Information Bureau in New York, which he founded circa 1909. Technically an independent news agency, the Bureau often functioned as a propaganda outlet for the Japanese government.

18 Matsujiro Honda (1866–1925) was a Japanese academic who taught for a time at the Higher Normal College in Tokyo and served as secretary of the Oriental Information Bureau.

Dear Sir: In the absence of Mr. Zumoto away in Japan, I beg to acknowledge your letter addressed to him and assure you that we have no accurate facts to tell you concerning the matter. It seems to me, however, that what you state in your paper greatly exaggerates things and misrepresents Japan. Only we can tell you that Japan is a legally governed country, and whatever is done will be done in accordance with the provisions of the constitution and laws of the country, which, we think, are humane and just. I am, etc.,

M. Honda.
P. S.:

1. Kotoku was not editor-in-chief of the *Yorozu*, but a member on the staff.

2. The organization of a special court is regulated in Article 59 of the Constitution promulgated more than twenty years ago.

3. 'Intellectual' is hardly a name to be given to Kotoku by us Japanese. There are several professors in the Imperial University and the Waseda University who uphold and propagate Socialist doctrines, but they are tolerated by the authorities and respected by the people. Kotoku's party are more of destroyers of social orders and moral stability of the country, and therefore even the opposition papers have no sympathy at all with him and his followers. On the contrary, the people in general are thoroughly in disgust with them—hence their

difficulty to get any respectable work. If
you outsiders agitate for those people, not
only it does not help them, but will, I fear,
induce the people of Japan to doubt the
true friendship of your country.

Mr. Honda assures us that he has "no accurate facts"
How then does he know that our statement of the case is
"greatly exaggerated and misrepresents Japan"?

The Consul General, as well as the vanished Mr.
Zumoto, tells us that the strict censorship in their country
would make it impossible to discuss the case of the prisoners, so that even the Japanese people are kept in complete
ignorance about the persecution.

We know only too well the meaning of Japanese censorship. Those who are unfamiliar with its great benefits,
will recall the system of espionage practiced by the government during the Russo-Japanese war. Certainly the
foreign war correspondents had a fine opportunity of fa-
miliarizing themselves with the liberalism of the Japanese
statesmen.[19]

It is strange that Mr. Honda did not come to the rescue of his country when Mr. Katayama protested to the
International Socialist Bureau and to the radical press of
the Western world against the brutal persecution of the
Socialists in Japan. Is it that the gentleman did not dare to
charge that Mr. Katayama, himself a Japanese, also misrepresented his country?

As a matter of fact the intent of misrepresentation is all
on the part of the officials representing Japan. It expresses itself in stamping the growing indignation against the

---

19   During the Russo-Japanese War the Japanese military authorities
      implemented a series of extremely heavy-handed policies includ-
      ing, but not limited to, transportation bans and aggressive cen-
      sorship campaigns. The latter was especially of foreign journalists,
      many of whom were imprisoned.

sentence as exclusively Anarchistic, in order to discredit that movement and at the same time to blacken the character of Kotoku. No doubt there is method in this madness. But as we do not mean to invite the sympathy of the American capitalists to help save our friends, it does not matter.

True, Mr. Honda and his colleagues assure us that Socialism is being taught in the Imperial and in the Waseda University, but they forget to mention the kind of Socialism that is being inculcated in the students. It is not the international revolutionary Socialism of Marx and Engels, but a loyal conservative State Socialism of the weakest dye, a brand of Socialism which may be espoused by such men as Mallock, Leroy-Beaulieu, and Wesley Hill.[20]

That the ruling class of Japan is out of sympathy with Denjiro Kotoku is readily understood. It has its reasons—evidently the same as the French bourgeoise has in keeping Hervé in prison, the German in distrusting Bebel, or as our own ruling powers have for their dislike of Debs or Warren.[21] The truly amusing part, however, is the reference in Mr. Honda's letter, that the Japanese people in general are in disgust with Kotoku and his comrades—"hence their difficulty to get any respectable work." Does Mr.

---

20 Havel is referring, respectively, to William Mallock (1849–1923), an English novelist and economist; Henry Leroy-Beaulieu (1842–1912), a French historian and publicist; and John Wesley Hill (c. 1860–1934), an American clergyman and writer. As Havel suggests, all three men were essentially social democrats who advocated cautious, even conservative, forms of socialism.

21 Havel is referring, respectively, to Gustave Hervé (1871–1944), a French socialist and anti-militarist writer who at the time of writing was in prison for his anti-militarist ideas; August Bebel (1840–1913), a German Marxist politician and writer; Eugene Debs (1855–1926), an American labor leader and socialist politician; and Fred Warren (1872–1959), an American socialist writer.

Honda mean to imply that work on the editorial staff of the *Yorozu*—even if not in the capacity of editor-in-chief—or translating sociologic books is not respectable?

Poor Kotoku! He will have to be content to be classed with the Garrisons, Tolstoys, Mazzinis,[22] yea, even with Jesus and Buddha, who also had no respectable work and with whom the ruling classes of their time were also disgusted.

Life is too precious to quibble over technicalities as to whether the death sentence has been "recommended" or pronounced. The fact is that Kotoku and friends are in immediate danger of their lives. That is sufficient for us to call, in the name of justice and international human solidarity, for a mighty protest. Dreyfus and Ferrer should serve us as a warning.

* * *

Just before going to press, we read the following cable in the daily papers:

> TOKIO, December 8.—Hontai and Uzawa, two distinguished Japanese lawyers, were threatened with instant execution to-day if they undertook to defend twenty-six Japanese radicals arrested recently on charges of conspiring to assassinate the Mikado and the royal family.
>
> The government takes the ground that the twenty-six men are Anarchists and should be killed and that they are not, therefore, entitled to any defense.
>
> The trials of the men will begin soon, and public excitement is increasing as the date of the trial approaches.

---

22 Giuseppe Mazzini (1805–1872) was an Italian revolutionary and politician.

JUSTICE IN JAPAN (1911)[1]

THE FATE OF OUR JAPANESE COMRADES IS STILL IN THE balance. The Supreme Court of Tokyo is at present deliberating upon the case and a decision is to be expected soon. Will our friends fall victims to reaction? Will they suffer a sacrificial death?

It will not happen if we energetically continue the protests which have already assumed an international character. The government of Japan at first thought to ignore this protest movement; it had no conception to what dimensions it would grow. The appeal to international solidarity has found a mighty echo. The revolutionists of all countries instinctively felt that it was *their* cause which was being decided at Tokyo, and that the condemnation of Denjiro Kotoku and comrades was a direct challenge to modern thought.

Will the government of Japan consider the international protest? It has at last been forced to break its silence and to issue an official statement, published by the leading papers of America and Europe. The government of the Mikado has evidently played what it thought a trump card by characterizing the condemned as Communist Anarchists. But it has merely succeeded in proving itself barbaric and brutal; nay, more—very stupid. We have never asserted the contrary regarding our condemned comrades; indeed, in our original appeal we clearly stated that Denjiro Kotoku was an Anarchist, known in Japan as the leader of the "Kropotkinists." Every intelligent man

---

1   This article originally appeared in *Mother Earth* 5, no. 11 (January 1911). A follow up to "The Kotoku Case," which was published the previous month, "Justice in Japan" provides a detailed account of the public relations fallout from the High Treason Incident.

who is conversant with modern social thought is aware of
the fact that Kropotkin is not a monarchist. We are proud
to count among our comrades a writer like Kotoku, a physician like Dr. Oishi, an artist like Takeda, or a translator
like Miss Sugano-Kano.[2] The twenty-six condemned
represent the intellectual element of Japan, among them
being workingmen, farmers, artists, physicians, and three
Buddhist priests.

The whole statement of the Japanese government is
quite one-sided. It has purposely omitted to mention the
fact that not only Anarchists, but also over two hundred
Socialists are languishing in Japanese prisons since June
of last year. The French Socialist daily, *L'Humanite*, publishes a letter received by Jean Longuet from S. Katayama,
the leading Socialist of Japan, in which he relates the
series of terrible persecutions and oppressions to which
the Japanese Socialists are being subjected.[3] Katayama
implores Longuet to lift up his voice against the brutal
treatment of the Japanese Socialists, and to assist them in
their terrible struggle. He begs him to give it the utmost
publicity all over the world.

In the face of these facts the spokesmen of the Japanese
government, Messrs. Masujiro Honda and Tsunego Baba,
of the Oriental Information Bureau, declare in the *Oriental*

---

2   Havel is referring, respectively, to Seinosuke Oishi (1867–1911),
    Takeda Kyuhei (1875–1911), and Kanno Sugako (1881–1911).
    Kanno, who was Kōtoku's one-time partner, was among those ini-
    tially arrested, the others being Miyashita Takichi (1875–1911),
    Nitta Toru (1880–1911), Niimura Tadao (1887–1911), and
    Furukawa Rikisaku (1884–1911). Oishi and Kyuhei were subse-
    quently rounded up as part of the alleged national conspiracy that
    the state claimed to have uncovered.

3   *L'Humanité*, July 9, 1910. Jean Longuet (1876–1938) was a
    French socialist and Karl Marx's grandson. *L'Humanité* was
    formerly the daily newspaper of the French Communist Party
    (PCF), published from 1904 to the present.

Economic Review (Vol. I, Number 3) that "a political persecution is impossible in Japan." But other prominent Japanese quite disagree with Messrs. Honda and Baba.[4] Count Hayashi, former Minister of Foreign Affairs, is one of seven scholars and publicists who contribute a group of strong articles to the *Taiyo* on Socialism.[5] Count Hayashi goes so far as to assert that the policy of the Minister of Education, aimed at the suppression of Socialist publications, is narrow-minded, dangerous, and inadequate to attain the object intended. The other six contributors, while censuring the "Anarchistic tendency" of Japanese Socialists, warn the government not to take any measure which will virtually drive the radicals and discontents into underhand agitation. One contributor, Mr. Inukai, a leader of the opposition party, holds the government itself responsible for the present dangerous tendency of the Socialist movement in Japan.[6] The police authorities put every Socialist under such strict espionage, he says, that his friends and relatives are forced to shun him in order not to be suspected by the police of being in sympathy with Socialism.

The official statement of Japan further lays particular stress on the legality of the procedure against Kotoku et al. Let us hear what an impartial observer has to say regarding the alleged legality.

Mr. Robert Young, the editor of the *Japan Chronicle* (a capitalist publication appearing in Japan), declared in an

---

4   Tsunego Baba (1875–1956) was a Japanese journalist, publicist, and politician. Baba served as associate editor of *The Oriental Review*, a publication of the Oriental Information Bureau.

5   Hayashi Tadasu (1850–1913) was a Japanese diplomat who served as ambassador to Russia and Britain and as Foreign Minister from 1906 to 1908. *Taiyō* ("The Sun") was a general interest magazine published in Japan from 1895 to 1928.

6   Inukai Tsuyoshi (1855–1932) was a Japanese politician who served as Prime Minister from 1931 to 1932, when he was assassinated.

interview with a representative of the London *Daily News*, published in that paper December 9, as follows:

> It is necessary that your readers should understand that in Japan the preliminary court, whose investigations are always secret, gives a decision on a case which virtually amounts to a verdict (it is really a finding), but it cannot sentence. There must follow a public trial, and after the public trial there can be an appeal to the higher court, and still another appeal is permissible from that court's decision to the Court of Cassation, whose decision is irrevocable.
>
> Now, in the case of these twenty-six Socialists, it must be clearly understood that so far they have only been examined by the preliminary court, and that instead of having the three public trials to which they are entitled, their case is to go at once to the Court of Cassation—-this court will try them to-morrow— from whose decision there is no appeal.
>
> I cannot understand this departure from the law of the land; it is both unconstitutional and unprecedented. Nor is this all. I understand that the Court of Cassation will try the twenty-six men and women in camera so that they are to have no public trial, and no chance of appeal, and we shall never know the facts. Since these people have been arrested they have had no opportunity whatever of placing their case before the public.
>
> On the other hand, when they were arrested, instructions were sent to every newspaper in Japan—my own included—that

no mention whatever was to be made either of the arrest or of anything connected with the arrest. This did not prevent the Japanese police authorities from shortly afterwards giving interviews to Japanese newspapers in which the authorities made the most serious charges against those arrested, though even then there was no mention of there being any plot against the Imperial House.[7]

Messrs. Honda and Baba do not merely seek to justify the action of their government. They attempt to strengthen their case by blackening the characters of the condemned. Till recently Mr. Honda masqueraded as a libertarian among the radical elements of New York. But now he has revealed himself in his true colors. And his colleague, Mr. Baba, is fitly stigmatized by his reply to the protest of Miss Alice Stone Blackwell in the Boston *Transcript*.[8] He states that the condemned "practiced some of the doctrines of communism of property on their friends and thus totally alienated all sympathy. The conduct of the female Socialist (Miss Sugano-Kano) in particular was such that the Japanese women could not speak of Socialism without a blush." Mr. Baba could not have selected a surer means of branding himself a liar and defamer. Only a scoundrel of the lowest type would stoop

---

7   The interview was republished as "The Japanese 'Anarchists'" in *The North-China Herald and Supreme Court & Consular Gazette* 97.2264 (December 30, 1910). Robert Young (1855–1932) was a British writer and publisher. *Japan Chronicle* was an English-language newspaper published in Japan from 1891 to 1940.

8   Alice Stone Blackwell (1857–1950) was an American feminist, suffragist, and journalist. The letter Havel references appears under the title "A Backward Step in Japan" in the December 2, 1910 issue of *The Boston Evening Transcript*. Baba's reply appears under the title "Japanese Anarchists" in the December 13, 1910 issue.

to such calumny of a noble woman on the threshold of death. What would the civilized world think of a man who would thus slander a Perovskaia or a Spiridonova?[9]

In answer to these calumnies we can say of Kotoku, Dr. Oishi, and Miss Sugano-Kano—with whom we have been in correspondence—that they are noble and beautiful characters. We do not stand alone in that opinion. Mr. L. Fleishman, of Pasadena, who was war-correspondent in the Russo-Japanese war, related at a protest meeting in Los Angeles his visit to Kotoku and the cordial welcome he received at the homes of our Japanese comrades.[10] Kotoku he described as the leading poetical writer of Japan, equal in literary style to the best writers in other countries, as unassuming and gentle as a lady.

Sasha Kropotkin Lebedeff,[11] the daughter of our beloved comrade, Peter Kropotkin, writes to us:

---

9 Sophia Perovskaya (1853–1881) and Maria Spiridonova (1884–1941) were Russian revolutionaries, often cited by anarchists as exemplary female representatives of the revolutionary socialist movement.

10 Leopold Fleischmann (1876–1951) was a radical Austrian-American journalist who befriended Kōtoku while working as a war correspondent during the Russo-Japanese War (see Notehelfer, *Kōtoku Shūsui*, p. 123, note 4). Although it is uncertain when the event Havel describes took place, similar protest meetings were organized by anarchists and socialists throughout the country in 1910 and 1911. Goldman, for example, spoke at such a meeting at Lloyd Hall in New York on 12 November 1910.

11 Alexandra Kropotkin-Lebedeff (1877–1966) was a Russian writer and translator and the daughter of Peter Kropotkin. Though not an anarchist herself, Kropotkin was a lifelong friend and associate of many anarchists, especially in New York, where she settled in the 1920s. It is not clear whether Havel knew her personally. Kōtoku translated Peter Kropotkin's *The Conquest of Bread* into Japanese in 1909; the letter suggests he was planning/had begun to translate *Fields, Factories and Workshops* as well.

My father thinks that, judging from what Kotoku used to say in his letters to him, Kotoku is far more of a teacher than a man of violent action. He is evidently a highly educated man and a deep thinker. I myself had some correspondence with him about the translations of my father's book, *Fields, Factories, and Workshops*. He must be an exceptionally gentle and courteous man, and he often wrote about the desperate conditions of the Japanese peasants. "No land, no food—a few grains of rice only," were his words.

How desperate is the case of the Japanese government is further evidenced by its tampering with the mails. It is guilty of breaking the international postal agreement in reference to the sanctity of private correspondence. Letters sent from America and Europe to persons suspected in Japan, are confiscated by the government and their contents examined. The government is straining every effort to suppress the truth regarding the condemned.

We hope that the friends of liberty will not cease their efforts in behalf of the intended victims. Should the government of Japan succeed in this dastardly plot, the struggle for social and economic emancipation would receive a terrible blow. We must save Kotoku and his friends.

LONG LIVE ANARCHY! (1911)[1]

> The greatest men of a nation are those whom
> it puts to death.
> —Ernest Renan[2]

THE BLACK DEED IS DONE. THE BEST AND NOBLEST OF THE
people have fallen, murdered in the most fiendish and
barbaric manner.

A crime, unparalleled in atrocity, has been committed
on January twenty-fourth, nineteen hundred and eleven.
A terrible blow has been dealt humanity, and the gauntlet thrown in the face of civilization. Ruthless barbarism
cold-bloodedly strangled the heroic pioneers of a new idea
and gloated over the agony of its helpless victims.

Yet we mourn not. Rather is it our task to discover to
the world the innocence and purity, the honesty and faith-
fulness, the self-sacrifice and devotion of our murdered
comrades. We mourn not: our friends have achieved
immortality.

A new epoch has struck for Japan with the date of their
martyrdom. When the era of Mikado Mutsuhito shall
have passed from man's memory, when *bushido* is but a
fable and a myth, the names of the martyred Anarchists

---

1   This article originally appeared in *Mother Earth* 5, no. 12
    (February 1911). It is a response to the execution of Kōtoku and
    ten others, which took place on January 24, 1911.

2   Ernest Renan (1823–1892) was a French orientalist scholar
    and freethinker. The quote appears in *The Life of Jesus* (London:
    Epiphany, 1864), p. 65. The work in question was extremely in-
    fluential in the nineteenth century freethought movement.

will be glorified on the pages of human progress.[3] When the members of the *Daishinin*, who delivered the noblest of mankind into the hangman's hands, shall have been long forgotten, the martyrs of Tokyo will be respected and admired by future generations.[4]

The revolutionary movement in the Orient has received its baptism of blood. The barbaric rulers think to have eradicated the movement for emancipation. What stupidity! They have destroyed the bodies of twelve representatives of the new, world-conquering idea, and silenced other representatives in the dungeons; but the spirit lives! That spirit, the eternal cry for liberty—it is not to be silenced, it cannot be killed. It was, it is, and will be. Conquering, it marches onward, ever onward, toward liberty and life.

Long live Anarchy! The historic cry has found its echo in the Far East. Often it has resounded, from the lips of the martyrs of Chicago, Paris, Buenos Ayres, Vienna, St. Petersburg, Barcelona, and numerous other places. For decades it has been terrifying the tyrants and oppressors of every land. They have tortured, beheaded, electrocuted, quartered, shot, and strangled the pioneers of the new idea. But their voices have not been silenced.

Long live Anarchy! On the twenty-fourth of January the cry once more rang from the lips of twelve new martyrs. The solidarity of the international proletariat has been crowned. The West and the East have found each other.

Proudly and joyfully our comrades faced death. *Long live Anarchy!* cried Denjiro Kotoku. *Banzai* (i.e., forever) replied his companions in struggle and death.

They were very dear to us. We mourn not; yet our hearts are saddened at the thought of the charming Sugano. Lovingly we call upon her memory. We see the tender lotus ruthlessly destroyed by the hand of the hangman; we

---

3   Mutshito is the Emperor Meiji (1852–1912), the 122nd Emperor of Japan. *Bushido* is the warrior code of the samurai.

4   The *Diashin-in* is the Japanese Court of Cassation.

behold her, weakened through illness, broken by long imprisonment, yet joyfully and calmly meeting her terrible doom. *I have lived for liberty and will die for liberty, for liberty is my life.* Thus she wrote but recently to her English teacher in San Francisco.

Gentle Sugano! You, the daughter of a Samurai, daughter of a member of your country's Parliament, talented author and writer, you went, like your Russian sisters, into the people, voluntarily exposing yourself to danger, hardships, and hunger. They have sought to besmirch your character and name. The representatives of a Mutsuhito, himself leading a life of polygamy; his son, the heir apparent, offspring of a concubine; the lackeys of Premier Katsura, who chose the daughter of a brothel keeper for his wife—all these honorable men have sought to besmirch you, lovely lotus flower, because of your friendship for Denjiro Kotoku.

What contemptible scoundrels! But some day there will arise a Turgeniev in the land of Nippon, and the name of Sugano Kano will be hailed with the Sophia Perovskaias, the Vera Figners, and Maria Spiridonovas.[5]

In Denjiro Kotoku the international movement has lost one of its noblest representatives. He was the pioneer of Socialist and Anarchist thought in the Far East. His numerous translations—Karl Marx's *Capital*, Peter Kropotkin's *Mutual Aid, Conquest of Bread, Fields, Factories, and Workshops*, and *Appeal to the Young*, as well as of other modern works—have accomplished the *real* opening of Japan to Western civilization.

Denjiro Kotoku was, next to Tolstoy, the severest opponent of war; and—like Hervé—a most courageous, uncompromising propagator of anti-militarist ideas. While the patriotic jingoes celebrated, during the Russo-Japanese

---

5   Vera Figner (1852–1942) was a Russian revolutionary and assassin who was involved in the plot to assassinate Tsar Alexander II (just as Kanno was involved in the plot to assassinate the Emperor).

war, orgies of wholesale man-killing, Kotoku was engaged in exposing the murderous business by his brilliant articles in the *Yorozu-Choho*. But the voice of the prophet was lost in the wilderness. Like Victor Hugo, Mazzini, Blanqui, Bakunin, Marx, and scores of other pioneers of liberty before him, he was forced to flee his native land, to live in exile at San Francisco, and here, in the land of Patrick Henry, Thomas Paine, and Jefferson, he was to suffer new persecutions at the hands of the government of Washington.[6] O shame, O disgrace!

Denjiro Kotoku, Sugano Kano, Dr. Oishi, and their comrades legally assassinated; these, the noblest and most intelligent of their people: writers, physicians, representatives of pure Buddhist philosophy of human brotherhood, and awakened, intellectual proletarians—these are the men slaughtered in the hope of annihilating every vestige of modern world-thought.

Great, brave men. Lovingly and tenderly we peruse over again an old letter from Dr. Oishi, a reader of *Mother Earth*. In strong, clear English he sends greetings to his American comrades and requests Anarchist literature for distribution among his countrymen. The much beloved, genial physician of Shingo-Key, bringing cheer and relief to the thousands of sick and afflicted. His only reward, the gallows.

Our eyes have at last been opened to the true character of the government of the Mikado. We know now the infamous conspiracy hatched by the Japanese government. We realize the full significance of the atrocious plot. We

---

6   Kōtoku came to the attention of U.S. authorities when the Social Revolutionary Party—a group he helped organize in San Francisco in 1906—openly advocated the assassination of the Emperor in its organ. Although he was actively surveilled, it is not clear that he suffered any real "persecutions" at the hands of the government. (On the contrary, it seems Kōtoku's return to Japan was entirely voluntary.)

can follow to their source the false reports, misrepresentations, and lies put in circulation by Reuter's Agency, the Japanese Ambassadors and Consuls, and especially by the Oriental Information Bureau of New York. The mysterious Oriental veil has been partly lifted. The civilized world is now aware that the trial of our martyred comrades was conducted in secret; that the accused were deprived of impartial hearing or defense; that the claim that they had confessed their guilt was pure fabrication; and that, finally, the official statement regarding the presence at the trial of the members of foreign embassies was also absolutely false.

The trial of Francisco Ferrer was ideal justice in comparison with this judicial wholesale slaughter. Since the days of the Dekabrists in Russia humanity has witnessed no crime so monstrous, so monumental as that committed by the government of Japan.[7]

The rulers of Japan have succeeded in accomplishing one thing. They have drawn upon themselves the hatred of the libertarian elements of every country, who will join hands with the awakening proletariat of Japan in the great work of social emancipation.

The massacre has not only made our comrades martyrs; it has made them immortal. Out of their blood will rise new rebels, avengers who will sweep off the face of the earth the murderers and their institutions.

---

7   The Decembrists were a Russian revolutionary movement which opposed Tsar Nicholas I's assumption of the throne in 1825.

KOTOKU'S CORRESPONDENCE WITH ALBERT JOHNSON (1911)[1]

ONE OF THE PLEASANT MEMORIES OF OUR MARTYRED Japanese comrades must have been their friendship with European and American radicals, among whom were Leopold Fleischmann and Albert Johnson, the veteran Anarchist of California.[2] Thanks to Leopold Fleischmann, Denjiro Kotoku, T. Sakai, Sen Katayama, Dr. Kato, and others came in closer touch with the social struggle in America.[3] It was also through Mr. Fleischmann that Denjiro Kotoku met our old friend Albert Johnson, the acquaintance soon ripening into a

---

1   This article appeared in *Mother Earth* 6, no. 6 (August 1911). It is the first of a three-part series intended to pay tribute to Kōtoku in the aftermath of his execution.

2   According to Notehelfer little is known about Albert Johnson (see *Kōtoku Shūsui*, p. 122). Born in 1844 in Vermont, he was evidently a freethinker and anarchist who worked as a fireman on the ferries that ran between San Francisco and Oakland (p. 123).

3   Fleischmann met and befriended several of these individuals while working as a war correspondent during the Russo-Japanese War. Toshihiko Sakai (1871–1933), a socialist historian and writer, collaborated with Katayama, Kōtoku, and others in founding the Japanese Social Democratic Party in 1901 and helped Kōtoku launch the newspaper *Heimin Shinbu* in 1903. Kato Tokijiro (1858–1930), also a socialist, was Kōtoku's physician. In 1905 he nursed Kōtoku back to health in his own home after the latter completed a five-month prison sentence; he also personally financed Kōtoku's trip to the United States.

friendship which continued even after Kotoku returned to Japan. The result of their intimacy now comes to us in the form of an extensive correspondence. I am indebted for these valuable letters to Leonard D. Abbott, of the *Current Literature*, and am very happy indeed to be able to submit them to the readers of *Mother Earth*.

The letters are reproduced as written, since any attempt to edit them would but detract from their charm and simple grandeur. One can readily see that Denjiro Kotoku had joined the army of the social revolution and that as thinker, fighter and organizer he gave himself unreservedly to the cause of human emancipation.

Of great value is the letter wherein Kotoku speaks of his development to Anarchism and the reasons therefor. Evidently the economic and social conditions which act as a leaven in Europe and America operate with the same force in Japan. Even as we, the Japanese are confronted with identical pressing problems demanding solution.

Denjiro Kotoku was a scholar engaged with deep philosophic questions. Like Renan, Strauss, and Bruno Bauer, our Comrade was devoting himself during his last imprisonment to a work containing a severe arraignment of Christianity.[4] What a strange coincidence that at the very moment when Professor Drews' work on Jesus Christ was causing such a furor in Germany, the Japanese Anarchist thinker, in a Japanese prison, with death staring him in the face, was elaborating the same theme.[5]

---

4   David Strauss (1808–1874) and Bruno Bauer (1809–1882) were German philosophers. Renan, Strauss, and Bauer all published famous controversial works in "radical" theology and/or Biblical criticism which were extremely influential in the nineteenth-century freethought movement.

5   Christian Drews (1865–1935) was a German historian, philosopher, and theologian. Havel is presumably referring to *Die Christusmythe* ("The Christ Myth"), trans. C. Delisle Burns (London ,1910).

Tokyo, Japan, Nov. 25th, 1904

Dear Comrade,

I feel very happy to inform you that this picture[6] was reproduced from that which you sent me, and is published from *Heimin Shimbun* office, a Socialist weekly. I have been prosecuted on the charge of publishing a treasonable article and sentenced to five months' imprisonment. When this card is in your hand I will be in Sugano Prison of Tokyo.

Yours fraternally,

D. Kotoku

Tokyo, Dec. 30th, 1904

Mr. A. Johnson

Dear Comrade,

In replying I thank you very much, for I have received Mr. Kropotkin's address and many valuable literatures which you sent to me.

Both as a source of argument and reference, Mr. Ladd's work, "Commentaries on Hebrew," should be of great value for me, because I am an atheist or agnostic, and always fighting against the dogma of Christian and all other religions.[7]

I regret that I did not have a chance of reading late Mr. Hearn's work, but I think it should be a good authority, as he lived himself a complete Japanese life during many years till his death.

As already informed, I was prosecuted by barbarous government on the charge of inciting to the alteration of the Dynastic Institution and sentenced to five months' imprisonment, but I soon appealed and second trial was postponed until January 6th.

Beside this I was sentenced on 20th inst. to a fine of 80 yen on the charge of translating and publishing

---

6   [Havel's note] Picture of Peter Kropotkin

7   Parish B. Ladd (died 1912) was an American freethinker. Kōtoku is referring to *Commentaries on Hebrew and Christian Mythology*, published by the Truthseeker Company (New York) in 1896.

Marx's "Communist Manifesto." What beautiful Japanese Government is! Is it not quite same to Russian despotism? I ever remain,

Yours fraternally,

D. Kotoku

Odawara, Japan, Aug. 10th, 1905

Mr. A. Johnson

Dear Comrade,

I have just received your letter of July 16th, and translated it orally with great pleasure for my wife, who listened very attentively with most gratitude for your friendship and kindness.

We could not help shedding tears of sympathy with your youngest daughter having lost her husband recently, and of thankfulness in knowing that you would have had the dinner in your house to celebrate my release.

August 6th we came to the sea-shore of Odawara, a town about fifty miles south-westernward from Tokyo, to restore my health. The building in which we are now staying is a villa owned by Dr. Kato, who is devoted Socialist and is kindly attending my sickness.

Five months' imprisonment not a little injured my health, but it gave me many lessons of the social questions. I have seen and studied great many of so-called "criminals" and became convinced that the governmental institutions—court, law, prison—are only responsible for them—poverty and crime.

Among the many books which I have read in the prison were Draper's "Conflict Between Religion and Science," Haeckel's "The Riddle of the Universe," Renan's "Life of Jesus," and so forth. [8] Besides I repeated again

---

8   John William Draper (1811–1882) was an English scientist, historian, and philosopher whose *History of the Conflict Between Religion and Science* was published by D. Appleton (New York) in 1874. Ernst Haeckel (1834–1919) was a German scientist, philosopher,

two interesting books which you sent me—Mr. Ladd's "Hebrew and Christian Mythology" and Mr. Kropotkin's "Fields, Factories and Workshops."[9] (By the way, Mr. Ladd often mentions Buddha as a Chinese philosopher. It is true that the greater part of Chinese population is now Buddhist, but Buddha or Gautama is not Chinese. He was born in India. He is Hindu. Several centuries after the death of Buddha his religion was introduced into China.)

Indeed, I had gone as a Marxian Socialist and returned as a radical Anarchist. To propagate Anarchism in this country, however, it means the death or lifelong, at least several years', imprisonment. Therefore its movement must be entirely secret, and its progress and success will need long, long time and endurance.

I am now intending to live in America and Europe during several years for the following purpose:

(1) To study foreign conversation and writing which are most important instruments for the International Movement of Communists or Anarchists. I can only read English literature, but cannot speak. And writing in English, as you see, is very hard for me.

(2) To visit the leaders of many foreign revolutionists and learn something from their movements.

(3) To criticize freely the position of the "His Majesty" and the political, economic and institutions from foreign land where the pernicious hand of "His Majesty" cannot reach.

If my health allows and money, that is to be borrowed from my relations and friends, could be raised I will start in the coming winter or next spring.

Although we are now at Odawara, we will return to Tokyo at next month.

---

and academic whose *The Riddle of the Universe* (*Die Welträthsel*) was published by Alfred Kröner Verlag (Stuttgart) in 1899.

9   *Fields, Factories and Workshops* was published by Putnam's (New York) in 1898.

Yours fraternally,

Denjiro Kotoku

P. S. My wife was pleased very much with many pictures enveloped in your letter.

Tokyo, Sept. 5th, 1905

Dear Comrade,

I thank you very much for the present of Kelso's "Government Analyzed," which I received last night.[10] I soon read the preface of the author. I think it is a very valuable book and I will learn many things of the evil of government and the good of Anarchy from it.

My health is recovering day by day, and I am intending to start for America in the next November. In haste.

Yours fraternally,

D. Kotoku

I have read Mr. Ladd's article, "Japan Leads the World," in *Searchlight* of July.[11]

Tokyo, Sept. 8th, 1905

Dear Comrade,

Japanese Government is now receiving natural, but dreadful result of the patriotism and jingoism which were stirred up by the hands of themselves. During the last four

---

10 John Russell Kelso (1831–1891) was an American politician, author, and lecturer. *Government Analyzed*, which was published by Etta Kelso (Longmont, Colorado) in 1892, offers a critique of the concept of government from what is essentially a philosophical or individualist anarchist perspective. It is mentioned in a number of anarchist periodicals, including *Liberty*, *Lucifer the Lightbearer*, and *Firebrand*, and was evidently quite popular.

11 George Ladd (1842–1921) was an American philosopher and educator. A professor at Yale, Ladd traveled in and wrote about Japan extensively. Kōtoku is possibly referring to an article entitled "Professor Ladd Educating Japan" from the July 15, 1905 issue of *The Search-light*.

days the city of Tokyo has been drowned by the sea of fire and blood.[12] The state of siege has been proclaimed, many publications suspended, and to the Postmaster given the right of confiscating any letter.

D. Kotoku

Tokyo, Oct. 11th, 1905

Mr. A. Johnson

Dear Comrade,

Our weekly is still suspended and our office has been compelled to dissolve ourselves owing to the barbarous persecution and financial difficulties.

I'm now intending to organize the Japanese laborers in America. There is no other means to get freedom of speech and press than to quit the soil of the state of siege and go to a more civilized country.

Yours fraternally,

D. Kotoku

October 11th, 1905

Dear Comrade,

Many thanks for books and literature. We were pleased very much with the pictures of the foreign ladies and children. I have decided to start on the N. Y. K.'s ship November 14th, for Seattle and San Francisco, with my nephew.

How pleasantly and happy it would be to shake hands with you and all comrades early in next December!

Yours fraternally,

D. Kotoku

(To be Continued.)

---

12   Kōtoku is evidently referring to the widespread public unrest that erupted in Tokyo a few days earlier in response to the conclusion of the Russo-Japanese War.

SURPRISED POLITICIANS
(1911)[1]

THE REVOLT OF THE BRITISH WORKINGMEN IS ONE OF THE most encouraging and important signs in the struggle of the international proletariat for emancipation. Significant lessons may be drawn from this struggle. We beheld the triumph of the general strike idea and witnessed the downfall of political leadership. The upstarts of the labor movement, corrupted in the swamp of parliamentarism, were as much surprised by the revolt and the splendid solidarity of the wage slaves as their colleagues and masters of the capitalist camp.

Never before was there an opportunity to see so clearly and convincingly how little sympathy the so-called leaders and the political parties have with the man of toil, or how poor their understanding concerning the condition of the people and the latter's soul. They are blind to the revolutionary activity of the Anarchists, Syndicalists, and industrialists. What gross ignorance, for instance, is displayed in the editorial observations of the N. Y. *Call:*

> "That the strike should approach the magnitude of an almost universal cessation of work, is hardly to be accounted for by any

---

1   This article, which appeared in *Mother Earth* 6, no. 7 (September 1911), was written in response to the Liverpool General Transport Strike (June 14 to August 21, 1911), which began as a nationwide strike of merchant sailors called by the National Seamen's and Firemen's Union and swiftly expanded in scope owing to a series of solidarity actions by dockworkers, railmen, and other laborers. For more information see H. Hikins, *The Liverpool General Transport Strike, 1911* (Liverpool: Toulouse Press, 1980).

widespread and long sustained propaganda advocating the general strike. Certainly neither of the two bodies professedly representing the Socialism of England, have laid any particular stress upon it as a weapon in the labor struggle, nor has there been any special organization of importance advocating it outside these two bodies. Rather does it seem a spontaneous and largely unexpected revolt on the part of the workers, in which direct agitation and organization do not appear to have played a distinct part in bringing about."[2]

The editor of the *Call* evidently knows nothing of any organizations outside the political Socialist parties of England. Is it sheer stupidity or the willful ignoring of facts? Perhaps the editor agrees with the London *Times* which seeks to explain the General Strike with this wisdom:

"Anarchy reigns and the so-called labor members of Parliament know nothing about the whole mad business. Indeed, the movement is said to be largely directed against them by agitators who have been less successful in public life than themselves."[3]

Tom Mann, who together with Ben Tillett conducted the strike, turned his back upon the Socialist party about a month ago.[4] In his resignation he gives the following reasons:

---

2   "England's Hunger Revolt," *The New York Call* (Wednesday August 16, 1911). *The New York Call* was the official outlet of the Socialist Party of America, published from 1908 to 1923.

3   "Labour Agitation Gone Mad," *The Times* (August 16, 1911).

4   Ben Tillett (1860–1943), British socialist, trade unionist, and politician.

"My experiences have driven me more and more into the non-parliamentary position; and this I find is most unwelcome to most members of the party. After the most careful reflection, I am driven to the belief that the real reason why the trades-unionist movement of this country is in such a deplorable state of inefficiency is to be found in the fictitious importance which the workers have been encouraged to attach to parliamentary action.

"I find nearly all the serious-minded young men of the Labor and Socialist movement have their minds centered upon obtaining some position in public life, such as local, municipal or county councillorship, or filling some governmental office, or aspiring to become members of Parliament.

"I am driven to the belief that this is entirely wrong, and that economic liberty will never be realized by such means. So I declare in favor of Direct Industrial Organization, not as a means, but as the means whereby the workers can ultimately overthrow the capitalist system and become the actual controllers of their own industrial and social destiny.

"I am of the opinion that the workers' fight must be carried out on the industrial plane, free from entanglements with the plutocratic enemy."[5]

---

5   The letter was addressed to H.W. Lee (1865–1932), Secretary of the Social Democratic Federation. It was reprinted in *The Agitator* 1, no. 16 (July 1, 1911) and in *The Social-Democrat* 15, no. 9 (September 15, 1911). See André Tiron, *The New Unionism* (New York: B.W. Huebsch, 1913), p. 131.

No one enjoys greater respect among the workers of England than Tom Mann. Deservedly so: has he not been an active participant within the last twenty-five years in every struggle of the proletariat in England, Australia, and South Africa? Like so many other Socialists, he has become convinced through experience of the uselessness of parliamentary activity and he has learned the importance of direct action and the General Strike.

The methods which the Anarchists have been propagating for a score of years have finally triumphed in England. Thus an important bond has been formed between the toilers of Great Britain and the revolutionary movement on the Continent.

By means of direct action and the General Strike the English workers have accomplished more in a few days than their leaders have succeeded in doing in the year-long "activity" in Parliament. They have not only carried their demands, but also caused tremendous injury to their masters, the capitalists. This strike, in which various organizations participated, involved not merely conciliation boards, but mainly practical demands: increase of pay, reduction of working hours, and the recognition of the right to organize—all of which have been won. Quite correctly the San Francisco *Revolt* remarks:

> "Five days of the general strike in the British Isles has served to win the respectful and favorable attention of the British Parliament to the demands and needs of the workingmen involved in the mighty demonstration of class solidarity. A commission has been called which, ostensibly, is to 'arbitrate,' but actually is to come into existence with instructions all ready for it under which it will have but one thing to do, and that to adjust the hours and the pay of the militant workers *in accordance with their demands*."[6]

6   "Class Unionism Wins!," *The Revolt* (August 26, 1911). *The Revolt*

Even such bitter enemies of the Syndicalists and Anarchists as the members of the Socialist Labor party must recognize the success of the direct Anarchist action of the English workers. Thus its London correspondent writes to the N. Y. *People*:

> "The moral value of the strike will prove lasting. More important than the commission inquiry is the discovery of the tremendous weapon possessed in simultaneous sympathetic strikes. It is likely to appeal to the workmen and procure thousands of recruits for the unions. A detached strike, financed by a single organization, will be abandoned as a rusty implement no longer serviceable, and the federated strike will be taken up as the method of redressing the grievances of the British workmen. They have learned from their first trial of strength that they have in their possession a better method of compelling the masters to make concessions and to reinstate strikers than they had heretofore. The general effect of the labor crisis has been the creation of a feeling of insecurity among capitalists and employers."[7]

The confession loses none of its significance by the change of the General Strike into a "federated" strike.

---

was a socialist newspaper published in San Francisco from 1911 to 1912. It was founded and edited by Tom Mooney.

7   "Labor Feels Its Power," *The Weekly People* (September 2, 1911). *The People* was an official outlet of the Socialist Labor Party, published from 1891 to 2008.

KOTOKU'S CORRESPONDENCE WITH ALBERT JOHNSON— CONTINUATION (1911)

San Francisco, May 29th, 5 p.m

Mr. Johnson

Dear Comrade,

I came here to-day (afternoon). I regret that I could not call on you, because I did not know where you are.

I have composed a poem of farewell[1] in Chinese language. It is in style of ancient classic. I will write it on Chinese paper and send you. I think I can post it to-morrow. It will be addressed to the Alameda.

I will stay in Oakland till June 1st. On that day we are going to hold a meeting for the organization of Japanese Social Revolutionary Party[2] at the Oakland Socialist headquarters.

Yours for the revolution,

D. Kotoku.

Japan, Dec. 18th, 1906

---

1   [Havel's note] Kotoku's sojourn in America lasted only a few months. He organized the Japanese workingmen on the coast and returned to his native land to continue his propagandistic work. H. H.

2   The Social Revolutionary Party (*Shakai Kakumeitô*) was founded by Kōtoku and a group of some 50 or so Japanese immigrants in Oakland, California on June 1, 1906. During its brief existence (approximately one year) the group published a journal entitled *Revolution* (*Kakumei*).

Dear Old Friend and Comrade,

The winter has come, the leaves have fallen. It is, however, very fine weather. The sky is blue, the sunlight is warm. So I am very happy at my village home.

My wife went to the law-court to attend as a hearer to the trial of Comrade Osugi[3] this morning. Comrade Osugi is a young Anarchist student and a best friend of mine. When I was in San Francisco he wrote to you in French language and Mrs. Ladd translated it for you. Do you remember it? Well, Mr. Osugi is now under the trial on the charge of "violence of the press law." He translated an article titled "To the Conscripts" from a French Anarchist paper and published it in *Hikari*, Japanese Socialist paper.[4] This anti-militaristic deed was prosecuted by the public officials. I am now anxious to hear the result of that trial. I think it will be probable the sentence of several months' imprisonment and the confiscation of printing machine. How good law and government are!

The most comical fact of the results of the late war is the conciliation (or rather embrace) of Christianity with Buddhism and Shintoism. The history of Christianity in Japan was until now a history of horrible persecutions. The Japanese diplomatists, however, earnestly desiring to silence the rumors caused and spread in Europe during the war that "Japan is a yellow peril" or "Japan is a pagan country," suddenly began to put on the mask of Western civilization, and eagerly welcome and protect, and use it as a means of introducing Japan to European and American

---

3   Sakae Ōsugi (1885–1923) was a Japanese anarchist. Ōsugi was exposed to radical ideas through Kōtoku's paper, *Yoruzo Chozo*.

4   *Hikari* ("Light")—Japanese socialist newspaper published from 1905 to 1906. The article in question was originally written by Gustave Hervé circa 1900. Portions of it were evidently reproduced as a poster which was circulated widely in 1905, including in the French anarchist newspaper *L'Anarchie*. Ōsugi's translation was published in the November 26, 1906 issue of *Hikari*.

powers as a civilized Christendom. On the other hand, Christian priests, taking advantage of the weakness of the government, got a great monetary aid from the State, and under its protection they are propagating in full vigor the Gospel of Patriotism. Thus Japanese Christianity, which was before the war the religion of poor, literally now changed within only two years to a great bourgeois religion and a machine of the State and militarism!

The preparation for the Socialist daily is almost completed. I hope the daily will have a success. The Japanese Socialist Party consists, as you know, of many different elements. Social-Democrats, Social Revolutionists, and even Christian Socialists. So the daily would be a very strange paper.

Most of our comrades are inclined to take the tactics of Parliamentalism rather than Syndicalism or Anarchism. But it is not because they are assuredly convinced which is true, but because of their ignorance of Anarchist Communism. Therefore our most important work at present is the translation and publication of Anarchist and Free-thought literature. I will do my best, and use our paper as an organ for the libertarian propaganda.

In China the rebellions and insurrections are spreading.[5] The social and political conditions of China are just same to that of Russia in last century. I think China will be within the coming ten years a land of great rebellion and terrorism. A group of Chinese students in Tokyo is becoming the center of Chinese Revolutionary movement.

Yours very truly,
D. Kotoku

Yugawara, Sagami, May 3rd, 1907
Dear Comrade and Friend,

Please forgive me for not writing to you for a long time. During last few months I was very busy, owing to

---

5   Kōtoku is presumably referring to the Hunan uprising, a series of anti-government activities which took place in December 1906.

the persecutions of the Government. Now that our daily has been suppressed and our many comrades have gone to the prison, I have no work, no business, so I got leisure to write. I am now alone, at an inn in Yugawara, a famous watering place, one day's ride from Tokyo. I came here to improve my health and am now translating a pamphlet, Arnold Roller's "Social General Strike."[6] My book, in which are collected my essays on Anti-militarism, Communism, and other Radicalism, has been prohibited and many copies seized by the Government, but the cunning publisher secretly sold 1,500 copies before the policemen came.[7]

Mrs. Yamanouchi is living with her mother and grandmother in a country villa near Tokyo. Her family is rich, but she is preparing to live an independent life. She says she does not like to live a parasite's life. I am now looking for her work. My wife and Magara Sakai[8] were very pleased with the fine cards from you. Magara is now with her father. She is four years old and a very amiable child.

Have you seen the Japanese students in Berkeley who are publishing a magazine which caused a sensation last January?[9] They are all clever and devoted libertarians.

---

6   Siegfried Nacht (1878–1956) was a German anarchist who wrote under the pen name "Arnold Roller." *The Social General Strike* (*Der Sociale Generalstreik*), published by the Chicago Debating Club in 1905, was circulated by Max Baginski (who also wrote the introduction) and other anarchists at the founding convention of the Industrial Workers of the World.

7   *Heimin Shugi* ("Democracy") was published by Ryobunkan (Tokyo, 1907).

8   Sakai Magara (1903–1983) was the daughter of Sakae Toshihiko. She eventually became an important socialist and feminist activist.

9   The magazine in question was none other than *Revolution* (*Kakumei*), the outlet of the short-lived Social Revolutionary Party mentioned above. It was published by Shigeki Oka (1878–1959), a former contributor to *Yorozu Choho* and a longtime friend of

I hope the future revolution in Japan will be caused by their hands. Please teach them, educate them, instruct them. Mr. Sakai is working on an "Encyclopedia of Social Problems" with a few young comrades.[10] Its accomplishment will take five or six months after this. It will have great effect for the education of our people. I am going to translate Kropotkin's works.

I am very anxious to hear of your eyes. Eyes are very important organs for all men. Take care of yourself. Remember me to your daughter and granddaughter. I ever remain,

Yours fraternally,

D. Kotoku

Kōtoku who helped facilitate the latter's visit to San Francisco. In January 1906, *Revolution* generated a furor when it published an article that appeared to call for the assassination of President Theodore Roosevelt. See "No Law to Publish Editor Oka," *San Francisco Call* (January 1, 1907), p. 3.

10   It is not clear that Sakai ever completed this work.

FRANCISCO FERRER (1911)[1]

"Distorted by partisan hate and favoritism, the image of his character fluctuated in history," Schiller writes of Wallenstein in the tragedy bearing that name.[2]

These words can be applied to all personalities who, standing in the forefront of the struggle of their epoch between the New and the Old, seal their faith and their convictions with their blood. Many waters pass into the ocean of time, often centuries elapse, ere the legends woven about the names of great men and women are destroyed.

The image of Francisco Ferrer y Guardia is also in danger of being distorted by partisan hatred and favoritism. Smoothly-lying clericalism, not content with the death of the great humanitarian, exerted every effort to blacken the name of its victim. But in vain. Immediately upon the dark deed of Montjuich, modern inquiry inserted its probe into the jesuitic legend and exposed it in all its details.

Two men of international fame—L. Simarro, Professor of Psychology at the University of Madrid, and the English

---

1   This article originally appeared in *Mother Earth* 6, no. 8 (October 1911). The publication date coincides with the second anniversary of Ferrer's execution.

2   Friedrich Schiller (1759–1805) was a German poet, historian, philosopher, and playwright. Havel is referring to Schiller's 1799 dramatic trilogy consisting of "Wallenstein's Camp," "The Piccolomini," and "Wallenstein's Death." The plays are loosely based on the decline of Albrecht von Wallenstein (1583–1684), a Bohemian general who commanded a large army during the Thirty Years' War. He was ultimately accused of treachery against the Holy Roman Empire and assassinated. See *Schiller's Wallenstein's Camp*, trans. M. Verkrüzen (Hamburg, 1899), p. 15.

author William Archer—working independently of each other, discover to us the origin, the development, and the culmination of the clerical conspiracy against Francisco Ferrer.[3] The book of Archer, *The Life, Trial, and Death of Francisco Ferrer*, is of vital significance for the American public. Is not the Catholic Church zealously at work to found a new dominion in the New World? It is, therefore, of great importance to call the attention of the people to the results of her activity in the Old World.

The Life of Ferrer is a masterpiece of scientific research—it testifies to rigid impartiality in every direction. Mr. Archer seeks original sources and supports every scene of the drama, every conclusion in the book, with documents clearly proving the innocence of Ferrer. As Zola demonstrated the innocence of Dreyfus, so have Professor Simarro and Mr. Archer unmasked to the contemporary world the crime perpetrated by the Catholic Church against Ferrer. The sower of darkness was caught in its own trap. It is his enemies, says Mr. Archer, that have enabled to display the true greatness of his character, and have thrust immortality upon him. First, the Madrid trial[4] secured him a certain measure of fame, but it was still restricted to people who took a special interest in rationalist and humanitarian education. Had he then been left in peace to pursue his publishing schemes, and even to re-open the *Escuela Moderna*, he might have gone to the grave twenty years hence, leaving behind him, among the Latin nations, a certain repute as an

---

3   Luis Simarro Lacabra (1851–1921) was a Spanish psychiatrist and William Archer (1856–1923) was a Scottish journalist and critic. Lacabra's book *El proceso Ferrer y la opinión europea* was published by Eduardo Arias (Madrid) in 1910. Archer's book was published by Moffett, Yard & Company (New York) in 1911.

4   On June 4, 1906, Ferrer was arrested for planning the attempted assassination of King Alfonso XIII, which took place on May 31. Although he was subsequently acquitted at trial, the *Escuela Moderna* was closed on June 15.

educator, but certainly nothing like world-wide fame. His whole life-work would have done less damage to Spanish Catholicism than the mere mention of his name does today. For by dragging him through a travesty of trial to a plainly unmerited doom, his enemies gave him an opportunity of showing to all the world his one supreme virtue—a high and unflinching courage. His dogmatic rationalism was a somewhat arid creed, but in his death he touched it with emotion. His executioners, from Sr. Maura downwards, conferred on him a patent of undying nobility.[5] The man who wrote his letters from prison, and who faced the great enigma—to his mind no enigma, but night and nothingness—with such serene, unfaltering resolution, is certainly not the least among the victims of obscurantism, the martyrs of free thought.

The enemies of Ferrer stand in the pillory. The question now arises whether another danger does not threaten his name—a danger from his friends, especially from the pure-and-simple freethinkers. As the clericals have attempted to proclaim Ferrer a vicious evil-doer, so have the bourgeois liberals painted him as simply a reformer, merely an educator. It is an open question which view is the worse—that of the clericals or of the freethinkers. Ferrer was indeed a great educator; but he was also much more. Education was to him but a means of liberating mankind from slavery, the path to ultimate Anarchy. A man who entrusted an old revolutionary like Anselmo Lorenzo with the work of a teacher in his schools, made use of Jean Grave's "Adventures of Nono," and who on the very eve of his death was engaged in translating Peter Kropotkin's "The Great French Revolution,"[6] must surely have been more than merely an educator. Ferrer

---

5   Antonio Maura y Montaner (1853–1925) was Prime Minister of Spain at the time of Ferrer's execution.

6   Jean Grave (1854–1939) was a French anarchist writer and journalist. *The Adventures of Nono* (*Les Aventures de Nono*) was published by Stock (Paris) in 1901.

was from first to last an ardent Revolutionist. He had come to think that Spain was not yet ripe for revolution; but the whole object of his work was to correct her unripeness by educating Revolutionists.

Ever since the revolution of 1868, writes William Heaford in his pamphlet "L'Ecole Moderne," sporadic efforts had been made by intelligent members of the Spanish working class to secure for their children something better than the miserable instruction given in the official schools.[7] The revolt against the distressing conditions above described began to make headway about 1885, and by the end of last century there were many "Republican schools" in various towns of Spain. What was new in the *Escuela Moderna* was, in the first place, the application of (more or less) modern and scientific methods of pedagogy; in the second place, the inculcation of definitely rationalistic, humanitarian, anti-military and anti-patriotic doctrine. Ferrer did not at all take the view that his mission was simply to supply his countrymen with something better than the deplorable education furnished by the State. He conceived his system to be an improvement, not only on Spanish education (which would have been a modest claim), but on education as commonly practiced in the world at large. He was conscious enough of the difficulty of getting his ideas carried out—of securing teachers, textbooks, and school material suited to his views. But that the views themselves were absolutely right, not for Spain alone, but for humanity, he had no doubt at all. He could not, as he said, "conceive life without propaganda"; and propaganda could not begin too early. Having attained absolute clearness on all things mundane, and convinced himself that things extra-mundane

---

7　The Revolution of 1868, known as the Glorious Revolution, led to the deposition of Queen Isabella II and, eventually, to the creation of the First Spanish Republic. William Heaford (1855–1937) was an English secularist and socialist; his pamphlet was published by Bibliothèque de Propagande (Brussels) in 1909.

either did not exist or did not matter, he felt that the first duty of the educator was to bring this gospel home to the infant mind, before any shades of the prison-house of supernaturalism had begun to gather round it. There is not the least doubt that his teaching was not merely anti-clerical but anti-religious. And even deeper than the rebellion against supernaturalism lay the rebellion against class domination and exploitation. State education was in Ferrer's eyes at least as noxious as church education.

What results Ferrer achieved by his instruction can be seen from the following extracts from essays of his pupils published in the *Boletines* of the *Escuela Moderna*:

KISSING THE PRIEST'S HAND.

There are many children with whom this is a habit though they know that priests are men like any one else, and that they preach what they do not believe. Moreover, they invite religious persons to drop coins into a box for the souls of the dead, and as there are no souls to receive them, it follows that the real object is that the priests may enjoy themselves at the expense of the ignorant.

EDUCATION.

Education may be very good or very bad, according to what is taught. It is good when rational things are taught, such as science. It is bad when metaphysical things are taught, such as religion.

LOS TOROS.

In the Roman times, human slaves fought with lions and tigers. On other occasions men fought with each other, and the brutalized public compelled the victor to kill the vanquished. Today we no longer do that, but we still have bullfights, in which men first enrage and then kill the poor animals. What sort of a public is it which enjoys this spectacle of torture and death!

THE GOVERNMENT AND THE SOLDIERS.

The Government commands and authorizes what is not just. For example: it forces into the army and sends to the war those who have not money to pay for their release. If the soldiers whom they command to kill men and burn villages remembered that they do not need to kill or burn any one or anything, then those who enjoy the benefits of war would have to do their own fighting.

INSTRUCTION.

Instruction is to the intelligence what food is to the body. It perfects the human race, elevates the spirit of man, purifies and embellishes it. By its means we must solve the social question which is agitating us, and establish the empire of justice, now so necessary in order that the human race may consider itself a true family, and men may reach the point of loving each other like real brothers.

THE PIOUS.

The pious say that we must not believe in science or practice its teachings. They say there is an all-powerful God; in that, case, if he can do everything, why does he suffer the rich to exploit the poor?

THE POLICE.

The police arrest unhappy people who have stolen a loaf for their family; they take them to prison, and thus make the misery greater.

THE TAVERN,

What a pity that there exist an infinity of taverns, instead of free schools! In the tavern men brutalize themselves, and squander the resources of their families. Women, too, suffer and degenerate, and children run about the streets neglected, badly fed and badly clothed; and when they come to be men, not knowing how to read or write, they go the same way as their parents.

PARASITES.

Certain vegetable and animal organisms, which live at the expense of others, and do nothing for themselves, are called parasites. There are parasites, too, in human society. The rich men and the priests live upon the workman until he is completely exhausted.

THE INQUISITION.

. . . But are these times really past, and only matters of history? We have still, not very far from this truth-teaching school (*verdadera Escuela*), a castle which is the centre of infection, with moats, subterranean passages, and dungeons. Even in the cultivated republic of the United States, a prisoner seated in a chair prepared for the purpose, and carbonized by electricity. In all countries there is some example of this Inquisition. It is time that this relic of barbarism should disappear. Catalonia is dishonored by the presence of that castle, whose history strikes horror to the traveler. It is necessary that we should destroy that phantasm, and on its site lay out a beautiful park; and surely the free people who enjoy it will sometimes think with of the martyrs who rest under its verdure.

The "castle" thus stigmatized was, of course, Montjuich. It waited patiently for five years and then it had its revenge.

Some Dutch schoolmasters expressed doubts as to the genuineness of the utterances of these young philosophers, who were thereupon asked to state their reflections upon this wholly gratuitous scepticism. A girl of 13 wrote—

"The thoughts which are printed in the *Boletine* are the work of our own intelligence; otherwise it would be a deception to publish them, and our teachers would be hypocrites."

A boy of twelve thus expressed himself—

"We can speak of the evils of society, such as religion, property, war, and government, not only because of the explanations of our teachers, but because we have arrived at an understanding of justice and truth. We adopt the ideas which we maintain because we know the truth, because we know what are the sources humanity, and because we want to lead an industrious and happy life, uniting ourselves with the whole human race in indissoluble bonds of fraternity, accompanied by liberty and equality."

Another girl of 13—

"We write down these thoughts because every day we receive lessons on some subjects connected with society, religion, property, government, etc., and we understand them, or if sometimes we don 't, they are repeated to us until we grasp them well."

Now listen to a boy of 10—

"Perhaps those professors think our brain is not yet sufficiently developed, and I say nothing to the contrary; but if a child is always given rational explanations, he will acquire as much intelligence as some grown-up persons—if not more."

A shrewd rap for the Dutch professors!

IMPRESSIONS FROM PARIS, PART 1 (1911)[1]

OUR FOREFATHERS DREAMT OF ROME. THEY HAD IRRE-sistible desire to see the Eternal City. The classical education which they had received in their youth gave them an impulse toward the great mother of cities on the Tiber.

A change in ideals took place toward the middle the last century. Paris became the dream of the new generation. It became the center of modern thought. The apostle of new ideas, the revolutionist as well as the artist and the scientist, found here a congenial atmosphere. The German Heine, the Englishman Thackeray, the Russian Turgenieff felt themselves at home.[2]

Why this longing toward Paris? Certainly it is not the life on the boulevards which attracts the social student, the scientist, or the artist. It is the atmosphere which cannot be easily described through the medium the pen, brush or chisel. "When I returned last time to America," said an American author to me only a few days ago, "I lived in the same way as I do here. Yet I missed something. It was the atmosphere of Paris."

One feels himself in the midst of full, pulsating life, a life which springs from the earth like the marvelous figures of Rodin. Paris is the city of new impressions, the melting-pot of new ideas. Art and Revolution, in the broader sense Art and Life, have here a closer connection than anywhere else.

---

1   This article—the first of a two-part series—originally appeared in *Mother Earth* 6, no. 9 (November 1911) and was evidently written in the aftermath of a trip Havel took to France in 1911.

2   In addition to the previously cited individuals, Havel is referring to William Makepeace Thackeray (1811–1863), an English novelist.

One must go not only to the *Salon d'Automne* or to the *Independants* but also to the gatherings of the Socialist and Anarchist groups in order to understand what an influence art has on revolution or vice versa.[3] Modern French art is an expression of revolt not only against old forms but also against degrading social conditions. The greater part of the now recognized artists had their early works reproduced in Anarchist, in revolutionary publications.

This connection between the artist and the revolutionary movement has a striking influence upon the workingman. A short time ago I attended a meeting of a group of former victims of Biribi.[4] The word Biribi has a terrible meaning in France. It is a synonym for all the crimes perpetrated by the Cossacks of the bourgeoisie on the unhappy soldiers who break the rules of military discipline, and are punished in a terrible manner.[5] Comrade Aubain, one of the victims of Biribi, describes in simple,

---

3   The *Salon d'Automne* ("Autumn Salon") is an annual art exhibition held in Paris since 1903. In its initial conception it was a reaction to the conservative Paris Salon and served as a means to showcase modernist art. The *Salon des Indépendants* was another series of large-scale exhibitions—also of modernist art—initiated by the Society of Independent Artists, an organization founded in Paris in 1884.

4   Havel is evidently referring to the *Groupe des Libérés des Bagnes Militaires* (Former Military Prisoners' Group), formed in May 1910 by Émile Aubin (b. 1886, known as "Marat"), an electrical worker and anarchist.

5   "Biribi" was a French game of chance, played for low stakes, which was outlawed in the early nineteenth century. As Havel intimates, the expression "to be sent to Biribi" referred to the disciplinary battalions in Algeria (the so-called, *Bataillons d'Infanterie Légère d'Afrique*, or Light Infantry Batallions of Africa) to which criminals and soldiers with disciplinary problems were sent as a punishment. The batallions were instituted in the 1830s and disbanded after the Second World War.

straightforward language his experiences in the military hell.[6] Yet his spirit was not broken. His voice was full of defiance and challenge to the leaders of the ruling class. Only a few days after the meeting he was sentenced to another term for anti-military propaganda expressed in a former meeting. The most interesting part of the meeting I attended was the participation of the *Chansonniers Révolutionnaires*, a special organization of comrades for "propaganda par le chanson."[7] My dream of a "Cabaret Artistique et Revolutionnaire" found an echo.[8] I saw what a factor artistic expression could be in the spreading of the Gospel of Anarchy. These comrades are all hardworking proletarians, yet notwithstanding the struggle for daily bread they show considerable talent. They inspire their hearers far more than a speaker can do. The audience takes part in some of the songs. As to the text of the "chansons"! They are the bitterest satire on contemporary events and conditions, on politicians and exploiters. One can feel the approach of the stormy petrel.

No wonder then that the bourgeoisie is alarmed at the revolutionary tendencies in modern art. The authorities try to suppress these tendencies through legal prosecution. Many artists are being prosecuted at present. Comrade Grandjouan received recently a sentence of eighteen months' imprisonment.[9] He prefers to live in exile rather

---

6   Émile Aubin.

7   Presumably Havel is referring to the Group of Socialist Poets and Singers (*Groupe des poètes et chansonniers socialistes*), later known as the Group of Revolutionary Poets and Singers (*Groupe des poètes chansonniers révolutionnaires*) and, ultimately the Red Muse (*La Muse Rouge*). The group was founded in 1901 by various anarchists and socialists and disbanded in 1939. Its purpose, as Havel suggests, was to promote "propaganda by song."

8   "An artistic and revolutionary cabaret."

9   Jules-Félix Grandjouan (1875–1968) was a French anarchist and artist whose drawings and paintings figured prominently in the

than eat the prison fare and has left for England. I had the luck to find him at his home just five minutes before he went to the depot to depart into exile. He was full of hope and enthusiasm. I am inclined to think that the government was glad to let him go. To send such an artist to prison would be a disagreeable task—even for such hardened politicians as are now at the helm. Still the cartoonists Auglay and Poulbot are now in the line for prosecution, notwithstanding the protest on the part of artists of world renown.[10] This protest gained a new impetus through the prosecution of the novelist Charles Henry Hirsch for "offense against morals" in one of his novels appearing now in *Le Journal*.[11] With great emphasis the signers of the protest state that while nothing is so far from the literary mind of France as to propagate pornography, yet it is just as far from it to tolerate puritanism. It is to be hoped that the spirit of France today is not the same as that which allowed the persecution of men like Flaubert, Gautier and Baudelaire a few decades ago.[12] There is no doubt that the Intellectuals will never acquiesce in any kind of persecution for ideas. Tolerance of ideas, no matter how revolutionary or how strange they may seem to the multitude or to the rulers, is the slogan of the artists of France.

This tolerance can be observed at present in connection with the *Salon d'Automne*. While the honest critic

---

revolutionary press of the early twentieth century. Baginski and Goldman met him in Paris in 1907 and he had drawn the cover art for the November 1907 issue of *Mother Earth*. In 1911, Grandjouan was sentenced to eighteen months in jail for antimilitarist cartoons published in *La Voix du Peuple*.

10   Havel is referring to the French illustrators August Auglay (1853–1925) and Francisque Poulbot (1879–1946).

11   Charles-Henry Hirsch (1870–1948) was a French poet, novelist, and playwright.

12   Théophile Gautier (1811–1872) was a French poet, novelist, and critic.

tries to understand the new tendencies in art, the bourgeois on the contrary revels in his own narrowminded
bigotry. The bourgeois mind exists not only among the
possessing classes—it can be found among the artists
themselves—even, indeed, among many revolutionists.
The inability to receive or to digest new ideas is typical of
the bourgeois mind. One has only to witness the stupid
attitude of the public in the room of "les Cubists" to see
an example of it. These people look with contemptuous
indifference or amusement at pictures which, to say the
least, are consistently worked out according to perfectly logical formulae—whatever the individual opinion of
their aesthetic value may be. As to the reactionists, they
simply demand the suppression of the new art, and they
accuse the good bourgeois minister Desjardin-Beaumetz
of giving a helping hand to "Revolution" and "Anarchy"
in art.[13] It is, after all, but a repetition of an old story.
As in former years Manet, Pissaro, Monet, Sisley, Renoir
and Cezanne were the *bêtes noirs* of the classicists so today
Matisse and Picasso, not to speak of "Les Cubists," are the
laughing stock of the conservative public. But as Manet
found an interpreter in Emile Zola, so will the modern
artist find his literary interpreter in our day. Still there is
some ground for the apprehension of the reactionist. In
the preface of the catalogue of the *Salon* they find incendiary thoughts: they are told that the modern artist does
not express life as they wish to see it, but as he himself sees
it; that art is the expression of life, and that art knows no
bounds; it is international. Instinctively they call it the
"Revolutionary Art."

To be sure, dignified the revolutionary paintings seldom are, at least to eyes accustomed to the old style. The
new art is startling, but it impresses one. How dull in
comparison is the old Salon with its miles of canvasses,

13 Étienne Dujardin-Beaumetz (1852–1913) was a French painter
who served as Minister of Fine Arts from 1905 to 1910.

correctly, or at least conventionally, drawn and composed, but utterly lacking in feeling. The modern painters have a message to the world and their art is a mighty protest against the tenets of the old dry school.

The well-known publishers Schleicher Freres are placing Élisée Reclus' "Correspondance" on the book market.[14] These letters are a valuable contribution to contemporary thought and to revolutionary literature. The critics pay high tribute to the dead anarchist thinker and scientist. Élisée Reclus and Elie Reclus were the sons of a liberty-living protestant priest who had a small parish at Sainte-Fay in the valley of Dordogne.[15] Educated in the colony of the Moravian brothers at Neuwied in Germany, there they imbibed humanitarian and cosmopolitan ideas, and took part in the Revolution of 1848. After the *coup d'etat* of Napoleon III they were sent into exile. Élisée Reclus was a great traveler. He traversed North and South America, Europe and Africa. For the great publishing house of the Hachettes he wrote his profound "Geographie Universelle" and "La Terre."[16] Sentenced to death for participation in the Commune, he was pardoned because of a protest from the scientific world. Of his anarchist writings only two small pamphlets have been as yet translated into English. The "Correspondance" ought easily to find a publisher in the United States.

The *Confederation Generale du Travail* inaugurated a great protest action against the abominable "Lois Scelerats," made by the frightened bourgeoisie after the

---

14 The first volume of Reclus's *Correspondance*, which covers the years 1855 to 1870 was published by Librairie Schleicher Frères in 1911. Volumes 2 (1870–1888) and 3 (1890–1905) were published in 1914 and 1915, respectively.

15 Reclus' brother Élie (1827–1904) was a journalist, ethnologist, and—like Élisée—an anarchist.

16 *Geographie Universelle* was published in 19 volumes between 1876 and 1894. *La Terre* was published in 1868.

attentats of Ravachol, Henry, Vaillant and Caserio in 1893 and 1894.[17] These dastardly laws are now being used for the suppression of syndicalist and anti-military propaganda. The *Ligue des Droits de l'Homme* founded in the stormy period of the Dreyfus agitation, directed a mighty protest against the new application of these laws.[18]

The attitude of the intellectuals could again be seen in the meeting held at the *Hotel de Société des Savants* protesting against the act of brigandage on the part of Italy in appropriating Tripoli.[19] Anatole France, Francis de Pressensé, Pierre Quillard, Gabriel Seailles and others took part in the protest.[20] I was forcibly struck by the presence on the platform of the Turkish State Secretary Haladjian Effendi.[21] I wonder whether, when he saw the

---

17 The *Confédération générale du travail* (General Federation of Labor, or CGT), was a French trade union federation founded in 1895. The CGT was an anarcho-syndicalist federation from 1895 until the outbreak of the First World War. The term *lois scélérates* ("villainous laws") refers to a series of French laws which severely restricted free speech. As Havel correctly notes, they were passed in the aftermath of various bombings and assassination attempts, most notably Vaillant's bombing attack on the French Chamber of Deputies on December 9, 1893. In 1911, the French government began to invoke the laws as a pretense for repressing the labor movement and was met with an outpouring of protest.

18 The *Ligue des Droits de l'Homme* (Human Rights League) was founded in 1898 by Ludovic Trarieux (1840–1904), a French Republic statesman, to defend Alfred Dreyfus.

19 The *Hôtel des sociétés savantes* ("the hotel of learned societies") is a kind of convention center founded in 1864 to host meetings of scholarly and scientific societies. Italy attempted to forcibly wrest Tripoli from the Ottoman Empire in October 1911.

20 Havel is referring, respectively, to Francis de Pressensé (1853–1914), a politician and journalist; Pierre Quillard (1864–1912), a symbolist poet and anarchist; and Gabriel Séailles, a philosopher.

21 Halajian Effendi was the Ottoman Minister of Public Works.

protest of the French workingmen, he thought of the oppression by his order of the striking Turkish workingmen.
A voice from the gallery, which called the attention of the
audience to the solidarity of the exploiters in all countries,
must have reminded him of his crime as a member of the
possessing class.

The influence of the literary world also played an important part in the trial of the editors of *La Guerre Sociale*,
who unmasked the spy Metivier and two of his colleagues.[22]
The trial was a *cause célèbre* and ended with the defeat of the
prosecuting government. The former premiers Clemenceau
and Briand, who hired these detestable creatures and used
them as *agents provocateurs* in order to discredit the syndicalist movement, stood in the public pillory.[23] The speech
of Miguel Almereyda, the chief defendant, was magnificent.[24] Even the capitalist press had to recognize the grandeur of the orator and the force of his arguments.

The prosecution tried to prove that the defendants
in unmasking the spies acted in the capacity of public

---

22 Havel is referring to Lucien Métivier (born 1884, death unknown)
    who was personally hired in May 1908 by Georges Clemenceau
    (1841–1929, French Radical Prime Minister from 1906 to
    1909 and 1917 to 1920) to serve as an *agent provocateur* within
    the French labor movement—a fact which Clemenceau himself
    admitted in November 1911. Métivier was exposed by various
    editors of *La Guerre Sociale* who had convened a "revolutionary
    court." They published his confession in June 1911 and, as Havel
    notes, were subsequently charged with "sequestration" and "breach
    of privacy." Their trial took place on October 10, 1911. For more
    information, see "Impressions from Paris, Part 2" below.

23 Aristide Briand (1862–1932) was French Republican-Socialist
    Prime Minister from 1909–1911; 21 January 1913–22 March
    1913; 1915–1917; 1921–1922; 1925–1926; and July 29, 1929
    until November 2, 1929.

24 Eugène Vigo (1883–1917), known as Miguel Almereyda, was a
    French socialist journalist.

judges, assumed official authority, broke the right of domicile and restricted the personal liberty of the spies. The jury acquitted the defendants of the charges. Deafening applause followed. All shades of political opinion were represented on the witness stand—Royalist and Bonapartist, Republican, Socialist and Anarchist, all declared in emphatic terms their contempt for the *mouchards* and their employers.[25] It was a memorable sight: Maurice Pujo, leader of the *Camelots du Roi*, Henri Rochefort, de Pressensé, Griffuelhés, former Secretary of denouncing the Napoleonic methods of Clemenceau and Briand.[26] The system of agents provocateurs, the *Confederation du Travail*, Pouget, de la Chapelle of the *Journal des Debuts* and many others received a terrific chastisement.[27]

Gustave Hervé, who is serving a term of five years in the prison of Clairvaux for his anti-militaristic and revolutionary propaganda, has received two additional years for an article in *La Guerre Sociale*.[28] He edits the paper from the prison under the nom-de-plume of "Un Sans

---

25 *Mouchard* (literally, "fly") refers to an undercover police informant or spy.

26 Maurice Pujo (1872–1955) was a French journalist who co-founded the monarchist group *Comité d'Action Française* in 1898. *Camelots du roi*—literally, "pages of the king"—was the youth organization affiliated with *Action Française*. Henri Rochefort (1831–1913) was a French politician and journalist. Victor Griffuelhes (1874–1922) was a revolutionary anarcho-syndicalist who served as Secretary General of the CGT from 1903 to 1909.

27 Havel is presumably referring to *Le Journal des Débats*, a French newspaper published from 1789 to 1944. It is not clear who "de la Chapelle" is.

28 Havel is presumably referring to Hervé's conviction in December 1905 for the publication and dissemination of an anti-militarist poster allegedly based on an article he had written in 1900. He was sentenced again in June 1911.

Patrie."[29] Hervé inspires great admiration among the revolutionary youth and has many enthusiastic followers. Although daily accused and attacked by the Guesdeist wing of the Socialist Party for his leanings toward Anarchy and his collaboration with the Syndicalists and Anarchists, his strength in the party seems to grow from day to day.[30] On the other hand, some Anarchists accuse Hervé of Blanquistic tendencies.[31] Undoubtedly there is great danger in the methods practised and propagated by Hervé and his school. The cloven hoof of the proletarian dictatur is visible. But notwithstanding all theoretical differences this must be recognized: Hervé has awakened an immense enthusiasm among the younger generation; he has inspired the movement with a new spirit, the spirit of active rebellion. The young generation is tired of dogmas and theories. What it wants is active participation, vital ideas and a life full of vibration.

---

29 Literally, "one without a country."

30 The Guesdeists—followers of Jules Guesde—were essentially orthodox Marxists.

31 By "Blanquistic tendencies," Havel is presumably referring to vanguardist tactics.

IMPRESSIONS FROM PARIS, PART 2 (1911)[1]

THERE MAY BE HONOR EVEN AMONG THIEVES, BUT THERE is certainly neither honor nor honesty among politicians. So long as it suits his purpose the politician may use direct and honorable means to achieve his ends, but the very moment he encounters an obstacle honest methods are forgotten, and brutality and sycophancy become his weapons. The new campaign against the *Confederation General du Travail* shows that the henchmen of the possessing class will stoop to anything to crush the militant organization of the producing class.[2] At the same time one may observe the deep-rooted antagonism between the French workingmen and the parasitical politicians. The latest savior of the French bourgeoisie is the present Premier Caillaux.[3] The spirit of the vindictive Versaillesians is strongly alive in this son of a traitor. It was his father who thirty years ago tried a *coup d'etat* in favor of the reigning oligarchy.[4] He

---

1   This article originally appeared in *Mother Earth* 6, no. 10 (December 1911).

2   Havel explains the nature of this campaign below.

3   Joseph-Marie-Auguste Caillaux (1863–1944) was French premier from 1911 to 1912. Caillaux was a member of the liberal-centrist Radical Party.

4   Eugene Caillaux (1822–1896), the father of Joseph-Marie-Auguste Caillaux, was a monarchist politician. In 1873, he and other Royalists attempted to restore the Bourbon monarchy under Henri Comte de Chambord (1820–1883) but the plan failed when the Comte refused to cooperate. The coup was led by led by Marie Edme Patrice Maurice de MacMahon, 1st Duke of Magenta (1808–1893)—a French general and Marshal of France

did not succeed. The Royalists and their tool, MacMahon, lost their position, probably through cowardice, and had to abandon their project.[5] But in one direction they succeeded all too well: they accumulated an immense fortune, which is now used by their sons to crush the working class. Caillaux *fils* is moreover the president of several large banks, and as such has outside of his private fortune a yearly income of 750,000 francs. No wonder then that he fears for his fatherland!

In a great speech, delivered before the opening of the Chambers at Saint-Calais, he proclaimed his intention of annihilating the Anarchistic tendencies among the French people. He not only proposes to use all the oppressive laws passed in former years by the political bandits of the Third Republic, but he threatens to introduce far more draconic laws should the former prove insufficient. Aye, he proves to be even a better servant than the Socialist traitors Viviani, Briand, and Millerand.[6] Clemenceau and Briand employed spies in the ranks of the militant workers; Caillaux, being a disciple of Machiavelli, has formed a plan which undoubtedly would have found a sympathetic echo in the heart

---

who served as chief of state of France and later President of the Third Republic (1875–1879).

5   Havel's claim is slightly inaccurate. MacMahon became President within two years of the abortive *coup* and, on May 16, 1877, proceeded to dismiss his own Prime Minister, the republican Jules Simon, and replace him with the monarchist Duke of Broglie (1821–1901). When parliament objected, he responded by dissolving the government. Ultimately MacMahon was ousted and the Royalist movement fell apart.

6   In addition to Briand and Millerand (previously cited), Havel is referring to René Viviani (1863–1925), French Republican-Socialist Prime Minister from 1914–1915. Havel deems these men "traitors" for compromising their socialist principles and selling out in various ways to bourgeois interests (for example, by deploying spies to infiltrate the radical labor movement).

of the great Florentine. The case of the labor leader Louis Métivier, recently exposed as a spy, gives him sufficient ground for his attack.[7] In an interview with the Socialist deputy Lauche he insinuated that Metivier is by no means the only traitor in the ranks of the *Confederation* and announced that he intends to expose the other spies one by one.[8] His object is clear: he is trying to spread distrust and general demoralization among the organized workers.

The first man to be denounced by Caillaux as a spy in the employ of the police is Edouard Ricardeau, a labor leader who has taken part in many strikes and in the bloody collisions with the police at Vigneux and Villeneuve-Saint-Georges.[9] The accused Ricardeau emphatically denies the charge and asks for proofs, which Caillaux refuses to produce.[10] If we remember what a havoc the exposure of Azeff caused among the Revolutionists of Russia, we cannot wonder at the present intense excitement among the French Syndicalists.[11]

7   See "Impressions from Paris, Part 1" above.

8   The interview in question appears in "Le Cas Ricordeau," *L'Humanité*, November 23, 1911. Jacques Lauche (1872–1920) was a French socialist politician.

9   Ricordeau (born 1877, death unknown) was the secretary of a roadworkers' union and an avowed radical with anarchistic tendencies. In June 1908 strikes in the Parisian suburbs of Draveil-Vigneux and Villeneuve-Saint-George were brutally repressed by the Clemenceau government. The strikes—which the government helped to instigate, at least in part, through the use of *agents provocateurs*—provided an excuse to arrest the radical leadership of the CGT. This move facilitated the takeover of the union by moderates and reformists following its October 1908 congress in Marseilles.

10   Ricordeau was tried in the Chamber of Deputies in November 1911. Although initially convicted and sentenced to banishment, he was subsequently exonerated.

11   Yevno Azef (1869–1918) was a Russian double agent who worked for the Socialist-Revolutionary Party as well as the Tsarist secret police.

Explanations and recriminations follow each other in the columns of *La Guerre Sociale*, the organ of Gustave Hervé, and *La Bataille Syndicaliste*, the daily of the *Confederation du Travail*.[12] L. Jouhaux, the president, and V. Griffulhes, the former secretary of the *Confederation*, warn the comrades against the dastardly tactics of Caillaux, and advise them to keep their heads cool in the present crisis.[13]

As usual, the Socialist politicians try to make capital for themselves out of this affair. Both wings of the Socialist party implore the Syndicalists to give up their anti-parliamentary policy and to combine with the Socialists against the "common enemy." But the comrades of the *Confederation* have no intention of following the songs of the Socialist sirens. During the last forty years politicians have used the workingmen as a stepping stone to a higher position, and their end attained, have invariably betrayed the cause of the proletariat. Of this principle Clemenceau himself is a classic example. Socialist politicians proved to be even worse than the brilliant man of letters. Millerand, Viviani, Turot, Gerault-Richard and Briand, traitors to the working-class as well as to the Socialist movement, were all intimate personal friends of Jaurés, the present leader of the party.[14]

---

12 *La Guerre Sociale* ("The Social War") was a weekly journal created by the Hervéists intended to unite the extreme French left. *La Bataille Syndicaliste* ("The Syndicalist Battle") was the daily journal of the *Confederation du Travail*.

13 Léon Jouhaux (1879–1954) was a French trade unionist and 1951 winner of the Nobel Peace Prize. Jouhaux was made Secretary General of the CGT in 1909 following the arrest and ouster of the previous secretary, Victor Griffuelhes (1874–1922)—a revolutionary anarcho-syndicalist who first took up the position in 1903. Jouhaux served in this capacity until 1947. Initially a revolutionary, Jouhaux eventually followed many radicals of his generation in becoming a moderate and a reformist.

14 In addition to the individuals previously cited, Havel is referring

One of the reproaches against the Anarchists and Syndicalists is that they do not pay enough attention to the struggle against clericalism. It is a favorite trick of the radical politicians to divert the attention of the working-man from his own misery and direct it toward an imaginary enemy—a dead lion. So long as there was necessity for a fight against the clerical-nationalistic enemy, the militant proletarian formed the vanguard in the struggle, but today he is tired of the cry "*A bas la calotte!*"[15] The church in France is dead and has absolutely no influence upon the life of the people. With the exception of the aristocracy and the small bourgeoisie, the churches are visited only by tourists. Like museums and ruins they are the haunts of sightseers. Writers and artists like Huysmans, Coppee, Bourget and Forain, disgusted with life and conditions, may return to the bosom of the mother church; Leon Daudet may produce his daily lampoons in the *Action Francaise*, but their efforts are appreciated only in the small artistocratic and royalist circles.[16] The propaganda of a Marc Sangnier, subsidized by the reactionists, and the noisy demonstrations of the *Camelots du Roi* play a certain role in the phantasy of foreign correspondents, but are not noticeable in the public life of France.[17]

---

to Henri Turot (1865–1920) and Alfred Léon Gérault-Richard (1860–1911), both of whom were socialist politicians and journalists.

15   "Down with the skullcap!"

16   Havel is referring, respectively, to J.K. Husymans (previously cited); François Coppée (1842–1908), a French poet and novelist; Paul Bourget (1852–1935), a French novelist and critic; and Jean-Louis Forain (1852–1931). Each of these men converted (or re-converted) to Roman Catholicism. Léon Daudet (1867–1942) was a French writer and journalist who edited *Action Française*, a monarchist and nationalist periodical founded in 1898 which served as the mouthpiece of the eponymous *Action Française* movement.

17   Marc Sangnier (1873–1950) was a French liberal Catholic

On the other hand, many of the anti-clerical politicians have proved to be gentlemen of shady character. Victor Flachon, director of *La Lanterne*, friend of Ex-Premier Combes and a most fiery opponent of the *Calotte*, is at present involved in a great scandal.[18] In company with other pillars of society he satisfied his sexual passions by ruining children of tender age and of both sexes in resorts on Montmartre and at his villa on the Cote d'Azur.[19] Briand is mentioned as being one of the visitors at the villa while the orgies were going on. The late King Edward has many disciples among the upstarts of France.[20] The present scandal will probably have grave political consequences.

Another reproach against the Syndicalists expressed recently by the literary quack Nordau is that they are men and women without idealism and lacking in respect for art, culture, and civilization.[21] Only a bombastic ignoramus like the author of *Degeneration* could make such a statement.[22] True, the Syndicalists have no respect for the

---

thinker, writer, and politician.

18 *La Lanterne* was a French anti-clerical periodical founded in 1877. Victor Flachon (1884–1934) was its editor from 1902 to 1911. Émile Combes (1835–1921) was French Radical Prime Minister from 1902 to 1905. *La Calotte* was an anti-clerical magazine published from 1906 to 1911; it was *La Lanterne*'s principal rival.

19 Montmarte and the Cote d'Azur (i.e., the French Riviera) are renowned as affluent areas. The former is a hill on the north side of Paris, now in the 18th arrondissement on the right bank of the Seine.

20 Edward VII (1841–1910) of the United Kingdom was involved in several sex-related scandals throughout his reign.

21 Max Nordau (1848–1923) was a Hungarian-Jewish writer and social critic. With Theodore Herzl, Nordau played a major role in the development of the Zionist movement. Nordau's book *Degeneration* was extremely controversial, especially within the burgeoning modern art milieu.

22 *Degeneration* (*"Entartung,"* Berlin: C. Duncker, 1892) accuses

culture of a class which condemns them to perpetual slavery, but they dream of a culture too high to be appreciated by the Nordaus of our time. To be sure, a Nordau is neglected in the columns of the Syndicalist publications, but a classic like Balzac, or an exquisite portrayer of human nature such as Charles-Louis Phillippe, Octave Mirbeau or Anatole France, find full appreciation.[23] Not the Syndicalist *Bataille*, but the journals to which Monsieur Nordau is a contributor have recently dragged Madame Curie's[24] private life through the gutter. True again, the Syndicalists preach and practice sabotage against their exploiters, but on the other hand they advertise in their publications the best obtainable text books on every trade and urge their comrades to perfect themselves in their line of work in order to achieve the most excellent type of artisanship.

The report upon the status of the population of France for the first half of the year 1911, published this month in *Le Journal Officiel*, gives the patriots an opportunity to raise a cry for the suppression of the Neo-Malthusian propaganda.[25] The good bourgeoisie

---

modern art of being immoral, perverse, and "degenerate." It was extremely controversial at the time of its publication, especially within the burgeoning modern art milieu.

23 Charles-Louis Philippe (1874–1909) was a French novelist.

24 Marie Skłodowska Curie (1867–1934) was a French-Polish physicist and chemist renowned for her groundbreaking research on radioactivity. In 1910, when Curie was a candidate for admittance to the French Academy of Sciences, she was repeatedly made the subject of humiliating exposés in the press, many of them centering on her relationship with the physicist Paul Langevin (1872–1946) following the death of her husband.

25 *La Journal Officiel*—i.e., *La Journal Officiel de La République Française*—is the official gazette of the French government. "Neo-Malthusian" refers to advocacy of population control programs in the vein of Thomas Malthus (1766–1834), an English scholar and

practice themselves the two-child system to perfection, but are horrified to see the working people follow their example. The French women refuse to furnish slaves and cannon-fodder for the capitalistic system. A healthy instinct tells the proletarian woman that it is a crime against herself and against her class to bring sickly children into the world. Not prevention but conception leaves her only too often in an unhealthy and dangerous condition. What the Neo-Malthusian propaganda tries to do is, first, to educate the woman along scientific lines and, second, to give her proper means for prevention. Needless to say, the man needs education on the subject just as much as the woman. The monthly *Generation Consciente*, published by our friends Humbert and Grandidier, does useful propaganda along these lines.[26] All means of prevention may be had at the offices of the paper, to which A. Naquet, Sebastian Faure, Jean Marestan, Paul Robin, Mme. Nelly Roussel,[27] V. Grandjouan and many other well-known Libertarians are contributors.[28] Means

cleric whose *Essay on the Principle of Population* (1798) warned against the dangers of overpopulation.

26 *Génération Consciente* was a French pro-contraception journal, founded in 1908 by Eugène Humbert (1870–1944), a French anarchist, pacifist, and birth control advocate. Louis Auguste Grandidier (1873–1931) was a French anarchist and revolutionary syndicalist.

27 Nelly Roussel (1878–1922) was a French anarchist, feminist, and birth-control advocate.

28 Havel is referring, respectively, to Alfred Naquet (1834–1916), a French-Jewish writer, politician, and chemist; Sébastien Faure (1858–1942), a French anarchist writer, journalist, and militant; and Jean Marestan (1874–1951), Paul Robin (1837–1912), and Nelly Roussel (1878–1922), French anarchists and birth control advocates. "V. Grandjouan" is presumably Jules-Félix Grandjouan, cited previously.

for the prevention of conception may also be had in any French drug-store and are to be seen in many show windows. O shades of holy Anthony![29]

However, the cry of the nationalists about the depopulation of France is a bugaboo. No signs of depopulation can be noticed so far; on the contrary, a slow but steady growth is statistically proven. At the worst, it could be said that the population remains stationary. To the same category of bugaboos belongs the theory of Germanophiles in regard to the decadence of the Latin races, especially of the French. No more ridiculous supposition could have been formed. The students of all countries still flock to the Sorbonne. In art France indisputably leads the nations. Bergson's philosophy occupies the minds of contemporary thinkers.[30] The center of the new musical movement is in Paris. Maeterlinck and France are our two most prominent living writers. French aeronauts have conquered the air. The French peasant is the most successful tiller of the soil. And finally, the French workingman leads the proletariat of the world in his revolutionary fire, his enthusiasm, and his ideal of a free society.

---

29 "Holy Anthony" is a reference to Anthony Comstock (1873–1915), the infamously puritanical U.S. Postal Inspector who helped ban birth control materials from the mail.

30 Henri-Louis Bergson (1859–1941) was a French philosopher. Although he has since passed into relative obscurity, he was a major philosophical figure at the time of Havel's writing. His writings on time and memory are especially notable.

THE FAITH AND RECORD OF ANARCHISTS (1912)[1]

THE GREAT SPREAD OF ANARCHIST IDEAS IN THE LAST DE-
cade seems to afford the capitalist press a good opportunity to emit a great deal of matter on the subject. This
in itself is a good sign: it proves that the idea of Anarchy
is taking root in the life of the people. The Anarchists
are accustomed to having their faith misrepresented; every scribbler can earn his weekly bread by penning an
article against the propagandists of the new gospel. The
Anarchists welcome the honest critic, and are glad indeed
to present their theories and practice to the impartial.
But they resent it strongly if a writer, under the mask of

---

1   This article appeared in *Mother Earth* 6, no. 12 (February 1912).
    As Richard Bach Jensen notes, "Alfred Vizetelly's popular and
    influential *The Anarchists*... attributes to the anarchists every
    assassination and many acts of popular violence that took place
    during the last quarter of the nineteenth century up until the eve
    of World War I, although the authors of these deeds were clear-
    ly revolutionaries and nationalists who did not share the anar-
    chists' desire to abolish hierarchical forms of centralized authority.
    Vizetelly continues to influence and confuse authors today, e.g.,
    Barton Ingraham, *Political Crime in Europe* (Berkeley: University
    of California Press, 1979), p. 180n, attributes the assassination
    of Alexander II of Russia (1881) and the assassination attempts
    against Kaiser Wilhelm I (1878), King Humbert of Italy (1878),
    and Alexander III (1887) to the anarchists, although the cul-
    prits were in fact revolutionary socialists or deranged persons"
    ("The United States, International Policing, and the War against
    Anarchist Terrorism, 1900–1914; *Terrorism and Political Violence*
    13, no. 1 (2001): pp. 15–46: 39–40n6).

impartiality, offers to the public a work on Anarchy which is tainted with dishonesty. Such a writer is far more dangerous than the ignorant penny-a-liner who fills up his columns with misinformation and false statements. To damn with faint praise is a favorite trick of some of our opponents.

To this class of opponents belongs Mr. Ernest Alfred Vizetelly, whose work "The Anarchists: Their Faith and their Record," has just been published.[2] Nobody will accuse Mr. Vizetelly of great modesty. In the preface to his book he remarks quite diffidently that there are numerous works on the subject of the theories or doctrines of the Anarchists, but that his volume is the first to supply a history of their doings from the days of Bakunin, who may be regarded as the founder of the sect, down to the present time. In connection with this important subject the author deems it necessary to prove to his readers in a footnote that he comes from old English stock and that his great-grandfather was a member of the Stationers Company and constable of the united parishes of St. Ann Blackfriars and St. Andrew by the Wardrobe.[3] This indeed predestines him to be a competent historian of the Anarchist movement. The truth is that Mr. Vizetelly is a worn-out British war-reporter, who in former years also dabbled in literature, but who has great difficulty nowadays to find a publisher for his sensational stuff. For many years he succeeded in living on Zola's fame. His heyday was when Zola, forced to leave France on account of the Dreyfus affair, spent a year in exile in England. An article in which he described graphically

---

2   [Havel's note] John Land Co., New York.

3   The Worshipful Company of Stationers and Newspaper Makers was one of the Livery Companies of the City of London, founded in 1403. St. Ann Blackfriars was a parish in the City of London in the ward of Farringdon Within. It was destroyed in the Great London of Fire of 1666 and united with the parish of St. Andrew-by-the-Wardrobe.

how Zola went to the London shops to buy some socks was reprinted innumerable times by the Philistine press of Europe and America. What a sensation! The great romancier had to leave France without a pair of extra socks! The great war-reporter Vizetelly would never have committed such an act of imprudence. His socks are undoubtedly always carefully packed away in his Gladstone.

The Houndsditch affair, called the battle of Sydney Street in the military annals of Great Britain, in which another famous war-reporter, Mr. Winston Churchill, made an ass of himself by calling out the military force of London against two desperados, gave Mr. Vizetelly a golden opportunity to perpetrate his book on Anarchists, their faith and their record.[4] To call his pasquil a history of Anarchist doings is quite as just as to call the rhymes of the present poet-laureate poems.[5] The book is nothing more than a compilation made from old newspaper files. The interpretation of Anarchist deeds by the author is full of bias and dictated by his prejudices as a law-abiding Philistine, and as to his conclusions, they read like the prognostication from some old almanac. Whatever value the book may possess is taken from the sensational work "Le Peril Anarchiste," by Felix Dubois, published at Paris in 1894.[6] The theoretical

---

4   In December 1910, anarchists killed three police officers who had interrupted them during an attempted burglary at 119 Houndsditch in London. The following month two of the anarchists were cornered in Sidney Street. Winston Churchill (1851–1955), who was Home Secretary at the time, gave permission to dispatch soldiers to the scene and, after a protracted gun battle, the anarchists were killed. Churchill was subsequently criticized at great length for meddling in police affairs and giving orders at the scene.

5   Presumably Havel is referring to Alfred Austin (1835–1913), who was Poet Laureate of England from 1896 to his death.

6   Félix Dubois (1862–1945) was a French journalist and explorer. *Le Péril Anarchiste* was published by E. Flammarion (Paris) in 1894. The first English translation was published by T.F. Unwin

information is taken from Paul Eltzbacher's valuable work "Anarchism."[7] The present book cannot compare with the work on Anarchy by Professor Zoccoli, of which Mr. Vizetelly seems to be quite ignorant.[8] As to the real history of Anarchists, their faith and their deeds, nothing can be compared with the excellent and sympathetic account by Alvan F. Sanborn in his "Paris and the Social Revolution," published in 1905 at Boston and inscribed to the Proletariat of America.[9] In this work the Anarchist propagandist has found an adequate interpretation.

Vizetelly stands stupid and blind before the heroism and sacrifice of the Anarchist propagandist. He heaps abuse on the heads of all the men and women who sacrificed themselves for their ideal. Ravachol is for him a monster; Henry a coldblooded coward; Caserio narrow-minded and imperfectly educated; Emile Pouget an "ex-counter-jumper" (a nice remark for a historian!);[10] Louise Michel is "a female notoriety, an ex-schoolmistress called *La Vierge Rouge*. She had been mixed up in the Commune of 1871 and was transported to New Caledonia. It is quite certain, however, that her case was one for treatment in a hospital or asylum. Subject to hysteria, she had lost her mental balance."[11]

(London) in 1894.

7   Paul Eltzbacher (1868–1925) was a German law professor. *Der Anarchismus* was published by Topos Verlag (Berlin) in 1900. The first English translation, by Stephan Byington, was published by Benjamin Tucker (New York) in 1908.

8   Ettore Zoccoli (1872–1958), Italian scholar and philosopher. *L'Anarchia* was published by Fratelli Bocca (Turin) in 1907.

9   Alvan Sanborn (1866–1966) was an American journalist and author. *Paris and the Social Revolution* was published by Small, Maynard & Company (Boston) in 1905. Extracts were published in *Mother Earth* in 1906.

10   Émile Pouget (1860–1931), French anarcho-syndicalist.

11   François Claudius Koenigstein (1859–1892) was a French

This description of Louise Michel thoroughly characterizes Mr. Vizetelly. No comment is necessary. On
the other hand, his tender heart nearly breaks with pity
when he writes of the bitter loss of the good rulers, who
suffer for their subjects and who are ever in danger from
the dastardly Anarchists. One of his beloved monarchs,
King Umberto of Italy, thought otherwise. At the time
of the attempt on his life in 1897 by Pietro Accierito he
remarked to his minister Ponzio Vaglia: *Sono gli incerti del
mestiere*! (Those are the risks of the calling!)[12] His calling
was terminated a few years later by the revolver shots of
Gaetano Bresci. Vizetelly repeats the old story, disproved
long ago, of Bresci having been well-provided with money
and clothes by his confederates in Paterson.

What are the sources of the author's historic information? In the account of the assassination of President Sadi
Carnot by Caserio in Lyons he narrates that several of his
wife's relatives were at that time residing: at Lyons. In preparing his story of the assassination he "has utilized some
notes sent to him by one of his brothers-in-law." Such are
the facts of the historian Vizetelly! As to the character of
Caserio, we possess a tender little study by Ada Negri, the
greatest living Italian poetess, whose school the idealistic
youth attended. But what does a Vizetelly care for the
opinion of a poetess?

True, he repudiates in his book some misconceptions about the Anarchists and their supposed secret

---

anarchist known as Ravachol. Like Henry and Caserio (previously
cited) he was tried and executed for a series of politically-motivated assassination attempts. Émile Pouget (1860–1931) was a
French anarcho-syndicalist. Viztelly mentions him, along with
Michel and the others, in a calculated attempt to smear and discredit notable anarchists.

12 Pietro Acciarito (1871–1943) was an Italian anarchist. Acciarito
made an unsuccessful attempt on the life of King Umberto I of
Italy in 1897.

organizations. But he himself is guilty of many misstatements and false conceptions. Referring to the *Mano Negro* affair in Andalusia he remarks naively: "We ourselves perpetuated a romance of the Black Hand several years ago—'The Scorpion,' We introduced into it some of the characters of the Jerez affair of 1882–1883, blending with episodes of that period others which occurred during the Federalist troubles of 1873 and the Anarchist rising of 1892, as well as others existent only in our imagination."[13]

Imagination and secrecy play a great part in Mr. Vizetelly's writings. He gave us a "true" story of the Chevalier d'Eon[14]—"with the aid of state and secret papers." No doubt he knows the worthlessness of secrecy. Yet his imagination leads him again to state and to repeat that Leon Czolgosz was influenced by Emma Goldman.[15] His imagination leads him also state that "There is some reason to think that Prince Kropotkin does not hold quite the same opinions on some matters (violence and social revolution) as he used to do." Yet he forgets to prove his statement.

---

13 *La Mano Negra* was a violent, secretive anarchist society which allegedly existed in Spain in the late nineteenth century. In 1882 several crimes in Jerez were attributed to *La Mano Negra*, leading to a severe police repression. As a result of the subsequent riots, seven peasants were condemned to death and executed in 1884. Similar repression occurred in 1892—again owing to alleged anarchist activity—culminating in the torture and execution of several people at Montjuich in Barcelona. "The Federalist troubles of 1873" refers to the political turmoil surrounding the declaration of the Democratic Federal Republic on June 7, 1873.

14 Havel is alluding to Viztelly's book *The True Story of the Chevalier d'Éon* (London: Tylston and Edwards, 1895). Charles-Geneviève-Louis-Auguste-André-Timothée d'Éon de Beaumont (1728–1810), usually known as the Chevalier d'Éon, was a French spy and diplomat who lived the last 33 years of his life as a woman.

15 While Czolgosz made it clear that Goldman didn't instruct him to do anything, it is not true that she had no influence on him.

Still as sometimes even a blind pig may find an acorn, so has Mr. Vizetelly a slight understanding of our ideas. To be sure this is the result of the fear of a loyal British bourgeois. His distinction between the Anti-militarism of the Anarchists and that of the Socialists is well taken. He says: "Nowadays Socialists as well as Anarchists denounce militarism, but we entertain no doubt that if Socialist rule should ever be established in Great Britain it will find itself constrained to establish some form of universal military service (if only by virtue of the principle that the same obligations rest on one and all) even if such service should not come before that time. Virtually all the Socialist theories embody principles of authority and compulsion. It is only the Anarchist theory which rejects both; and Anti-militarism is the first step on the road to Anarchism. That is a point to be remembered by many pious folk, and selfish folk, and utopian dreamers also. So well is it understood by the members of the Anarchist fraternity that of more recent years all of their greatest, most determined and persistent efforts have been directed against Militarism in every form. If the Socialists on their side also oppose it, that is because, such as it exists, it forms an obstacle to their ascendency. Once in power, however, they would revive and strengthen it for their own purposes."

And the good patriot empties his heart of the following commonplaces: "Whilst we continue to love our country, whilst we are beholden to the State for good and orderly government and protection and the furtherance of all the interests of the community, it is our duty to guard our country from those who may wish it ill, and to support the State by personal service."

To this outpouring we say Amen!

SOCIALISM AS IT IS (1912)[1]

LIKE THE SOCIALIST PARTIES IN EUROPE, THE SOCIALIST Party in America has its two prominent tendencies: the "opportunistic" and the "revolutionary." These two tendencies have nothing in common with the controversy between the "intellectuals" and the "proletarians." Proletarians can be found in the ranks of the opportunists, and intellectuals in those of the revolutionists. Innumerable articles, pamphlets, and books have been written on this subject.

In following the division in the Socialist camp, the Anarchist feels a kind of diabolical joy. The intellectual strife between the hostile brethren reminds him of the disputations of the Scholastics. Hard as he may try, he fails to find the great fundamental difference between the opportunistic and the revolutionary Socialists.

What is the ultimate goal for which the social rebels today are striving? Is it a free society based on voluntary cooperation and social harmony—Anarchism; or is it a new form of State based on the wage system, representation, and majority rule—Socialism? An answer to either question decides in which camp you belong. Either you are libertarian or authoritarian—an Anarchist or a Socialist. The Socialists are strong believers in a State and in governmentalism; they emphasize their belief in representation; the wage system is the cornerstone of their future economic organization.

What, then, is the position of the "revolutionists" in the Socialist movement? Is the radical Kautsky more libertarian than the revisionist Bernstein, Guesde more

---

1   This article originally appeared in *Mother Earth* 7, no. 6 (August 1912).

than Jaurés, Quelch more than Keir Hardie, Turati more than Bissolati?[2] All of them, whether they are theoreticians or practical workers, whether they are Radicals or Revisionists, Marxists or Neo-Marxists, Revolutionists or Opportunists, Possibilists or Impossibilists, Proletarians or Intellectuals—all of them are governmentalists and believers in majority rule. The question of tactics—how and by what means to attain the Socialist State—is the only object of dissention between them.

If any one wishes a proof of this statement, he need only read the latest contribution to the Socialist literature: "Socialism as It Is," by William English Walling, published by the Macmillan Company, New York.[3]

William English Walling belongs to the group of idealists in the Socialist Party of America who, through their intellectual honesty and revolutionary sincerity, try to save the party from total stagnation and political corruption. In "Russia's Message" he gave us an excellent description of the gigantic struggle of the Russian people. What a pity to find a man still in the ranks of governmentalists and parliamentarians! No matter how hard he strikes at tactics

---

2   In addition to the previously cited figures, Havel is referring to Karl Johann Kautsky (1854–1938), a Czech-German philosopher, journalist, and Marxist theorist who was recognized as one of the most authoritative proponents of Orthodox Marxism after Engels's death in 1895; Jules Basile Guesde (1845–1922), a French socialist journalist and politician; James Keir Hardie (1856–1915), a Scottish socialist and labor leader who is recognized as one of the primary founders of the Independent Labour Party (later the Labour Party) in the United Kingdom; Filippo Turati (1857–1932), an Italian sociologist, criminologist, and socialist politician who, along with his wife, Anna Kulischov (1857–1925), was instrumental in founding the Italian Socialist Party; and Leonida Bissolati (1857–1920), the founder of the Italian Reformist Socialist Party.

3   Published in 1912.

of the Opportunists, in principle he is one of them. A Socialist democracy is his ideal.

The title of the book, "Socialism as It Is," as well as the sub-title, "A Survey of the Worldwide Revolutionary Movement," is misleading. "Socialism as It Ought to be" or "Socialism as I Would Like to Have It" would be a more fitting and apropos. In an elaborate array of proofs he annihilates the arguments of the Opportunists and Reformists. He proves convincingly the uselessness of reform in the midst of capitalist society. No matter how far a social reform may go, it does not improve the conditions of the working class, but only helps to strengthen capitalist system. For every advance awarded labor an advance will be gained by the capitalist class. The most important effect of reform is to increase the relative power of the possessing class. The Socialist politicians are simply tools in the hands of capitalists.

But what a fundamental mistake to believe that the revolutionary and not the opportunistic tactics are gaining in the ranks of the Socialist movement! I cannot conceive by what by what imaginary and fantastic deductions Wailing comes to such a conclusion. The tendency in the Socialist movement in every country goes exactly in the opposite direction—toward Reformism.

The Reformists in the Socialist Party do not trouble themselves very much about the decisions of the Socialist organizations or about the programs adopted by conventions, on which Walling's assertion of the spread of Revolutionism is based. If it fits in their working system, the Reformists vote for the most intransigent policy; if it does not suit them, they simply ignore the program and continue their "practical" work. And they prove by it that they are much more logical than their opponents in the movement, the Revolutionists. Opportunism and compromise is the logical consequence of the participation on the part of Socialists—Opportunists as well as Revolutionists—in the institutions of the bourgeoisie.

One cannot participate in parliamentary cretinism and be a Revolutionist at the same time. Parliamentarism has transformed the Socialist movement into a reform movement with all its vices and intellectual corruption. The Briands, Millerands, Ferris, Bissolatis, Bergers, and Hillquits are the logical representatives of this evolution. The "revolutionary" Socialists are the last Mohicans in the movement. But they don't realize it.[4]

The "revolutionary" Socialist Eugene Debs declares that: "When the political or economic leaders of the wage workers are recommended for their good sense and wise action by capitalists, it is proof that they have become misleaders and cannot be trusted." Yet at the same time he works hand in glove with the Bergers, Seidels, and Hillquits, who are applauded by the capitalists and the bourgeoisie politicians for good sense and wise action.[5]

The real revolutionary, anti-parliamentary, and an-ti-governmental world-wide social movement is to be found outside the Socialist parties, and is being vilified, abused and persecuted by Socialist politicians just as

---

4   Havel is referring, respectively, to Aristide Briand (previous-ly cited); Alexandre Millerand (previously cited); Enrico Ferri (1856–1929), an Italian criminologist and sociologist who re-searched social causes of and was the author of *Criminal Sociology* (1884); Leonida Bissolati (previously cited); Victor Luitpold Berger (1860–1929), a founding member of the Socialist Party of America and the first socialist elected to the U.S. House of Representatives in 1911; and Morris Hillquit (1869–1933), a New York-based lawyer who helped found the Socialist Party of America alongside Berger. All of these figures were reformist so-cial democrats who opposed revolutionary or militant forms of socialism on principle.

5   Emil Seidel (1864–1947) was the first socialist mayor of a major city in the United States. He was mayor of Milwaukee from 1910 to 1912. The quote is taken from *Socialism as It Is*, p. 151. Walling does not cite a source.

much as by the capitalists and their police and judiciary authorities.

The revolutionary spirit of the Socialist movement was lost the very moment Karl Marx and his satellites succeeded in splitting and killing the old Internationale at the Hague Congress of 1872. It was driven out from the Congress at Halle, in 1890, by the "revolutionist" Bebel and his followers, and it was annihilated at the congresses at Zurich in 1893, at London in 1896, and at Paris in 1900.[6]

In truth, the Marxian Socialists never tolerated the revolutionary spirit, and whenever it appeared they tried to strangle and exterminate it by any means in their power. At times they succeeded only too well. Socialism, as it really is today, and the revolutionary movement are contradictory.

---

6 Havel is referring, respectively, to the Fifth International Workingmen's Association Congress; the Congress of Halle; the Third Congress of the Second International; the Fourth Congress of the Second International; and the Fifth Congress of the Second International. Bakunin and his followers were expelled from the Hague Congress in 1872, thus marking the end of the alliance between the anarchists and the Marxists, and anarchists were expelled or marginalized at each of the subsequent international congresses. The reference to Bebel refers to the Congress of Halle, during which several young socialists who wished to abandon parliamentary action were expelled—an event known as the "Zurich Revolution."

AFTER TWENTY-FIVE YEARS
(1912)[1]

THE PROPHETIC WORDS OF AUGUST SPIES—"THERE WILL
come a time when our silence will be more powerful than
the voices you strangle today"—find their fulfillment now,
twenty-five years after the tragedy of Chicago. The intellectual seeds planted by our comrades and watered with
their lifeblood have been absorbed by the proletariat of
America. The red banner of the Social Revolution, struck
down by the janissaries of the ruling class on November
11th, 1887, is floating today over the hills and valleys of
the country. The young generation carries the unconquerable message of rebellion from town to town, from field
to field, from coast to coast, calling upon the enslaved and
oppressed to break their mental chains and fetters and to
prepare for the final struggle with the powers of darkness
and exploitation. The clarion of the social vanguard can be
heard at San Diego, at Los Angeles, at Lawrence—in the
East and in the West, in the North and in the South of the
Republic of Mammon. The battle is not waged by a handful of rebels as it was in Chicago twenty-five years ago;
no, the whole country is aflame with the spirit of social
unrest. The ideas for which our comrades Parsons, Spies,
Lingg, Fischer, and Engel, died on the gallows in 1887—
those very same ideas strike terror to the heart of the enemy of our time. And blind as were the rulers a quarter of
a century ago, blind they are today. Still they hope to be

---

1   This article originally appeared in *Mother Earth* 7, no. 9
     (November 1912). It was written on the occasion of the twen-
     ty-fifth anniversary of the Haymarket executions, which took
     place on November 11, 1887.

able to garrote those ideas by strangling the pioneers of the social movement. The stormy petrel screams over the heads of our financial pirates, and their helmsmen try to reach the haven of safety by steering their ship through a sea of blood and desolation.

In vain, in vain! The powerful voice from the grave of the martyrs urges the social rebels to greater and ever greater effort. The lesson they taught us is not forgotten; it went into our very souls and is part of our life—yea, is life itself.

* * *

Many of the fighters have become disillusioned and disappointed. Their vision has been obscured by a number of defeats. The very intensity with which they fought for the Ideal brought about a sharp reaction. They await the Social Revolution and do not notice that they are living in its very midst. If only their vision could expand; if they could but look freely at the social horizon! They would behold an immense change since the fateful day of 1887. Only a few years ago in many countries we had to meet in secret to commemorate the Eleventh of November. Today the speeches of our martyrs are read by the youth of China, Egypt, Japan, Persia—not to speak of Europe and America. Only a decade ago the Anarchist speaker or writer was the pariah of mankind; today thousands and thousands of earnest men and women listen to our message. Social life in every phase—literature, art, science and education—is transvalued through the irresistible force of Anarchy. Our direct tactics are not only being adopted by the fighting proletariat, but they are used in every sincere and passionate protest against inequality.

* * *

Every time an Anarchist agitator is killed or imprisoned, every time an Anarchist paper succumbs to circumstance, the enemy cries: "Anarchy is dead!" What blindness, what folly! The idea of Anarchy is inherent in the soul of man. To destroy this idea would mean to destroy every aspiration for a higher life, every hope for freedom; it would mean to destroy life itself. Anarchy was from the beginning, is now, and will be forever. Our self-imposed duty is to make mankind conscious of it. In this work we find ourselves in company with the best and the greatest spirits of any time. Our Chicago martyrs knew for what they died; they went to death in a serene and joyful state of mind. Our pleasure it is to follow in their footsteps—not whining for our dead friends, but proud to be their companions in the struggle for emancipation.

> *Many loved Truth and lavished life's best oil*
> *Amid the dust of books to find her,*
> *Content at last for guerdon of their toil*
> *With the cast mantle she has left behind her;*
>
> *Many in sad faith sought her,*
> *Many with crossed hands sighed for her,*
> *But these, our brothers, fought for her,*
> *At life's dear peril wrought for her,*
> *So loved her that they died for her.*[2]

---

2   These are the first nine lines of the Harvard Commemoration Ode (July 21, 1865), written and delivered by James Russell Lowell (1819–1891). Lowell was a Romantic poet associated with the Fireside Poets. He advocated for better conditions for factory workers and was an early abolitionist.

THE SYNDICALIST EDUCATIONAL LEAGUE (1912)[1]

Hippolyte Havel & Harry Kelly[2]

A NUMBER OF ACTIVE REVOLUTIONISTS REALIZING THE NE-cessity for a league to spread the idea of Syndicalism in the United States sent out a call for a meeting to discuss the question. In response to the call about sixty friends and sympathizers assembled at the Ferrer Center, New York City, on the evening of October 4th, and after a discussion lasting several hours it was decided to form such an association.[3]

On October 11th the second meeting was held and the League formally launched. The Syndicalist League is to be purely educational in character, placing itself, however, at

---

1   This article originally appeared in *Mother Earth* 7, no. 9 (November 1912). Hippolyte Havel was the Secretary of the Syndicalist Educational League and Harry Kelly acted as the treasurer. It is unclear when, and under what circumstances, the League was dissolved; however, there is some evidence to suggest it was still in existence in 1914.

2   Harry Kelly (1871–1952) was an Irish-born anarchist and trade unionist. For more information, see "Harry Kelly: A Celebration" below.

3   The Ferrer Center was the first, and most notable, of the American Modern Schools. It was founded in New York City in 1911 and relocated to the Stelton Colony in Piscataway Township, New Jersey in 1914.

the disposal of workingmen who request information and assistance in organizing unions in those industries which at present are unorganized. The basis of membership is adherence to the subjoined Aims and Purposes. It was decided that monthly dues of twenty-five cents should be paid, with no initiation fee, and that a secretary and treasurer, both without salary, were sufficient to transact the business of the League. A campaign of education is under way, and a large mass meeting will be held on November 14th, at Lenox Casino, at which a number of prominent speakers will explain the aims and purposes of the League. Subsequently a series of meetings will be held in different parts of the city and speakers will visit labor organizations for the same purpose.

Aims and Purposes

The Syndicalist League is an organization of active propagandists formed for the purpose of spreading the ideas of Syndicalism, Direct Action, and the General Strike among the organized and unorganized workers of America.

Syndicalism aims to abolish wage slavery and to substitute in its place a new economic system based on the free cooperation of the productive syndicates. The purpose of the Syndicalist League is therefore to educate the proletariat, organized and unorganized, to the necessity of effective, revolutionary action in the conduct of labor's struggle against capitalism, as well as to prepare the workers for their mission of taking charge of production and distribution in the future society. The Syndicalist League is not a new rival to the existing labor organizations; it is not formed with the purpose of splitting these organizations or of antagonizing organized labor. But as we realize that all indirect political activity serves only to mislead and dupe the workers, robs them of their initiative and weakens their power of resistance, and as furthermore all economic compromises with capital are based on the fundamental fallacy of the identity of interests between master and slave and are detrimental to the cause of labor, therefore we will fight with all our energy against indirect political tactics and all other reactionary and corrupting tendencies in the labor movement which are so harmful to the solidarity of the workers.

The Syndicalist League represents the modern revolutionary labor movement in its aim of expropriating the possessing class and of establishing a free economic society based on voluntary cooperation and the principle: To each according to his needs, from each according to his ability.

Letters of Information should be addressed to the Secretary, 61 E. 107th St., New York City.

Hippolyte Havel, Scry.

Harry Kelly, Treas.

THE DRAMA OF LIFE AND DEATH (1912)

IN HIS FASCINATING BOOK ON INDIA, PIERRE LOTI DESCRIBES his quest after the solution of the riddle of life.[1] Skeptical towards Christianity, he tries to fathom the mystery by means of the ancient wisdom of India as interpreted by the Brahmins or their theosophic disciples. Alas! The search is vain. The portal of the shrine is closed to him. Neither the priest of the ancient gods nor the followers of Madame Blavatsky can quench his thirst for knowledge.[2] Yet, notwithstanding his disappointment, a transformation took place in his soul. His views and beliefs underwent a change. Pierre Loti, after a visit to India, was a different man from the one who started out on the quest the previous year.

A similar experience you can have if you undertake a journey with Edward Carpenter through his new book, *The Drama of Love and Death*.[3] You may not find the solution of the riddle, but you will return from an interesting excursion into the invisible world with new vistas of life. Though you may not agree with the author in all his conclusions, you will confess that he has given you a new view of the everlasting problem of life and death.

1   The book in question is *India* (London: T. Werner Laurie, 1913).

2   Helena Petrovna Blavatsky (1831–1891), born Helena von Hahn, was a Russian occultist.

3   Edward Carpenter (1844–1929) was an English socialist poet, philosopher, and early gay activist. A lifelong antiauthoritarian, Carpenter was extremely sympathetic to anarchism and was personal friends with several anarchist notables, including Kropotkin. *The Drama of Life and Death* was published by Mitchell Kennerley (London) in 1912.

To be sure, if you still swear by Büchner and Moleschott, if the theological disputes of Bruno Bauer, Feuerbach, Strauss, and Renan are your spiritual armory and Bradlaugh and Ingersoll your leaders in the realm of thought, then you will be disappointed.[4] Carpenter is a heretic in the opposite direction. There is much in the book that may shock your prejudices; some statements will bring a sarcastic smile to your face; some hypotheses will seem to you far-fetched; still you will not return the same from the journey.

The priest of India and Edward Carpenter arrive by different means at the same conclusion. "The dewdrop slips into the shining sea"; the microcosm, released from the finite body, "pervades the universe." The ancient philosophers of the East arrived just as surely at the idea of continuous life in infinite divisions as the most modern philosopher with all his biological proofs before him. The fear of death can only be eliminated by the sublime knowledge that what we regard as death is merely the disintegration of the particles which make up the individual body—after which they are free to pervade all things. "Death is the necessary door by which we pass from one phase to another; and Love is a similar door."

---

4   In addition to previously cited individuals, Havel is referring, respectively, to Karl Georg Büchner (1813–1837), a German dramatist, writer, and natural scientist; Jacob Moleschott (1822–1893), a Dutch physiologist known for his advocacy of "scientific materialism"; Ludwig Andreas von Feuerbach (1804–1872), a German philosopher known for his critique of Christianity; Charles Bradlaugh (1833–1891), an English political activist who founded the National Secular Society in 1866; and Robert Green "Bob" Ingersoll (1833–1899), an American lawyer, political leader, and orator during the Golden Age of Freethought who was known as "The Great Agnostic." All of these figures were atheists and/or critics of religion.

The fear of death is the enemy of life. Disperse the fear of death and you will lead a full life—a life of love, beauty, and harmony. This is the essence of Carpenter's book. He expresses the longings and feelings of thousands and thousands of seekers after harmonious life. These ideas are vibrating throughout the spiritual life of our time. Maxim Gorky expresses a similar idea in his drama "The Children of the Sun"; Protossoff, the main character, cries out:

> "The fear of death, this is the only thing which keeps men from being bold, beautiful, and free. It impends over them like a black cloud. It covers the earth with its shadows; it gives birth to spectres. It compels them to stray from the straight path to freedom, from the broad road of experience. It moves them to create hasty and monstrous notions concerning the meaning of life, it frightens the reason, and thought then creates superstitions. But we, we are people, we are the children of the sun, of the radiant source of life, born of the sun, we shall conquer the dark fear of death. We are children of the sun. It is the sun glowing in our veins which gives birth to proud and fiery ideas, illuminating the darkness of our ignorance, it is an ocean of energy, beauty and joy that intoxicates the soul."[5]

* * *

There can be no life without sex. To know life one must understand sex. But when we do gain the knowledge

---

5   Maxim Gorky, "The Children of the Sun," trans. Archibald Wolfe, *Poet Lore* 17, no. 2 (1906), pp. 1–77: 35.

of sex? Only after years of frightful experience, surrounded by the ignorance and stupidity of our parents, wading
through muddy streams of lies and hypocrisy. Shall the
new generation suffer the same agonies, tramp the same
hard road to Golgotha?

A great awakening on matters of sex education is per-
ceptible in all countries—even among professional educators, usually the last to catch up with current thought. The
third International Congress for School Hygiene, meeting last year in the Sorbonne, occupied itself mainly with
the burning question of sexual initiation.[6] Dr. Chotzen,
of Breslau, a German delegate, was in favor of full information, based both on intelligence and sentiment, about
sexual functions.[7] Dr. Chotzen's views were supported by
Dr. Doleris, who gave an excellent expose of the subject, by
Professor Lanson, the President of the Congress, as well as
by a great number of the delegates.[8] The discussion caused
an attack on the part of *Le Temps* and a spirited reply from
Professor Lanson.[9] The eminent savant had no difficulty
in crushing the ridiculous arguments of the editor of *Le
Temps* in favor of "*le prix infini de la virginite de dame*" and
"*la poesie de la pudeur et 1 'adorable mystere de l 'amour.*"[10]

---

6   The congress took place in Paris, August 2–7, 1910.

7   Dr. Martin Chotzen (d.1921) was an early twentieth centu-
     ry Prussian dermatologist, professor, and lecturer operating in
     Breslau. He also researched treatments for a number of venere-
     al diseases.

8   Jacques Amédée Doléris (1852–1938) was a French gynecologist,
     natalist, and hygienist who worked at the hospital Boucicaut in
     Paris. Professor Gustave Lanson (1857–1934) was a French histo-
     rian and literary critic.

9   Professor Gustave Lanson (1857–1934) was a French historian
     and literary critic. The attack in question was published as an
     editorial in *Le Temps* (*The Times*) on August 6, 1910. Lanson's
     response appeared in *La Grand Revue* on 10 September 1910.

10   *Le prix infini de a virginite de dame*—"the infinite value of women's

The result of the controversy is an admirable book from the pen of our comrade G. Bessede called *L'initiation Sexuelle* and containing a splendid preface by Dr. L. Brusselle.[11]

The author treats the difficult subject of sexual initiation with great tact and delicacy. His method, based on simple facts which are brought by everyday life to the notice of the child, and laying especial stress on the sexual evolution of the animal world, evolves step by step toward instruction in the human sexual relation. The tact, modesty, simplicity, and clarity with which Bessede treats his subject indicate a true pedagogue.

* * *

Some time ago I was obliged to listen to a lot of tommyrot about criminals. The participants in this discussion were mostly "radicals," among them a professional judge who was especially bitter against the criminal class. I embarrassed the goody-goody people with their cheap sympathy for the "lost brothers" when I asked the judge how he would make his living if there were no tramps, outcasts, or criminals. Still more shocked were they when I declared that a criminal is far superior to the man who sentences him. Most of them "saw the beauty of Jesus," and "admired Tolstoy tremendously," yet they were shocked. The pseudo-science of Lombroso, Nordau and their ilk haunted their brains.[12] The exposures of writ-

---

virginity"; *la poesie de la pudeur et l'adorable mystere de l'amour.*— "the poetry of modesty and the adorable mystery of love."

11 Gédéon Bessède (1878–1917) was an early twentieth century French anarchist writer. *L'initiation Sexuelle* ("Sexual Initiation"), which was published by Art and Science (Paris) in 1910, focuses on the sexuality of children from age three to age twenty.

12 Cesare Lombroso (1835–1909), born Ezechia Marco Lombroso, Italian criminologist, physician, and founder of the Italian School

ers like Brand Whitlock in his *Turn of the Balance*; Wm. C. Owen in *Crime and Criminals*; Messrs. Hopper and Bechdolt in *9009* have not had a great effect on them.[13] The confessions of a "real criminal," Donald Lowrie,[14] in *My Life in Prison*, may open their eyes.

Lowrie describes his experiences in St. Quentin prison. He might have served his time in any other prison. They are all alike; the treatment of the inmates is dastardly, cruel, inhuman, degenerating, and senseless. Lowrie has a fine understanding for his fellow prisoners. You find more humanity in prison than outside. In a criminal society like ours it is preferable to be a criminal than an "honest, decent citizen." Read Lowrie's description of "Ed" Morrell and you will discover a hero of sublime character. The "professional" criminal "Smoky" is a good Samaritan who would have a place of honor in a free society. The chapter on executions seems to me to be the best. The hangman hides his shame behind the criminal system which makes him a murderous tool. "He can't help it, you know," says the easy "radical," "he has to make his living."

Lowrie has no social views; as far as I can see, he thinks the system is all right, if we only had humane rulers and good jailers! Poor chap.

---

of Positivist Criminology. The pseudo-science to which Havel refers is phrenology, which maintained that human personality traits bore a direct relation to the size and shape of the skull.

13   The works in question were published, respectively, by Bobbs-Merrill (Indianapolis) in 1907; the Prison Reform League (Los Angeles) in 1910; and the Mcclure Company (New York) in 1908. James M. Hopper (1876–1956) and Frederick Bechdolt (1874–1950) were American authors. *9009: A Novel of Prison* in particular was wildly popular among members of the *Mother Earth* circle.

14   Donald Lowrie (1875–1925) was an American journalist, author, and outspoken advocate of prison reform. His book *My Life in Prison* was published by Mitchell Kennerley (New York) in 1912.

KROPOTKIN THE REVOLUTIONIST (1912)[1]

OF THE THOUSANDS OF CONGRATULATIONS AND GOOD wishes conveyed to-day to Peter Kropotkin by his admirers, friends and sympathizers, none will, I am sure, find in his heart such a responsive echo as those expressed—most of them in silence—by the simple workers in the Anarchist movement, the men who are neither writers nor speakers, whose names are unknown to the great public, the quiet, self-sacrificing comrades without whom there would be no movement. Those of us who have shared their bed and their last bit of bread know their feeling for the beloved teacher, their love for the man who gave up his position among the favored ones and stepped down to the lowly to share their daily struggle, their sorrows, their aspirations; the man who became their guide in the sacred cause of the Social Revolution. [2]

Many will speak of Kropotkin as the great natural scientist, the historian, the philologue, the litterateur; he is all this, but he is at the same time far more—he is an active revolutionist! He is not satisfied, like so many

---

1   This article originally appeared in *Mother Earth* 7, no. 10 (1912), a special issue commemorating Kropotkin's seventieth birthday (9 December 1912). Contributors included Tcherkesoff, Carpenter, Goldman, Fabbri, Abbott, Nieuwenhuis, Mann, Berkman, Grave, Baginski, and Kelly, among others. The newspapers *Golos Truda* and *Cronaca Sovversiva* also ran special issues, and *Mother Earth* and *Frei Arbeiter Stimme* organized a celebration at Carnegie Hall in Kropotkin's honor.

2   Kropotkin was born a Russian prince but later renounced his standing and his nobility.

scientists, merely to investigate natural phenomena and make deductions which ought to be of value to mankind; he knows that such discoveries cannot be applied as long as the system of exploitation exists, and he therefore works with all his power for the Social Revolution which shall abolish exploitation.

Were it not for men like Kropotkin, the pseudo-scientific Socialists would long since have succeeded in extinguishing the revolutionary flame in the hearts of the workers. It is to his lasting credit that he has used all his great knowledge to fight the demoralizing activities of these reformers, who use the name of Revolutionist to hide their mental corruption. It is this—the uncompromising attitude, his direct participation in social revolt, his firm belief in the proletariat—which distinguishes Peter Kropotkin from many other leaders of modern thought. He is the most widely read revolutionary author; the Bible and the *Communist Manifesto* are the only works which have been translated into so many tongues as *The Words of a* Rebel, *The Appeal to the Young*, and other writings of Kropotkin.[3] It would be impossible to state in how many editions and translations each of his pamphlets has appeared. Sometimes I wonder whether he would recognize his own children: the pamphlets go through so many transformations in their journeyings from one language to another!

Peter Kropotkin is the most beloved comrade in the Anarchist movement; his name is a household word in the revolutionary family in all parts of the world. Our

---

3   The original titles of these works, written in French, were *Paroles d'un révolté* and *Aux Jeunes Gens*. The former was published by Flammarion (Paris) in 1885. The latter appeared in several installments in *Le Révolté* (June 25, July 10, August 7, and August 21, 1880). Notwithstanding the popularity of these works, it is highly unlikely they were published in more languages than the Bible or the *Communist Manifesto*.

ill-fated Japanese comrades were proud of being called Kropotkinists.[4] This was no idolatry on their part, but simply the expression of deep appreciation of his work. Those who have had the opportunity of meeting Kropotkin in his home or in public know that simplicity and modesty are his chief characteristics. As he never fails to emphasize that our place is among the workers in the factories and in the fields, not among the so-called intellectuals, so he is never happier than when he sits with his comrades and fellow-workers. I remember his indignation several years ago in Chicago when he accepted an invitation to a social gathering, expecting to meet his comrades, and found himself instead among vulgar bourgeois women who pestered him for his autograph. The irony of it! The man who gave up gladly his position at the Russian court to go to the people being entertained by the porkocracy of Chicago!

One of the bitterest disappointments of his life, as he himself told me, was that he could not participate actively in the great Russian Revolution.[5] His friends and comrades decided that he could render the revolution far greater aid if he remained in London as one of the organizers of the gigantic struggle. But what arguments they had to use to convince him!

Peter Kropotkin's life and activities demolish the shallow arguments of our utilitarians, who judge all spiritual and intellectual life from their own narrow point of view. His work disproves the belief that ours is an age of specialists only. Like every great thinker, Kropotkin is many-sided in his intellectual activity; life and science as well as art find in him a great interpreter.

Looking back over the seventy years of his life, he must needs feel gratified with his work. The Anarchist brotherhood, to which he belongs, rejoices with him today.

---

4   See "The Kotoku Case" and related articles above.

5   Kropotkin is referring to the Revolution of 1905.

MILITARY PROTECTION FOR WALL STREET (1913)[1]

A DEEP SIGNIFICANCE MUST BE ATTACHED TO THE PETI-
tion of Wall Street for special military protection. Five
hundred bank presidents, manufacturers, stock-brokers,
and other prominent members of the Society of Mammon
signed a document asking the United States government
for an army guard for the great financial institutions. The
petitioners want adequate quarters for a full regiment of
infantry located on Governor's island, "so that in case of
mob outbreaks armed force could reach the downtown
banking center within twelve minutes."

This remarkable document is signed by Henry P.
Davidson, senior member of J. P. Morgan & Co.; Walter
E. Frew, president of the Corn Exchange Bank; Frank A.
Vanderlip, president of the National City Bank; Edward
Townsend, president of the Importers and Traders
National Bank; Francis L. Hine, president of the First
National Bank; W. C. Brown, president of the New York
Central Railroad, and other pillars of society.

The conditions of social harmony are then not so perfect as the believers in the golden rule daily assure us.
The fanciful tales of prosperity and material abundance
woven in the capitalist press do not seem to be of great
weight to the real rulers of the republic. They like to hear
the sweet lullaby of social peace, but at the same time
they want the social peace confirmed by the presence of
machine guns.

---

1   This article originally appeared in *Mother Earth* 8, no. 8 (October
     1913). For more information, see *The New York Times* (28
     September 1913), p. 47.

The traders in human flesh and the worshippers of the golden calf were always the first to see the scriptural *mene, mene, tekel upharsin* written on the wall.[2] They feel the sword of Damocles constantly over their heads. Their present uneasiness is a portentous omen of a deep social unrest. Though the times seem normal and exploitation goes on without unusual eruptions, the brains of the capitalistic system are given over to anxiety. They fear outbreaks of mobs—instinctively they sense the approach of a social upheaval.

Since time immemorial hired mercenaries have proved to be the best protection for tyrants and exploiters. Louis d'ors were ever the banner under which the military hirelings fought the battles of their employers.[3] The American capitalist has improved on the ancient system. He has realized the necessity of cultivating the raw material furnished him; to the louis d'ors he adds a mental obsession; with the help of other hirelings, political spellbinders, he succeeds in inoculating the brain of his mercenaries with the bacillus of patriotism. Seattle proved to be an admirable lesson.[4] The petition of Wall Street ought to convince even the most doubting Thomas of the need for an anti-militaristic propaganda, carried on a larger scale than heretofore.

Militarism is the last stronghold of capitalism. The leaders of the system count on the soldiery as the final and only arbiter of their destiny; let all other pillars which

---

2 This translates roughly to "you have been counted and found wanting."

3 *Louis d'ors*—i.e., filthy lucre, a type of French coin.

4 On July 17, 1913—the first day of the annual Golden Potlach Festival—a fistfight broke out between some soldiers and members of the IWW (one of the latter supposedly "insulted the uniforms" of the former during a speech). A newspaper story published the next day further agitated the soldiers, who proceeded to set fire to the offices of the IWW and the Socialist Party.

their rule rests crumble; so long as they can command their uniformed assassins, they feel safe in position. They have organized the system to such degree that they hope to continue their robbery with help of hordes driven to work by hunger, commanded by Jim Farleys, and protected by the bayonets and machine guns of the patriotic Hessians.[5] Their servants in Capitol are and always will be willing and anxious to give them the necessary security.

It will depend on the conscious workers, the men and women working in the revolutionary movement, whether this nefarious plan will succeed or fail. Efforts in the right direction will undermine this last bulwark of parasites who parade in the mask of Civilization. We have seen during the past few years, in China, in Portugal, in Mexico, in Turkey and in Persia that the armies are not immune against revolutionary propaganda, revolution.[6] The revolutions in those countries resulted in more than a mere change of rules; they had a strong socioeconomic significance. In Mexico especially we are witnessing social revolution on a broad basis. And even the clear revolutionary propaganda among soldiers proved in many countries to be a great success. In France, where the propaganda has been on in a systematic manner, whole battalions have refused to fire upon their brothers on the economic battlefield.[7] The act of our Italian comrade Masetti, who shot his colonel before the departure to Tunis, rather than take part in the murder of the natives of Africa, was an

---

5   Jim Farley (1873–1913) was a notorious private detective and strikebreaker.

6   Havel is referring to various revolutionary uprisings in China (1911–1912), Portugal (1910), Mexico (1910), and the Ottoman Empire (1908), each of which involved large scale military defections.

7   In the years leading up to the First World War the French antimilitarism movement helped provoke the several mutinies of the sort Havel describes.

inspiration to all revolutionists.[8] The case of Buwalda in San Francisco proves that the soldiers and sailors of the United States are not insensible to thoughts of freedom.[9] Wall Street may yet see the protection it yearns for become a boomerang for emancipation.

The social revolutionist should rejoice over the action of Wall Street; it shows that his work is not in vain. The ideas of social revolt are spreading—the preparations of the enemy are a convincing proof of it. The workers for a free society need not be discouraged by the pessimistic views of complacent wiseacres who have "outgrown" the idea of a social revolution. The revolution will come suddenly, in spite of them and to their great surprise.

---

8   Augusto Masetti (1888–1966) was an Italian anarchist. Masetti is reputed to have shouted "Down with the war! Long live anarchy!" during the act Havel describes.

9   See "The Coalition Against Anarchists" and "Introduction to *Anarchism and Other Essays*" above.

THE LESSON OF CHICAGO (1913)[1]

ONCE AGAIN WE APPROACH THE DAY OF MARTYRS. OUR thoughts are irresistibly drawn towards the Lake of Michigan, where in the City of Mammon and exploitation our brothers breathed their last on the historic Eleventh of November. At the behest of the ruling class of Chicago they were, murdered in the Cook County jail. The cowards and dupes of the laboring class acquiesced in the five-fold murder, and scoundrelism reigned supreme.

Brothers and sisters, let us beware of the wise soothsayers in the labor movement who appear each year to assure us that by commemorating the day of the execution of our comrades we imitate the Church which honors its alleged saints.

Parsons, Lingg, Engel, Spies and Fischer died for our cause; they lost their lives spreading our ideals and our inspiration. If in honoring the memory of these men we commit the crime of idolatry, let us plead guilty.

The sceptical critic who does not perceive the significance of this day, is beyond redemption. We are indeed aware that before and after November Eleventh men and women in every part of the world have sacrificed their lives by the hundreds and thousands for the good of humanity. But we also know that that infamous scoundrel Gary spoke the truth when in overruling the motion for a new trial he declared: "This case is without precedent.

---

1   This article originally appeared in *Mother Earth* 8, no. 9 (November 1913). Like "After Twenty-Five Years," published the previous year, it is a commemoration of the Haymarket executions (November 11, 1887).

There is no example in the law books of a case of this sort. No such occurrence has ever happened before in the history of the world." [2]

Verily the infamy of the five-fold murder is without parallel. It rang the death knell of the judicial system.

Yes, we plead guilty. We try to emulate our martyred comrades in their work and deeds—unworthy as we may otherwise be.

* * *

But what shall we say to those youthful wiseacres in the labor movement who, proud of their knowledge acquired in the School of Ignorance, fancy they have reached a better understanding of the social question than our comrades had in their hour of struggle; those clay-footed heroes who imagine that their methods in the fight with capitalism are far superior to those of the revolutionary workers of twenty-six years ago.

In reading the speeches of our comrades delivered on the threshold of death, and in glancing over the history of the famous trial by Dyer D. Lum, I am again and again impressed with the deep knowledge of these men, their broad vision, their intellectual attainment, and especially with their sound judgment of the social question. [3] In what have we improved on them? Compare their speeches with those delivered by Clarence Darrow in the trials of Moyer, Haywood, and Pettibone; with those in his own trial, and with those of Ettor and Giovannitti at their trial in Lawrence. [4] Neither

---

2 Joseph E. Gary (1821–1906) was the judge who presided over the trial of the Haymarket Martyrs.

3 Dyer D. Lum, *A Concise History of the Great Trial of the Chicago Anarchists in 1886* (Chicago: Socialistic Publishing Society, 1886).

4 Havel is referring, respectively, to Clarence Darrow (1857–1938), a famous trial lawyer and member of the American Civil Liberties Union; Charles Moyer (1866–1929), an American labor leader

Darrow nor Ettor and Giovannitti added a single item of sociological, intellectual, or economic worth to the speeches of
our comrades. The uncompromising attitude of the Chicago
Anarchists before the court cannot be surpassed. Jack Whyte's
defiance of the judge in San Diego is merely an echo of the
terrific thunder of Louis Lingg. [5] Has the preamble of any
organization improved on the program of the Anarchistic
Working People's Party founded in 1883, at Pittsburgh:

> "Destruction of the existing class rule by
> all means: by energetic, relentless, revolu-
> tionary and international action.

---

and president of the Western Federation of Miners from 1902
to 1926; William Dudley "Big Bill" Haywood (1869–1928), an
American trade unionist and founding member of the Industrial
Workers of the World; George Pettibone (1862–1908), an
American minor and trade unionist; Joseph James "Smiling Joe"
Ettor (1885–1948), an Italian-American trade unionist and leader
of the Industrial Workers of the World; and Arturo M. Giovannitti
(1884–1959), an Italian-American trade unionist and poet.
Moyer, who had led the WFM during the Colorado Labor Wars
(1903–1904), was charged alongside Haywood and Pettibone
with conspiracy to murder Frank Steunenberg, ex-governor of the
state of Idaho, in 1906. Ettor and Giovannitti were implicated in
a killing that occurred during the 1912 Lawrence Textile Strike.
Darrow served as defense attorney in both cases.

5   In an effort to radical organizing, especially by the IWW, the city
of San Diego passed an ordinance in January 1912 severely limiting freedom of speech and assembly. During the ensuing controversy scores of radicals were harassed and abused; a few were
even murdered. It was in this context that police arrested several
Wobblies on conspiracy to commit terroristic acts on March 18.
At his trial a few days later, the alleged ringleader Jack Whyte
(died 1915) exploded at the judge: "To hell with your courts; I
know what justice is!" For more information see "A Tribute to
Jack White," *Mother Earth* 10, no. 2 (April, 1915).

"Establishment of a free society based upon a cooperative system of production.

"Free exchange of equivalent products, by and between the productive organizations, without commerce and profit-mongery.

"Organization of education on a secular, scientific and equal basis for both sexes.

"Equal rights for all, without distinction of sex or race.

"Regulation of all public affairs by free contracts between the autonomous independent communes and associations, resting on a federalistic basis."[6]

Furthermore, the great railroad strike in 1877, the strike in East St. Louis, the strikes in Hocking Valley and in Monongahela Valley, the lock-out of the girls in the Merrimac Mills in Connecticut—struggles in which our comrades took such a prominent part, were not surpassed in their intensity, in the ferocity of the enemy, nor in the solidarity of the workers by the strikes at Lawrence, Little Falls, or Paterson.[7]

---

6   The so-called "Pittsburgh Manifesto" was drafted by several notable radicals including Johann Most, Albert Parsons, and August Spies. It was adopted by the Pittsburgh Congress of the International Working Peoples' Association in 1883.

7   Havel is referring, respectively, to the Great Railroad Strike of 1877, sometimes referred to as the Great Upheaval, which began on July 14 in Martinsburg, West Virginia, and lasted approximately 45 days; the 1877 St. Louis General Strike, which was organized by the Knights of Labor and the Workingmen's Party in response to the Great Railroad Strike and is generally accepted

In these days of cheap sensationalism and intellectual prostitution we are accustomed to sneers at the antiquated tactics of Anarchists. But we wish our critics would demonstrate where and how they have improved on our theory and methods as preached and propagated by our Chicago comrades and by the Anarchists since then. August Spies' words are as true today as they were twenty-six years ago:

> We have interpreted to the people their conditions and relations in society. We have explained to them the different social phenomena and the social laws and circumstances under which they occur. We have, by way of scientific investigation incontrovertibly proved and brought to their knowledge that the system of wages is the root of the present social iniquities— iniquities so monstrous that they cry to heaven. We have further said that the wage system, as a specific form of development, would, by the necessity of logic, have to give to higher forms of civilization; that the wage system must furnish the foundation for a social system of co-operation—that

---

as the first general strike in the United States; the Hocking Valley Coal Strike, which took place in Ohio for nine months in 1884 and 1885; the Homestead Strike, which took place in Homestead, Pennsylvania between June 30 and July 6, 1892; the Merrimack Mill lockout, which took place in Lowell, Massachusetts in 1903; the Lawrence Textile Strike, which took place in Lawrence, Massachusetts from January 1 to March 12, 1912; the Little Falls Textile Strike, which took place in Little Falls, New York from October 9, 1911 to January 3, 1912; and the Paterson Silk Strike, which took place in Paterson, New Jersey from February 1 to June 28, 1913.

is, Socialism. That whether this or that theory, this or that scheme regarding future arrangements were accepted was not a matter of choice, but one of historical necessity, and that to us the tendency of progress seemed to be Anarchism—that is, a future society without kings or classes—a society of sovereigns in which liberty and economic equality of all would furnish unshakable equilibrium as a foundation for natural order.

That our method and theory has proved to be correct, we see today. The spread of Anarchist ideas we can follow in all directions. In the ranks of the ruling class we witness a general disintegration. A daily which in 1887 howled for the blood of our comrades, writes now: "Recent events... invite the inquiry whether there is any law that anybody can understand; whether there is any law that its most powerful ministers can be made to recognize; whether there is any law that does not hang upon whim, caprice, or prejudice, and whether there is any law that cannot be twisted to meet the views of its expounders on the bench as well as at the bar."[8]

And this from the *New York World*!

---

8   "Judges Who Disagree," *New York World*, October 20, 1913.

THE BROTHERS KARAMAZOV
(1913)[1]

OF ALL THE GREAT RUSSIAN WRITERS OF THE LAST CENTU-
ry, none made so deep an impression upon his contemporaries as Fyodor Michailovitch Dostoievsky. His popularity was immense. When he died, forty thousand people
followed his body to the grave. Turgeniev and Tolstoy had
a great influence upon the artistic life of Western Europe,
but the most intellectual men of the time were fascinated
by the brilliant genius of Dostoievsky. He is the father of
the modern psychological novel. His influence one may
detect in the works of all modern writers. Nietzsche calls
him "my great master." And while the popularity of many
of his contemporaries is today on the wane, Dostoievsky's
fame is spreading from year to year, and his works find
ever greater appreciation and understanding. The author
who in his lifetime was labeled a Russian nationalist, even
the apostle of Slavophilism, is now recognized as a cosmopolitan genius, the greatest analyst of the human soul.[2]

To the English-reading public Dostoievsky has so far
remained a sealed book. To be sure, many are acquainted with *Crime and Punishment* and the *Memoirs from a
Dead House*; but only in abridged and mutilated translations.[3] Few people in this country are familiar with

---

1   This article originally appeared in *Mother Earth* 8, no. 2 (April
    1913). Havel is reviewing the 1912 edition.

2   *Slavophilism* was a nineteenth century intellectual and political
    movement which advocated Slavic culture over that of Western
    European culture.

3   These works were published in 1866 and 1862, respectively. The
    latter is more commonly known as *The House of the Dead*.

Vizetelly's series of Russian authors in which appeared *Injury and Insult, The Friend of the Family, The Idiot, Poor Folks, Uncle's Dream,* and *The Permanent Husband.*[4] Like so many foreign writers, Dostoievsky suffers much at the hands of translators. The English rendering is far inferior to those in the German language. Some of his works have been so distorted that they read more like dime novels than like psychological masterpieces.

It is praiseworthy, therefore, on the part of the Macmillan Company to have started the publication of Dostoievsky's novels in their entirety, and it was a wise selection of the literary editor to choose *The Brothers Karamazov* as the first of the series.[5] The novel, translated by Constance Garnett, appears in a complete, un-abridged form.[6] If we consider that a translation of *The Brothers Karamazov* appeared in French as early as 1887 (the German translation even earlier), we see how long it takes the English-speaking public to get acquainted with the masterpieces of the world's literature. A synopsis of the novel was made for Pavel Orleneff several years ago by Miss Isabel Hapgood, and a French dramatization, made by J. Copeau and J. Croue, appeared in 1911 in *L'Illustration Theatrale,* while the play was being produced

---

4   Henry Vizetelly (1820–1894) was an English publisher. The works Havel cites were published in 1861, 1859, 1868, 1844, 1859, and 1870, respectively. *The Friend of the Family* is also known as *The Village of Stepanchikovo* and *The Permanent Husband* is also known as *The Eternal Husband.*

5   *The Brothers Karamazov,* completed in 1880, was Dostoyevsky's final novel.

6   Constance Clara Garnett (1861–1946) was an English translator of nineteenth-century Russian literature. Garnett was one of the first English translators of Tolstoy, Dostoyevsky, Anton Chekhov. Her unabridged translation was published by Macmillan (New York) in 1912.

at a Paris theatre.[7] Dostoievsky planned *The Brothers Karamazov* when he lived in exile in Dresden, in the utmost misery, poverty, and sickness. The work was never finished. Dostoievsky intended to write a novel of five volumes, but only two were completed. In the latter half of 1880 when he worked on the novel he was, as his friend Strakhov informs us, entirely exhausted. "He lived, it was plain, solely on his nerves. His body had become so frail that the first slight blow might destroy it."[8] Yet his mental power was untiring.

Is *The Brothers Karamazov* a great novel, a novel which can be compared with *War and Peace* or *Fathers and Sons*? Opinions of the work vary considerably. The best critics of Russian literature disagree in their estimation. K. Waliszewski in his *Russian Literature* characterizes the novel as a "most invaluable treasury of information concerning the contemporary life of Russia, moral, intellectual, and social."[9] Dmitri Mereshkovski, in his essays on "Tolstoy and Dostoievsky as Artists," says that "there is no

---

7   Isabel Florence Hapgood (1851–1928) was an American writer and translator of French and Russian texts. Her translation of *The Brothers Karamazov* from the French was published by Orleneff's *Russian Lyceum* series in 1905. Jacques Copeau (1879–1949)—a French theatre director, producer, actor, dramatist, and founder of the famous Théâtre du Vieux-Colombier—and Jean Croué (1878–1952)—a French actor and writer—published their dramatization in *L'Illustration Theatrale* ("Theatrical Illustration") 179 (May 1911). *L'illustration* magazine, published weekly in France from 1843 to 1944, was a magazine in which new theatrical works were reviewed.

8   Nikolay Nikolayevich Strakhov (1828–1896) was a Russian philosopher and literary critic. Strahkov was a close friend and collaborator of Dostoyevsky.

9   *A History of Russian Literature* (New York: D. Appleton, 1900), p. 351. Kazimierz Klemens Waliszewski (1849–1935) was a Polish author and historian.

doubt that 'The Brothers Karamazov' is one of the greatest creations of Dostoievsky, unlike anything else in the
world's literature, a creation that has its roots in the inmost recesses of his consciousness and of his unconscious-
ness."[10] On the other hand, Peter Kropotkin in his *Russian
Literature* finds the novel "so unnatural, so much fabricat-
ed for the purpose of introducing—here a bit of morals,
there some abominable character taken from a psycho-
pathic hospital, or again in order to analyze the feelings
of some purely imaginary criminal, that a few good pages
scattered here and there do not compensate the reader for
the hard task of reading these two volumes."[11] Melchier
de Vogue agrees with Kropotkin. In his *Russian Novelists*
he finds many parts of the work "intolerably tedious. The
plot amounts to nothing but a framework upon which to
hang all the author's favorite theories, and display every
type of his eccentric fancy."[12]

How can we reconcile such diverse opinions, such
diametrically opposed views? Is it overvaluation or un-
derestimation; prejudice in favor of or against the author? To me the criterion is simply this: does the book
give one new values, a new view of life, does it disturb
one's soul to the utmost depth? If it succeed in accomplishing this, it is a great book. I am convinced that
The Brothers Karamazov are a part of every one of us;
we all are more or less either an Alyosha or Dmitri, an
Ivan or a Smerdyakov. The brothers Karamazov live not
only in Russia, but everywhere; we find them in every

---

10   *Tolstoi as Man and Artist* (London: Archibald Constable & Co.,
     1902), p. 287. Dmitri Sergeyevich Merezhkovsky (1866–1941)
     was a Russian novelist, poet, and literary critic.

11   *Russian Literature* (New York: McClure, Phillips & Co.,
     1905), p. 169.

12   *The Russian Novelists* (Boston: D. Lothrop Company, 1887), p.
     185. Charles-Jean-Melchior de Vogüé (1829–1916) was a French
     archaeologist and diplomat.

country, in every station of society. Their portrayal by Dostoievsky is true and lifelike.

In making comparison between the art of Tolstoy and that of the author of *The Brothers Karamazov*, Mereshkovski expresses the opinion that Dostoievsky has no rival in the art of gradual tension, accumulation, increase, and alarming concentration of dramatic power. No doubt this characterization of Dostoievsky's art is correct. The boundless picture which is enfolded in *The Brothers Karamazov* is condensed, if we do not count the intervals between the acts, into a few days. But even in one day, in one hour, and that almost on one and the same spot, the characters of the novel pass through experiences which ordinary mortals do not taste in a lifetime. Dostoievsky has no need to describe the appearance of his characters, for by their peculiar form of language and tone of voice they themselves depict, not only their thoughts and feelings, but their faces and bodies.

When the elder Karamazov, suddenly getting quite animated, addresses his sons thus:

> "Ah, you boys! You children, little sucking pigs, to my thinking. ... I never thought a woman ugly in my life—that's been my rule! Can you understand that? How could you understand it? You've milk in your veins, not blood. You're not out of your shells yet. My rule has been that you can always find something devilishly interesting in every woman that you wouldn't find in any other. Only, one must know how to find it, that's the point! That's a talent! To my mind there are no ugly women. The very fact that she is a woman is half the battle ... but how could you understand that? Even in vielles lilies, even in them you may discover something that makes

you simply wonder that men have been such fools as to let them grow old without noticing them. Barefooted girls or unattractive ones, you must take them by surprise. Didn't you know that? You must astound them till they're fascinated, upset, ashamed that such a gentleman should fall in love with such a little slut. It's a jolly good thing that there always are and will be masters and slaves in the world, so there always will be a little maid-of-all and her master, and you know that's all that's needed for happiness."

We see the heart of the old man, and also his fat, shaking Adam's apple, and his moist, thin lips; the tiny, shamelessly piercing eyes, and his whole savage figure—the figure of an old Roman of the times of the decadence. When we learn that on a packet of money, sealed and tied with ribbon, there was also written in his own hand, "To my angel Grushenka, if she will come to me," and that three days later he added "for my little chicken," he suddenly stands before us alive. We could not explain how, or why, but we feel that in this belated "for my little chicken" we have caught some subtle, sensual wrinkle on his face. It is just that last little touch which makes the portrait so lifelike, as if the painter, going beyond the bounds of his art, had created a portrait which is ever on the point of stirring and coming out of the frame like a specter or a ghost.

The wonderful portrait of the Grand Inquisitor will ever live in the world's literature. What a portrait!—Jesus appears again on earth at the time when heretics are daily being burned at the stake; he is recognized by the people—a deep offence to the Grand Inquisitor, who has Jesus arrested and brought before him. The admonition the Grand Inquisitor gives to Jesus is penetrating. Why has he come back to disturb the peace and the rule of the Church?

> "It is Thou? Thou? Don't answer, be silent. What canst Thou say, indeed? I know too well what Thou wouldst say. And Thou hast no right to add anything to what Thou hadst said of old. Why, then, art Thou come to hinder us? For Thou hast come to hinder us, and Thou knowest that. But dost Thou know what will be to-morrow? I know not who Thou art and care not to know whether it is Thou or only a semblance of Him, but to-morrow I shall condemn Thee and burn Thee at the stake as the worst of heretics. And the very people who have today kissed Thy feet, to-morrow at the faintest sign from me will rush to heap up the embers of Thy fire. Knowest Thou that?"

The whole monologue of the Grand Inquisitor should be reprinted for the edification of the Church. After all, the question whether *The Brothers Karamazov* is a masterpiece or whether it belongs to morbid literature, stands and falls with the attitude one takes toward Dostoievsky himself, his life and his philosophy. Estimates of *The Brothers Karamazov* differ as fundamentally as opinions concerning Dostoievsky. Neither the judgment of the Englishman A. T. Lloyd, or of the German Julius Bierbaum, of the Frenchman Andre Gide, or the valuation of that universal connoisseur of literature, George Brandes—not to speak of the Russian critics—will help one to form a true estimate of Dostoievsky.[13]

---

13   Havel is referring, respectively, to the writers John Arthur Thomas Lloyd (1870–1856), Otto Julius Bierbaum (1865–1910), André

The problem is the same as with Schopenhauer. Those who understand and accept Schopenhauer will also understand and accept Dostoievsky. To be sure, as it would be as inappropriate to compare the political views of Schopenhauer with those of a Metternich, as to draw a parallel between the philosophy of Dostoievsky with the opinions of the Slavophiles Shterbatov, Kirejevsky, Tchomykov, or the brothers Aksakov.[14] Dostoievsky was considered a nationalist in the narrowest and most anti-European sense; in reality he was a cosmopolitan in the broadest conception. Throughout his life he preserved his feeling for universal culture ("omni-human" culture, he called it), the capacity to feel at home everywhere, to live the vital ideas of all ages and peoples. True, he believed the Russian genius to be more universal in its assimilative capacity, and therefore superior to the genius of other nations, but in this respect Mereshkovski says, "He, being next to Pushkin, the most Russian of Russian authors, was at the same time the greatest of our cosmopolitans."[15]

Paul Guillaume Gide (1869–1951), and Georg Morris Cohen Brandes (1842–1927), each of whom published critical works on Dostoyevsky—e.g., *A Great Russian Realist* (Lloyd, 1912); "Dostoyevsky and Nietzsche" (Bierbaum, 1910), *Dostoevsky* (Gide, 1923, a collection of earlier essays), and *Impressions of Russia* (Brandes, 1889).

14 Arthur Schopenhauer (1788–1860) was a German philosopher. Presumably Havel is referring to Schopenhauer's appropriation by German nationalists (hence the reference to Metternich, a notorious early advocate of this ideology). In a similar fashion, Havel wants to distinguish Dostoyevsky's cosmopolitanism from the deeply nationalistic ideas of Mikhail Shcherbatov (1733–1790), Ivan Kireyevsky (1806–1856), Aleksey Khomyakov (1804–1860), Konstantin Aksakov (1817–1860), Ivan Askasov (1823–1886), and other writers and critics associated with the Slavophile movement.

15 *Tolstoi as Man and Artist*, p. 126.

Primarily he was, as no other writer before or since, the poet of the humiliated and the oppressed. He knew the people, felt and suffered with them. In his essay on the bourgeoisie, wherein he flays the superficial rationalism and the false sentiments of the middle class, he writes: "The theorists, burying themselves in their doctrinaire wisdom, not only fail to understand the people, but even despise them; not, be it understood, with evil intention, but almost instinctively. We are convinced that even the most intelligent among them believes that when occasion offered he would only have to talk ten minutes with the people in order to understand them thoroughly, while the people might probably not even be listening to what he was talking about."[16] Born in poverty, he died in poverty. The spirit of ownership, of detachment from the great mass of one's fellows seemed to Dostoievsky the supreme sin. In his material and mental suffering he reminds one of another great analyst of the human soul, the Dutch writer Douvers Deckker-Multatuli.[17]

---

16 The essay in question appears in Dostoevsky's "Winter Notes on Summer Impressions," published in *Vremya* in 1863.

17 Like Dostoevsky, Multatuli was a depressive personality who lived in extreme poverty for most of his adult life.

THE CIVIL WAR IN COLORADO (1914)[1]

THE YEAR ONE THOUSAND NINE HUNDRED AND FOURTEEN will stand out in the annals of the proletariat of America in letters of fire. At the time when many hundreds and thousands of hungry and homeless workers tramped through the streets of the cities begging for work, for the privilege of producing wealth for their exploiters, triumphant Capitalism committed its greatest crime—the massacre of workers in Colorado. All former outrages perpetrated by the masters upon labor sink into insignificance in comparison with the slaughter of the miners, their wives and children at Ludlow, on the twentieth of April. The exploiting monster, represented by its chief tool, revealed itself in its full bestiality.

Capitalism has proved once more that its power is the supreme law, and that it recognizes nothing else but its own might. And what a sight! The President of the mightiest republic in the world begging for concessions in Wall Street![2]

---

1   This essay originally appeared in *Mother Earth* 9, no. 3 (May 1914). It was written in response to the Ludlow Massacre, a violent attack by the Colorado National Guard against striking miners and their families ordered by the Colorado Fuel and Iron Company. Approximately two dozen people (including women and children, as Havel notes) were killed. Among other things, the miners were striking for the enforcement of the eight-hour day law and the recognition of their union.

2   Havel is presumably referring to Woodrow Wilson's "New Freedom," a series of progressive policies enacted by Wilson and the Democrats beginning in 1913. The stated goal of many of these policies was to curb the power of Wall Street financiers.

But he received only a well-deserved kick. Even the most doubting Thomas must now perceive where the real seat of the government is located. And the shame of it! Organized labor, misled by cowardly leaders, quietly continues its work, while its members are being massacred. Verily, we progress phenomenally. Has all the sweat and all the blood of the workers of this country been sacrificed in vain?

Has the agitation of the last decades accomplished nothing?

If there ever was a time when labor had cause to proclaim a general uprising, now is such a time. A massacre like that in Colorado can be answered only by general destruction.

The miners in Colorado proved their manhood. Their fellow workers have yet to prove theirs. If they acquiesce in this crime today, they will be slaughtered like their brothers in Colorado tomorrow. If they do not rise and destroy the tyranny of Capitalism, the monster will wallow in the blood of their mothers and children. Will they merely await another investigation by political harlots? Never before has the theory of peaceful and legal agitation suffered such a breakdown as in Colorado. Never before has political action been proven a greater fallacy. The law mills of the State worked overtime, yet the condition of the workers became more unbearable from day to day. It is the irony of fate that such conditions should prevail in a State where laws for the protection of labor abound. The miners of Colorado found out of how much value they are.

Then the glory of suffrage! The women of Colorado have been in possession of the ballot since 1891, yet economic conditions in their State are worse than anywhere else in the nation.

The secret lies in this: while plenty of laws for the protection of labor have been enacted, the capitalists have shown nothing but contempt for the paper statutes.

The miners went on strike on the 22nd of last September [1913] to enforce certain demands which are granted by the laws of the State.[3] Colorado has on its statute books a large number of laws especially designed to prevent just such situations as have arisen in that plutocratic commonwealth. To mention a few of these laws:

It is against the law to discharge an employee between the age of eighteen and sixty years solely on account of age.

It is unlawful for any person, company or corporation to prevent any employee from joining a labor union or other organization, or for such person or corporation to coerce employees by discharging or threatening to discharge them for joining labor or other unions or organizations.

It is unlawful for persons or corporations to import "scab" labor by misrepresentation, or to engage such labor without previous warning that strikes are on in the districts in which it is proposed to employ such labor.

It is against the law in Colorado to employ armed guards, or to possess arms for the purpose of using same to defend mining or other property without the express permission of the Governor of the Slate.

The Eight-Hour law is legally required throughout the State in all mining industry. Employers cannot "blacklist" labor, or refuse to give proper references of efficient employees when so required.

Labor laws require also that coal mines shall be rendered safe for workers and supplied with all necessary devices for preventing accidents.

The Colorado statutes are also very explicit in regard to "company stores," and there is a comprehensive "truck act" in existence.[4]

---

3   Actually, the strike began on September 23, 1913.

4   Company stores were retail outlets that sold a limited range of food, clothing and daily necessities to employees of a company, often at extremely high prices. They were widely regarded as exploitative. "Truck acts" refers to legislation that outlaws truck systems, also known as "company store" systems. In Colorado,

There are numerous laws as to employment of women and children.

The Colorado Fuel and Iron Company (the Rockefeller interests) has for many years exercised undisputed political control in the counties of southern Colorado where the strike is underway. The functions of civil government have been carried on by the hirelings of the company, and it is a well-known fact that the corporation's will is the dominating influence in all matters where its interests are involved. The accidents and catastrophes which have occurred in its mines during the past decade have exacted a fearful toll in life and brought untold desolation to widows and children.

Since 1900 the effort to form unions has been constantly broken up by the C. F. and I. Company and other combinations of coal operators, though to prevent employees from forming such unions is a misdemeanor in that State. The lowest possible wages have been paid. The average wage for an eight-hour day paid by the Berwind mine, owned by the C. F. and I. Company, is $1.58. During 1912, the average net wage per year in this mine was $615.32. A decent life, everyone must admit, cannot be lived on such wages. Through the company's stores much of this money returns to the corporation.

The right of the miners of the C. F. and I. Company to form or join a union is said by John D. Rockefeller, Jr., to be the one right which he cannot "concede."[5] He

truck systems were outlawed in the Revised Statutes of 1908, Section 6989.

5   John Davidson Rockefeller, Jr. (1874–1960) was an American financier. In the months after Havel published this essay his house was targeted for a bombing attack by anarchists in New York seeking vengeance for his role in the Massacre. On July 4, 1914, the bomb detonated during manufacture, killing at least four people. The statement to which Havel alludes was issued on April 28, 1914.

lays great stress upon the constitutional privilege of every citizen "to be protected in his life and liberty." It is singular to find, however, that unorganized miners are treated worse by the C. F. and I. Company than those who belong to a union.

In order to throw some light upon general conditions in the coal mines of Colorado, it might be well to quote from a report by the Secretary of State and Commissioner of Labor to the Governor of Colorado.[6] Speaking of the employment of armed guards to break up miners' unions, to enforce labor by imported strikebreakers, and to deny miners the rights of citizenship in Colorado, the Secretary of State declares:

"The system as employed by the C.F. and I. Company in Las Animas County is not only in open defiance of all the laws of the State of Colorado, but it maintains, under the thin guise of law, an armed force, consisting of deputy sheriffs, in all its camps, who are used not only to violate all the laws, but to maltreat anyone who attempts in any way to assert his rights as a citizen. The county officials of Las Animas County are in league with this Company, so that it is absolutely impossible to get anything like justice from the hands of the legally elected officials of that county.

"In order to thoroughly understand to what extremes these so-called officials of the law go, I shall state that after the Company exacts a rent for their houses from their employees, no home is sacred or has any privacy, the Company taking the ground that, as they own the property, they have the right to enter it at all times, and I have been told by women in Primers that there was no privacy in their home life, that whenever a representative of the Company or a deputy sheriff desired, they entered the house unannounced.

---

6   Elias M. Ammons (1860–1925) was governor of Colorado from 1913 to 1915. He was responsible for deploying the National Guard at Ludlow.

"We find that children are employed in the mines, at the coal washers and at the coke ovens, in direct violation of the laws of Colorado, which make it unlawful to employ any child under sixteen years of age in any dangerous occupation, and the only excuse offered by the officials of the Company is that it is none of their business, that these children are working with the consent of their parents."[7]

Further evidence in the report refers to boys under sixteen years old engaged as "trappers" in the mines of the C. F. and I. Company, who lost their lives after working only six months in these mines. One of the boys was killed on his fifteenth birthday. Other children working in the Rockefeller mines were as young as ten years.

Even before the strike broke out, the mine owners imported strikebreakers and employed a detective agency whose specialty is breaking strikes. This agency shipped in a large number of gunmen, who tried their best to break the strike. The strikers resisted, and at the request of the mine owners the militia was sent to the strike district.

The militia is the tool of the companies, and though the miners first welcomed it in preference to the hired thugs of the Baldwin-Feltz Detective Agency, they soon learned to fear the militia more than the gunmen.[8] When the militia came into the strike district, they tried to compel the miners to submit to measurement by the Bertillion system.[9]

---

7   Havel is referring to James Pearce (1865–1950), who served as Colorado Secretary of State from 1909 to 1915. The quote appears in the *Biennial Report of the Bureau of Labor Statistics, Colorado, 1909–1910* (1911), pp. 27–28. The relevant section was actually authored by a state inspector named E.G. Coray.

8   A detective agency formed in 1890 by William Gibboney Baldwin as the Baldwin Detective Agency. Like the Pinkerton Agency, the Baldwin-Feltz Agency was commonly employed to infiltrate and break up labor strikes.

9   A system formerly used for identifying persons by means of a detailed record of body measurements, physical description, and

The miners rebelled at this, whereupon they were herded by batches of cavalry—the miners being on foot—and taken from Aguilar to Trinidad, a distance of twenty miles, without food or drink. One of the miners fell on the road, and after being struck by the soldiers was left to die.

The militia acted with total disregard for human rights. Women were assaulted at night, and even in broad daylight; houses were entered by the soldiery and pillaged; saloons were invaded and their proprietors robbed. Searches of miners' houses were made, ostensibly to discover arms, but actually for the purpose of robbery.

It would be beyond human power to endure such outrages. The miners, many of them veterans of the Balkan War, armed themselves and asserted their manhood.[10] A terrific struggle was the result, culminating in the attack by the gunmen and the militia upon Ludlow.

The tent colony of the strikers at Ludlow was attacked by the uniformed murderers on the night of the 20th of April. The thugs were provided with machine guns. After a bombardment they fiendishly saturated the tents with coal oil and applied the torch. Twenty-five persons, among them two women and eleven children, were burned to death. That the colony at Ludlow was deliberately attacked and destroyed is admitted by the coroner's jury:

"We, the jury, find that the deceased came to their deaths by asphyxiation or fire, or both, caused by the burning of the tents of the Ludlow tent colony, and that the fire on the tents was started by militiamen under Major Hamrock and Lieut. Linderfelt, or mine guards, or both, on the 20th day of April, 1914."

Linderfelt is the paid thug of the Baldwin-Feltz Detective Agency, and at the same time he is an officer in

---

photographs. The Bertillon system was superseded by the more accurate procedure of fingerprinting.

10 There were two conflicts in the Balkans near this time (in 1912 and 1913), both directed against the Ottoman Empire.

the militia. It is Linderfelt who in cold blood killed heroic Greek leader, Louis Tikas, after the latter was arrested and put in his charge.[11]

The terrible massacre dumbfounded everybody for a moment. But then the miners arose in rebellion. Blood for blood! Vengeance for Ludlow was the battle cry. Mine after mine was attacked and destroyed. The whole district was devastated. The hirelings of the exploiters paid heavily for their crimes. In a few days the miners were masters of the country. The victory was won.

And now we see history repeat itself. The doctrinaire in the White House, who dared not take a stand against the butchery of workingmen, sends federal troops to help crush the victorious miners. Like an obedient lackey the President carries out the orders of his masters.

Will the workers of America stand by quietly and allow the exploiters to force their brothers in Colorado into the old subjugation? If they do, they sign their doom

This is no time for wise and deliberate discussion. Now is the time for action. We have only one duty: to destroy the parasites, to exterminate the bloodsuckers and their hirelings.

---

11 On April 20, soldiers confronted Louis Tikas (1886–1914), a trade unionist and leader of the Greek miners, demanding that he hand over three individuals who were allegedly being detained in the camp against their will. Tikas responded by arranging a meeting with one of the militia commanders. While this was happening, Patrick Hamrock (1874–1939) and Karl Linderfelt (1876–1957), both officers in the Colorado National Guard, positioned machine guns above the tent colony of Ludlow. A short time later a gunfight broke out and the National Guard opened fire on the tent colony. Tikas was later apprehended and killed by soldiers.

THE NEW UNIONISM (1914)[1]

SYNDICALISM IS THE LATEST VICTIM OF JOURNALISTIC EN-
terprise. The book mart is being flooded with works dealing with the new phase of the labor movement. In innumerable articles, pamphlets and books we are supposed
to get the genesis, the true meaning, and the aim of the
new Unionism. What an army of interpreters, expositors,
and annotators! Like mushrooms after rain the journalistic sympathizers appeared on the scene after the recent
strikes in England and America. Syndicalism must indeed
be a healthy growth if it can withstand such a parasitical invasion.

The unhappy reader wading through this jungle of
printed leaves gathers, unfortunately, very little information. Most of the books consist merely of a mass of more
or less cleverly written-up misstatement and misinformation. Unable to comprehend a militant movement of
intelligent, conscious workers, these well-wishers describe
Syndicalism as the discovery of some great thinker or philosopher. Ignorant of the fact that the movement existed
in the brains and hearts of the proletarians ere Messrs.
Berth, Lagardelle, Leone *e tutti quanti* appeared on the
stage, these bourgeois scriveners attribute it to some
hero or other, and multiply their ignorance by quoting
one another.[2]

---

1   This essay originally appeared in *Mother Earth* 8, no. 7
    (September 1914).

2   Havel is referring, respectively, to the French syndicalists Edouard
    Berth (1875–1939) and Hubert Lagardelle (1874–1958) as well
    as the Italian economist Enrico Leone (1875–1940). Havel's
    point is that these men "and all the rest" (*e tutti quanti*) are es-
    sentially "Johnny-come-latelies" whose significance with regard to

Yet far more dangerous for the evolution of the Syndicalist movement are those writers who are well-informed on the subject, but who interpret it from a partisan, prejudiced standpoint. By ignoring certain facts, or if they cannot ignore them, by perverting or distorting them, they give a far worse survey of the movement than the ignorant penny-a-liner who does not know better. A past-master of this cheap art of misinformation is Mr. Andre Tridon, whose book, *The New Unionism*,[3] has just appeared.[4] Tridon can claim the distinction of having succeeded in producing the most dishonest book on Syndicalism which has so far appeared on the book market. In a polemic with Robert Allerton Parker in the *St. Louis Mirror* concerning the mental dishonesty of his work, Tridon informs us that he is an ex-Anarchist: he, too, has had the Anarchist measles, having graduated to Anarchism from Monarchism and Catholicism for purely sentimental reasons.[5] 'Tis too bad. He forgets to inform us what reasons led him into journalistic prostitution. No wonder he finds that Rousseau,

---

the development of syndicalism has been greatly exaggerated.

3   [Havel's note] *The New Unionism*. By Andre Tridon. B. M. Huebsch, Publisher. Price 25 cents net.

4   André Tridon (1877–1922) was a French-born anarcho-syndicalist, an active member of the New York anarchist milieu of the early twentieth century, and a regular at the New York Modern School. He was secretary of the Socialist and literary magazine *Masses* for a time and later became a psychoanalyst. Allan Antliff suggests in his book *Anarchist Modernism* (University of Chicago Press, 2007) that Havel and Tridon were friends and collaborators who saw eye to eye on political and artistic matters (pp. 102–105). Tridon's book, however, was rather critical of anarchism—hence this rather acerbic review.

5   Robert Allerton Parker (1888–1970) was an American journalist and critic who contributed to *Mother Earth* and helped Margaret Sanger edit various publications. Like Havel and Tridon, he was part of the New York radical milieu.

Proudhon, Tolstoy, and Stirner have no message for the practical man.[6] No, dear Andre, they have not.

To be sure, even by studying the Anarchist movement most diligently and by perusing the Anarchist literature minutely, one would search in vain for marks left through the activity of Mr. Tridon, but then such characters as Tridon are omnipotent; he may have influenced the Anarchist movement indirectly, by astral activity. As an exponent of the new Unionism he is in the company of ex-priests and ex-gold-mine-swindle-promoters who imagine they have discovered a new gold mine in Syndicalism.[7] Still, Tridon may dislike the Anarchists as much as he likes: that is his privilege; but he is mistaken if he thinks that he can treat them as a negligent quantity by fighting them with the methods of the ostrich: by ignoring, hiding, and minimizing their activity and their influence in the revolutionary labor movement. The trouble with Andre is that he is too well-informed. Were he less well-informed he would not destroy his arguments with his own statements. "To give credit to the Anarchists," declares Tridon, "for the development of Syndicalism reveals a deep ignorance of Syndicalism's status of the present day."[8] Really? Now let us see what

---

6   *The New Unionism*, p. 2.

7   The identity of the "ex-priest" is unclear. Although it is possible Havel is referring to Thomas Hagerty (born 1862, death unknown), a Roman Catholic priest and trade union activist who was credited with writing the preamble to the to the IWW Constitution, Hagerty had been inactive in the trade union movement for nearly ten years at the time this article was published. Presumably the "ex-gold-mine-swindle-promoter" is Henry Gaylord Wilshire (1861–1927), a former land developer who espoused revolutionary syndicalism in 1911. In 1910 Wilshire was accused of using his magazine to sell shares in a non-existent gold mine.

8   At the highest level of generality, syndicalism is a socialist economic system which advocates for the organization of industries

the same Tridon has to say on this subject on page 70 of his book:

> "To Fernand Pelloutier more than to any other leader is due the present revolutionary connotation of the word Syndicalism.[9] In the course of his short life (1867-1901), he showed himself an unremitting foe of parliamentary action. In 1897 he coined the word which now sums up the methods of New Unionism, 'Direct Action' ... all his life Pelloutier adhered to this militant policy. When Millerand came forward with a programme of reforms, Pelloutier attacked savagely what he called 'the half-baked projects of that self-styled socialist.' Although suffering from tuberculosis in an advanced stage, he did not hesitate in the last years of his life to court persecution. His book *La vie ouvriere en France* called upon his head governmental thunder and he died a pauper in 1901."[10]

---

into productive confederations or syndicates. It is to be distinguished as such from anarcho-syndicalism, a tactical orientation which seeks to realize the distinctive ends of anarchism, including the abolition of capitalism and the state, through militant forms of direct action within the trade union movement, most notably the general strike.

9 Fernand Pelloutier (1867–1901) was a French anarcho-syndicalist and leader of the *Fédération des Bourses du Travail* (Federation of Workers' Councils) from 1895 until his death. Pelloutier was extremely influential in the political and intellectual development of revolutionary syndicalism.

10 *La vie ouvrière en France* ("The Workers Life in France") was published by Schleicher Frères (Paris) in 1900.

On the next page Tridon writes: "Fernand Pelloutier did his best to gather the Anarchists into the syndicates," and on page 189, "at the very time (1903) Pelloutier's efforts were bearing fruit and the Anarchists elements introduced by Pelloutier were on the point of imposing their views and tactics upon the more conservative Federations of Unions." To the Anarchists must be given then some credit, *est-ce-pas*? Though Tridon succeeds in writing his confession in such a manner that the average reader may well remain in ignorance as to Pelloutier's Anarchist beliefs and activity.

And how does Tridon's denial of Anarchist influence on Syndicalism compare with the declaration of Georges Yvetot, then the Secretary of the section of Bourses du Travail at the Congress of the French Federation of Labor at Toulouse: "I am reproached with confusing Syndicalism with Anarchism. It is not my fault if Anarchism and Syndicalism have the same ends in view. The former pursues the integral emancipation of the individual; the latter the integral emancipation of the workingman. I find the whole of Syndicalism in Anarchism."[11] Furthermore: in describing the different shades of opinion in the Confederal Committee of the French Confederation, Tridon declares: "It is the Left which has steadily directed the destinies of the Confederation since the fusion of 1902."[12] The Left, which is composed of Anarchists and whose most prominent member is Yvetot!

---

11 Georges Yvetot (1868–1942) was a French trade unionist and anarcho-syndicalist who served as the Secretary of the *Bourses du Travail* from 1901 to 1918. The congress in question (the 25th National Cooperative Congress, the 11th Congress of the General Federation of Labor, and the 4th Congress of the Federation of Workers' Councils) took place in Toulouse from October 3 through October 10, 1910. The quotation appears in the on page 226 of the congress proceedings (*Compte Rendu des Travaux*), which were published by Imprimeie Ouvrière (Toulouse) in 1911.

12 *The New Unionism*, p. 73.

Tridon quotes Yvetot repeatedly, yet he never mentions the fact that Yvetot is an active Anarchist and that in addition to his work as editor of *La Voix du Peuple*, the official organ of the *Confederation*, he is a diligent contributor to various Anarchist publications.[13] The same contemptible ostrich policy Tridon follows in quoting Pouget, Pierrot, Faure, the Italian de Ambris, the German Friedeberg, the Hollander Cornelissen, and other Anarchists active in the Syndicalist movement.[14] "The various New Unionist groups keep in touch with one another through the publication of *Le Bulletin International du mouvement Syndicaliste*, edited, by Christiaan Cornelissen, a well-known sociologist," writes Tridon.[15] Quite true, but why hide the fact that Cornelissen is not only a well-known sociologist but an active Anarchist as well? *Le Pere Peinard* was according to Tridon a "revolutionary" organ, and its editor, Pouget, became after his days in exile a "convert to Syndicalism."[16] What ingenuity in keeping Anarchists in obscurity! Pouget "converted" to Syndicalism! Here indeed ignorance is bliss!

---

13 *La Voix du Peuple* ("The Voice of the People") was the official organ of the General Confederation of Labor, published from 1900 to 1946.

14 Havel is referring, respectively, to Marc Pierrot (1871–1950), a French anarchist and physician; Alceste De Ambris (1874–1934), an Italian syndicalist; Raphael Friedeberg (1863–1940), a German physician and socialist (later an anarchist) and Christiaan Cornelissen (1864–1942), a Dutch syndicalist writer and trade unionist.

15 *The New Unionism*, p. 182. *La Bulletin International du mouvement Syndicaliste* ("International Bulletin of the Syndicalist Movement") was a French-language syndicalist periodical published from 1907 to 1915.

16 *The New Unionism*, p. 85. *Le Pere Peinard* (meaning, roughly, "Cool Daddy") was a French anarchist periodical published from 1882 to 1902.

In his over-anxiety to annihilate Anarchism our good Andre makes one blunder after another. So when he states apodictically: "Kropotkin recently wrote a preface for Pouget and Pataud's book on Syndicalism. It does not imply that Syndicalism is being modified by Kropotkin; it means that after all these years Kropotkin is realizing the positive trend of the new movement."[17] Can anyone explain to us poor mortals what interest Kropotkin could have in "modifying Syndicalism"? Too bad Pouget and Pataud didn't ask Andre to write the preface to their work instead of Kropotkin.

The joke is on Tridon when he quotes Cornelissen's repudiation of the so-called intellectual interpreters of Syndicalism with approval. Cornelissen writes: "Instead of studying the French movement through its official organ *La Voix du Peuple*, or through pamphlets written by militant Syndicalists, the authors of articles on Syndicalism prefer to quote French and Italian writers who are outside the movement, and with whom the French unions have nothing to do."[18] Now these remarks of Cornelissen are directed precisely against such scriveners as Tridon, and especially they point at Berth, Lagardelle, Leone, and other writers of the Neo-Marxian school, the very same men Tridon accepts as his authorities. Indeed, the first chapter of his book commences with a lengthy quotation directed against Anarchism from Berth's book, *Le Nouveaux Aspects du Socialisme*.[19]

---

17 Tridon is referring to *Comment nous ferons la Révolution* ("How We Will Make the Revolution"), published by Tallandier (Paris) in 1909 and written by Emile Pouget and Emile Pataud. Emile Pataud (1860–1935) was a French syndicalist and revolutionary. Pataud earned the nickname "Prince of Darkness" for organizing several strikes among electrical workers in the first three decades of the twentieth century. (The strikes in question often involved forced power outages.)

18 *The New Unionism*, p. 186.

19 "New Aspects of Socialism," published by Rivière (Paris) in 1908.

He is quite enraptured with the silly harangue of that Neo-Marxian blatherskite.

As long as Tridon stands on the soil of France, Italy, or Spain he is familiar with the subject of his book notwithstanding his clumsy attempts to ignore the work of Anarchists. But once he leaves the Latin world he finds himself in a *terra incognita*. He makes pitiful attempts to describe the new Unionism in other countries. Speaking of Austria, he informs us that the "Austrian Syndicalists are absolutely independent in their action from the Anarchists and Socialist groups. The three groups refused to combine in organizing the anti-war manifestation which took place on November 10, 1912, in Vienna."[20] This will be "some news" to Comrade Grossmann, the editor of the Anarchist organ *Wohlstand fur Alle*, at the same time official organ of the syndicalist *Freie Gewerkschafts-Vereinigung*.[21] At the invitation of the French *Confederation* Comrade Grossmann goes nearly every year to France to explain to the German workers in Paris the purpose and tactics of Syndicalism, and he was the principle speaker on the occasion of which Tridon speaks. In truth Syndicalism and Anarchism mean the same to Austrian workers as far as they are educated.

As to Bohemia there is no revolutionary movement whatever which is not inspired by Anarchists. The organ of the miners, *Hornicke Listy*, is edited by Anarchists.[22] Our comrades in Holland too will be surprised to learn

---

20 *The New Unionism*, p. 174.

21 Rudolf Grossman (1882–1942), known as Pierre Ramus, was a German anarchist and pacifist. *Wohlstand fur Alle* ("Prosperity for All") was a German anarchist newspaper published from 1907 to 1914. As Havel notes, it was the official outlet of the *Freie Gewerkschafts-Vereinigung* ("Free Trade Union Association"), an anarcho-syndicalist organization which existed from 1911 to 1914.

22 *Hornické Listy* ("Miners' Journal") was a Czech-language radical newspaper, published from 1906 to c. 1912.

that "the Dutch Syndicalists are being attacked by both the Anarchists and the Socialists."[23] It depends on which Syndicalists Mr. Tridon means. In the Anarchist papers, *Vrye Socialist*, *Toekomst*, *Recht voor Allen*, *Arbeider*, *Vryheidsvann*, *Nar de Vryheid* and *De wapens neder*, he would look in vain for attacks on the real revolutionary Syndicalists.[24]

We learn from Tridon that Sabotage was applied by the Japanese workers in the course of several strikes which took place in 1912, but he fails to inform his readers of the work of Denjiro Kotoku, Suga Kano and their fellow-workers who died on the gallows because of their propaganda and for spreading the idea of Syndicalism and Direct Action.

The movement "in other countries" our author dismisses with a few lines, but his courage revives the very moment he enters the United States. But this excursion requires another chapter. Here Andre becomes rhapsodical—the prophet of the I. W. W. "The most radical Syndicalist body on earth," cries our modern Sir Galahad, "the American I. W. W. owes absolutely nothing to Anarchism."[25] No, it sprang pure from Nirvana. I wonder what the hundreds of Anarchists working loyally and energetically in the ranks of that organization think of Tridon's statement, born of ignorance and of hatred of the Anarchist movement in America? But there is a humorous

---

23   *The New Unionism*, p. 177.

24   Havel is referring, respectively, to *De Vrije Socialist* ("The Free Socialist"), published from 1898 to 1995; *Toekomst* ("The Future"), published from 1893 to 1923; *Recht voor Allen* ("Justice for All"), published from 1879 to 1900; *Arbeider* ("The Worker"), published from 1892 to 1940; *Vrijheidsvaan* ("The Banner of Freedom"), published from c. 1910 to c. 1914; *Naar de Vrijheid* ("To Freedom"), published from 1903 to 1922; and *De wapens neder* ("Down with Weapons"), published from 1903 to 1940.

25   This quote does not appear in the book; it is not clear where Havel is getting it from.

phase to the situation. No matter how hard Andre works, the members of the I. W. W. do not seem to appreciate his efforts. Last winter he offered his great knowledge of the labor question to the I. W. W. local in New York. But lo! who didn't care were the members of the organization. The nicely advertized lectures had to be cancelled. Does he expect they will read his book?

INTRODUCTION TO *THE SELECTED WORKS OF VOLTAIRINE DE CLEYRE* (1914)[1]

"NATURE HAS THE HABIT OF NOW AND THEN PRODUCING a type of human being far in advance of the times; an ideal for us to emulate; a being devoid of sham, uncompromising, and to whom the truth is sacred; a being whose selfishness is so large that it takes in the whole human race and treats self only as one of the great mass; a being keen to sense all forms of wrong, and powerful in denunciation of it; one who can reach into the future and draw it nearer. Such a being was Voltairine de Cleyre."[2]

What could be added to this splendid tribute by Jay Fox to the memory of Voltairine De Cleyre? These admirable words express the sentiments of all the friends and

---

1   *The Selected Works of Voltairine de Cleyre* was edited by Alexander Berkman and published by Mother Earth Publishing Association in 1914. For more on Voltairine's life, see Paul Avrich, *An American Anarchist: The Life of Voltairine de Cleyre* (Chico, CA: AK Press, 2018); Sharon Presley and Crispin Sartwell, eds., *Exquisite Rebel: The Essays of Voltairine de Cleyre* (Buffalo, NY: SUNY Press, 2005).

2   Jay Fox (1870–1961) was an American trade unionist and anarchist. In his tribute (*The Agitator*, 15 July 1912), Fox also writes: "She has left the stage, but her memory will linger long, like the odor of a fragrant rose crushed at full bloom; like the impression of a great thought flashed on the mind."

comrades of that remarkable woman whose whole life was dedicated to a dominant idea.

Like many other women in public life, Voltairine De Cleyre was a voluminous letter writer. Those letters addressed to her comrades, friends, and admirers would form her real biography; in them we trace her heroic struggles, her activity, her beliefs, her doubts, her mental changes—in short, her whole life, mirrored in a manner no biographer will ever be able to equal. To collect and publish this correspondence as a part of Voltairine De Cleyre's works is impossible; the task is too big for the present undertaking. But let us hope that we will find time and means to publish at least a part of this correspondence in the near future.

The average American still holds to the belief that Anarchism is a foreign poison imported into the States from decadent Europe by criminal paranoiacs. Hence the ridiculous attempt of our lawmakers to stamp out Anarchy, by passing a statute which forbids Anarchists from other lands to enter the country. Those wise Solons are ignorant of the fact that Anarchist theories and ideas were propounded in our Commonwealth ere Proudhon or Bakunin entered the arena of intellectual struggle and formulated their thesis of perfect freedom and economic independence in Anarchy. Neither are they acquainted with the writings of Lysander Spooner, Josiah Warren, Stephen Pearl Andrews, William B. Greene, or Benjamin Tucker, nor familiar with the propagandist work of Albert R. Parsons, Dyer D. Lum, C. L. James, Moses Harman, Ross Winn, and a host of other Anarchists who sprang from the native stock and soil. To call their attention to these facts is quite as futile as to point out that the tocsin of revolt resounds in the writings of Emerson, Thoreau, Hawthorne, Whitman, Garrison, Wendell Phillips, and other seers of America; just as futile as to prove to them that the pioneers in the movement for woman's emancipation in America were permeated with Anarchist thoughts and feelings. Hardened by a fierce struggle and strengthened by a vicious persecution, those brave champions of sex-freedom defied the respectable mob by proclaiming their independence from prevailing cant and hypocrisy. They inaugurated the tremendous sex revolt among the American women— a purely native movement which has yet to find its historian.[3]

Voltairine De Cleyre belongs to this gallant array of rebels who swore allegiance to the cause of universal liberty, thus forfeiting the respect of all "honorable citizens," and bringing upon their heads the persecution of the ruling class. In the real history of the struggle for human emancipation, her name will be found among the foremost of her time. Born shortly after the close of the Civil War, she witnessed during her life the most momentous transformation of the nation; she saw the change from an agricultural community into an industrial empire; the tremendous development of capital in this country, with the accompanying misery and degradation of labor. Her life path was sketched ere she reached the age of womanhood: she had to become a rebel! To stand outside of the struggle would have meant intellectual death. She chose the only way.

Voltairine De Cleyre was born on November 17, 1866, in the town of Leslie, Michigan. She died on June 6, 1912, in Chicago. She came from French-American stock, on her mother's side of Puritan descent. Her father, Auguste de Cleyre, was a native of western Flanders, but his family was of French origin.[4] He emigrated to America in

---

3   Of those note already cited earlier, Havel is referring, respectively, to William Batchelder Greene (1819–1878), an American individualist anarchist, abolitionist, and Unitarian minister; Charles L. James (1846–1911), an American anarchist writer and propagandist; and Ross Winn (1871–1912), an American anarchist writer and publisher.

4   De Cleyre's father was named Hector, not Auguste.

1854. Being a freethinker and a great admirer of Voltaire, he insisted on the birthday of the child that the new member of the family should be called Voltairine. Though born in Leslie, the earliest recollections of Voltairine were of the small town of St. John's, in Clinton County, her parents having removed to that place a year after her birth. Voltairine did not have a happy childhood; her earliest life was embittered by want of the common necessities, which her parents, hard as they tried, could not provide. A vein of sadness can be traced in her earliest poems—the songs of a child of talent and great fantasy. A deep sorrow fell into her heart at the age of four, when the teacher of the primary school refused to admit her because she was too young. But she soon succeeded in forcing her entrance into the temple of knowledge. An earnest student, she was graduated from the grammar school at the age of twelve.

Strength of mind does not seem to have been a characteristic of Auguste de Cleyre, for he recanted his libertarian ideas, returned to the fold of the church, and became obsessed with the idea that the highest vocation for a woman was the life of a nun. He determined to put the child into a convent. Thus began the great tragedy of Voltairine's *early life*. Her beloved mother, a member of the Presbyterian Church, opposed this idea with all her strength, but in vain: the will of the lord of the household prevailed, and the child was sent to the Convent of Our Lady of Lake Huron, at Sarnia, in the Province of Ontario, Canada. Here she experienced four years of terrible ordeal; only after much repression, insubordination, and atonement, she forced her way back into the living world. In the sketch, "The Making of an Anarchist", she tells us of the strain she underwent in that living tomb:

"How I pity myself now, when I remember it, poor lonesome little soul, battling solitary in the murk of religious superstition, unable to believe and yet in hourly fear of damnation, hot, savage, and eternal, if I do not instantly confess and profess! How well I recall the bitter energy with which I repelled my teacher's enjoinder, when I told her I did not wish to apologize for an adjudged fault as I could not see that I had been wrong and would not feel my words. 'It is not necessary', said she, 'that we should feel what we say, but it is always necessary that we obey our superiors.' 'I will not lie,' I answered hotly, and at the same time trembled lest my disobedience had finally consigned me to torment! I struggled my way out at last, and was a freethinker when I left the institution, three years later, though I had never seen a book or heard a word to help me in my loneliness. It had been like the Valley of the Shadow of Death, and there are white scars on my soul yet, where Ignorance and Superstition burnt me with their hell-fire in those stifling days. Am I blasphemous? It is their word, not mine. Beside that battle of my young days all others have been easy, for whatever was without, within my own Will was supreme. It has owed no allegiance, and never shall; it has moved steadily in one direction, the knowledge and assertion of its own liberty, with all the responsibility falling thereon."[5]

During her stay at the convent there was little communication between her and her parents. In a letter from Mrs. Eliza de Cleyre, the mother of Voltairine, we are informed that she decided to run away from the convent after she had been there a few weeks. She escaped before breakfast, and crossed the river to Port Huron; but, as she had no money, she started to walk home. After covering seventeen miles, she realized that she never could do it; so she turned around and walked back, and entering the house of an acquaintance in Port Huron asked for something to eat. They sent for her father, who afterwards took her back to the convent. What penance they inflicted she never told, but at sixteen her health was so bad that the convent authorities let her come home for a vacation, telling

---

5   The essay originally appeared in *The Independent* 55 (September 1903), pp. 2276–2280. The quote appears on p. 2277.

her, however, that she would find her every movement watched, and that everything she said would be reported to them. The result was that she started at every sound, her hands shaking and her face as pale as death. She was about five weeks from graduating at that time. When her vacation was over, she went back and finished her studies. And then she started for home again, but this time she had money enough for her fare, and she got home to stay, never to go back to the place that had been a prison to her. She had seen enough of the convent to decide for herself that she could not be a nun.

The child who had sung:

> "There's a love supreme in the Great Hereafter,
> The buds of Earth are bloom in Heaven,
> The smiles of the world are ripples of laughter
> When back to its Aidenn the soul is given,
> And the tears of the world, though long in flowing,
> Water the fields of the bye-and-bye;
> They fall as dews on the sweet grass growing,
> When the fountains of sorrow and grief run dry.
> Though clouds hang over the furrows now sowing
> There's a harvest sun-wreath in the After-sky.
> "No love is wasted, no heart beats vainly,
> There's a vast perfection beyond the grave;
> Up the bays of heaven the stars shine plainly—
> The stars lying dim on the brow of the wave.
> And the lights of our loves, though they flicker and wane, they
> Shall shine all undimmed in the ether nave.
> For the altars of God are lit with souls
> Fanned to flaming with love where the star-wind rolls"[6]

---

6   "The Christian's Faith," which de Cleyre wrote in 1887. It is reproduced on p. 18 of the *Selected Works*.

[She] returned from the convent a strong-minded free-thinker. She was received with open arms by her mother, almost as one returned from the grave. With the exception of the education derived from books, she knew no more than a child, having almost no knowledge of practical things.

Already in the convent she had succeeded in impressing her strong personality upon her surroundings. Her teachers could not break her; they were therefore forced to respect her. In a polemic with the editor of the Catholic *Buffalo Union and Times*, a few years ago, Voltairine wrote: "If you think that I, as your opponent, deserve the benefit of truth, but as a stranger you doubt my veracity, I respectfully request you to submit this letter to Sister Mary Medard, my former teacher, now Superioress at Windsor, or to my revered friend, Father Siegfried, Overbrook Seminary, Overbrook, Pa., who will tell you whether, in their opinion, my disposition to tell the truth may be trusted."[7]

Reaction from the repression and the cruel discipline of the Catholic Church helped to develop Voltairine's inherent tendency toward free-thought; the five-fold murder of the labor leaders in Chicago, in 1887, shocked her mind so deeply that from that moment dates her development toward Anarchism. When in 1886 the bomb fell on the Haymarket Square, and the Anarchists were arrested, Voltairine De Cleyre, who at that time was a free-thought lecturer, shouted: "They ought to be hanged!"[8] They were

---

7   The *Union and Times* was published in Buffalo, New York, from 1881 to 1939.

8   See "Introduction to *Anarchism and Other Essays*," "After Twenty-Five Years," and "The Lessons of Chicago" above. In her memorial oration "The Eleventh of November, 1887," Voltairine writes: "This is my confession: fifteen years ago last May when the echoes of the Haymarket bomb rolled through the little Michigan village where I then lived, I, like the rest of the credulous and brutal,

hanged, and now her body rests in Waldheim Cemetery, near the grave of those martyrs.[9] Speaking at a memorial meeting in honor of those comrades, in 1901, she said: "For that ignorant, outrageous, bloodthirsty sentence I shall never forgive myself, though I know the dead men would have forgiven me, though I know those who loved them forgive me. But my own voice, as it sounded that night, will sound so in my ears till I die—a bitter reproach and a shame. I have only one word of extenuation for myself and the millions of others who did as I did that night— ignorance."

She did not remain long in ignorance. In "The Making of an Anarchist" she describes why she became a convert to the idea and why she entered the movement. "Till then," she writes, "I believed in the essential justice of the American law and trial by jury. After that I never could. The infamy of that trial has passed into history, and the question it awakened as to the possibility of justice under law has passed into clamorous crying across the world."

At the age of nineteen Voltairine had consecrated herself to the service of humanity. In her poem, "The Burial of My Past Self," she thus bids farewell to her youthful life:

"And now. Humanity, I turn to you;
I consecrate my service to the world!
Perish the old love, welcome to the new—
Broad as the space-aisles where the stars are whirled!"

---

read one lying newspaper headline, 'Anarchists throw a bomb in a crowd in the Haymarket in Chicago,' and immediately cried out, 'They ought to be hung'" (*Selected Works*, p. 164).

9   Waldheim Cemetery is the former name of Forest Home Cemetery in Forest Park, Illinois. Several anarchist notables including Emma Goldman and Lucy Parsons are buried there near the Haymarket Martyrs Monument.

Yet the pure and simple free-thought agitation in its narrow circle could not suffice her. The spirit of rebellion, the spirit of Anarchy, took hold of her soul. The idea of universal rebellion saved her; otherwise she might have stagnated like so many of her contemporaries, suffocated in the narrow surroundings of their intellectual life. A lecture of Clarence Darrow, which she heard in 1887, led her to the study of Socialism, and then there was for her but one step to Anarchism. Dyer D. Lum, the fellow worker of the Chicago martyrs, had undoubtedly the greatest influence in shaping her development; he was her teacher, her confidant, and comrade; his death in 1893 was a terrible blow to Voltairine. [10]

Voltairine spent the greater part of her life in Philadelphia. Here, among congenial friends, and later among the Jewish emigrants, she did her best work. In 1897 she went on a lecture tour to England and Scotland, and in 1902, after an insane youth had tried to take her life, she went for a short trip to Norway to recuperate from her wounds. [11] Hers was a life of bitter economic struggle and an unceasing fight with physical weakness, partly resulting from this very economic struggle. One wonders how, under such circumstances, she could have produced such an amount of work. Her poems, sketches, propagandistic articles and essays may be found in the *Open Court, Twentieth Century, Magazine of Poetry, Truth, Lucifer, Boston Investigator, Rights of Labor, Truth Seeker, Liberty, Chicago Liberal, Free Society, Mother Earth,* and in *The Independent.* [12] She translated Jean Grave's "Moribund

---

10   Lum committed suicide April 6, 1893. Nearly thirty years her senior, he was a kind of father figure to de Cleyre and the two enjoyed an extremely close friendship for several years.

11   The attack occurred on December 19, 1902. The assailant was Herman Helcher, a former pupil of de Cleyre's who suffered from fever-induced mental illness.

12   In addition to the previously cited publications, Havel is referring,

Society and Anarchy" from the French, and left an unfinished translation of Louise Michel's work on the Paris Commune.[13] In *Mother Earth* appeared her translations from the Jewish of Libin and Peretz.[14] In collaboration with Dyer D. Lum she wrote a novel on social questions, which has unfortunately remained unfinished.

Voltairine De Cleyre's views on the sex-question, on agnosticism and free-thought, on individualism and communism, on non-resistance and direct action, underwent many changes. In the year 1902 she wrote: "The spread of Tolstoy's 'War and Peace'" and "The Slavery of Our Times," and the growth of the numerous Tolstoy clubs having for their purpose the dissemination of the

---

respectively, to *The Open Court*, a Chicago-based scholarly journal published between 1887 and 1936; *The Twentieth Century*, a social reform-oriented magazine published in Boston from 1909 to 1911; *Truth*, a Boston-based weekly (later monthly) magazine published between 1881 and 1905; *The Boston Investigator*, an American freethought newspaper published between 1831 and 1904; *The Rights of Labor*, a trade unionist newspaper published in Chicago between 1890 and 1893; *The Truth Seeker* is a freethought magazine published (mostly) in New York since 1873; *The Chicago Liberal* was a women's freethought newspaper published between 1881 and 1898; and *The Independent*

13 Jean Grave's *La société mourante et l'anarchie* was published by Tresse and Stock (Paris) in 1893. De Cleyre's translation was published as "Moribund Society and Anarchism" by A. Isaak (San Francisco) in 1899. Louis Michel's *La Commune, Histoire et souvenirs* was published by P.V. Stock (Paris) in 1898.

14 Havel is referring to Israel Hurewitz (1872–1955), known as Zalmon Libin, a Russian-Jewish playwright and short story writer; and Peretz Hirschbien (1880–1948), a Yiddish-language playwright, novelist and journalist. Voltairine's translation of Libin's "Little Albert's Punishment" and Hirschbein's "Hope and Fear" appeared in *Mother Earth* 2, no. 4 (June 1907) and 1, no. 2 (April 1906), respectively.

literature of non-resistance, is an evidence that many receive the idea that it is easier to conquer war with peace. I am one of these. I can see no end of retaliation, unless someone ceases to retaliate." She adds, however: "But let no one mistake this for servile submission or meek abnegation; my right shall be asserted no matter at what cost to me, and none shall trench upon it without my protest." But as she used to quote her comrade, Dyer D. Lum: "Events proved to be the true schoolmasters." The last years of her life were filled with the spirit of direct action, and especially with the social importance of the Mexican Revolution. The splendid propaganda work of Wm. C. Owen in behalf of this tremendous upheaval inspired her to great effort.[15] She, too, had found out by experience that only action counts, that only a direct participation in the struggle makes life worthwhile.

Voltairine De Cleyre was one of the most remarkable personalities of our time. She was a born iconoclast; her spirit was too free, her taste too refined, to accept any idea that has the slightest degree of limitation. A great sadness, a knowledge that there is a universal pain, filled her heart. Through her own suffering and through the suffering of others she reached the highest exaltation of mind; she was conscious of all the vanities of life. In the service of the poor and oppressed she found her life mission. In an exquisite tribute to her memory, Leonard D. Abbott calls Voltairine De Cleyre a priestess of Pity and of Vengeance, whose voice has a vibrant quality that is unique in literature.[16] We are convinced that her writings will live as long as humanity exists.

---

15   From 1911, William C. Owen edited the English language section of *Regeneración*, the newspaper of the paper of the *Partido Liberal Mexicano* ("Mexican Liberal Party"). After de Cleyre's death he went on to edit *Land and Liberty: An Anti Slavery Journal* from May 1914 to July 1915.

16   Leonard Abbott, "A Priestess of Pity and Vengeance," *Mother Earth* 7, no. 7 (September 1912).

BAKUNIN (1914)[1]

No man can emancipate himself, except
by emancipating with him all the men
around him. My liberty is the liberty of
everyone, for I am not truly free, free
not only in thought but in deed, except
when my liberty and my rights find their
confirmation, their sanction, in the liberty
and the rights of all men, my equals.[2]
—Bakunin

MIKHAIL ALEXANDROVITCH BAKUNIN WAS DESCENDED
from an old aristocratic family, which according to tradition had emigrated to Russia from Transylvania. He
was born on his father's estate at Pryamukhino, district
of Torshok, in the province of Tver, on the 8th of May
in the year 1814. Bakunin's father was a former diplomat
who at the age of forty-five married a young girl of the
poor but aristocratic family of Muraviev. One of her uncles was the infamous General Muraviev, who drowned
the Polish Revolution in blood and gained the name "the
hangman of Warsaw."

Bakunin was the oldest of eleven children. In a fragmen-
tary autobiography, "*La [L']Histoire de ma vie*," Bakunin

---

1   This pamphlet was published in celebration of the centenary of
    Bakunin's birth by "The Centenary Commemoration Committee"
    (New York). For an authoritative account of Bakunin's life, see Mark
    Leier, *Bakunin: The Creative Passion* (New York: St. Martin's, 2006).

2   From "Solidarity in Liberty: The Workers' Path to Freedom"
    (1867).

describes his father as a man of intellect and culture, a true philanthropist, possessed of a broad mind and generous sympathies.[3] He belonged to a revolutionary society which tried to undermine the autocratic despotism which oppressed Russia, but changed his mind after the unsuccessful conspiracy of the Decembrists in 1825. From then on he tried with all his might to make of his children true servants and good subjects of the Czar. Bakunin's father was very rich. He was the owner of a thousand "souls." Including women and children he was the unrestricted ruler of three thousand human beings.

Bakunin spent his early youth at Pryamukhino, where he received instruction in languages, history and arithmetic from his father and one of his uncles. Religious instruction was almost entirely overlooked, as the father was a freethinker. His moral education suffered through the knowledge that his entire material and intellectual existence was founded on injustice, on the system of serfdom. The youth possessed an instinctive feeling of hatred for all injustice: the sense for truth and right was strongly developed in him.

At the age of 14 Bakunin entered the Artillery School at St. Petersburg. He graduated in 1832 and was sent as an officer to a regiment in the province of Minsk. Here he spent two years, witnessing the oppression of the Polish inhabitants after the suppression of the insurrection of 1830. The vocation of a soldier soon became repulsive to him and he quit the army in 1834, in his twentieth year. The next six years he spent either in Moscow or St. Petersburg with friends or with his family at his father's estate. During these years he devoted himself passionately to the study of philosophy, and came in contact with the most progressive and sympathetic representatives of the universities of Moscow

---

3   *L'Histoire de ma vie*, "The History of My Life," was written in 1871. Evidently the first part was published by Marie Stromberg in *La Revue Socialiste* 28, no. 167 (November 28, 1898).

and St. Petersburg. This generation lived in a purely intellectual atmosphere and had little interest in the practical aspects of life. The German philosopher Hegel had nowhere such enthusiastic disciples as in Russia; his philosophic system played regular havoc among the Russian intellectuals of that period. Bakunin, who had already studied the French Encyclopedists and had in 1836 translated Fichte's *Einige Vorlesungen ueber die lestimmung des Gelehrten*, became in 1837 a thorough Hegelian.[4] He wrote a preface to a translation of Hegel's lectures, and published shortly after an article "On Philosophy."

In the fall of 1839 Bakunin and his friends Stankevitch and Bjelinski became acquainted with Alexander Herzen and his followers, who had returned from their exile in the provinces to Moscow.[5] Fierce discussions were the result. The Moscow Hegelians represented the most reactionary standpoint, while the circle of Herzen propagated the ideas of Western republicanism and French socialism. In 1840 Bakunin went to Berlin and entered the University. Soon he developed from a conservative to a revolutionary Hegelian. Ludwig Feuerbach, the great critic of Christianity, was the cause of this transformation. In a

---

4   *Einige Vorlesungen ueber die lestimmung des Gelehrten* ("Some Lectures Concerning the Scholar's Vocation") was published in 1794.

5   Havel is referring, respectively, to Nikolai Stankevich (1813–1840), a Russian philosopher and poet; Vissarion Belinsky (1811–1848), a Russian literary critic; and Alexander Herzen (1812–1870), a Russian writer and thinker known as the "father of Russian socialism." Herzen was an important influence on the young Bakunin and, despite their myriad political disagreements—particularly as concerns tactics—the two remained lifelong friends. Stankevich headed a Moscow intellectual circle which Bakunin joined in 1836. Belinsky, another member of this circle, would go on to become one of Russia's most important literary critics.

pamphlet entitled "Schelling and the Book of Revelations" Bakunin for the first time shows his revolutionary view of life. From 1840 till 1843 Bakunin spent his time in Germany, first in Berlin, where for a time he lived with Turgenjev, and later in Dresden. He was in close contact with the most progressive Germans; with Arnold Ruge and his friends; with Adolph Reichel, who proved to be a true friend through his whole life; with Georg Herwegh, and other free spirits of that time.[6]

Bakunin's next literary work, an essay called "The Reaction in Germany; a fragment by a Frenchman," published in Ruge's *Deutsche Jahrbuecher* under the pseudonym Jules Elysard, was an attack upon all compromise in the revolutionary ranks.[7] This work, known principally because of the last sentence, "The zeal for destruction is at the same time a producing zeal," called the attention of the police to Bakunin's activity. The result was that he no longer felt secure in Saxony. He left Leipzig with Herwegh in January, 1843, and they travelled to Zurich by way of Strassburg. In Zurich Bakunin became acquainted with the German radicals Julius Froebel, August Follen, and their friends; later he came to know the Communist Wilhelm Weitling and his followers.[8] He published sev-

---

6   Havel is referring, respectively, to Arnold Ruge (1802–1880), a philosopher and political theorist; Adolf Reichel (1820–1896), a composer; and Georg Friedrich Herwegh (1817–1875), a poet—all of whom Bakunin met and befriended upon moving to Dresden in 1842. Ruge, like Marx, was a Young Hegelian and an important figure in the early German Left. Bakunin collaborated with Ruge on *Die Hallische Jarbücher* ("The Halle Yearbook"), a radical newspaper published between 1838 and 1843.

7   "*Die Reaction in Deutschland, ein Fragment von einem Franzosen*" was actually published in *Die Hallische Jarbücher* 17 (October 1942).

8   Havel is referring, respectively, to Julius Fröbel (1805–1893), a journalist, diplomat, and author; August Ludwig Follen

eral articles on Communism in Froebel's *Schweizerischer Republikaner*. Weitling was presently arrested and among his papers the police found Bakunin's name. The Russian ambassador asked for information concerning him, and Bakunin was obliged to leave Zurich as quickly as possible. He went to Geneva and later to Berne.

Here in February, 1844, the Russian ambassador informed him that his government insisted upon his immediate return to Russia. Bakunin decided otherwise; he went to Brussels, where he met Lelewel, the Polish historian and revolutionist, and many other Polish and Russian exiles.[9] From Brussels he went to Paris, where he met and became friendly with the Anarchist philosopher Pierre Joseph Proudhon, the novelist George Sand, and many prominent Frenchmen. Herzen, Reichel, Bjelinski, and the naturalist Karl Vogt, all personal friends of Bakunin, lived at this time in France.[10] In December, 1844, Bakunin got information from Russia that on account of his revolutionary activity and his refusal to return to Russia he had been sentenced to exile in Siberia for life and that his entire fortune had been confiscated by the government of the Czar.

(1794–1855), a poet; and Wilhelm Weitling (1808–1871), a communist writer and activist. Fröbel, a radical democrat, edited for a time the *Schweizerischer Republikaner* ("The Swiss Republican"), a Swiss radical newspaper published from 1830 and 1846, and again from 1848 to 1851. Bakunin was probably introduced to communist theory by Weitling.

9   Joachim Lelewel (1786–1861) was a Polish historian and politician. Lelewel co-founded and served as vice the *Demokratische Gesellschaft zur Einigung und Verbrüderung aller Völker* (Democratic Society for Unity and Brotherhood of All Peoples) with Marx and Engels in 1847.

10 Karl Christoph Vogt (1817–1895) was a German scientist and early supporter of evolutionary theory. He served as a left-wing delegate to the Frankfurt Parliament.

In March, 1846, Bakunin wrote in *The Constitutional* on the Russian horror in Poland; in November, 1847, he spoke on the same theme in a Polish meeting. The result was that at the request of the Russian ambassador he was expelled by the French government from French territory. He went to Brussels, but only a short time. In Paris the Revolution broke out, and soon the whole of Europe was aflame. The long awaited Revolution had arrived! Bakunin saw clearly that the success of the Revolution of 1848 could only be assured if the democratic parties of all the countries of Europe should unite. This the Reaction tried by all the means in its power to prevent. Bakunin took upon himself the mission of agitation among the Slavs; no man could have been better fitted for the work than he. He planned to join the Polish revolutionists with the intention of spreading the movement to Russia. From Paris he journeyed to Cologne, Leipzig and Breslau, and in each city he met the revolutionary leaders and participated in all important discussions. From Breslau he went to the Slavic Congress at Prague, hoping to be able to convert the delegates to the Revolutionary cause. While Bakunin was in Prague the Revolution broke out in that city. He was in the thick of the fight; and it was only after the Revolution had been suppressed that he left for Breslau.

Thence he went to Berlin, where he became acquainted with Max Stirner, the author of *The Ego and His Own*. In October he was expelled from Prussia; three days later from Saxony. He found a place of comparative security in the small liberal state of Anhalt. In Koethen and Dessau he revealed a feverish activity, mostly of conspirative character. He was preparing for a general uprising in the spring of 1849. In the eyes of the reactionary powers he became the most feared and most hated personality in the ranks of the Revolutionists.

From January till March Bakunin lived in secret in Leipzig, whence he conspired with Bohemian revolutionists. In May the Revolution broke out in Dresden.

Bakunin was one of the leaders, fighting on the barricades, in close contact with the provisory government. Active day and night, he became terror incarnate in the eyes of the Saxon philistines. After the suppression of the Revolution he marched with Richard Wagner and other rebels to Freiberg, where the last attempt at an invasion of Bohemia was made. Then Bakunin and some friends marched to Chemnitz, where they hoped to find refuge. They were received hospitably, but in the night the good citizens attacked Bakunin and his followers in bed, arrested them and turned them over to the Prussian soldiers in Altenburg. Here begins Bakunin's prison life.

Bakunin and his comrades Heubner and Roeckel were brought in irons to the fortress of Konigstein.[11] Heubner and Roeckel were sentenced to death, but the sentence was later commuted to a life term in the penitentiary. Bakunin was kept in the fortress until June, 1850; on the 13th of June he was extradited to Austria. He was first kept in Prague, and later transferred to the horrible prison in Olmutz, where he was inhumanly treated. On the 15th of May, 1851, he was sentenced to death, but the sentence was changed to life imprisonment. Shortly after Bakunin was extradited to Russia; a welcome change, as nowhere had he been so maltreated as in the Austrian prisons.

In St. Petersburg he was first incarcerated in the fortress of Peter and Paul; at the beginning of the Crimean War he was transferred to the fortress of Schlusselburg. He suffered from scurvy and lost his teeth. Deep melancholy

---

11   Havel is referring to Otto Leonhard Heubner (1812–1893), a German lawyer, politician and poet; and Carl August Röckel (1814–1876), a German composer and conductor. Bakunin, Heubner, and Röckel were arrested in Chemnitz on May 9, 1849. Heuber and Röckel were convicted of high treason in January 1850 and sentenced to death. The sentence was commuted to life imprisonment in May 1850 and the two men were eventually released in 1859 and 1862, respectively.

took hold of him, and he would have ended his life by suicide if his family had not succeeded, in March, 1857, in having his sentence changed to exile in Siberia. In Tomsk in Western Siberia and later in the eastern part of the country he enjoyed comparative freedom, although he was constantly under police surveillance; he came in close contact with many exiles, and lost no opportunity for the propaganda of revolutionary ideas. He even gained a great deal of influence over his relative Muraviev-Amurski, who was then acting as Governor of Eastern Siberia.[12] Bakunin tried to convert him to the idea of a United States of Siberia.

Muraviev-Amurski tried to get an amnesty for Bakunin, but did not succeed; later he was recalled to European Russia, and Bakunin made preparations for escape. He succeeded in outwitting the authorities and left Irkutsk on the 5th of June 1861. He traveled down the Amur to Nikolajevsk, and from there to Japan. On the 17th of September he landed in San Francisco, having sailed from Yokohama. The news of the escape and safe landing of the great revolutionist caused an intense international sensation. In San Francisco and later in New York Bakunin found many old friends and former co-workers. But he did not stay long in the United States. On the 15th of November he embarked for Liverpool, and on the 27th of September he was received with open arms by his old friends Herzen and Ogarjev in London.[13]

---

12 Nikolay Muravyov-Amursky (1809–1881) was a Russian states-man and diplomat. Kropotkin praises Muravyov for his enlight-ened approach to governance in Siberia—a possible, even likely, consequence of Bakunin's influence.

13 Nikolaï Platonovitch Ogarev (1813–1877) was a Russian socialist poet and journalist. Ogarev was an early associate of Herzen's, with whom he founded an intellectual circle (the so-called "Herzen-Ogarev Circle") in Moscow in the 1830s. He and Bakunin collaborated on a wide array of revolutionary activities throughout the 1860s.

During his exile in Tomsk (in 1858) Bakunin had married the daughter of a Polish revolutionist, but it was not until two years after his arrival in London that he was able to rejoin his wife at Stockholm. After his escape from Siberia Bakunin threw himself with his old energy into the revolutionary propaganda. He had the confidence of the revolutionary elements of all countries. At this time he still hoped for a general European uprising; Garibaldi's expedition to Sicily and Naples produced great enthusiasm, and the exiles in London, among them the Frenchmen Louis Blanc and Talandier, the Italians Mazzini and Saffi, the Russians Herzen and Ogarjev, the radical Englishmen Linton and Holyoake, and especially the Polish leaders had great hopes for an international revolt.[14] Bakunin attempted to establish a closer connection between the Russian and the Polish revolutionists.

He issued several appeals, among them "To the Russian, Polish and all Slavic friends" and "The People's Cause: Romanov, Pugatchev or Pestel," urging all rebels to a concerted action; but unfortunately his efforts did not meet with success.[15] The aristocratic element in the Polish movement made a friendly cooperation with the Russian revolutionist impossible. When the Polish Revolution of 1863 broke out Bakunin himself went to Helsingfors with a Polish expedition on the steamer *Ward Jackson*, and

---

14 In addition to previously cited individuals, Havel is referring, respectively, to Giuseppe Garibaldi (1807–1882), an Italian general and politician and a leading figure in the Italian *Risorgimento*; Louis Blanc (1811–1882), a French socialist politician and historian; Alfred Talandier (1822–1890), a French politician; Aurelio Saffi (1819–1890), an Italian politician active during the period of Italian unification; and William James Linton (1812–1897), an English-born American artist, author, and political reformer.

15 Both appeals were issued in 1862. The former was published in a supplement to *Kolokol* 122/12 (February), the latter as a pamphlet by Trübner (London).

thence to Sweden, where he tried to influence the Swedish radicals to an action against Russia.[16]

The breakdown of the Polish Revolution showed that the era of national uprisings was over. A new epoch had begun. The movement of the proletariat now became the dominant factor. Bakunin, who was the true incarnation of the revolutionary spirit, felt this; from now on he entered the international workingmen's movement, to display here the same indomitable energy he had used in the national uprisings before the prison doors had closed upon him. His ideas were now clarified; he had developed to a true conception of the philosophy of Anarchism. All former inconsistencies disappeared; destruction of the State, of every authority based upon force, of every superstition, even if it should mask itself under the name of Socialism, now became his goal. The most interesting and significant part of his life had begun.

After his return from London Bakunin settled down in Italy. His revolutionary efforts were now directed toward organizing a secret society of the most intelligent, honest,

---

16 Bakunin's plan to participate in the Polish insurrection failed. He ended up in Stockholm, where he stayed briefly before returning to London. In an August 1863 letter sent to Herzen and Ogarev, he writes: "More than once, I have tried to return to Poland. I had no luck. Currently, the feelings in Poland towards us are altogether different, such that in wishing them success, we Russians have the duty to abstain from all direct participation in their affairs, which have become very complicated because of the interests of Western Europe, always hostile to both the imperialist system and even more so to the Russian people. This is why I stayed in Sweden and I devoted myself to finding friends sympathetic to our Russian cause, who are ready to struggle with us. My efforts have been rewarded with success. From now on, Stockholm and all of Sweden will be a secure refuge for Russian revolutionary action and immigration. The Russian publicity and propaganda will find here solid footing, supporters and a wealth of resources."

and energetic men from all libertarian movements for the purpose of spreading atheistic-anarchistic ideas and of influencing the next uprisings in a social revolutionary direction. This society, whose members were mainly his personal friends and co-workers, was called the "*Fraternite Internationale*."[17] It was the real basis of the libertarian International in Italy, Spain, Southern France, and the Latin part of Switzerland. The International Workingmen's Association was founded in September, 1864, in London. Bakunin had in the beginning no direct connection with that organization. He and his friends worked in their own way among the revolutionary elements of all countries. They participated in the Peace Congress held at Geneva in September, 1867.[18] Bakunin and his intimate comrades Joukovski, Mroczkovski, Naguet, and others made great efforts to win the Congress to their side.[19] Bakunin was

---

17 *Fraternite Internationale* ("International Brotherhood") was a se-
    cret revolutionary organization which Bakunin founded in 1866
    and dissolved three years later. Its objective, according to a gran-
    diose 1869 manifesto, was "a revolution that shall be at the same
    time universal, social, philosophical, and economic, so that no
    stone may remain unturned, in all of Europe first, and then in
    the rest of the world, to change the present order of things found-
    ed on property, on exploitation, domination, and the principle
    of authority, be it religious, metaphysical, and doctrinaire in the
    bourgeois manner or even revolutionary in the Jacobin manner."
    Evidently the Brotherhood never amounted to more than an in-
    formal group of some of Bakunin's followers.

18 Havel is referring to the Inaugural Congress of the League of
    Peace and Freedom, which was held in September 1867. His
    famous essay, "Federalism, Socialism, and Anti-Theologism," is
    based on a speech he gave at this congress.

19 Havel is referring, respectively, to Nikolai Ivanovich Zhukovsky
    (1833–1895) and Félix Walery Mroczkovski (1867–1937), both
    political revolutionaries and followers of Bakunin. "Naguet" is
    Alfred Naquet, previously cited.

elected a member of the Central Committee at Berne. The majority of the League, however, consisted of bourgeois republicans who had no sympathy with the workingmen's movement.

The next Congress voted down the proposal of Bakunin to recognize the social question as the supreme question; Bakunin, Élisée Reclus, Aristide Rey, Joukovski, Mroczkovski, Fanelli, and others (18 members in all) left the organization and founded the "*Alliance internationale de la democratic socialiste*."[20] Bakunin proposed that they should join the International Workingmen's Association, and he and his friends became members of the Jura Section of the International. The General Council of the International, which was under the influence of Karl Marx, refused membership to the "Alliance," and the latter organization dissolved. But Marx and his faction accused Bakunin and his friends of keeping a secret organization among themselves to work against the General Council.

It would take volumes to describe the great historic struggle between Marx and Bakunin in the International. There was concerned not only personal antagonism, but at the same time a struggle between two diametrically opposite conceptions—that of the authoritarian Socialism of Marx, and that of the libertarian Anarchistic Socialism of Bakunin. The Jura Federation was the stronghold of those in the International whose tendency was against the state and toward direct economic revolutionary action. Karl Marx and Frederick Engels, the leading spirits of the

---

20 In addition to previously cited individuals, Havel is referring to Aristide Rey (1834–1901) and Giuseppe Fanelli, both political revolutionaries and followers of Bakunin. The second congress took place in Bern in 1868. Bakunin and 79 others founded the *Alliance internationale de la democratic socialiste*, a revolutionary socialist organization, on October 28, 1868. As Havel notes, it dissolved shortly thereafter as members joined various national sections of the International Workingmen's Association.

General Council in London, were working to divert the International from the direct economic struggle and make of it a parliamentary fighting machine. Bakunin opposed this movement with all his power. He declared that every political movement which has not for its immediate and direct object the final and complete economic emancipation of the workers, which has not inscribed upon its banner quite definitely and clearly, the principle of "economic equality," that is, the integral restitution of capital to labor, or else social liquidation—every such movement is a bourgeois one, and as such must be excluded from the International.

> "Without mercy the policy of the democratic bourgeois, or bourgeois-Socialists, must be excluded, which, when these declare that political freedom is a necessary condition of economic emancipation, can only mean this: political reforms, or political revolutions must precede economic reforms or economic revolutions; the workers must therefore join hands with the more or less Radical bourgeois, in order to carry out the former together with them, then, being free, to turn the latter into a reality against them. We protest loudly against this unfortunate theory, which, so far as the workers are concerned, can only result in their again letting themselves be used as tools against themselves, and handing them over once more to bourgeois exploitation."[21]

Bakunin, the fearless fighter for the social and economic emancipation of the working class, presents a

---

21 "The Politics of the International," part 4, *L'Égalité*, August 28, 1869.

direct antithesis to the social democratic spirit and petty bourgeois cowardice of political life. In Karl Marx he found a mean antagonist. Even in the midst of the revolutionary struggles of 1848, Marx published in his *New Rhenish Gazette* articles accusing Bakunin of being a secret agent of Czar Nicholas and the Panslavists.[22] Marx and his friends were at that time forced to stammer their apologies. Whilst Bakunin suffered imprisonment at Olmutz and in other Austrian jails, Herzen, the great Russian political writer, and Mazzini, forced Marx to take back his calumnies. But Marx was not the man to forgive them this humiliation.

Many years later, after Bakunin had suffered imprisonment in the subterranean cells of the Schlusselberg and exile to Siberia, Marx and his satellites started the despicable game anew. Anonymous denunciations appeared in Social Democratic papers, under the editorship of Liebknecht, Hess, and others.[23] But at the congress of the International at Basle in 1869 the slanderers were forced to compromise themselves and to declare the entire baselessness of their charge. No wonder Marx flew into a rage, and resolved to kill Bakunin morally.

At the Hague Congress of the International, in 1872, Marx succeeded, with the aid of a fictitious majority, in having the Jura Federation and its leading spirits, Bakunin and James Guillaume,[24] excluded from the International,

---

22 The *New Rhenish Gazette* (*Neue Rheinische Zeitung*) was revolutionary newspaper published by Karl Marx from 1848 to 1849. The accusation in question was published on 6 July 1848.

23 Havel is referring to Karl Liebknecht (1871–1919), a German socialist who co-founded the Spartacist League and the Communist Party of Germany with Rosa Luxemburg; and Moses Hess (1812–1875), a Jewish socialist philosopher and a founder of labor Zionism.

24 James Guillaume (1844–1916) was an English-born anarchist and a leading member of the Jura Federation. Along with Bakunin, he

whereupon the Jura, the Spanish, the Italian, and the East Belgian (Vesdre) Federations broke entirely with the General Council, which was transferred next year to New York, where it died; while the Federations just mentioned, concluding a federative alliance among themselves, and abolishing all central authority, continued the work of the International Workingmen's Association on federalist principles, and up to 1878 held regular yearly congresses, until this became impossible, owing to Government prosecutions.

In the history of the revolutionary movement there is no personality who has been so much slandered and maligned as was Bakunin by his antagonists. His enemies stooped to the lowest depths to besmirch the character of the man who represented the true revolutionary spirit of his time. In his essay on Bakunin's influence Peter Kropotkin says truly: "Those who gathered around him were men who stood on a high moral plane. I never knew him personally, but I made the acquaintance of most of those who worked with him in the International, and were pursued with the most bitter hatred of Karl Marx and Friedrich Engels. And in the face of those who hated and slandered them, I assert that every one of Bakunin's comrades represented a moral personality of the highest value. I am convinced that history will confirm my assertion. Posterity will no doubt recognize that his personal enemies, though gifted with intelligence, entertained a less moral outlook on life than those who called themselves Bakunin's friends."[25]

After October, 1868, Bakunin lived in Geneva, later in Locarno. He edited the "*Egalite*," the organ of the Jura Federation, and busied himself with general propaganda in the Federation. He took a prominent part in the

---

played a leading role in founding the Anarchist International of St. Imier in 1872.

25 "Bakunin," *Freedom* (June/July 1905), pp. 18–19.

Congress of the International held at Basle in September, 1869. He kept up a correspondence with comrades in Russia, Italy, Spain, and other countries.

The war between Germany and France called Bakunin again to action. He saw clearly the terrible result the triumph of German militarism would have on the revolutionary movement. Unlike many others, who spent their time preparing peace manifestos, he immediately began to prepare for insurrections. He himself went to Lyons where he made ready for an uprising. The city was taken by the revolutionists on September 28th, 1870, but as there was a lack of solidarity and logical co-operation the attempt to proclaim a Commune failed. Bakunin was for a short time in danger; he was incarcerated and brutally mistreated. Comrades succeeded in freeing him from prison, but he had to leave the city the next day. He went to Marseilles, then to Genoa, and then back to Locarno. When the Parisians proclaimed the Commune Bakunin was on his way to Florence. The defeat of the Commune and the slaughter of 35,000 workers threw Bakunin into a mood of deepest pessimism. He retired from public action for a short time to make a resume of his ideas. The result was two brilliant works: "God and the State" and "The Knouto-German Empire."[26]

Bakunin's activities during the years 1871-72-73 were concentrated upon Russia, Italy, and Spain. In 1871 commenced his great polemic with Mazzini. As a result we have his forceful "*Risposta*" to Mazzini; also the "*Risposta All Unita Italiana*" and the pamphlet "*La Theologie politique de Mazzini, et l'Internationale*."[27] Mazzini died in

---

26 "God and the State" is actually part of "The Knouto-German Empire," published in 1870–1871.

27 Havel is referring, respectively to *Risposta d'un Internazionale a Giuseppe Mazzini* ("Response of an Internationalist to Giuseppe Mazzini"), published in *Il Gazzettino Rosa* on August 16, 1871; *Risposta All Unita Italiana* ("Response to a Unified Italy"),

1872, but his followers continued the discussion with bitter animosity. Bakunin found staunch friends and comrades in Cafiero, Malatesta, and other Italians.[28] In Spain he was in correspondence with Lorenzo, Pellicer, Morago, Vinas, and others; a Slavic section of the International was founded in Zurich.[29] Karl Marx and his faction had succeeded in excluding Bakunin and his followers from the International, but they did not succeed in capturing the spirit of the organization. The Italian, Spanish, French, and the Jura Sections met at St. Imier in the Jura on the 15th and 16th of September, 1872, and reorganized the International on a federalistic basis with a collectivist-anarchist program. In April, 1873, appeared the "*Memoire de la Federation Jurassienne*" in which Bakunin impartially gives the history of the International, and of the split in the organization.[30] The Marxians also published a pam-

---

published in *Il Gazzettino Rosa* on October 10–12, 1871; and *La Theologie politique de Mazzini, et l'Internationale* ("The Political Theology of Mazzini and the International") published by James Guillaume (Neuchâtel) in 1871. In these writings, Bakunin accuses Mazzini of being a political reactionary and an authoritarian.

28 Carlo Cafiero (1846–1892) was an Italian anarchist. Cafiero was a close friend and associate of Bakunin's (among other things, he purchased a house for Bakunin in 1873) and one of the chief proponents of anarcho-communism during the First International.

29 Havel is referring, respectively, to the Catalan anarchist Rafael Farga i Pellicer (1844–1890), a printer who was responsible for publishing most of the anarchist propaganda in Spain during the First International period; and the Spanish anarchists Tomás González Morago (died 1885) and José García Viñas (1848–1931), both of whom played a role in founding the Spanish section of the IWA. Both Morago and Viñas were collectivists.

30 *Mémoire présenté par la Fédération Jurassienne* ("Memoir of the Jura Federation") was published by Comité Fédéral Jurassien (Sonvillier) in 1873. Although the book describes Bakunin's ideas and activities, he was not the author.

phlet full of lies and attacks upon Bakunin. It appeared in July, 1873, under the title "*L'Alliance de la democratie socialiste et l'association international des travailleurs.*"[31] Bakunin answered in a letter published in the *Journal de Geneve* on September 25th, 1873.

After the reorganization of the libertarian International Bakunin announced in the *Bulletin of the Jura Federation* (October 12, 1873) his resignation from the International and his retirement from political to private life. This announcement was made for the special purpose of hood-winking the authorities.[32] A revolutionary movement of great strength had developed in Spain, and the Spanish members of the International had invited Bakunin to that country. Unfortunately, material circumstances and the arrest of certain comrades made the journey impossible. The uprisings were crushed, and in 1874 the International was proscribed in Spain, although it continued to exist in secret organizations for seven years.

From "*Baronata,*" the estate on the Lake of Maggiore which Cafiero had purchased as a refuge for revolution-ists, Bakunin and Cafiero, together with other members of the International, particularly with A. Costa, orga-nized an insurrection in Italy.[33] Bakunin left Switzerland in July, 1874 and travelled by way of Brescia, Bergamo, and Verona to Bologna, where he met Costa and other conspirators. Unfortunately Costa was arrested on the

---

31 *L'Alliance de la démocratie socialiste et l'association internation-al des travailleurs* ("The Alliance for Social Democracy and the International Workingmen's Association") was published anony-mously by Darson (London) in 1873. It has been variously attribut-ed to Marx, Marx and Engels, and Marx, Engels, and Lafargue.

32 The source of this claim is unclear. In 1873 Bakunin was in ex-tremely poor health; by all reasonable appearances his intention to retire was completely sincere.

33 Andrea Costa (1851–1910) was an Italian socialist. He renounced anarchism in 1879.

5th of August, and the uprisings in Bologna and other Italian cities ended in failure.[34] Bakunin left the country dressed in the garb of a priest, and returned to Locarno, disappointed, in very poor health, and in a bad pecuniary situation. He now retired entirely from the revolutionary movement, and lived with his family in Locarno until his death on the 1st of July, 1876, at a private hospital at Berne. His old friends Professor Adolph Vogt and the Reichel family were near him when he ended his phenomenal journey on this planet.[35]

Quoting the great French revolutionist, Auguste Blanqui, Kropotkin says that it is easier to measure accurately the influence of events by their indirect consequences rather than their direct results, for the former are always more important than the latter. We must likewise estimate Bakunin's influence, not so much by what he personally attained, but by the influence he exerted upon the thoughts and actions of his immediate disciples. For his literary legacy is small. "Communism and the State," "The Historical Development of the International Worker's Association," "God and the State"—these are the three books he wrote.[36] These originated in the same

---

34 The insurrections were supposed to take place in cities throughout Italy on August 7–8, 1874. Only a small handful of revolutionaries turned out, and those who did not manage to escape (Bakunin fled in disguise) were arrested.

35 Adolf Vogt (1823–1907), the son of Karl Vogt (previously cited), was a professor of medicine at the University of Bern and Bakunin's personal physician. Adolf Reichel (1816–1896) was a musician and composer whom Bakunin had known since the 1840s.

36 Presumably Havel is referring to *Gosudarstvennost i Anarkhiya* ("Statism and Anarchy"), published by Ross (Zurich) in 1874; *Istoricheskoye Razvitiye Internatsionala* ("The Historical Development of the International"), published by Ross (Zurich) in 1873; and *Dieu l'État* ("God and the State"), written in 1871,

way as his other pamphlets, which were written in order to answer questions of the day, or addressed as letters to friends, but reached the length of pamphlets owing to their author's discursive style of writing. In this way arose "The Knouto-German Empire," "Report of a Frenchman on the Present Crisis," "The Political Theology of Mazzini and the International," "The Bears of Berne," and other works.[37]

As a rule, Bakunin sat down to write a letter dealing with some question of the moment. But the letter quickly grew to the size of a pamphlet, and the pamphlet to that of a book. For the author wrote so fluently, had so thorough a conception of the philosophy of history, such a vast store of knowledge relating to the events of the time, that the pages soon filled themselves. If we only consider what he and his friends—Herzen, Ogarjev, Mazzini, and Ledru-Rollin[38] amongst others, the best men of action in that revolutionary period of the forties—thought about the questions of the day; what they felt during the hopeful years which preceded the red year, 1871–2, and the despair which followed it: if we call this to mind we will understand readily how the thoughts, conceptions, facts and arguments borrowed from real life must have invaded Bakunin's spirit. We learn to understand also how his

---

discovered posthumously by Cafiero and Reclus, and published by Imprimerie Jurassiene (Geneva) in 1882. "God and the State" was originally intended to be the second part of a larger work entitled *L'Empire knouto-germanique et la Révolution Sociale* ("The Knouto-Germanic Empire and the Social Revolution"), written between 1870 and 1872. The first part was published by Imprimerie Coopérative (Genva) in 1871.

37 In addition to the previously cited works, Havel is referring to *Lettres à un Français sur la crise actuelle*, and *Les Ours de Berne*, both published by Guillaume (Neuchâtel) in 1870.

38 Alexandre Ledru-Rollin (1807–1874) was a French politician and an important figure in the early French socialist movement.

generalization of historical philosophy, so richly adorned with facts and brilliant thoughts, could only be taken from contemporary reality.

Every pamphlet of Bakunin signifies a crisis in the history of revolutionary thought in Europe. His speeches at the congress of the Peace and Liberty League were so many challenges to all the radicals of Europe.[39] In them Bakunin declared that the radicalism of 1848 had had its day, that the new era, the epoch of Socialism and Labor, had dawned. Another question besides political liberty, that of economic independence, had raised its head. This question would become the dominating factor in European history. The pamphlet addressed to Mazzini announces the end of conspiracy for the purpose of waging wars of national independence, and the advent of the social revolution.[40] Bakunin proclaimed the end of sentimental Christian Socialism and the dawn of atheistic realistic communism. And his famous letter to Herzen concerning the International had the same significance for Russia as the other had for Italy[41].

In "The Bears of Berne" Bakunin bids farewell to the philistine Swiss democracy, while his "Letters to a Frenchman," written during the Franco-German War of 1870-1, were a dirge to Gambetta's radicalism and an enthusiastic appeal for the new epoch which found its expression soon after in the Paris Commune, a movement which overthrew the old State-Socialist ideas of Louis Blanc and proclaimed the new idea of Communism, the Commune taking up arms for the defense of its territory to inaugurate the social revolution within their own

---

39 As noted previously, the most famous of these speeches formed the basis of *Federalism, Socialism, and Anti-Theologism* (1867).

40 Presumably Havel is referring to *The Political Theology of Mazzini and the International* (1871).

41 Presumably Havel is referring to Bakunin's October 28, 1869 letter to Herzen, which severely criticizes Marx, among other things.

walls—this was Bakunin's advice, in order to repel the German invasion.[42]

His "Knouto-German Empire and the Social Revolution" was the prophetic vision of an old revolutionist. Then already, in 1871, Bakunin foresaw that, resulting from the triumph of Bismarck's military state, a, forty to fifty years' reaction would descend upon Europe.[43] Likewise Bakunin prophesied the rise of German State Socialism, to which Bismarck also stood sponsor. At the same time, Bakunin aimed at winning the Latin countries for Stateless Communism or Anarchism.

Finally we have "Communism and the State," "The Historical Development of the International," and "God and the State." These contain, for the thinking reader, in spite of their fighting tendency, attributable to the fact that they were written on the spur of the moment, more profound political thought, a higher philosophic conception of history, than whole volumes of university or Socialist treatises, which distinguish themselves as a rule, by the fact that they try to conceal the lack of deep thought and ideas in a mist of dialectic. Bakunin's writings contain no ready-made recipe for a political cookshop. Those who expect to find the solution of all their doubts in one book, without exercising their thinking capacity, will get no satisfaction out of his works. But should the reader be accustomed to independent thinking and used to looking upon books

---

42   Léon Gambetta (1838–1882) was a French statesman prominent during and after the Franco-Prussian War. In "Letters to a Frenchman on the Present Crisis" Bakunin chides Gambetta, who was at one time an avowed radical, for selling out the working class.

43   Otto Von Bismarck (1815–1898) was a Prussian statesman who unified the German states. In "The Knouto-Germanic Empire" Bakunin argued that Bismarck's state socialism would set the stage for the eventual emergence of a counter-revolution in Germany. Some have interpreted this as a prediction of the rise of fascism.

as material over which he must reflect individually—as if in conversation with an intelligent man who awakens his intellect—the sometimes unarranged, but always brilliant generalizations of Bakunin will be more useful than all the works of the authoritarian Socialists.

The ideas which Bakunin spread in the middle of the last century form today the social philosophy of the most advanced part of the international proletariat. Those ideas, which went through the crucible of hostile criticism shine today in greater-clarity than ever, and form the basis on which free humanity will build its social structure.

THE NOVEL OF THE REVOLUTION (1915)[1]

AT LAST WE HAVE AN ENGLISH VERSION OF *SANIN*. FIVE years ago I pointed out the importance of Artzibashev among Russian writers and the great value of *Sanin* as a mirror of the present generation. But to our translators, contemporary Russian literature ends with Gorki and Andrejev. They regard the young school of writers as obscene and immoral. Their brains are filled with Comstockism; therefore they boycotted *Sanin*. So the English-speaking public had to wait many years ere the publishers of "The Trend" were inspired to publish a translation of that important novel—unfortunately not a translation from the original Russian but an adaptation from the French. Still, better than nothing, and better late than never.

Meanwhile a new star has appeared in the Russian literary firmament. Two years ago the review *Zavjety* startled the revolutionary and artistic world by the publication of a novel by V. Ropshin, a young writer who was formerly an active member of the Socialist Revolutionary Party of Russia. The author uses a symbolic title for his work; he calls the novel *That Which Never Existed*.[2] The book

---

1   This article was originally published in *Greenwich Village* 1, no. 3 (February 22, 1915), pp. 18–19. See "An Immoral Writer" above.

2   Boris Viktorovich Savinkov (1879–1825) was a Russian author who wrote under the pseudonym "Ropshin." *To, chego ne Bilo* was originally published in the magazine *Zavjety* (numbers 1 through 8, April–November 1912; and number 1 in January 1903). The English version (*What Never Happened: A Novel of the Revolution*), translated by Thomas Seltzer, was published by Alfred Knopf (New York) in 1917.

is a remarkable study of the revolutionary movement in Russia and specifically of the revolutionary uprising following, or rather concurring with, the Russo-Japanese War. Ropshin is not a newcomer; he made his debut with the novel *The Pale Horse*, a book which did not attract much attention.[3] The appearance of *That Which Never Existed*, however, made him at once the center of a bitter and passionate feud. Not since the days of Turgenjev's *Fathers and Sons* has the intelligentsia in Russia been in such an uproar on account of a book. The first installments produced immediately a vehement discussion. The author was accused, first, of having imitated Tolstoy's idea: some critics even went so far as to accuse Ropshin of plagiarizing *War and Peace*; second, he was said to have travestied the revolutionary movement.

Only those who are acquainted with the intellectual life of the Russian people can grasp the importance of literature in the daily social life of the Russian. The appearance of a novel by a great writer is an historic event. Tchernichevsky's *What's to be Done?* influenced an entire generation.[4] The writer in Russia is the truest exponent of new ideals, he is the herald of the social reconstruction and the prophet of the future social order. The fiercer the contemporary struggle the more lofty an expression it will find in the works of the Russian men of letters.

No wonder then that Ropshin's novel created so great a sensation. The author sets out to prove nothing less than that the whole revolutionary movement broke down because it was built on false premises—it "never existed":

---

3   *Kon bledny* was originally published in the magazine *Russkaya Mysl* 1 (1909). The English version, translated by Z. Vengerova, was published by Alfred Knopf (New York) in 1919.

4   *Chto dielat* was published in 1863. The English version was translated and published by Benjamin Tucker (Boston) in 1886. On the influence of "What's To Be Done?" see footnote 8 in "Introduction to Anarchism and Other Essays."

"All our work our sacrifices, our suffering have been in vain. Why? Because our philosophy was founded upon hatred and vanity instead of upon love and pity and truth." According to this view, Ropshin is undoubtedly a true Tolstoyan; as to this charge of direct plagiarism from Tolstoy, even such pedantic Marxians as Plechanov have defended the writer against this accusation. The novel is written in three parts, and gives us a broad panorama of the revolutionary movement with the war in the Far East as a background. The characters are real; we feel them. They are part of our own life. In the family Bolatov we find the old, perpetual struggle between the old generation and the new. Three sons are drawn one after the other into the maelstrom of the Revolution. The self-appointed executioners of Von Plehve, Grand Duke Sergius, Premier Stolypin, and other dignitaries of autocracy stand in a clear light before our vision. The killing of the chief of the gendarme by the ruthless revolutionist Volodya is a masterful piece of psychological description. In other types we find the traitor Azev, the indefatigable Gershun, and other well known leaders of the Revolution portrayed in forceful strokes. We follow the nerve-racking preparations of the terrorists, and participate in that wonderful uprising in Moscow. And in the third part of the novel we follow the great movement toward expropriation, in the desperate attempts to revive the revolutionary spirit, and the inevitable failure, according to the author, of the gigantic movement. Ropshin tries to give an impartial view of the differences between the various revolutionary parties: the Social Democrats, the Social Revolutionists, the Anarchists and the Expropriators pure and simple. He uses subtle satire in describing the childlike inanity of the decrepit historic ruins who masquerade as leaders of the revolution, and the highbrow behavior of the Marxian Socialists.

A striking characteristic of the book is the great number of Jewish revolutionists portrayed as participating in the movement for liberation and playing an important role in the Revolution. As the reactionists in Prussia denounced in their time Heine and Borne, so the representatives of the autocratic regime in Ropshin's book cries out: "The Jews, the Jews, they are our ruin!"[5]

When, I wonder, will our translators and publishers discover Ropshin?

---

5   Karl Ludwig Börne (1786–1836) was a German political writer and satirist.

THE SPIRIT OF THE VILLAGE (1915)[1]

WHEN I SPEAK OF GREENWICH VILLAGE I HAVE NO GEO-graphical conception in view. The term Greenwich Village is to me a spiritual zone of the mind. Is there any *raison d'etre* for the existence of a spiritual Greenwich Village? I believe there is. Those fellow wanderers who pawned their last coat in rue Franc Bourgeois, who shivered in rue St. Jacques and searched for the cheapest brasserie in rue Lepic, those who crowded the Olympe in rue de la Gaîté, will understand the charm of the Village.[2] A ramble along Charlton and Varick Streets is a reverie, not to speak of the sounds of—how do Minetta Lane, Patchin Place, Sheridan Square and Gay Street strike you?[3]

To be sure the native of the Village has no especial distinction. He is just as dull as the native of the Bronx,

---

1   This essay originally appeared in *Greenwich Village* 1 (January 20, 1915), pp. 1–2. At this time Havel was working as a cook and waiter at a restaurant owned by his companion, fellow anarchist Polly Holladay. "Polly's" was located on MacDougall Street in the Village.

2   Havel is referring, respectively, to various bohemian neighbor-hoods in Paris—viz., Rue des Francs-Bourgeois, an affluent and trendy neighborhood in the Le Marais region of Paris; Rue St. Jacques, a street in the Latin Quarter of Paris, on which the Sorbonne is located; Rue Lepic, a street in Montmartre, a district of Paris, which was well-known for its famous inhabitants—including Vincent Van Gogh, Pablo Picasso, and Erik Satie; and Rue de la Gaîté, a street in the Montparnasse Quarter of Paris famous for its numerous theaters, including *l'Olympe*.

3   These are all streets in New York City's Greenwich Village.

or the native of Hoboken. The apaches of the Village are more crude than the gangs of upper Riverside. So are, in proportion, the *alguaciles*[4] of the Village more vicious and brutal than their confreres in other precincts. The Village has also its speaking reformers and neighborhood centers full of apostles in male and female petticoats, good people who clean out certain parts of their territory from outcasts and drive out those poor dregs of humanity into others parts of the city. The joints of the Village compare favorably with Doctor's and Barney Flynn's emporiums on the Bowery and Chatham Square.

The soothsayers of yesteryear assured us that the Village is doomed... No danger so far, though the subterranean barbarians are busy reconstructing Seventh Avenue and building a subway for the men in a hurry. True, also, "The Grapevine" has disappeared and we miss the pewters of creamy ale.[5] But take courage, ye tipplers, there are heavenly retreats in the Village. "Griffou"[6] is dead, but there is a new brasserie de Lilla, yes, even a café Grossenwahn.[7] Josiah Flint, if he should awaken from his grave, would not be lonesome in the Village.[8]

---

4 A Spanish term indicating a kind of legal magistrate carried over from the time of Muslim Spain. In this instance, Havel seems to be using it as a collective term for law enforcement in general.

5 A famous Greenwich Village landmark, the "Old Grapevine" was a popular destination for artists, businessmen and, during the American Civil War, southern spies.

6 The Griffou was a popular restaurant and boarding house in Greenwich Village. Famous residents and guests included Ida Tarbell, Oscar Wilde, and Mark Twain. It has since reopened.

7 It is uncertain what Havel is referring to here. However, the *Brasserie des Lilas* and the *Café Grossenwahn* were famous bohemian haunts in Paris and Berlin, respectively.

8 Josiah Flynt (1869–1907) was an American sociologist and vagrant by choice whose best-known work is *Tramping with Tramps* (New York: Century, 1899). Then, as now, homeless people had a

If you lose your illusions and the devil takes hold of your soul, you leave your garret on the sacred Butte and rent a studio Parc Monceau, you leave the Soho and take your domicile in Chelsea, or you become a traitor to Greenwich Village and move into an apartment on Riverside Drive.[9] You will smile pityingly over the folly of the poor devils who lose their lives in ugly holes on Washington Square, or find pleasure in cheap restaurants among pickpockets on Carmine Street. But some evening, after the West Indian has pushed you up to your steamheated apartment and after you have gone over your bank account, you will sigh for the dear old haunts of the Village. Old reminiscences will float before your vision and old names will strikes chords in your damned soul, and you will envy the silly chaps and maidens who remained true to the Village.

Like a sneakthief you will return secretly one evening and you will look up the dear old places. But the charm will be gone. Even the caravanserie on Thirty-first Street and the Zukunftstatt[10] on Seventy-seventh Street will close their portals to you. Then you have lost your

---

reputation for drinking. Havel's point is either that the Village is cheap, or else that it has much to offer to "tramps" in the way of opportunities to drink.

9 Havel is contrasting bohemian neighborhoods—e.g., Montmarte ("the Butte") in Paris, Soho in London, Greenwich Village in New York—with affluent neighborhoods—e.g., Parc Monceau in Paris's 8th Arrondissement; Chelsea in London, and Riverside Drive in northern Manhattan.

10 "Caravanserie"—i.e., cheap hotels (in this case, on West 31st Street in the vicinity of Penn Station)—is probably a misspelling of the term *caravanserai*, a kind of road-side inn common along the Silk Road. "Zukunftstatt" is a misspelling of the German word *Zukunftstadt*, meaning "city of the future." The "Seventy-seventh Street" Havel refers to is most likely W. 77th Street, though his reference is otherwise unclear.

illusions, your enthusiasm and your idealism. Greenwich Village is a spiritual conception and shopkeepers are not interested in dreamers. The Village is the rallying point for new ideas. Its spirit reaches the heathenish bellyworshippers of Harlem, even nature fakers near the Zoo in the Bronx.[11] The Bronxite points proudly to Poe's cottage, but come to the Village, young man, *caro mio*, and I will point out to you "Grub Street" where another iconoclast, Thomas Paine, earned his bread and his fame in daily struggles with the economic devil.[12]

True, there are literary and artistic coteries and cliques in the Village. Pity, envy, and spiteful enmity reign in certain circles. Gossip seems supreme. Ye gods, what an avalanche of gossip! To quote that illustrious gentleman, Don Quixote of La Mancha, "there is more mischief in the Village than comes to one's ears." Also the braggart, the fumiste, the chevalier d'Industrie are to be found here. George Moore would have found in the Village more material and more gossip than he discovered in Paris or in Dublin.[13]

But notwithstanding all these human traits, there is a wonderful atmosphere in this part of Manhattan. In the squalid studios and garrets, ideas are forged into new forms. If your eyes are open and your heart sympathetic, you will see Francois Villon spending the borrowed dime in the

---

11 "Bellyworshippers" is probably an allusion to Philippians 3:19, meaning those with hedonistic lifestyles.

12 "*Caro mio*" means "my dear" in Italian. "Grub Street" is the name of a now non-existent street in London associated with hack writers. It became a general term for low-quality publishing houses. Paine lived in Greenwich Village during the last few years of his life.

13 George Moore (1852–1933) was an Irish novelist who was controversial during Havel's lifetime because of the scandalous nature of his books. Moore is sometimes considered the first modern Irish novelist.

"Working-girl's Home."[14] You will note Villers de L'Isle
Adam contemplating his twentieth attempt at suicide.[15]
With Peter Hille you could tramp towards Nirvana.[16]
Raskolnikoff pursues his own shadow and Bassaroff pro-
claims here his philosophy while Sanin celebrates his
orgies.[17] The "Grub Street" of Greenwich Village has as
many tragedies as Boul' Mich and Soho.[18] Chatteron and
Francis Thompson are here but you must look carefully
for them.[19] Elusive and shy they are. Even Aretino could

14　Francois Villon (born 1431) was a French writer best known for
　　cataloging his own criminal behavior in his poetry. Villon disap-
　　peared in 1463 after he was banished from the city of Paris when
　　he continued his criminal behavior while free on bail.

15　Auguste Villiers de l'Isle-Adam (1838–1889) was a French sym-
　　bolist writer. Havel is probably referring to Villiers de l'Isle-
　　Adam's regular use of suicide as a plot point in his novels.

16　Peter Hille (1854–1904) was a German writer and social dem-
　　ocrat who was known to associate with the anarchist "New
　　Community" in Berlin. Hille was involved with the naturalistic
　　movement, and spent many years homeless, in deep poverty, or
　　on the run from the German police.

17　Havel is referring, respectively, to Rodion Romanovich
　　Roskolnikov, the protagonist of Fyodor Dostoyevsky's *Crime and
　　Punishment*; Yevgeny Bazarov, the antagonist of Ivan Turgenev's
　　Fathers and Sons; and the eponymous protagonist of the novel by
　　Mikhail Artsybashev.

18　Havel is referring to the Boulevard Saint-Michel in the Latin
　　Quarter of Paris,

19　Thomas Chatterton (1752–1770) was an English poet who pub-
　　lished the majority of his work under the pseudonym of Thomas
　　Rawley, a fictional fifteenth century monk. Chatterton's poems,
　　fake identity, and suicide at the age of seventeen contributed to
　　his becoming a romanticized figure among later poets, includ-
　　ing Keats and Shelley. Francis Thompson (1859–1907) was an
　　English poet. Homeless and addicted to opium, Thompson was
　　rescued from the streets by his editors. Later, he attempted suicide

add here a few tricks to his Bible of eroticism.[20] Van Gogh and Gauguin are formulating their ideas. And Verlaine is to be met, if you have the divine spark in your soul.[21] The city which hasn't a Greenwich Village is to be pitied. It has no life, no illusion, no art. Greenwich Village is a world in itself. It has its own ethics, its special morals, its distinct individuality.

We have suffered with the men and women in the attics and studios. We know them well and I am sure of their sincerity and their enthusiasm for a higher form of life. They try to forge their ideas, revolutionary ideas, mind you, into new rhythmic forms, and this, to me, is the supreme effort. The knights errant of the social revolution, those fighters against capitalistic society are also to be met in Greenwich Village; they are the boon companions of the craftsmen of the chisel, the brush, and the pen.

This, indeed, is a revelation. Experienced connoisseurs have told us many times that we do not need to worship at the shrines of the Old World. Here in our sordid surroundings we find the materials and thought a-plenty to discover our artistic soul. If you have the artistic spark, you will find in Greenwich Village a sympathetic echo and splendid fellow workers. A Greenwich Village can be found in every part of the world: on the Seine, on the

---

but allegedly experienced a mystical vision of Thomas Chatterton and survived.

20 Pietro Aretino (1492–1556) was an Italian writer. Aretino was a particularly controversial figure, being a public homosexual who wrote graphic material that parodied famous writers of the day and mocked the papacy. Aretino is sometimes regarded as the first modern writer of erotic prose.

21 Paul Verlaine (1844–1896) was a French symbolist poet whose most famous work is *Clair de Lune*, later set to music by Claude Debussy. Apart from his poetry, Verlaine is perhaps best known for his struggle with drug addiction and for shooting his lover, the poet Arthur Rimbaud, during an argument.

Thames, on the Yser,[22] on the Danube, on the Tiber. Why, my friend Ben Ali Yussef assures me that there is a Greenwich Village in Jerusalem![23]

If the Village did not exist, we would have to invent it.

---

22 The Yser is a river that flows from French Flanders into Belgium.

23 The identity of this individual is uncertain.

TO OUR READERS! (1917)[1]

We are late with the current issue. The reason?

First: the federal authorities took kindly charge of our manuscripts.

Second: our printer got cold feet. In fact, we are boycotted by the printing trade of Chicago.

The printers would not mind to take our money, but they insist on a censorship of their own; they want to decide what articles or items should or should not appear in the columns of *The Social War*! We cannot prevent a censorship forced upon the press by the executive of the ruling class, but we strenuously oppose a censorship exercised through fear and cowardice by private individuals in the printing trade.

The Social War will appear in Chicago, if possible, or in another city if necessary. And if we should be forced to change our name, it will not be *La Victoire* but *La Victoire Sociale*![2]

Comrades and Readers of the Social War:

A few words of explanation. When we started to publish *The Social War* we knew that we would have no plain sailing with our publication. We had enough experience in the revolutionary movement to know what to expect

---

1   This article originally appeared in *The Social War* 1, no. 5 (May 1917). Edited by Havel and others, *The Social War* was published by the International Propaganda Group of Chicago from 1917 to 1918. Another periodical by this name had been published briefly by Havel and the Belgian anarchist Edward Mylius (born 1878) in New York in 1913. Like *The Revolutionary Almanac* (1914) it was published by the Rabelais Press, founded by the Greek anarchist John Rompapas (born c. 1876).

2   "The Social Victory."

on the part of authorities. Still I did not expect to be arrested on the plain and simple charge of "being an anarchist." This happened to me and to comrade Appel on the 13th of May when we were taken into custody by detectives Patrick Alcock and Jim Mullin.[3] I have sufficient humor to appreciate any kind of adventure, but I must confess: this charge was too ambiguous for my understanding.

We were shadowed since the first issue of our publication made its appearance; evidently the police of Chicago had to wait for the declaration of war to declare war on *The Social War*.

Somehow my inner consciousness tells me that we are suspected to be in a secret understanding with these "willful men" La Follette, Champ Clark, Kilchin, and other upholders of America traditions.[4]

Proud like peacocks, officers Alcock and Mullin took us in a patrol wagon before the magistrate in the Shakespeare Station. (Yes, dear readers, a police station in Chicago is named after the Swan of Avon.) Here the first hitch occurred: the magistrate in this police court seems to be in possession of a good portion of common sense.

"What's the charge?" asked the magistrate.

---

3   Theodore Appel (1857–1943) was a German-American anarchist and co-editor (with Havel) of *The Social War*. Among other things, he served as Chicago agent for *Free Society*, manager of *The Alarm*, and secretary of the International Federation of Chicago.

4   Havel is referring, respectively, to Robert La Follette (1855–1925), an American Republican (and, later, Progressive) politician from Wisconsin; James Beauchamp "Champ" Clark (1850–1921), a Democratic politician from Missouri who served as Speaker of the House of Representatives from 1911 to 1919; and Claude Kitchin (1869–1923), a Democratic politician from North Carolina. Wilson denounced these and other politicians who opposed his "preparedness" campaign as "a little group of willful men." Havel is alluding to the American tradition of isolationism.

"Them are anarchists, Your Honor" answered Patrick Alcock.

"Very well, but what is the charge?" asked again His Honor.

"Well, they do not deny that they are anarchists," replied Alcock, somehow surprised and hurt in his patriotism imported from County Doneghal in Ireland.

"I hear, I hear, but you must have some charge against them, officer. Do you understand?"

"Well, it does not matter, Your Honor. Their case is now transferred into the hands of federal authorities."

So ended the preliminary hearing in the Shakespeare police court. The judge had to bow before the federal dictum and, notwithstanding of my protest, we were turned over to Hinton G. Glabaugh, chief of the federal district of the Middle West. In the federal building we were kept incommunicado and to go for hours through a regular third degree. Mr. Glabaugh brought some kind of photo in order to prove that he has my "record." With triumphant braggadocio he announced that he know how many years I had served in Russia, Austria, and other European countries. But notwithstanding all bulldozing and browbeating we withstood the verbal onslaught with good grace. Dignity was on our side.

While we were taken to the Harrison police station to be measured and fingerprints to be taken according to the system of Monsieur Bertillon the office of *The Social War* was raided and all my correspondence and manuscripts confiscated.

My correspondence aroused great curiosity on the part of the inquisitors: they were astonished to find out that there are in this country distinguished authors and artists who are not afraid to honor an anarchist with their friendship.

But the picture changed the very moment the inquisitor beheld copies of the *Revolt* and *The Revolutionary Almanac*. He began to rave like a maniac. "So, that's the kind of literature you are producing. You don't believe in organized government. You believe in anarchy. Well, I will show you. Neither will we believe in organized government; we will give you your own medicine. I will send men after you and they will beat you to pieces"—and so the raving went on.

I had to smile over his logic, but as I was a prisoner I was not allowed to answer. I was told to "shut up with the artistic stuff." A man who does not believe in organized government belongs to Dunnin (asylum for the insane)—such was the final dictum of this excellent representative of organized government.[5]

And here we sat, each criminal in a different corner in the office of the Holy Inquisition. I tried to amuse myself with "Essays of Elia" but the noise around me was neither conducive to reading nor to contemplation.[6]

Yet every episode must have an end. No matter how hard the federal officers tried they could not produce any charge against us. So Patrick Alcock had to be called in again. And now his ingenious brain started to work. He remembered suddenly that I had made some disrespectful remarks about President Wilson. These remarks against Wilson I am supposed to have made after my arrest and before I entered the patrol wagon.

This was the stupidest frame-up I ever heard of. Alcock did not bring this charge against me in the Shakespeare Station. It occurred to him only after he saw that our arrest was illegal—without a warrant and without any charge whatsoever.

We were taken back to the police station, where we had the greatest difficulty to get in communication with

5   Havel is referring to Dunning, a neighborhood on the northwest side of Chicago and the location of the former Cook County Insane Asylum (known simply as "Dunning").

6   *The Essays of Elia* is an essay collection published in 1823 by the English writer Charles Lamb (1775–1834).

our friends outside. Alcock made now a charge of "disorderly conduct" against us and he threatened that we shall not be allowed to go free on bonds. Of course, he thought because we are anarchists we have no legal rights. After we had spent two nights in the police station, we were brought before a magistrate in the municipal court in the county building. We insisted on a jury trial and the case was set for the 4th of May.

Graced with heavy handcuffs, we now proceeded to the County Jail. Next day comrade Sarah Gruber succeeded in getting us out on bonds.[7] Mr. Cunnea, a prominent member of the Chicago Bar and candidate for District Attorney on the Socialist ticket in the last election, has taken up our defense.[8]

When we appeared in the Court on May 4th our accuser, Mr. Alcock, was not present, but instead we saw the federal inquisitor on the spot. On advice of Mr. Cunnea the case was postponed till 17th of May. We shall see and hear then what our crime is.[9] The jury will have to decide whether a citizen of this country has the right to call himself an anarchist, or in that matter, socialist, Republican, Episcopalian, Baptist, or Quaker.

Mr. Cunnea takes up this fight for free thought; it is a case of principle with him. But, friends, there are expenses to meet in connection with the trial. We appeal to you to help us to carry on the battle; remember we are living in portent times and the prejudice against anarchists is being worked up by the police.

---

7   Sarah Gruber (birth and death dates unknown) was a friend of Emma Goldman's who later raised funds for Goldman's autobiography.

8   William Cunnea (1868–1937) was a Socialist Party politician and Eugene Debs's attorney.

9   On May 25th Havel and Appel were found not guilty by Judge Gemmill in the Municipal Court of Chicago.

NO COMPROMISE (1917)[1]

SOCIAL IDEAS HAVE ALSO THEIR MARTYRDOM—A MARTYRdom as intense as that of individuals.

It is the martyrdom of aspirations misapplied of characteristics misinterpreted, of attempts miscarried—on through dismal disappointment.

It took centuries to transform the simple vision of Jesus of Nazareth into the form of a pompous tyrannical State Church, but only a few decades were needed to transform the ideal of voluntary socialism into the shape of bureaucratic state machinery.

Today we stand on the threshold of a new era—the era of triumphant democracy.[2] And the anarchists, the representatives of the greatest effort for individual freedom, are confronted with a big problem: the problem of anarchy versus democracy.

It is a clear issue and no amount of sophistry will be able to dodge the issue: either we remain true to the anarchist ideal or we shall enter the muddy waters of compromise with democracy.

I notice many signs of retrogression in the anarchist movement. The clearness of vision of some comrades seems to be obscured by shallow, hollow phrases about the rights of small nationalities, representation of minorities, and other postulates of democracy of many, many years ago.

These comrades with atavistic, nationalistic tendencies, in taking part in the present rampant lunacy, entered

---

1   This essay originally appeared in *The Social War* 1, no. 6 (June 1917).

2   Here and throughout, Havel is using the term "democracy" to refer to representative government or parliamentarism.

already the ranks of democracy: there can be no room for them in the anarchist movement.

The anarchist keeps to the straight road toward liberty—bold and uncompromising he attacks the smooth respectability of social democracy no matter under what guise it may hide itself.

The representatives of plutocracy and bureaucracy in all capitalistic countries unfurl the oriflamme of democracy. A bureau-democratic state-socialistic program—this is the message of Wilson to the contemporary world. No wonder that this message is praised and applauded by all believers in the state-socialistic straitjacket.

Anarchists cannot be misled by side issues: there is no or very little difference between the "libertarian" ideal of Wilson-Walling-Gompers-Balfour-Henderson[3] and that of Bethmann Holleg-Scheidermann-David and Kaiser Wilhelm.[4] They all pretend to strive for freedom of mankind—they are all good democrats.

Never before stood the anarchists before a more severe test. Now is the time to ask ourselves: are we true to our principles of the greatest individual liberty—anarchy? For only liberty—untrammeled, free development—can serve as a safe foundation for further progress of mankind.

---

3   Presumably Havel is referring to the "liberal" politicians Alfred Balfour (1848–1930), a British Conservative who served as Prime Minister from 1902 to 1905 and later as Foreign Secretary; and Arthur Henderson (1863–1935), a leader of the British Labour Party.

4   Presumably Havel is referring to Theobald von Bethmann-Hollweg (1856–1921), who served as German Chancellor from 1909 to 1921; Philipp Scheidemann (1865–1939), a German Social Democratic politician who proclaimed Germany a republic 1918 and subsequently served as chancellor; and Eduard David (1863–1930), a German Social Democratic politician and first president of the Weimar assembly.

Let those whose brain is befuddled by chauvinistic phrases follow the easy path of democracy, but they should not hide their democratic tendencies from the ranks of the anarchist movement.

The present butchery will cease sooner or later, but it may take centuries to overthrow the system of entrenched democratic state socialism—a far more dangerous foe than Caesarism.

Autocracy in its purest form cannot be overthrown overnight—history teaches this—but it will take centuries to destroy an autocratic system built upon majority rule and democratic representation.

There is only one choice for a libertarian: anarchy or democracy.

HARRY KELLY: AN APPRECIATION AT THE CELEBRATION OF HIS FIFTIETH BIRTHDAY (1921)[1]

FERRER COLONY
Stelton, New Jersey
Sunday, January 23, 1921

Some men are endowed with a personality which makes them superior to their fellow citizens. The names of such men seldom gleam from the front page of the daily press, yet they excel in themselves and find their recognition amongst those who are able to appreciate their characteristic qualities. Their inherent modesty never creates jealousy or envy, and their lives have greater influence and are of greater reality than the lives of those who achieve their fame and fulfill their ambition by kowtowing before their masters and rulers.

Such a man who excels through his personality among his fellows, is Harry Kelly, at present the organizer of the Ferrer Modern School at Stelton in New Jersey. By birth and occupation Kelly belongs to the working class. Those who are not acquainted with his life fancy that his cradle stood on Emerald Isle of Erin;[2] they are mistaken; Harry

---

1   This essay originally appeared as a brochure published at the Ferrer Colony (Stelton, New Jersey) in January 1921. Kelly and Havel were close friends and collaborators. Among other things, both were instrumental in the founding of the first American Modern School in New York in 1911.

2   Ireland.

May Kelly—to give him his full name— was born in the city of Saint Louis in Missouri. His early years were spent on the banks of the Mississippi. Figuratively speaking, he piloted like Mark Twain a great part of his life on the Father of Waters. Undoubtedly he could relate as many accidents and adventures as did Mark Twain in his *Life on the Mississippi*.[3]

On his mother's side Kelly comes from the well-known Calvert clan, whose members to this very day claim as heirloom from Lord Baltimore the site on which is built the city proudly carrying the name of that Colonial Governor.[4]

Among the trades Kelly had to choose from on reaching the wage-earning age, he preferred the art of Gutenberg; he became a printer.[5] As such he had a greater opportunity to get acquainted with social ideas than workers in other trades. It was the period of the Knights of Labor[6] and no thinking worker could stand outside the organized movement against exploitation of labor. Anarchist ideas gained a strong foothold among progressive workers at that time and Anarchist thought soon permeated Kelly's social vision. He became the collaborator of Charles Mowbrey on *The Rebel* in Boston. After the disappearance of that paper, he lighted his own candle; he published a paper called *The Match*. *The Match* went out all too suddenly, but while it burned it gave Kelly great pleasure and satisfaction.[7]

---

3   *Life on the Mississippi* was published by J.R. Osgood & Company (Boston) in 1883.

4   The Calverts were a noble British family who were instrumental in founding the Maryland colony.

5   Johannes Gutenberg (1395–1468) was the German inventor of the printing press.

6   Originally called the Noble and Holy Order of the Knights of Labor, the Knights of Labor was an early American labor organization formed after the collapse of the National Labor Union in 1873.

7   *The Match* was only published twice, in 1896.

A journey to England gave Kelly the impatiently awaited opportunity to get in closer touch with the revolutionary movement in Europe. There, among congenial friends
and comrades, he without doubt spent the happiest days
of his life.[8] There, among thinkers and propagandists
of Anarchism, he fortified his ideal with historical, eco-
nomical and social facts and data. In Peter Kropotkin he
not only found an enthusiastic comrade, but also a great
teacher and a sincere friend. His journeys to Bromley in
Kent, where Kropotkin lived at that period, Kelly counts
as the most blessed hours of his experience in England.
He was a collaborator on the *Freedom*, now the oldest Anarchist journal in existence; here lie worked with
mind and brawn among such well-known Anarchists as
Kropotkin, Tcherkesow, Louise Michel, Dr. Max Nettlau,
and John Turner. [9] A great meeting place for all shades
of social rebels was then Tom Mann's hostelry Enterprise
in Longacre. One is apt to paraphrase Keats' "Ode to the
Mermaid Tavern" of Marlowe's and Shakespeare's fame:

> Souls of rebels dead and gone,
> What Elysium have you known,
> Happy fields or mossy cavern,
> Choicer than Tom Mann's Tavern?

Often it has been stated with some levity, and a great
deal of acrimony, that Anarchism is the offspring of
the ignorance, vice and tyranny of Europe. Even if this

---

8   Emma Goldman, for example, stayed with Kelly in London in
    1899. It was during this time that she (and presumably Kelly as
    well) met and befriended Havel, who had recently been expelled
    from France and Austria-Hungary for his political activities.

9   Max Nettlau (1865–1944) was a German anarchist and historian.
    Nettlau was a founding contributor to Freedom Press and wrote
    influential biographies of many of important classical anarchists,
    including his friends Peter Kropotkin and Errico Malatesta.

were true it would not affect the truth or falsity of what Anarchism represents. Such names as Godwin, Bakunin, Reclus, Kropotkin, Stirner, Proudhon, and Tolstoy can lend only luster to any cause with which they are coupled.[10] But it happens that America has contributed more than her share to the intellectual labor that hat has made Anarchism the most consistent theory, the most beautiful ideal, and the only practical method of solving the social problem.

* * *

The American pedigree includes such names as Josiah Warren, Lysander Spooner, Nathaniel Greene, Dyer D. Lum, Albert R. Parsons, Voltairine De Cleyre, Ross Winn—to mention only those who went their way into Nirvana, and who during their lifetime achieved prominence as writers, orators, or organizers in the labor movement.[11]

Among those who follow in the footsteps of these, pioneers, Harry Kelly holds a prominent position. Max Nettlau the historian of the Anarchist movement says truly:

---

10 William Godwin (1756–1836) was an English journalist, novelist, and political theorist, widely considered to be one of the first proponents of political anarchism. While famous in his own right, Godwin is perhaps best known as the husband of Mary Wollstonecraft, an important feminist writer, and as the father of Mary Shelley, the author of *Frankenstein*.

11 In addition to previously cited individuals, Havel is referring to Nathaniel Greene (1797–1877), an American journalist and politician. Greene was not an anarchist, having been a prominent part of the Democratic Party's media campaign. Havel is probably associating him with William Batchelder Greene, his son, who was an individualist anarchist, abolitionist, and Unitarian minister.

> Kelly is one of the living Anarchists who
> contributes real thought to the movement,
> a man who can state his theory of society
> in scientific, logical and precise manner
> and in convincing language.

It is the fashion nowadays to change one's convictions from day to day. Those "followers of fashion" in social ideas maintain with La Rochefoucauld that only jackasses stick to their convictions through life.[12] Those wiseacres forget, though, that the readiness to leave off one set of convictions in order to assume another set shows a complete indifference to convictions altogether, this weakness of will is a disease which consists not merely in the loss of desire, but in the loss of the capacity to translate desire into deed. Harry Kelly does not belong to those weathercocks; he does not change his convictions according to fleeting fashions; he remains true to his ideals—for that ideal is his very life.

> ...To thine own self be true,
> And it must follow, as the night the day,
> Thou canst not then be false to any man.

Yet Kelly is not satisfied with having merely a desire; what he is longing for is to translate his desire into deeds. He is not content in having an ideal— lie works for the realization of his ideal. Consequently he is always willing to put aside his private life and to act at every opportunity as speaker, organizer or writer, as the occasion requires. Like Francisco Ferrer, the martyred founder of the Modern Schools in Spain, he has to preach the gospel at all times

It would hardly be possible to enumerate all the occasions on which Kelly participated during the years he

---

12 Francois de La Rochefoucauld (1613–1680) was a French writer famous for his aphorisms.

spent in the revolutionary movement, at protest meetings, in strikes and demonstrations; and, in the all too often underestimated work of organizing, he always stands in the forefront. A staunch friend of Emma Goldman and Alexander Berkman, he worked with these comrades through many years, ere our wise rulers made the decision to deport them from the shores of America to Soviet Russia on the day of the tercentenary of the landing of the Pilgrim Fathers from the Mayflower. We humans realize only a small part of our dreams; Kelly is fortunate to have realized one of his supreme dreams: a social community and a school for children of proletarian parents in the country, far from the nerve-racking influence of the modern city.

The Ferrer Colony in Stelton is to a great part Harry Kelly's Achievement.[13] What an amount of sacrifice, labor and enthusiasm it took to organize a libertarian community only those can estimate who worked with Kelly in that undertaking. Due mainly to the efforts of Harry Kelly, we see today a free community and a free school based on rational education—a free community on a free soil.

Harry Kelly is only fifty years old, and notwithstanding all hardships he encountered during these years, just as young in spirit as on the day be entered the ranks of the militant labor movement. His best work is still ahead of him.

---

13 The Ferrer Colony was an anarchist colony which operated in Stelton, New Jersey from 1915 to 1953. Havel helped found the colony and lived there from 1924 until he was committed to the Marlboro State Psychiatric Hospital near the end of his life.

INTRODUCTION TO *THE BIOGRAPHY OF AN ANARCHIST* (1924)[1]

THIS SHORT SKETCH OF MALATESTA'S LIFE IS BASED ON THE exhaustive study of Max Nettlau, published in Italian translation by "Il Martello" in New York under the title *Vita e Pensieri di Errico Malatesta*, and in German translation issued at Berlin by the publishers of *The Syndicalist*.[2] Max Nettlau, the profound scholar of the Anarchist movement, biographer of Michael Bakunin and author of *Bibliographie de l'Anarchie*, lives in Vienna, and like so many intellectuals in Europe, in distressing economic condition.[3] May I express here the hope that he will find sufficient encouragement to continue his valuable task in the Anarchist movement? He was in contact with the most remarkable men and women in the revolutionary movement of our time and his own reminiscences should prove of great value to the younger generation.

---

1   This pamphlet was originally published in 1924 by the Jewish Anarchist Federation (New York). Essentially a continuation of the Pioneers of Liberty, the Federation was founded in 1921 by the *Freie Arbeiter Shtimme* group.

2   *Il Martello* ("The Hammer") was an Italian anarchist and anti-fascist newspaper edited by Carlo Tresca and published in New York from 1917 to 1946. Published in Berlin from 1918 to 1932, *Der Syndikalist* was a German anarcho-syndicalist newspaper and the principal organ of the Freien Arbeiter-Union Deutschlands (Free Workers Union of Germany).

3   Nettlau's *Bibliographie de l'Anarchie* was published by Bibliothèque des "Temps Nouveaux" (Brussels) in 1897.

The American publishers refuse to print the Biography on the pretext that it would not pay. No doubt, should an upheaval occur in Italy and Malatesta's name appear in the foreground, the same publishers would be only to eager to get hold of the manuscript. Meanwhile our comrades of the Jewish Anarchist Federation offer the short sketch as a homage to Malatesta on his seventieth birthday.

In a very sympathetic review of the *Vita e Pensieri* in the New York *Nation*, Eugene Lyons states that Malatesta's life symbolized the romantic age of rebellion.[4] True, but it is not the romance of self-conscious knight-errantry, of adventure for adventure's sake. It is rather the inevitable unfolding of a character unswerving in its devotion to a philosophy of action. Even at the peaks of his adventures Malatesta has remained kindly, retiring, modest in his habits.

Against the background of a Europe misruled by renegade Millerands, Lloyd Georges, Mussolinis, Eberts, Pilsudskis, and other of the fraternity of ex-idealists, the personality of Errico Malatesta attains an idyllic grandeur.[5] At the age of seventy he can look back upon fifty years of intensive revolutionary work, thirty-six of them spent in busy exile. His life has a consistency, an almost

---

4   "A Great Rebel," *The Nation* (May 16, 1923). Eugene Lyons (1898–1985) was an American editor and writer who edited both *Reader's Digest* and the *National Review*. A socialist as a young man, Lyons eventually burned out on Communism and shifted to the political right, becoming an ardent critic of communism.

5   Havel is referring, respectively, to Alexandre Mitterand (previously cited); David Lloyd George (1863–1945), Prime Minister of the United Kingdom from 1916 to 1922; Friedrich Ebert (1871–1925), the first President of Germany after the end of the First World War (1919 to 1925); and Józef Piłsudski (1867–1935), Polish dictator who led the military effort to re-establish the state in the aftermath of the First World War. All of these figures were leftists in their youth who subsequently drifted to the right.

apocalyptic directness which more than explains the ad-
ulation with which he is regarded among the comrades.
It coincides, moreover, with a concentrated half century
of social development. Its threads are woven closely into
lives of the leaders during this period—Mazzini, Bakunin,
Cafiero, William Morris, the brothers Reclus, James
Guillaume, Stepniak, Kropotkin, and many others.[6] It
is a life that bridges the time of the Paris Commune and
the Russian Revolution. Its course consequently has a tremendous significance.

When Malatesta returned to Italy in October, 1919,
after being smuggled out of England on a coal boat by
the head of the Italian Seamen's Federation, all the ships
in the port of Genoa saluted his arrival, the city stopped
work and turned out to greet him. His arrest soon after
and the events in Italy which have forced him temporarily
into the background of national life are recent enough to
be generally known.[7] Despite his age, Malatesta is still a
vigorous social rebel, and the most stirring chapters of his
life may still have to be written.

---

6   In additional to previously cited figures, Havel is referring to
     Sergey Stepnyak-Kravchinsky (1851–1895), a Russian anarchist
     revolutionary. In 1878 Stepnyak assassinated Nikolay Mezentsov,
     commander of the Russian secret police. Stepnyak died crossing a
     train track in 1895.

7   Malatesta was arrested in 1921 and released two months before
     the fascists came to power.

SPEECH TO THE ANARCHIST CONFERENCE (1925)[1]

Kropotkin Institute, Stelton, NJ

4 July 1925

Comrades:

I believe in simplicity in movement. I do not think that there is any value whatsoever in resolutions.[2] We passed resolutions in the last fifty years and we never got anything out of it.

We ought to start with a very small beginning and grow up into a broader organization. I am afraid that our comrades are only to liable to be influenced by the American advertising. Our press, everything, is based on this advertising idea. This is influencing the movement in wrong directions. Anarchist ideas cannot be sold by advertizing like soap or Ford's flivvers.

---

1   Conferences of this sort were held at Stelton nearly every summer of the colony's existence. The 1925 conference included delegates from the Road to Freedom Group, the Anarchist Aid Society, the New Society Group, and the Spanish-language anarchist newspaper *Cultura Obrera*. Topics discussed included strategies for propaganda, means to support *The Road to Freedom* (a newspaper edited by Walter Starr Van Valkenburgh with Havel's assistance and published at Stelton from 1924 to 1932), and the relation of anarchism to the labor movement. Havel's speech, given at the opening of the conference, is particularly concerned with the question—still very much relevant today—of whom to reach and how.

2   Havel's criticisms notwithstanding, the conference passed six resolutions on issues ranging from Sacco and Vanzetti to international anarchist regroupment.

As to the policy of the paper: many of the comrades mentioned that it should be a live workingmen's paper. Other comrades thought it should be a literary paper. Some comrades thought we should print all kinds of subjects, one page for the labor movement, one for current events and so on. In a monthly paper of eight pages you will have to get the primary idea propagated and that is Anarchism. A monthly paper cannot take part in all small problems, though these might be important for the unions and social life. The most important thing for us is to bring the "idea" to people. The paper should not be for comrades only; they imagine that they know all our ideas and secondly they do not even read the paper. As mentioned by our Italian comrade, Tanuzzo, papers are not even distributed. Therefore, if we want to reach the people we must go outside with the paper. Most of our comrades are so wise that they do not want to read anything. Do not let us use big words and make resolutions unless we are ready to carry them out. We will have to have some organization among our own group. The work always goes to a few comrades. It is always the few who carry on the movement; it is only camouflage of a movement. If we could afford to publish a weekly paper we could give more space and go more deeply into the workingmen's life; but if we could publish a weekly paper we would have to be more active comrades. This is the problem for us. Do not believe that a paper can make a movement. It is a movement that produces papers. But most of our comrades imagine that a speaker or an editor can make a movement. The movement must come from comrades and inevitably then we will have a good press.

Since the paper exists, Anna Sasnovsky was the only one to send an article.[3] Many of our comrades seem to

---

3   Anna Sosnovsky (1900–1949) was a Jewish-American trade unionist and anarchist. A member of the International Ladies Garment Workers Union, she published the newspaper *Der*

think they are "ubermenschen" (supermen). To get articles which have to do with the movement—with life, that is the greatest difficulty. Every editor will tell you the same thing. Los Angeles is the only city which sometimes sends reports. Personally, I hope to be not the only responsible man for the publication. If the paper is supported by comrades, it should be in the hands of the comrades. It should not rely upon one individual, I have always said the paper must belong to the movement, not be a one-man paper. Today it is a one-man paper.

We have to have groups in different cities, otherwise the paper will die down in time. As a monthly publication, it has a very limited field. We have comrades in San Francisco, in Los Angeles, in Detroit, in Cleveland, in Boston, in Chicago and Philadelphia, who support the paper but so far we did not get support from other cities. When I look at the Italian or Spanish press, I notice at least fifty men who can write articles and express their ideas. One man cannot full up a paper entirely with his own ideas and very few men are able to express themselves in different ways. Therefore, comrades should try to get interested and write for the paper, to give a certain impression of the movement. Most of our comrades are ignorant of our own ideas. I am surprised how little they know of our own theory. If you ask them what kind of a society we want to establish, they will talk about Bakunin, Kropotkin, Tucker, but they have never read their books.

Some of our young comrades have never heard of the Chicago Anarchists. I do not mean to say that everyone should be a Max Nettlau and be able to quote all authors, but every comrade should be acquainted with the general movement. He should be able to express his ideas.

Yunyon Arbeiter ("The Union Worker") with Rose Pesotta and others from 1923 to 1927. Sosnovsky was married to fellow anarchist Abe Winokour (1894–1969); the two lived at Stelton in the 1920s and 30s.

If the comrades will take interest in the paper, then we will be able to have a good press. In connection with this, international connections will naturally arise from our own movement. Today the international connection we have is mainly through correspondence—exchanges or private correspondence.

Perhaps you will make it possible to publish a weekly paper; if we could do that we also could give out publication like a yearly almanac.[4] We could publish theoretical articles there and in the weekly paper have articles dealing with the working class. No paper can exist with 580 subscribers. I do not only mean financially, but also spiritually. At least we ought to have so many groups that we could print 5,000 copies and spread them in different localities.[5] No security for the paper. The problem is, how to get subscribers and connections with comrades in all parts of the country.

I have no objection to treat the daily topics in our small paper, but if we take part in the everyday life of the working people, we will have no space to propagate our ideas. Anarchism would be lost just as it is lost in the unions.

---

4   Havel attempted something similar with his *Revolutionary Almanac*, published by the Rabelais Press (New York) in 1914.

5   According to Kenyon Zimmer, the newspaper's circulation was about 1,200 in 1925. By 1932 it had reached approximately 3,000. See "Anarchist Newspaper Circulation," http://katesharpleylibrary .pbworks.com/w/page/13175715/Anarchist%20newspaper%20 circulation.

THE VOICE OF GARY (1928)

HAVING SENTENCED OUR COMRADES TO DEATH, JUDGE Gary cried out in 1887, "Anarchy is crushed."

Forty years after Webster Thayer cried out, "Did you see what I did to those anarchist bastards!"[1]

Thus spewed out their hatred towards the apostles of a new society, the paid representatives of the moribund society.

And the organs of the codfish aristocracy wrote smugly, "Let us forget the incident; let us return to normalcy."

But, lo, and behold, neither is Anarchy crushed nor are the "Anarchist bastards" silent.

The voices of Sacco and Vanzetti have not been burned in the electric chair.

They can be heard in a play, "Gods of the Lightning," a Broadway sensation, and it is crying out in the pages of the *Outlook and Independent*, from whose columns the rough riding Roosevelt used to denounce Anarchists as "undesirable citizens."[2]

---

1   Webster Thayer (1857–1933) was the Boston-based judge who presided over the Sacco and Vanzetti trial.

2   "Gods of the Lightning" was written by Maxwell Anderson and Harold Hickerson in 1928. It ran for 29 performances at the Little Theatre in October and November of that year. The *Outlook* was a weekly newspaper published in New York City from 1870 to 1928. Roosevelt was the editor of the *Outlook* for a time after he left the Presidency, but the *Outlook* is most famous for its involvement in the publication of Booker T. Washington's *Up From Slavery*. The *Independent* was published from 1848 to 1928, and advocated for abolition, women's suffrage and numerous causes of the mainstream American left. The two papers were merged into one in 1928.

And now comes Upton Sinclair with his powerful arraignment of Fuller, Lowell, and Thayer in his panoramic novel entitled *Boston*.[3] It is a most searching exposè of the ruling clique of Massachusetts and of the callous, premeditated murder of our comrades.

Yes, "Massachusetts, there she stands." Not the Massachusetts of the whisky boozer Daniel Webster but the Massachusetts of a trio of murderers: Fuller, Lowell and Thayer.[4]

From an Anarchist standpoint, many objections could be made against Sinclair's latest work. His criticism of the

---

3   *Boston* was published by Albert and Charles Boni (New York) in 1928. Alvan Fuller (1878–1958) was an American politician who served as Governor of Massachusetts from 1925 to 1929, concurrent with the Sacco and Vanzetti trial. While Fuller was criticized for his handling of the case, he later presided over a reform of the Massachusetts legal system due to fallout from the trial. Abbott Lawrence Lowell (1856–1943) was an American legal scholar who was President of Harvard University from 1909 to 1933. Lowell was appointed to the Advisory Committee on Sacco and Vanzetti, a body created to determine whether Governor Fuller should grant the pair clemency. Ultimately, Lowell advised against clemency. Lowell was heavily criticized for his involvement in the trial, and his decision greatly damaged his relationship with Harvard alumni groups.

4   Daniel Webster (1782–1852) was one of the most influential politicians in American history. Webster served only five years in the United States Senate, but acted as Secretary of State for three presidents: Fillmore, Harrison, and Tyler. "Whisky boozer" is a reference to Webster's reputation as a drinker, if not an alcoholic. The line "there she stands" is a misquoting of Webster's Second Speech on Foote's Resolution (U.S. Senate, 26 January 1830). The actual quote is, "I shall enter on no encomium of Massachusetts; she needs none. There she is." Havel's point is that the noble Massachusetts so valorized by Webster has become a breeding ground for murderers and thugs.

Defense Committee and his sneer at the lack and disbelief of organization among Anarchists shows the Socialistic politician. There are other kinds of organizations than a centralized pyramid in charge of Marxian dictators.

Historical novels dealing with Anarchists, like *The Bomb* by Frank Harris, *The Anarchist Woman* by Hutchins Hapgood, and now *Boston* by Upton Sinclair, are written in sympathetic vein towards certain individual Anarchists, but the authors have small understanding of the Anarchist movement.[5] Though they have associated with some Anarchists, they cannot grasp the spirit of the movement.

Yet, Sinclair has accomplished a great work in *Boston*. The novel will reach thousands of men and women we could never approach with our press and will show them the sublime heroism and the unconquerable spirit of Sacco and Vanzetti.

As to the impossible character of "Cornelia" in the novel, we leave it to the Artistic conscience of the author.[6]

---

5   *The Bomb* was published by Mitchell Kennerley (New York) in 1909. Frank Harris (1856–1931) was an Irish-born American journalist, writer and editor. He is best known for his autobiography, which was banned on the grounds that it contained graphic sexual material.

6   Cornelia Thornwell—the main character in *Boston*—is portrayed as the matriarch of a wealthy, aristocratic Boston family. Repulsed by her late husband's heirs and their squabbling over his inheritance, she "runs away" to Plymouth under an assumed identity and begins to fraternize with working class Italian immigrants who expose her to radical political ideas. Cornelia subsequently joins the anarchist movement and, as a result, becomes personally involved with Sacco and Vanzetti and their plight. Many critics regarded the character and her exploits as unbelievable at best and deeply patronizing at worst.

SOME REFLECTIONS ON THE SACCO-VANZETTI CASE (1929)[1]

THE DRAMA STAGED BY THE SPIRITUAL DESCENDANTS OF Cotton Mather in Boston two years ago had some unusually remarkable features.[2]

One item seems to me to have been overlooked in all the descriptions of that tragic affair, a small item, no doubt, but to me one of the utmost significance.

Organized labor supplied the executioner, Elliott, with the deadly "juice" which ended the lives of our comrades.[3] Yes, a member of the Electrical Workers Union turned on the switch for the electric chair.

Two years ago, the day after the tragedy, I stated that the supine ox-like indifference, the cowardly silence and spiritual corruption of American Labor, was mainly responsible for the deaths of Sacco and Vanzetti.

Ox-like! No: for even an ox kicks when he gives up his life.

Labor acquiesced by silence and timorousness, for it is spiritually dead.

---

1   This article originally appeared in *The Road to Freedom* (September 1929).

2   Cotton Mather (1663–1728) was an American colonial Puritan minister best known for his controversial involvement with the Salem Witch Trials.

3   Robert Greene Elliott (1874–1939) was the official "state electrician" of New York who operated electric chairs in New York and surrounding states from 1926 to his death.

A general stoppage of work on the part of two million organized workers would have prevented the martyrdom of our two brothers.

The labor leaders of a generation ago had less finesse than the present moguls of organized labor. Their social vision was also fixed on concrete achievement, but they were not supine.

They believed in crude lighting and when they went into action the ruling barons knew what to expect.

Of course, some of them were ample guzzlers of strong drink, lovers of many women and a roaring time, but they had within them, by Jove, the germs of real he-men.

Compare them with the lick-spittles and boot lickers of today, kowtowing before their lords and masters!

The editor of the *Industrial Worker* has a fine delineation in that paper of the subtle rationalization of class hatred in the minds of the ruling class as shown in the Centralia, the Mooney-Billings and the Sacco-Vanzetti cases.[4]

A true picture! But what about the moronizing efforts on the minds of the American workers by the rationalizing labor leaders?

Our intelligentsia stood the test in the Sacco-Vanzetti case much better than organized labor, far better, indeed, than we had any right to expect.

In *Thirteen Days* by Jeannette Marks, and in *America Arraigned* by Ralph Cheney and Lucia Trent are to be found a fine array of burning minds.[5]

---

4   *The Industrial Worker* is the official newspaper of the Industrial Workers of the World, published sporadically from 1905 to the present. C.B. Ellis was the editor from 1928 to 1929.

5   *Thirteen Days* was published by A. & C. Boni (New York) in 1929. *America Arraigned! An Anthology of Sacco-Vanzetti Verse* was published by Dean & Co. (New York) in 1929. Jeannette Marks (1875–1964) was an American writer and a professor of English at Mount Holyoke College. E. Ralph Cheney (1896–1941) and Lucia Trent (1897–1977) were American socialists and poets.

The subtle mind of capitalist rationalization imagined to have played comrades as "common criminals."

Yet the trick was soon discovered and was hurled back into the teeth of the traducers. To be sure, we have had in our own ranks, expropriators as well as propagandists by deed and we never disowned any of them. They ever found understanding and sympathy among the militants.

Yet, the innocence of Sacco and Vanzetti, the purity of their minds was so crystal clear that the accusation of robbery was generally disbelieved, even among those who stated that "they ought to hang anyway, because they were anarchists."

The Thayers, the Katzmanns, the Fullers and the Lowells well knew the role they had to play.[6] Sacco and Vanzetti represented the New Life, the New Society. In their bodies, the spirit of Revolt had to be crushed. But the Fullers and the rest did not work in any subtle fashion. They carried out a crude and beastly job.

Once again the Ideal stood face to face with the stand-patter. Witness the countenance of Thayer and compare its cruel, hard lines with the faces of Sacco and Vanzetti. It doesn't take a psychologist to determine which is possessed of the higher type of human feeling.

And what must we think of Alvan Fuller who went into the death cell of Vanzetti where he grasped his hand and gave him to understand that he would see to it that justice would be done only to turn about and sign his life away?

A typical example of bourgeois upstart, beginning his career as a vendor of bicycles and developing into a plutocratic connoisseur, buying old masters in Europe by the wholesale! *Malade Ho*!

Oh no! Nicola Sacco was not taken in by the legal farce. He knew they wanted his life. He knew the stamp

---

6   In addition to previously cited figures, Havel is referring to Frederick Katzmann (1875–1953), an American lawyer who prosecuted the Sacco and Vanzetti case.

of the *Bastardi Puritani*! He would have nothing to do with the legalistic sham and the appeals to the hangman.

Poor Bart, his faith in the humanity of his tormentors was his greatest glory! What a sublime view of comradeship and solidarity these two great comrades have set before us. Do we appreciate the tortures they endured for those seven long years of agony? The anguish and forlorn hope from day to day, from hour to hour, that finally an awakened labor movement would rescue them!

Sacco could have been rescued from Dedham by a single energetic act but he would not go without Bart. And Bart was imprisoned within the Charlestown fortress where any attempt at rescue was out of the question.

These two dear brothers of ours, the soul of our souls, left this great mission to us.

Woe to us if we become laggards: and preach not the gospel of anarchy and of a Free Society for which they worked so faithfully and died so nobly.

Do not let us live alone on memory, comrades; we have a self-imposed duty to perform in carrying on the message they left in our care. If we fail in this, the tragic death and suffering of our martyred comrades was all in vain.

NOW AND AFTER (1929)

"GIVE US NEW LITERATURE. OUR BOOKS AND PAMPHLETS are out of date; we need a restatement of our principles in a clear lucid and simple manner; we have to appeal to the working man in his language; our literature is too highbrow, too theoretical"—and so on.

This has been the cry of our active comrades for these many years past. A legitimate complaint on the part of our propagandists, though I think that they do not quite follow the work accomplished by our writers since the Russian Revolution. Let us see.

Max Nettlau in his historical researches; Sebastian Faure in the now appearing *Encyclopedia of Anarchism*;[1] Rudolf Rocker in the remarkable biography of Johann Most;[2] Pierre Ramus in his *Neuschopfung de Gesellschaft durch den Communistichen Anarchismus*;[3] Emma Goldman and Alexander Berkman in their books on Soviet Russia;[4] our Japanese comrade Ishikawa in his critique on

---

1   Faure's *Encyclopédie Anarchiste* was published in four volumes by E. Rivet (Limoges) between 1925 and 1934.

2   Rudolf Rocker (1873–1958) was a German anarcho-syndicalist writer and activist. His *Johann Most: Das Leben Eines Rebellen* ("Johann Most: The Life of a Rebel") was published by Verlag "Der Syndikalist" (Berlin) in 1924.

3   *Neuschöpfung de Gesellschaft durch den Communistichen Anarchismus* ("The Revival of Society under Anarchist Communism") was published by Verlag "Erkenntnis und Befreiung" (Vienna) in 1921.

4   Havel is referring, respectively, to *My Disillusionment in Russia*, published by Doubleday, Page & Co. (New York) in 1923; and *The Bolshevik Myth*, published by Boni & Liveright (New York) in 1925.

dialectic materialism;[5] the works of Armando Borghi;[6] A. de Santillan in *La Protesta* in Buenos Aires;[7] Urales and Montseny in *La Revista Blanca* in Barcelona;[8] the letters of our martyrs, Sacco and Vanzetti[9]—to mention but a few achievements of our publicists, and there are many more—prove conclusively that anarchism is not sterile in its literary output.

And now comes Alexander Berkman again with his latest work: *The A. B. C. of Anarchism*, just the work our comrades have been longing for.[10] Berkman has succeed-

---

5   Havel is possibly referring to *Hi-shinkaron to jinsei* ("Non-Evolution and Life") published in Tokyo in 1925. Sanshirō Ishikawa (1876–1956) was a Japanese anarchist and philosopher.

6   Armando Borghi (1882–1968) was an Italian anarchist and journalist, best known for organizing the Italian anarchist movement after the Second World War. Borghi's most important work from this period was *Mussolini in Camicia* (often translated "Mussolini in Red and Black"), published by Edizioni Libertarie (New York) in 1927.

7   Diego Abad de Santillán (1897–1983) was a Spanish-born anarchist, economist and writer known for his involvement in both the Spanish and Argentine anarchist movements. Founded in 1897, *La Protesta* is an Argentine anarcho-syndicalist newspaper and the principal organ of the Federación Obrera Regional Argentina ("Argentine Regional Workers' Federation"). Santillán edited the newspaper at various times.

8   Joan Montseny i Carret (1864–1942) was a Catalan anarchist and writer who wrote under his own name and the pseudonym Frederico Urales. *La Revista Blanca* was an anarchist individualist magazine published by Montseny in Madrid (1898–1905) and Barcelona (1923–1936).

9   *The Letters of Sacco and Vanzetti* were edited by Marion Frankfurter and Gardner Jackson and published by Viking Press (New York) in 1928.

10 Berkman was invited to write an introduction to anarchism by the Jewish Anarchist Federation in 1926. The result was *Now*

ed in restating the theory and practice of our ideal in the most clear, lucid and simple language. Truly, a great achievement. Only the pamphlets of Kropotkin and Tolstoi and the historic talk between two workers written by Malatesta, can be mentioned in comparison with Berkman's book.[11]

The hardest task for any writer is to write in a simple style especially on subject of theoretical concepts. Wiseacres, loaded down with tomes on economic and social theorists may find the book too simple. To me, the lucidity constitutes its greatness.

The book is addressed primarily to the American reader, the American worker. Now the average American worker, though highly specialized in his trade and cynical in his behavior, has the mind of a child when it comes to the understanding of social theories: the political boss is his teacher in economics. Of course, I do not speak of those holding membership in social organizations and political parties, but of the average man in the street, the man who knows little or nothing about social theories. To reach him, one must use the simplest terms in discussion.

The great value of Berkman's book, I emphasize again is just this simple, admirable language with which he approaches the reader.

Many of our comrades would do well to peruse the book thoroughly. Some of those who doubt the necessity of organization will find much wisdom here on this question—much that should be pondered over. Spontaneous action is all very well, but the mode of life with its

---

and After: The ABC of Communist Anarchism, was published by Vanguard Press (New York) in 1929.

11 Havel is referring to Fra Contadini ("Between Peasants"), which was first published Malatesta's newspaper La Questione Sociale in September 1884. An English translation (A Talk About Anarchist Communism Between Two Workers) was published by Freedom Press (London) in 1891.

application of technology to every human endeavor cries out for a closer cohesion in our ranks right now and will demand far more in the not far distant future.

The chapters on the preparation for the Social Revolution and how to defend the victorious revolution from its enemies and counter revolutionists are wonderfully clear and precise. So are those pages devoted to a thorough criticism of the Bolshevik position and their use of anarchist slogans for their own purposes.

These are points which have so far been sadly neglected in our literature, with the exception of Emile Pataud's and Emile Pouget's book, but Berkman provides some excellent illustrations on these gravely important problems.[12]

Propaganda means education, and Berkman's book will prove of great value for that purpose; we are neither religious cranks with a mission nor materialistic fatalists who expect a free society to grow by itself out of the present system. We are propagandists. All we can do is to expose the bankruptcy, the dissolution of existing institutions and demonstrate how the tendencies growing from this dissolution work along lines of the realization of the Anarchist Society. Berkman's book will prove of great help toward this realization. It is, indeed, the A.B.C. of Anarchism.

Comrade Berkman has given us three remarkable books: his *Prison Memoirs*, recognized as a great literary work and also of great value to students of penology; then, *The Bolshevik Myth*, a historical exposè of the Russian Revolution by an eye witness; and now this splendid work on Anarchist Communism. He has added luster to our movement and we are indeed happy to congratulate him upon his successful accomplishment of such an arduous task.

---

12 Havel is referring to *Comment nous ferons la Révolution* (cited previously).

GUSTAV LANDAUER (1930)[1]

THE UPRISING OF GERMAN WORKERS, SOLDIERS, AND SAIL-
ors in November, 1918, was directed not only against
the Nepmen and Junkers but also against the traitorous
leaders of the German Social Democracy.[2] And as these
upstarts from the working class had, during the war, supported the Kaiser, so they turned now against their own
flesh and blood and massacred their followers in order
to keep their social position among the bourgeoisie. The
assassins from Versailles had their bloodhound in the
aristocratic Marquis de Galliffet.[3] The assassins from

---

1   This essay originally appeared in *The Road to Freedom*.

2   The German Revolution (also known as the November
     Revolution) refers to a series of social and political conflicts which
     transpired in the aftermath of Germany's humiliating defeat in
     the First World War. The revolution began in earnest with the
     declaration of a republic on November 9, 1918 and the abdica-
     tion of Kaiser Wilhelm II shortly thereafter. This was followed by
     nearly a year of bloody conflicts between revolutionary leftists and
     the Social Democratic Party (including the Spartacist Uprising of
     January 1919), the latter of which refused to implement any form
     of soviet-style socialism and instead opted for a parliamentary
     system. The revolution ended on August 11, 1919 with the adop-
     tion of the Weimar Constitution. "Junkers" refers to the tradi-
     tional nobility of Prussia. The use of the term "Nepmen" (usually
     rendered "NEPmen") is unclear. It usually refers to industrialists
     and businessmen who took advantage of Lenin's New Economic
     Policy (or NEP) to make a profit. As the NEP wasn't instituted
     until 1921, however, Havel is evidently referring to a generic kind
     of person—presumably war profiteers.

3   Gaston Alexandre Auguste, Marquis de Galliffet (1830–1909) was a
     French military officer and politician best known for his involvement

Berlin found their bloodhound in the proletarian landsknecht, Noske.[4]

Thirty-five years ago I listened to Noske during a Commune celebration in Hanover, denouncing Galiffet. It did not take him a lifetime to imitate his forerunner. Among the victims of Noske was our beloved comrade Gustav Landauer. The Anarchist movement lost in him one of the most interesting and original personalities.

When the workers of Munich proclaimed a Rote Republik, the president of the Soviet, Kurt Eisner, called immediately upon his friend Gustav Landauer and invited him to come to Munich and to help in the reconstruction of society.[5] Landauer left his study and hastened to the field of action. Alas, to find there his Golgotha.

Eisner was killed by the Bavarian Fascisti and Landauer delivered the funeral oration over the body of his friend. Shortly after he followed Eisner in the

---

in the suppression of the Paris Commune (hence his being described as a "bloodhound" for the "assassins from Versailles").

4   Gustav Noske (1868–1946) was a German politician who served as the first Minister of Defense for the Weimar Republic. Ostensibly a socialist, Noske conspired with conservative politicians and military leaders to crush the communist uprisings of 1919–1920. The *landsknechte* (roughly, "lowland knights") were mercenaries, mainly German pikemen, in fifteenth and sixteenth century Europe. Havel is suggesting, in effect, that Noske is a thug for hire.

5   Kurt Eisner (1867–1919) was a German socialist politician and journalist. A member of the Independent Social Democratic Party, Eisner was instrumental in overthrowing the Bavarian monarchy and creating a short-lived social-democratic state in November 1918, for which he served as Prime Minister until February 1919. Strictly speaking, the revolutionary *Bayerische Räterepublik* (Bavarian Council Republic, also known as the Munich Soviet Republic was not declared until two months later, following Eisner's assassination by a right-wing nationalist on 21 February 1919.

Valhalla of immortal rebels. An aristocratic Junker, named Freiherr von Gagern, struck him with a whip over the face and his soldateska killed him with their bayonets.[6] One of the landsknechts tore from Landauer's finger an old ring—how well I remember that ring!—spat in Landauer's face and said, "that dog does not need it any more."[7]

Such was the end of one of the most spiritual thinkers and artists of modern Germany.

Landauer's correspondence with his contemporaries, his friends and admirers, has just been published, edited by Dr. Buber and published by Rutter & Loening in Frankfurt A.M.[8] In the correspondence we can follow the remarkable intellectual activity of our martyred friend and comrade. I only need to mention some of the names of his correspondents to elucidate Landauer's spiritual affinities. Here we find the poets Hugo von Hoffmannsthal and Richard Dehmel; Fritz Manthner, the author of the *The Origin of Language*; the critic Maximilian Harden; Walter Rathenau, also killed later by the Fascisti; the Dutch Sociologist, Van Eden, to mention only a few of the original minds who had great influence on contemporary thought.[9]

---

6   As Havel suggests, Major Baron Heinrich von Gagern (1878–1964) was a German soldier and aristocrat. He received a nominal fine for assaulting Landauer; no one was ever charged in the murder. *Soldetska* is a German word referring to a band of soldiers.

7   Landauer was arrested on May 1, 1919. The following day he was transported to the prison at Stadelheim, where, according to most accounts, he was savagely beaten by members of the reactionary Freikorps before being shot to death.

8   Martin Buber (1878–1965) was an Austrian-born Jewish existentialist philosopher and a close friend of Landauer's for much of his adult life. *Gustav Landauer: Sein Lebensgang in Briefen* ("Gustav Landauer: His Life in Letters") was published in 1929.

9   Havel is referring, respectively, to Hugo von Hofmannsthal

Gustav Landauer was born April 7th, 1870, in Karlsruhe, Wurttemberg, from middle class parents. After he had received the diploma as Doctor of Philosophy and Philology he intended to study medicine at the University in Freiburg, but was refused the matriculation because he had meanwhile served a prison term for his political activity and was considered a dangerous agitator. He went to Berlin where he became a collaborator on the *Sozialistischer Akademiker*.[10] In 1896 he published his first work, a novel called *Der Todesprediger*.[11] In 1892 he joined the revolt of the radical wing in the Social Democracy and became a member of the "Unabhamgigen," the Independents.[12] From there it took only a short time to Anarchism.

(1874–1929), an Austrian novelist, composer, poet and essayist; Richard Dehmel (1863–1920), a German writer and poet; Maximilian Harden (1861–1927), born Felix Ernst Witkoswki, a German journalist; Walter Rathenau (1867–1922), a German industrialist and politician who served as Foreign Minister for the Weimar Republic; and Frederik Van Eeden (1860–1932), a Dutch sociologist, psychologist and writer. It is unclear what these individuals had in common, or why Landauer had "spiritual affinities" with them.

10 *Sozialistischer Akademiker* ("Socialist Academics") was a German socialist newspaper published from 1895 to 1896.

11 *Der Todesprediger* ("The Preacher of Death") was published by Heinrich Minden (Dresden) in 1893, not 1896 as Havel claims. A parody of the *Bildungsroman* genre, it is highly influenced by Nietzschean and Schopenhauerian themes.

12 Havel is referring to the *Verein der unabhängiger Sozialisten* ("Association of Independent Socialists"), also known as the *Opposition der Jungen* ("The Youthful Oppositioin"), a German socialist organization which existed from 1891 to 1894. Other important members—all of them anarchists or Marxist revolutionaries who became disillusioned with social democratic politics—included Max Baginski (1864–1943), Wilhelm Werner (1859–1939), Bruno Wille, and Karl Wildberger (1855–1939).

Landauer became the editor of the *Sozialist*, published by the "Unabhamgigen," and with his co-workers Albert Weidner and Wilhelm Spohr, made that organ into one of the most outstanding Anarchist publications.[13] The *Sozialist* represented the theoretical part of Anarchism, a second paper, *Der Arme Konrad*, added to it, the propagandist view of our movement.[14]

Landauer translated Proudhon and Kropotkin at the same time continuing his work on Belle Lettres.[15] A new edition of Heinse's *Ardinghello*;[16] transvaluation of

13 *Der Sozialist* ("The Socialist") was a German socialist newspaper published from 1891 to 1899, and again from 1909 to 1915. Albert Weidner (1871–1948) and Wilhelm Spohr (1868–1959) were German anarchist writers and political activists. Along with Landauer, Baginski, Wille, and many others, they were members of the Friederichshagener Dichtkreis (Friederichshagener Poets' Circle). Spohr was a poet, a critic, and a translator (among other things, he translated Multatuli from the Dutch). Weidner lived with Landauer (and many others) in the Neue Gemeinschaft ("New Community") urban commune in Berlin (1900–1904).

14 *Der Arme Konrad* ("Poor Conrad") was a German socialist newspaper published from 1896 to 1899. Edited by Weidner, *Der Arme Konrad* was the result of a mutiny by staff members of *Der Sozialist*, who felt that the newspaper had become too theoretical. Landauer created *Der Arme Konrad* as a compromise.

15 See, for example, "Neuprägung der Worte 'Anarchie,' 'anarchisch,' und 'Anarchist,'" (excerpted from Proudhon's: *Was ist Eigentum?* [What Is Property?], 1840); Peter Kropotkin, *Landwirtschaft, Industrie und Handwerk* (Fields, Factories and Workshops), published S. Calvary and Company (Berlin) in 1904; and Peter Kropotkin, *Gegenseitige Hilfe in der Entwickelung* (Mutual Aid: A Factor of Evolution), published by T. Thomas (Leipzig) in 1904. My thanks to Dominique Miething for the Proudhon reference.

16 Wilhelm Heinse (1746–1803) was a German novelist and an important contributor to the Romantic *Sturm und Drang* movement. His novel *Ardinghello* was originally published in 1787.

the mediaeval mystics, Jacob Boehme and Ekkehard;[17] and a splendid delineation of Goethe's are his contributions to the German literature.[18] To the literature of revolt he contributed the remarkable exposition of *Die Revolution*.[19]

At the International Congress in Zurich in 1893, and in London in 1896, where the final break occurred between the political Socialists and the Anarchists, Landauer represented the German anarchist movement.[20] In

---

Although Landauer never produced a new edition of the text, he did reprint several excerpts in *Der Sozialist* in 1896, beginning with Vol. 2, No. 15 (April 11). My thanks to Dominique Miething for this reference.

17 Havel is referring to *Meister Eckharts mystische Schriften* (Meister Eckhart's Mystical Writings), published by Schnabel (Berlin) in 1903. Eckhart Von Hochheim (1260–1327), known as "Meister Eckhart," was a German theologian and mystic. Landauer discusses Böhme, among many others, in *Skepsis und Mystik* (Doubt and Mysticism), published by E. Fleischel (Berlin) in 1903.

18 Landauer wrote extensively on Goethe. His most important piece is most likely "*Goethes Politik*" ("Goethe's Politics"), which is included in *Der werdende Mensch: Aufsätze zur Literatur* (The Emerging Man: Essays on Literature), published by G. Kiepenheuer (Potsdam) in 1921.

19 *Die Revolution* (The Revolution) was published by Rütten and Loening (Frankfurt A.M.) in 1907. One of Landauer's most significant contributions to anarchist thought, it contains the famous and oft-quoted lines: "The state is a condition, a certain relationship among human beings, a mode of behaviour between them; we destroy it by contracting other relationships, by behaving differently toward one another . . . We are the state, and we shall continue to be the state until we have created the institutions that form a real community and society of men."

20 Havel is referring to the Congress of the Second International (Zurich, 1893), from which Landauer, along with fellow anarchists Wildberger and Wille, were expelled for criticizing parliamentary

1908 Landauer and some of his comrades founded the "Sozialische Bund" for the propaganda of "Siedlungs Genosenschaften"—Anarchist colonies in Germany—in connection with which he published the *Anfruf zum Freien Sozialismus.*[21]

The German Anarchist movement produced some of the most outstanding personalities in August Rainsdorf, the fierce terrorist;[22] in John Most, the powerful agitator; in Gustav Landauer, the intellectual pathfinder.

An original thinker, a great artist, a brave comrade, and a beloved friend gave up his life on May 2, 1919, for humanity and the Anarchist ideal.

---

politics. The same thing happened in London in 1896.

21 Havel is referring to the *Sozialisticher Bund* (Socialist Federation), which Landauer founded with Buber, Mühsam, and others as a network of decentralized communes (*siedlungs genossenschaften*, or cooperative settlements). The *Sozialisticher Bund* published Landauer's *Aufruf zum Socialismus* (Call to Socialism) in Berlin in 1911.

22 August Reinsdorf (1849–1885) was a German anarchist, sometimes known as the "Father of German Anarchism." He was executed for his attempt to assassinate Friedrich III.

GANDHI'S IDEAL (1930)[1]

THE GANDHI MOVEMENT IS OF GREAT SIGNIFICANCE AND it behooves us to get acquainted with the fundamental ideas of the Mahatma. What are his ideas? Gandhi's ideas are accessible in his own autobiography *The Story of My Experiments with Truth* and in other works from his own pen.[2] Rather than to depend on his interpreters, it is far better to read the remarkable man himself. If his gospel is still misunderstood it is not his fault; it is not because he lacks zeal for expounding it. The two volumes of his auto-biography and the story of his "Satya-graha" campaign for his compatriots in South Africa fill nearly 2,000 pages.[3] Besides that, he has, since 1904, been almost continuously editing a weekly paper to propagate and explain his ideas. Few men have exposed their souls more unflinchingly to the ordeal of publicity.

The reader who has ploughed steadily through the pages of his autobiography may reasonably feel that he knows most of what there is to know about the Mahatma, and he will accordingly consider his verdict on the question: Does or does not Gandhi deserve the title which has been accorded to him, viz.: "Mahatma, the Great Soul"?

---

1 This essay originally appeared in *The Road to Freedom* 6, no. 10 (June 1930). It was most likely written in response to Gandhi's famous "Salt March," which took place a few months earlier.

2 *The Story of My Experiments with Truth* was originally published in installments in Gandhi's journal *Navjivan* between 1925 and 1929. The first English translation was published by Mahadev Dasai in two volumes (1927 and 1929).

3 *Satyagraha* literally means "passive insistence on the truth." In the context of Mahatma Gandh's thought and practice, it can be equated to non-violent civil resistance.

But here Gandhi clearly interposes that the issue has been wrongly stated: he has never claimed, always disowned, the worshipful title. The question he brings before the reader is whether his ideas are true and valuable to humanity.

Gandhi's *a priori* statement is the declaration that "There is no other God than Truth; the end of man is to know Truth." Still, he does not claim himself to have more than caught "little fleeting glimpses of that mighty effulgence."

To get to know "Truth" man needs "Ahimsa," non-violence, which, as interpreted by Gandhi, is very much like the love of one's neighbor—but extended beyond the human species.

In popular Hinduism, "Ahimsa" is merely the refusal to destroy animal life. Gandhi, while seeking to avoid conflict with this popular notion, evidently regards "Ahimsa" as concerned less with action than with thought. Where there is no feeling of hatred there is no "himsa," violence, thus "Ahimsa" means for Gandhi "loving the meanest of creation as oneself."

To attain this state of mind self-purification is necessary, and, purification being highly infectious, this leads to purification of one's surroundings. Purification consists in becoming "absolutely passion-free, rising above the currents of love and hatred."

The zeal for purification of his surroundings and the devotion to the ideal of "Ahimsa" made Gandhi a rebel and brought him into the public arena to protest against "himsa," violence or injustice, wherever he sees it. And the greatest violence being the British rule over Hindustan leads Gandhi on his journey of civil disobedience. There is a striking similarity of Gandhi's ideal with that of Tolstoy.

OUR DUTY TO SACCO AND VANZETTI (1930)[1]

WEEK AFTER WEEK, MONTH AFTER MONTH, YEAR AFTER year we appealed, implored, exhorted, and pleaded with the American workers to prevent the murder of Sacco and Vanzetti.

All in vain, we could not penetrate through the stone wall of indifference. Why repeat? What does wailing amount to?

Our duty is simple, plain and clear. Our comrades left a powerful message to us: to spread the ideal of Anarchism as forcibly and energetically as they did in their lifetime.

Let us recognize the fact; by burning our comrades in the electric chair, the ruling class challenged the Anarchist movement in the United States.

It is our duty to take up the gauntlet thrown by the enemy into our teeth.

Counting on supine indifference, the ruling class considers the case closed.

It is up to us to keep it open. True, we are a small minority; but let not this reflection temper our spirit and dampen our ardor.

By spreading the ideal of Anarchism, we shall fulfill the hopes and dreams of our martyred comrades.

Their martyrdom shall not be in vain. Let us continue with the slogan of Paul of Tarsus: "WOE IS ME IF I SPREAD NOT THE GOSPEL."

---

1   This essay originally appeared in *The Road to Freedom* (August 1930).

AMONG THE BOOKS (1930)[1]

REVIEW OF *MY 30 YEARS WAR*: BY MARGARET ANDERSON.
Covici-Friede, N.Y., $4.

After she had given up the *Little Review*, Margaret Anderson, known among her friends as "Marty," went to Europe and settled down among the Franco-American expatriates. She has now published her autobiography and herewith ended her Odyssey in search of Ulysses. The book is caviar for the cognoscenti.

Autobiographies and psychographs are the latest literary rage and racket. Soon, I am afraid, we shall hear of embryos depicting their experience in the maternal prison. The more I browse among autobiographies, the less I find the real life of the authors. Whether I take St. Augustine, Benvenuto Cellini, Jean Jacques Rousseau, Henry Adams, Mary Bashkirtseff, Mme. Dubarry, or any of the hundreds of self-portraits, I only find puzzles.[2] Goethe, wise as

---

1   Margaret Anderson (1886–1973) was an American publisher who edited the famed *Little Review* from 1914 to 1929. An important outlet of literary modernism, the *Review* introduced many of the most prominent American and British writers of the twentieth century, including Ezra Pound, James Joyce, and T.S. Eliot. Although Havel's description of Anderson as a "dilettante" is fair (she never made any major literary or political contributions of her own), Anderson is significant figure in the history of the modernist movement who had valid differences of opinion with Goldman and other radicals of the time—many of whom failed to appreciate the political relevance of avant garde literature.

2   In addition to previously cited (or famous) individuals, Havel is referring, respectively, to Henry Adams (1838–1918), an American educator and historian known for his posthumously published memoir, *The Education of Henry Adams*; and Jeanne

ever, knew why he entitled his autobiography *"Dichtung und Wahrheit."*[3] It takes a great amount of *Dichtung* to hide the *Wahrheit.*

That guy who made up the blurb and jacket for Miss Anderson's book seems to have the mind of an ostrich. Judging from the jacket one would never imagine that the book deals at least a third part with Anarchism and Emma Goldman.

Burton Rascoe compares Miss Anderson's book with the autobiography of Isadora Duncan.[4] Quite unfair, for Marty has none of the vulgar exhibitionism of Isadora. She is reticent about her private life, too refined and sensitive to offer the mob spicy details about sex-life. She has the gift of sensitization.

The *Little Review* was the great opus of Marty's variegated attempts and the publication of Joyce's *Ulysses* her greatest achievement. Is this sufficient? Marty overestimates her artistic struggle. Her war was no war at all; it was not even an attack against windmills; it was a play with soap bubbles. She has that great zest for life and that lead her to all kinds of experimentation.

Clara Laughlin, Emma Goldman, Jane Heap, (her coworker on the *Little Review*), and Georgette Leblanc (former Mme. Maeterlinck) were the beacon lights in her life.[5]

Bécu, comtesse du Barry (1743–1793), a French memoirist and mistress of Louis XV and had a famously difficult relationship with his son and daughter in law, Louis XVI and Marie Antoinette.

3 *Dichtung und Wahrheit* ("Poetry and Truth") was published between 1811 and 1833.

4 Havel is referring, respectively, to Burton Rascoe (1892–1957), an American journalist, writer and literary critic; and Isadora Duncan (1877–1927), an American dancer. An avowed leftist, Duncan was part of the same broad bohemian and radical milieu as Havel. (It is worth noting, for example, that Alexander Berkman helped her write the autobiography mentioned here.)

5 Havel is referring, respectively, to Clara Laughlin (1873–1941),

She gave up Anarchism. Had she ever had it? Alas, she never understood Anarchism, she never grasped the philosophy, it was only an experiment with her. "All Anarchists I met," she declares, "were interested in Art."[6] Quite true, but she forgets that they are interested in something else besides Art: in social dynamics and economics. This part of Anarchism she never touched. She was skirmishing on the fringe.

I wish Miss Anderson had taken the advice of Clara Laughlin:[7] to stand on the bridges and to watch life. To feel the story of every vagabond she may meet mere, in every poor waif of a girl who may be wanting to throw herself into the river. In her Drang-und-Sturm period, after the killing of Joe Hill, she wrote in the *Little Review*: "Why doesn't someone shoot the Governor of Utah?"[8] Detectives went after her but an influential admirer of Marty persuaded the authorities that "Miss

---

an American writer and editor; Jane Heap (1883–1964), an American publisher who, like her long-term business associate and lover Anderson, was crucial to the development of literary modernism in the United States; and Georgette Leblanc (1869–1941), a French operatic singer and one-time lover of the Belgian writer Maurice Maeterlinck.

6   The actual quotation is "I have never known a people more rabid about art than anarchists" (*My Thirty Years' War*, p. 133).

7   Havel is paraphrasing the quotation slightly, which appears on p. 30 of *My Thirty Years' War*.

8   "Toward Revolution," *The Little Review* 2, no. 9 (December 1915). The actual quote was "Incidentally, why didn't someone shoot the governor of Utah before he could shoot Joe Hill?" Joe Hill (1879–1915) was a Swedish-born American labor activist and songwriter. Born Joseph Emmanuel Hagglund, Hill ultimately settled in Utah, where he was tried and executed for his supposed involvement in a murder. The trial was controversial at the time and remains so, as it was believed that Hill had been framed for the act.

Anderson was only a flighty society girl who meant nothing she said."

Was that admirer far from truth?

She helped to arrange lectures for Emma Goldman and was distressed when E.G. "refused to address the audience in the Fine Arts Building in a rough manner."[9] Like an emancipated Sorosis girl, Marty wanted to *etaper le bourgeois*.[10] In Denver she and Jane Heap "gave ourselves to reforming the anarchist mind."[11] *Sancta Simplicitas*.

And what kind of social philosophy has she acquired since she gave up Anarchism? Her spiritual farther is A. E. Orage, a former editor of the London *New Age*, now the commissioner for a Russian imitation Yogi.[12] Miss Anderson "went in ecstasy and wanted to weep, as a token of admiration" when Orage gave her this sublime advice: "Act, don't be acted upon. Remember, you are a pianist, not a piano."[13]

How sophomoric! And she states: "I like monarchies,

9   Anderson helped to arrange Goldman's lectures on drama at the Fine Arts Building in Chicago (November 1914). Although it is unclear where Havel is getting this quotation from, it accurately reflects the substance of Anderson's response as outlined on pp. 83–84 of *My Thirty Years' War* as well as her article "Emma Goldman in Chicago" (*Mother Earth* 9, no. 10, December 1914).

10   A "Sorosis girl" is a member of a female sorority. *Épater la bourgeoisie* ("shock the bourgeoisie") was a rallying cry of the French Decadents.

11   The actual quote is "We had a large revolutionary public in Denver and I shall always remember that city as the place where we gave ourselves seriously to reforming the anarchist mind" (*My Thirty Years' War*, p. 133).

12   Havel is referring, respectively, to Alfred Richard Orage (1873–1934), an English writer, editor, and socialist intellectual; and George Gurdjieff (1866–1949), a Russian-born mystic who combined the esoteric teachings of Christianity, Sufism and eastern mysticism into a philosophy he called "the Work" or "the Fourth Way."

13   Havel is running together and paraphrasing several quotes from *My Thirty Years' War*, pp. 269–270.

tyrants, prima donnas, the insane. I even like Mussolini. At least he is having fun, though Rome is a terrible place today."[14]

What a come down!

Miss Anderson never wanted to belong to a group, yet she spent all her life among literary cliques, and precious dilettante Ezra Pound is the high priest of the Cenacle of the expatriates she admires now.[15] The letters she publishes in her book as an example of Ezra's literary clairvoyance are Ga Ga, full of vanity and cattish spitefulness.

Art for Art's sake—yes, and dollars from Otto Kahn.[16]

Bernard Shaw has a fine characterization of these *l'art pour l'art* enthusiasts. He says:

> No men are greater sticklers for the arbitrary dominion of genius and talent than your artists. The great painter is not content with being sought after and admired because his hands can do more than ordinary hands, which they truly can, but he wants to be fed as if his stomach needed more food than ordinary stomachs, which it does not. A day's work is a day's work, neither more nor less, and the man who does it needs a day's sustenance, a night's repose, and due leisure, whether he be

---

14 *My Thirty Years' War*, p. 41.

15 Ezra Pound (1885–1972) was an American-born poet whose best known work was the *Cantos*, a large collection of poems. Outside of his poetry, Pound is probably best known for his conversion to the fascist movement and his defection to Italy. Arrested in the aftermath of World War II, Pound spent the final years of his life in a mental institution. The Cenacle is the upper room in which the Last Supper occurred.

16 Otto Kahn (1867–1934) was a British investment banker who devoted his wealth to collecting and funding artworks.

painter or ploughman. But the rascal of a painter, poet, novelist, or other voluptuary of labor, is not content with his advantage in popular esteem over the ploughman; he also wants an advantage in money, as if there were more hours in a day spent in a studio or library than in the field; or as if he needed more food to enable him to do his work than the ploughman to enable him to do his. He talks of the higher quality of his work, as if the higher quality of it was his own making—as if it gave him a right to work less for his neighbor than his neighbor works for him—as if the ploughman could not do better without him than he without the ploughman—as if the value of the most celebrated pictures has not been questioned more than that of any straight furrow in the arable world—as if it did not take an apprenticeship of as many years to train the hand and eye of a mason or blacksmith as of an artist—as if, in short, the fellow were a god, as canting brain worshippers have for years past been assuring him he is. Artists are the high priests of the modern Moloch.[17]

And Thomas Craven has this to say:

It is no wonder that the worker has no tolerance of artists. Look at the painter! A snob, a divine ignoramus who scatters the illusion that he is a superior being. A fantastic organism bawling out that he is

---

17 *An Unsocial Socialist* (London: Swan, Sonnenschein, Lowery & Co., 1887), p. 77.

a soul apart, that he has a peculiar intelligence—that he has nothing in common
with the human herd! Like all children
he learns to scratch on paper; he dabbles
in pigments. Vanity and laziness are the
twin stimulants to his nothing gifts; and
his highest ambition is to crawl into fash-
ionable society. He apes the commercial
hero and panders to the rich. He pursues
his trade with the bloodless cunning of the
hypocrite and spends his life imitating the
mannerisms of successful predecessors. He
does anything to carry popular favor, and
once he has gained his coveted position,
he goes repeating himself until merciful
death knocks him in the head. Sometimes
he is able to talk, and his speech is a ran-
dom idiocy of confusions. He makes a virtue of his weakness, crying lyrically that he
is sensitive, and reduces art to the level of
technical processes. A carpenter with clean
hands, he lacks the mechanic's honesty of
purpose and daily industry. He has nothing
to say, and his lymphatic disposition, not
balanced by sober toil, spits out temperament for dollars and cents. He has separated art from life and turned it into a bastard
occupation for dilettantes! He transcribes
nature and copies the human head, and the
camera, in one flash, makes rubbish of his
stupid efforts. He speaks with a French ac-
cent, and demands special privileges. When
befuddled, he is a symbolist; when literal, a
realist. He has not the courage to go back
to the crafts where he belongs. He has the
exuberance of a leper and the imagination
of a lap-dog. He worships the dealer, and

produces a commodity that is forced on the
public by stealth and misrepresentation. I
say it is not a wonderful that the artist is a
despicable figure in modern life.[18]

It would be cruel to add anything to it. The book is
illustrated with "spiritualized" likeness of the artistic intelligentsia—Margaret Anderson herself, Gertrude Stein,
James Joyce, Ezra Pound, Ben Hecht, Georgette Leblanc,
Jane Heap, George Antheil, Ernest Hemingway, and others.[19] It also contains a characteristic likeness of Emma
Goldman by Hutchinson.

The best morsel of the book is a quotation from the vale-
dictum of Jane Heap in the last issue of the *Little Review*: "It
is quite unlikely that there will have to be reorganization on
a large scale before we can have any thing approaching great
objective art... or approaching life . . . Perhaps it would be
more than an intellectual adventure to give up our obses-
sions about art, hopelessness, and *Little Reviews*, and take to
pursuits more becoming to human beings."[20]

---

18 *Paint* (New York: Harcourt Brace, 1923), p. 115. Thomas Craven
    (1888–1969) was an American author and critic well known for
    promoting American painters of the Regionalist school.

19 In addition to previously cited (and famous) individuals, Havel is
    referring, respectively, to Ben Hecht (1894–1964), an American
    screenwriter, director, producer, and occasionally contribu-
    tor to *Mother Earth*, sometimes known as the "Shakespeare of
    Hollywood"; and George Antheil (1900–1959), an American
    composer and inventor. Hecht's scripts include *Gunga Din, Some
    Like it Hot, Gone with the Wind,* and *His Girl Friday.* He was the
    first winner of the Academy Award for Best Screenplay.

20 The quote appears on p. 274 of *My Thirty Years' War.* The por-
    tion originally written by Heap in her final editorial for *The Little
    Review* ("Lost: A Renaissance," 12, no. 2, May 1929) begins
    "Perhaps it would be more than an intellectual adventure..."
    Everything before that appears to have been written by Anderson.

A VICTIM OF COMMUNIST TREACHERY (1930)[1]

PETER PETRELLA, A HIGHLY SENSITIVE VICTIM OF A CRUEL society, a fine comrade and untiring idealist, met his death in Detroit early last month. Trapped by the police through an "anonymous tip," he was killed by a detective while defending his life. Brave to death, he killed one of the officers before he in turn was shot.

The hunt for Petrella was the sequel of an affair at a communist meeting near Pittsburgh a few weeks previously.

Petrella went to that meeting dedicated to Sacco and Vanzetti to protest against the travesty of communists arranging a memorial meeting for Sacco and Vanzetti while they are at the same time killing and sending anarchists into exile in Russia.

He was attacked by the communists at the meeting and in self-defense he shot two of his assailants.

---

1   Little is known about Peter Petrella (referred to as "Pietri Petrelli" in several news stories). Evidently he was an Italian anarchist who had lived in Avella, Pennsylvania for five years at the time of the events described and had a longstanding feud with local communists. On August 22, 1930, Petrella attended a Sacco-Vanzetti meeting in Avella that had been organized by the communist-controlled National Miners Union. At some point he created a disturbance which culminated in his fatally shooting two communist miners named George Harkoff and Stephen Mina. Petrella fled the scene but was apprehended in Detroit on Sunday, September 7. Evidently the police were informed via an anonymous tip that Petrella had been involved in another, unrelated murder which had occurred earlier in the month. Havel, obviously, blames the communists for Petrella's death.

Petrella's father and a brother were killed by the Fascisti in Italy; another brother died in prison in Argentina.

Communist intolerance and treachery hunted the last member of this family of rebels to death at the hands of an American policeman. Anarchists will cherish the memory of Peter Petrella as a loyal friend, a brave comrade, and one whose heart was stout enough to die standing up rather than waste out his remaining years behind prison bars.

THE ANARCHIST RELATIONS COMMITTEE (1930)

In the January issue there appeared a statement of principles of the Anarchist Relations Committee. Have you read and taken that statement into consideration? We anxiously await your opinion.

Is anarchism a living ideal to be propagated with all our zeal, all our energy and enthusiasm, or is it but a precious jewel to be hidden away in a velvet casket and only to be displayed at socials, picnics, and entertainments?

Put metaphysical discussion aside for the moment and grasp the immensity of a full and useful life! Discouraged humanity is waiting for a new gospel. It is up to us to supply the disappointed workers with the weapon for their final deliverance. That weapon is the Ideal of Anarchism and its tactical application in the death struggle with the oppressors.

We expect you to join with your groups in & discussion of our proposition and to keep us informed of your progress. If the secretary of your group neglects our appeals, we urge individual members to stir him into action and insist upon results.

We want a live movement spreading among the people instead of stagnation and everlasting rag-chewing with cranks, hair-splitters, and sore-heads.

The New York members of the A. R. C. are working in conjunction with the Anarchist Aid Society and have recently held a protest meeting against the continued incarceration of Francesco Ghezzi by the Bolshevik Dictators in Russia masquerading under the name of Communists, and as these lines are being written, another joint meeting is taking place to determine further activities.[1]

Now *you* should go into action and report your plans and progress to S. Dolgoff, Secretary, care of *Road to Freedom*.[2]

---

1   Havel is referring to Francesco Ghezzi (1893–1942), an Italian anarchist. One of the many anarchists who moved to Russia after the Bolshevik Revolution, he was ultimately accused of counter-revolutionary activity and spent the last days of his life in a gulag. Ghezzi's conviction was overturned in 1956.

2   Sam Dolgoff (1902–1990) was an American anarchist. Part of a younger generation, Dolgoff played a critical role in connecting later anarchist thinkers to Havel's contemporaries.

THE SIGNIFICANCE OF MAY DAY (1931)

THE MAY IDEA—IN THE RELATION OF ITS REVOLUTIONARY spirit to labor struggles—first manifested itself in the economic battles of the Knights of Labor. The final theoretical aim of that organization—founded by Uriah S. Stephens and fellow-workers in 1869, and bearing a pronounced radical character in the beginning of its history—was the emancipation of the working classes by means of direct economic action.[1]

Its first practical demand was the eight-hour day, and the agitation to that end was an unusually strenuous one. Several strikes of the Knights of Labor were practically General Strikes. The various economic battles of that period, supported by the American Federation of Labor during its young days, culminated, on the first of May 1886, in a great strike, which gradually assumed almost national proportions.

The workingmen of a number of large cities, especially those of Chicago, ceased their work on that day and proclaimed a strike in favor of the eight-hour day.

The manly attitude of labor in 1886 was the result of a resolution passed by the Labor Congress held at St. Louis one year previously.[2] Great demonstrations of a

---

1 While the rank and file of the Knights of Labor included many militants and radicals, its founder Uriah Smith Stephens (1821–1882), like Terence Powderly and other important leaders of the union, were generally opposed to strikes and other forms of militant labor activity.

2 At its annual convention in December 1885, the Federation of Organized Trades and Labor Unions, a precursor to the AFL,

pronounced social revolutionary character took place all over the country, culminating in the strike of two hundred thousand workingmen, the majority of whom were successful in winning the eight-hour day.

The names of our murdered brothers, sacrificed to propitiate an enraged Moloch, will forever remain indivisibly linked with the idea of the first of May. *It was the Anarchists that bore the brunt of those economic battles.* In vain, however, did organized capital hope to strangle the labor movement on the scaffold; a bitter disappointment awaited the exploiters. True, the movement had suffered an eclipse, but only a temporary one. Quickly rallying its forces, it grew with renewed vigor and energy. In December, 1888, the American Federation of Labor decided to make another attempt to win the eight-hour day, and again by means of direct economic action.[3] The strike was to be initiated by a gigantic demonstration on the first of May, 1890. In the meantime there assembled at Paris (1889) an International Labor Congress.[4] A resolution was offered

---

resolved that May 1, 1886 would be the day on which the eight-hour workday would be implemented. The convention took place in Washington, D.C.—not St. Louis.

3   The convention took place in St. Louis, December 11–15, 1888.

4   Havel is referring to the International Workers Congress, which took place in Paris on July 14, 1889—the centenary of the fall of the Bastille. The Congress issued the following resolution: "The Congress decides to organize a great international demonstration, so that in all countries and in all cities on one appointed day the toiling masses shall demand of the state authorities the legal reduction of the working day to eight hours, as well as the carrying out of other decisions of the Paris Congress. Since a similar demonstration has already been decided upon for May 1, 1890, by the American Federation of Labor at its Convention in St. Louis, December, 1888, this day is accepted for the international demonstration. The workers of the various countries must organize this demonstration according to conditions prevailing in each country."

to join the demonstration, and the day which three years previously initiated the eight-hour movement, became the slogan of the international proletariat, awakened to the realization of the revolutionary character of its final emancipation. Chicago was to serve as an example.

Unfortunately, however, the direction was not followed. The majority of the congress consisting of political parliamentarists, believers in indirect action, they purposely ignored the essential import of the first of May, so dearly bought on the battlefield; they decided that henceforth the first of May was to be "consecrated to the dignity of labor," thus perverting the revolutionary significance of the great day into a mere appeal to the powers that be to grant the favor of an eight-hour day. Thus the parliamentarists degraded the noble meaning of the historic day...

The effect of the Paris resolution soon manifested itself: the revolutionary energy of the masses became dormant; the wage slaves limited their activity to mere appeals to their masters for alleviation and to political action, either independent of, or in fusion with, the bourgeois parties, as is the case in England and America. They quietly suffered their representatives in Parliament and Congress to defend and strengthen their enemy, the government... In 1914 the parliamentarians betrayed so shamefully and so completely the cause of Labor that class murder became rampant and May Day became an irony.

National patriotic "holidays" celebrate murder in the interests of the kings of money. But the holiday of the international proletariat —the First of May—glorifies the awakening of the brotherhood of man and prepares the way for the abolition of wholesale patriotic and industrial slaughter. What moots us the Fourth of July when we realize that the so-called War of Independence has only served to enable American lords the better to exploit the American masses?

The significance of the First of May is to further this grand conception of labor's mission and hasten its realization. It is a great and difficult task. But in spite of all obstacles, Forward! is our motto, and ever forward we progress.

WHAT'S ANARCHISM? (1932)[1]

Preface

EVERY GREAT MOVEMENT SINCE THE BEGINNING OF HISTORY has been a movement to lift the bottom dog and put him on his feet. And every such movement has been led by extremists. All the great names of history have been the names of extremists. The brave pioneers who blazed the trail through the unknown forest had to fight their way against the many dangers of wild nature, wild beasts, and wilder men. The heroic men who first raised their voices in the cause of religious liberty had to pass through years of cruel persecution. They were hounded to the scaffold or the state with execration and abuse. The wheel slowly turns full circle, and the malefactor of yesterday become the hero-martyr of today, and the faithful tread weary miles to his shrine to pay homage to his memory. Those who dared to raise a protest against political slavery had to face a tempest of slander and vituperation. Today the market-places that witnessed their humiliation are adorned with cherished monuments in their honor, and their names glow from the pedestals with an added brilliance bought by their belated recognition.

But the greatest, the bitterest, the fiercest fight of all the ages is now being fought. The struggle for economic freedom is being waged in every country, race and nation. Compared with this conflict, the contests of the past are as the mimic warfare of happy children marshalling their tiny tin warriors on the nursery floor. No passion is too sordid, no cruelty is too severe, no persecution is too fierce

---

1   Originally published by the Free Society Group of Chicago and the International Group of Detroit.

to find its place and use in this campaign. It began when the first chattel slave raised his voice in protest against a corroding chain. Right down the ages the din of its conflict has kept time like a Greek chorus to the discordant jazz that mars the harmony of the world's advance.

* * *

The working-class does not need leadership so much as it needs comradeship. The world has had enough of leaders. The hero and the leader, even the teacher and the prophet, will in time go the way of the king, the baron, and the capitalist. In the last analysis, it is the friend and companion that the people need; it is the co- operation and fellowship of all people working together for the exaltation of the common life.[2]

What's Anarchism?

The specter of Communism is haunting the world.[3] Not only the powers of Europe, but those of America and Asia as well have entered into a holy alliance to exercise this specter and—oh, cruel irony of history—the erstwhile followers of Marx and Engels, the Socialists of all countries, join the holy alliance against Communism. "Whence this Communism?" they cry out in despair, and exercising the specter they murmur pitifully *mea culpa, mea maxima culpa*.

What is this terrible specter of Communism? Is Communism a state of Society to be established and

---

2   The lines beginning with "The working-class" and ending with "common life" are taken from George D. Herron, *From Revolution to Revolution: An Address In Memory of the Paris Commune* (Chicago: Charles H. Kerr Co., 1907).

3   This is a reference to the opening of Marx and Engels's *Manifesto of the Communist Party* (1848).

managed by the people themselves or a new form of government over them? Is it Communism of the people when a political party captures the State power and decrees a set of laws for others to obey? Is it even a "Transition Stage" as Engels and Lenin prophesied?

State Capitalism—a Transition Stage from private Capitalism—is evolving right now in all countries. But will this transition period usher in a Communist society? On the contrary, we witness a gradual evolution of the State, wherein an all powerful political bureaucracy controls the life of the producers, by controlling the means of production and the products for consumption.

The Bolshevik State Communism is the last form of reaction fooling the workers. Anarchist-Communism is the antidote and protection against bureaucratic State slavery, and the only theory of a free society recognizing the just claim of each to the fullest satisfaction of all his needs, physical, moral and intellectual.

Anarchism is no hypocritical scheme. It cannot dupe men in the manner of political parties which pretend to be saviors of the working class, promising to do wonders if the workers will only give them their confidence. The Anarchists have the far more difficult mission of making the workers realize that neither this nor that political party can do naught for their salvation, and that the sole hope lies in their own insight and energy.

Anarchism may be briefly defined as the negation of all government and all authority of man over man; Communism as the recognition of the just claim of each to the fullest satisfaction of all his needs, physical, moral and intellectual. The Anarchist, therefore, whilst resisting as far as possible all forms of coercion and authority, repudiates just as firmly even the suggestion that he should impose himself upon others, realizing as he does that this fatal propensity in the majority of mankind has been the cause of nearly all the misery and bloodshed in the world.

He understands just as clearly that to satisfy his needs without contributing, to the best of his ability, his share of labor in maintaining the general well-being, would be to live at the expenses of others—to become an exploiter and to live as the rich drones live today. Obviously, then, government on the one hand and private ownership of the means of production on the other, complete the vicious circle—the present social system—which keeps mankind degraded and enslaved.

There will be no need to justify the Anarchist's attack upon all forms of government, history teaches the lesson he has learned on every page. But that lesson being concealed from the mass of the people by interested advocated of "law and order", and even by Social Democrats and the Bolsheviks, the Anarchist deals his hardest blows at the sophisms that uphold the State, and urges workers in striving for their emancipation to confine their efforts to the economic field.

It follows, therefore, that politically and economically his attitude is purely revolutionary; and hence arises the vilification and misrepresentation that Anarchism, which denounces all forms of social injustice, meets with in the press and from public speakers.

Rightly conceived, Anarchism is no mere abstract ideal theory of human society. It views life and social relations with eyes disillusioned. Making an end of all superstitions, prejudices and false sentiments it tries to see things as they really are; and without building castles in the air it finds by the simple correlation of established facts that the grandest possibilities of a full and free life can be placed within the reach of all, once that monstrous bulwark of all our social iniquities—the State—has been destroyed, and common property declared.[4]

---

4   The five paragraphs beginning with "Anarchism may be brief-
     ly defined" and ending with "common property declared" are
     taken from Alfred Marsh, "Anarchist Communism: Its Aims

Modern jurists frequently speak of the atomization of the State in the Middle Ages. In reality it was not atomic. The truth is that the Middle Ages were atomized in the centuries that followed them. The characteristic fact of European societies between the fifteenth and nineteenth centuries was that the corporations were abandoned by their most energetic members. And from this dissolution of the corporate life has arisen the modern unitary state, as an historic and temporal necessity; not as a category of social life. But if the State is not a category, if it is purely an historic institution which arises at the bidding of a momentary necessity, it runs the risk of vanishing from history with the necessity which has called it into existence. And that, in fact, was what occurred in the mentality of thinkers and was on the point of happening in reality.

When the war of 1914 broke out the institution of the State was on the point of disappearing from among the peoples of Western Europe. The thinkers, at least, had already ceased to believe in the necessity for it. It was defended only by the politicians; but there did not remain a single public man who enjoyed the confidence placed in his predecessors. This was not the fault of the men. Personally, they may have been as clever and good then as were the statesmen of old. But we called them politicians and not statesmen, for we no longer believed in the State.[5]

What, after all, is this State idea, this idea of the organized Community to which the individual has to be immolated? Theoretically it is the subordination of the individual to the good of all that is demanded; practically it

---

and Principles," the *Reformers' Year Book*, ed. Joseph Edwards (London: Clarion Company, 1902), p. 26.

5   The two paragraphs beginning with "Modern Jurists frequently speak" and ending with "no longer believed in the state" are taken from Ramiro de Maeztu, *Authority, Liberty and Function in the Light of the War* (London: Allen and Unwin, 1916), pp. 24–25.

is his subordination to a collective egoism, political, military, economic, which seeks to satisfy certain collective aims and ambitions shaped ad imposed on the great mass of the individuals by a smaller or larger number of ruling persons who are supposed in some way to represent the community. It is immaterial whether these belong to a governing class or emerge as in modern States from the mass partly by force of character, but much more by force of circumstances; are imposed more by hypnotism of verbal persuasion than by overt and actual force. In either case there is no guarantee that this ruling class or ruling body represents the best minds of a nation or its noblest or its highest instincts.

Nothing of the kind can be asserted of the modern politician in any part of the world; he does not represent the soul of the people or its aspirations; what he does usually represent is all the average pettiness, selfishness, egoism, self-deception that is about him and these he represents well enough as well as a great deal of mental incompetence and moral conventionality, timidity and pretence. Great issues often come to him for decision but he does not deal with them greatly; high words and noble ideas are on his lips, but they are only the clap-trap of a party. The disease and falsehood of modern political life is present in every country of the world and only the hypnotized acquiescence that men yield to everything that is habitual and makes the present atmosphere of their lives, cloaks and prolongs the malady. Yet it is by such minds that the good of all had to be decided, to such hands that it has to be entrusted, to such an agency calling itself the State the individual is being more and more called upon to give up his entire activity.

* * *

Even if the governing instrument were better constituted and of a higher and moral character, still the

State would not be what the State idea pretends to be. Theoretically, it is the collective wisdom and force of the community as the particular machinery of the State organization will allow to come to the surface which uses that machine but is also caught in it and hampered by it, and hampered also by the large among of folly and selfish weakness that comes up in the same wave. Things would be much worse if there were not a field left for a less trammeled individual effort doing what the State cannot do, employing and using the sincerity, energy, idealism of the best individuals to attempt that which the State has not the wisdom or courage to attempt, getting that done which a collective conservatism and imbecility leave undone or actively oppose and suppress. It is this which is the really effective agent of collective progress. But we are now tending towards such an increase of organized State-power and such a huge irresistible and complex State activity as will either eliminate or leave it dwarfed and cowed into helplessness. Thus the necessary corrective to the defects, limitations ad inefficiency of the State machine is rapidly disappearing.

The State is neither the best mind of the nation or is it even the sum of the communal energies. It leaves out voluntary action, suppresses the working force and thinking mind of important minorities often of those which represent that which is best in the present State of Society.[6]

The regeneration of Society, or better still, the formation of a new Society, is possible along through Anarchism, i.e. through the re-establishment of natural relations of men to one another. This can be accomplished by Anarchist Communism, guaranteeing to each individual

6   The four paragraphs beginning with "What after all is this State idea" and ending with "the present State of Society" are taken from Sri Aurobindo, *The Ideal of Human Unity* (Pondicherry: Sri Aurobindo Ashram Press, 1919), pp. 296–297.

full liberty. Each member of such a Society stands free and equal among his fellow beings, and any attempt to establish other standards will constitute an act of violence against the principle of a free Society. There is no natural right for the possession of private property, nor for authoritarian leadership; once permitted they inevitably destroy the peace and general welfare. The whole history of mankind proves this statement.

Let us consider Anarchism as the scientific teaching of the natural relationship of men. Realizing that our knowledge of the world reaches no further than our senses can reach the Anarchist rejects all fruitless dreams. All that takes place in the universe is the result of activity inherent in matter. Upon this view, is based our moral doctrine, which may be summarized as follows:

Every living being strives unceasingly for enjoyment of life; this endeavor is the basis of all his actions. Each human being seeks to learn by what ways and means he can attain the highest purpose of life.

Through experience and observation one arrives at the conclusion that the individual separated from the society of his fellow-men, produces the mere necessities of life by the utmost wearisome labor, but that through the common labor of many, these necessities are wearily readily obtained, allowing leisure for the pursuit of arts and sciences, by which life is made pleasanter and richer; this knowledge imposes upon one the duty of working for the common well, since each individual welfare is assured only through universal well being.

The fact that the gifts, powers and dispositions of men are very different, leads one to the conclusion that the participation in the various labors of a group or community must be entirely voluntary, free from outward pressure, as free as the right to use and enjoy in unlimited measure the goods produced by common labor.

By experience and clear knowledge of the qualities of man, we arrive at the firm conviction that a lasting welfare of Society can be established only through free fellowship, i.e. through Communistic-Anarchist Society.[7]

By what means can such a Society be accomplished? Through the propaganda in word and deed, i.e. through the distribution of Anarchist literature and the courageous determination of a sufficient number of men and women not to participate in the present system of exploitation and slavery.

Anarchism is not only a beautiful philosophy of life but it is also the only logical theory for an economically and intellectually free society. It is not the careless thinker or a wild theorizer who can appreciate the ideal of a society based on free agreements of equals without law and bureaucracy. It is the Socialist politician who believes that rule and laws are a necessary part of life.

At the back of every law is the element of coercion. It is impossible to escape from that fact. Politicians and bureaucrats may argue that it is coercion for the good of underdeveloped workers. This means that coercion is not merely pure despotism but something even worse—the driving about of helpless human sheep. All tyrants and priests use the same arguments.

Anarchism alone embodies these days' social revolutionary ideals, without trimming or compromising. It does not aim at success that spells Dictatorship; it does not seek to gain the reins of government, nor strives to rule workers organizations. It works for the real enlightenment of the toilers, aiding them to that mental maturity which will enable them to accomplish their won emancipation.

By education, by free organization, by individual and associated resistance to economic and political tyranny,

---

7   The six paragraphs beginning with "The regeneration of Society" and ending with "Communistic-Anarchist Society" are taken from E. Steinle, "An Essay on the Scientific Principles of the Theory of Anarchism," *The Age of Thought* 1, no. 4 (July 1896) / 1, no. 5 (August 1896).

the Anarchists hope to achieve their aims. The task may seem hopeless to many, but it should be remembered that our movement is spreading in all countries. Modern science, art and literature are imbued with distinct anarchist tendencies.[8]

There are certain things that cannot be left to other, to be attended to by proxy. One of them is thinking. Man had issued to divide Providence the mandate to direct fate—and came to grief as a result. Political providence has now crowded the divine into the background, and the subjects, citizens, voters are again the duped.

Man will have to recover the power with which his ignorance has invented gods, statesmen, priests, and politicians, before he can achieve maturity and independence. That is the ABC of Anarchism.

The educated man is revolted by the thought that men and women are such ill-mannered beings that they can only be kept in order by a system of rules which might be fairly tolerable inside the boundary walls of a lunatic asylum.

We can imagine a reasonable man thinking that there are so many lunatics and financiers, lazy gentlefolk, as present in the world, that it may be necessary to continue a system of laws until we have got rid of them all or reduced them to some kind of social discipline. But it seems utterly preposterous that anyone of education could believe that these temporary laws can be part of a permanent and ultimate ideal of life.

Men are very quick to repudiate submission to a man; but when the slavery comes in guise of submission to law or custom or to a government not directly personal, they are very likely not to recognize it. The divinity which was formerly thought to hedge a king is now thought to hedge

---

8   The paragraph beginning "By education" and ending with "anarchist tendencies" is taken from the essay by Alfred Marsh above (see note 3).

laws and to sanction them. But a life minutely regulated by laws and customs may be essentially as far from a free life as one regulated by the will of a depot. The statement frequently put forward as an axiom that men must sacrifice many of their liberties in order that they may live together is not true; that they *have* sacrificed them is certain; but to say that they *must*, betrays a confusion of thought. A man cannot walk through a crowded street as he would walk through one that is deserted, but neither can he walk through a tangled forest with the same freedom with which he would walk through an open meadow; and yet he can hardly be said to sacrifice his freedom in walking through a tangled forest. His liberty would be restricted in any of these places if another man should approach him and force him to turn back, whether the man happened to be a private citizen or a public officer, and the act would be tyrannical whether the officer acted in accordance with the will of a depot or with the will of the people or with the law.

Freedom implies that if a man is doing anything which does not threaten the freedom of others, no man and no body of men have any right to interfere with him. "What," cry many of our philanthropic friends, "If we are fully persuaded that a certain act is for a man's own advantage and for that of society, while another act is greatly for his disadvantage, shall we not compel him to do the one and to abstain from doing the other?" No, for it is of more importance that the principle of freedom shall be preserved than that what you are persuaded is for the best shall be enforced.

This, of course, simply amounts to saying that freedom will yield better results in the long run than slavery.[9]

---

9   The three paragraphs beginning with "Men are very quick" and ending with "long run than slavery" are taken from Anonymous, "Perfect Liberty the Best of All," *Mother Earth* 8, no. 5 (1913): pp. 130–131.

Civilization and progress are words much conjured with. We boast of our industrial development and speak with pride of our commercial growth and even our intellectual achievements. We point the finger of scorn at the "backward" nations and enlarger upon our own steady progress. But *what is progress?* Giants of stone and steel, reared on human bones; mills and factories, slaughter-houses of body and mind; successful corners in the necessaries of life; multiplied volumes of statue books; the perfection of man-killing weapons; increased navies and armies—are these the meaning of civilization, the acme of progress? We seem to have lost all sense of criterion. Scarlet piles of stone or gold upon the ruins of human souls are the measure of our success. We have been stricken with blindness by the glare of Mammon. We have lost our path on the Broadway of Success. Yet Life is more, far more than mere success. And Life is individual. The one purpose of being is development; in free expression alone is satisfaction. Expression is growth; growth in freedom, progress. In man alone is progress. The external and the social must but indicate the inner. Woe to them when they hinder instead of reflecting the soul. That is barbarism, slavery.[10]

Freedom, liberty, and such words are found in dictionaries, but each year marks a decrease of the original article. As a man surcingles or puts a band around a horse, and draws it till he kills the horse or breaks the band, so are the people of this country, by the chain of legislation, denying liberty and paving the way for the clouds of evil that arise from too much law. In this country it is already a fact that, when a man cannot personally force his ideas into the life of a neighbor, he sets about rigging up a

---

10 The paragraph beginning "Civilization and progress" and ending with "That is barbarism, slavery" are taken from Anonymous (probably Max Baginski), "Observations and Comments," *Mother Earth* 3, no. 6 (1908): p. 242.

legislative propellant that shall bind the victim, and then, with the help of those who skin on shares or work for fees, pump the objectionable in or draw the milk out. If you wish an appliance that will shorten the freedom of our neighbor, go to the legislature and have it made—that is, if there are none already in stock. There are some places on the skin not yet covered by some kind of legislative plaster. A very few breathing pores left open. A few places where the stomach pump of taxation has not been inserted for the benefit of the inserter, but these spots or places are fast disappearing under the operation of the legislative cauterizer and puncturer.[11]

From the respect paid to property flow, as from a poisoned fountain, most of the evils and vices which render this world such a dreary scene to the contemplative mind. For it is in the most polished society that noisome reptiles and venomous serpents lurk under the rank herbage; and there is voluptuousness pampered by the still sultry air, which relaxes every good disposition before it ripens into virtue.

One class presses on another, for all are aiming to procure respect due only to talents and virtue. Men neglect the duties incumbent on man, yet are treated like demigods. The world is almost, literally speaking, a den of sharpers or oppressors.

There is a homely proverb, which speaks a shrewd truth, that whoever the devil finds idle he will employ. And what but habitual idleness can hereditary wealth and titles produce? For man is so constituted that he can only attain a proper use of his faculties by exercising them, and will not exercise them unless necessity of some kind first set the wheels in motion. Virtue likewise can only be

---

11 The paragraph beginning "Freedom, liberty and such words" and ending with "cauterizer and puncture" is taken from Anonymous, "The Stupidity of Legislation," *Mother Earth* 8, no. 7 (1913), p. 201.

acquired by the discharge of relative duties; but the importance of these sacred duties will scarcely be felt by the being who is cajoled out of his humanity by the flattery of sycophants. There must be more equality established in society or morality will never gain ground, and this virtuous equality will not rest firmly even when founded on a rock, if one-half of mankind be chained to its bottom by fate, for they will be continually undermining it through ignorance or pride.[12]

No man or woman who has looked at society with open, honest eyes can blind the fact that crime, like all other human actions, is the inevitable product of existing causes; that it springs up in poverty-stricken surroundings as surely as the cactus blooms in the desert. But "society," the propertied class that for the moment dominated the situation, steadily refuses to acknowledge this most obvious of facts, although it bends the knee weekly to a teacher who said, with all the emphasis language could afford, that men cannot gather figs of thorns, or grapes of thistles.

This deliberate blindness will continue until the eyes that now remain obstinately closed are forced to open; and the opening can come only as the result of education—learned stupidly by the whip of events or wisely by voluntary acceptance of the truth.[13]

Were it possible for someone to secure full control of the air, leaving mankind the alternative of paying tribute or strangling or want of breath, we should all of us become the serfs of the air monopoly. We should be forced to comply with its conditions, or die. Our dependence

---

12   The three paragraphs beginning with "From the respect" and ending with "ignorance or pride" are taken from Mary Wollstonecraft, *Vindication of the Rights of Women*, Chapter 5.

13   The two paragraphs beginning with "No man or woman" and ending with "voluntary acceptance of the truth" are taken from C.D. Light, *Crime and Punishment* (New York: Mother Earth Publishing Company, 1910), pp. 11–12.

would be most absolute. This unbearable situation would be further aggravated by irony and scorn if the constitution of the land contained the solemn proviso: "All citizens are equal before the law; their liberty must not be abridged by special privileges." Could anyone but a fool believe in this constitution-guarantee liberty, always remembering the command of the air monopolist: Submit of die! The liberty of choosing between submission and strangulation is but a two-edged slavery with destruction at either end.

It is this kind of liberty that the people of the "most progressive countries" enjoy. Instead of air read food, shelter, clothing, and you have the same terrible dependence of the people on the monopolists of land, production and money. The existence of the great majority is today made possible only by their slavish submission to the conditions of these masters of the earth.

Private property with its thousand and one corrupting influences is today the ruling power on earth. It dictates to the propertyless masses the compulsory statutes, to refuse to submit or to sacrifice one's independence, means the loss of the means of existence. That is the punishment visited upon those who, though poor, strive to preserve their manhood and their individuality.

But—unfortunately? Fortunately?—almost everyone adapts himself to the slavery of existence, even though many suffer, hesitate, tremble, and frit their teeth. Some go insane; many—men and women without number—are crippled bodily or mentally or both; others—and those by no means the worst— resort to suicide. Statistics throw considerable light upon these results of our profit-civilization.

The "justice" of this civilization depends neither upon court nor judges; it works "of itself", quietly, but is more merciless and inexorable that the most hard-hearted judge. It is the fate of the modern man under the rule of a production-system which is not intended to satisfy the needs of mankind, but which blindly works for the enrichment of the few.

Whether you work with your hands or your brain, if you refuse to offer yourself for sale, this "inner justice" will immediately reduce your rations, will rob you of shelter and home, and finally deprive you even of the small means necessary to secure mere bread or a ten-cent lodging. Before long you will have become an outcast, because you have offended against the discipline of this order which demands absolute economic submission.

Therefore try hard to sell yourself somehow or other; else you're lost and you will become a pauper, or—if you possess courage enough—you will turn criminal.

Sell your labor, ability, and intelligence; lie, cheat and swindle for you existence. What matters manhood, personality, self-respect. You are a mere cog in the machine of the "higher powers"; you are a bond serf who hates his task, or—if you are a brain worker — an intellectual helot who propagates opinions not his own, and teaches "fats" he knows nothing of, but which in some way serve the interests of his bread-givers. All this must be borne is you are to "do well" in the world. Why not? Must not the prostitute also follow the business? The same conditions which force her to sell her body, cause also the journalist to write what he does not believe, the teacher to teach what he himself refuses to accept, or the physician to perform operations to which he would not submit himself.

The difference between the slavery of former days and the existence-bondage of today is that formerly the slaves were forcible driven to the market, while the serfs of today offer themselves for sale of "their own free will." It is ironically called "free competition"; but behind each miserable free competitor stand want, hunger, and anxiety, more effective and compelling than the slave-driver's whip.

The marketability of men and things impresses upon society the character of prostitution. It is prostitution to be forced, for mere existence, to sell oneself, physically or mentally, to manufacturers or publishers.

Under such conditions who can speak of the dignity of labor? Work which is forced and hateful, and of the products of which the worker is deprived, is shameful and unworthy of the thinking man.

This boundless general venality comprises all the vice, evil, and crime which is the despair of the moralist and reformer, and which serve as a text to exhort man to honesty, righteousness, and neighborly love. Empty phrases! Mankind does not live up to the moral laws down on paper, because the very conditions of existence are based on the principle of taking advantage of our fellow-men.

* * *

In place of the domination of private property, in place of the shameless tyranny of profit, we would put Anarchist Communism. Its basic principle is, first of all, to guarantee to each man the right of existence, making the necessaries of life as accessible and free as air and sunshine. Without this fundamental right man is a pariah, a pauper at the mercy of those who own the means of existence.

The propertyless masses forever plead with the lords of the each for compassion, for mercy and reforms, instead of depriving them of their robber-monopoly and proclaiming the earth the free homestead and storehouse of mankind. It is just as if the calves would plead with the tanner not to tan their skins too deep a hue. The tanners would ignore their plea, as the owners of the earth will continue their usury in human flesh so long as they are not deprived of their monopoly of property.

It is not the bitterest irony that under the domination of sacred private property the majority of mankind lack all property? Under Anarchist Communism, which strives to abolish private possession, there would be no millionaires, billionaires, or stockholders, but every one would enjoy the means necessary to a wholesome life. If we wished to express it in a paradox we should say: only Communism will secure a man the possession of the earth.[14]

Lack of clarity, pusillanimity, and compromise are the worst curse of the American Labor movement. Of what benefit, for instance, can it be to the social or economic improvement of the workers if they are represented in the political dens of the plutocracy? The sole effect of such "successes" is to supply capitalist exploitation and governmental tyranny with new supporters bearing the label of Labor or Socialist parties.

Of what use is it to the workers what here and there some branch strike is occasionally won? Capitalism possesses no end of means to nullify the success of such strikers. Its power to revenge itself economically upon the workers, to intensify exploitation, raise the cost of living, and so forth, is practically limitless. Local strikes, if conducted in a revolutionary spirit, with an eye to the ultimate destruction of the robber system of private property, have propagandistic value. But as a means to the essential, fundamental emancipation of the toilers, they can not be seriously considered by the intelligent student.

The solution of the problem of labor—the abolition of wage slavery—is not to be found within the State regime. Our thoughts and actions must transcend these narrow boundaries, we must attack the very sources of wage slavery. These sources are private property, the State and— the third in the holy trinity—the Church. The rule of this trinity absolutely excludes the producers from well-being justice and liberty. No diplomatizing and politicianizing can help in this matter. So long as this trinity is not overthrown, misery, dependence and slavery are unavoidable.

---

14 The fifteen paragraphs beginning with "Were it possible" and ending with "possession of the earth" are taken from Max Baginski, "Communism the Basis of Liberty," *Mother Earth* 6, no. 3 (1911): pp. 76–78.

That is the point where Anarchists and the labor movement must finally meet on common ground. If the workers are not to turn utter traitors to the ideal of the emancipation, they must prepare for the final struggle with this trinity, and in that struggle the Anarchists will be their staunchest fellow fighters. The movement that the social revolutionary philosophy of Anarchism will combine with the intelligence of the workers, with their energy and strength, the doom of the dominant institution will be sealed.

In the face of the many dangerous errors and false conceptions dominating the labor movement, we shall neither bless nor curse, but persistently continue our agitation toward the hour when the more intelligent element of the proletariat will learn to understand us and will hold out to the Anarchists the hand of brotherhood, together to battle with the common enemy.[15]

Investigations so loudly clamored for by the politicians can only have the effect of pacifying and weakening labor. These proceedings and their reports can tell nothing new to the proletarian, even if the investigations be honest and sincere, which is rarely the case. On the other hand, their tendency is to arouse vain hopes and false conceptions of the character of the governmental machinery. And that is highly injurious to the growth of the revolutionary spirit, in which alone there is guarantee that the people themselves will conquer industrial and social Justice.

The workers, grown to maturity, will energetically call "Hands off" to the politicians, wherever these may seek to fish for voter in the troubled waters of strikes and other large struggles. Politicians are to be measured with the

---

15 The five paragraphs beginning with "Lack of clarity, pusillanimity" and ending with "the common enemy" are taken from Anonymous, "Anarchism Applied," *Mother Earth* 8, no. 6 (1913): p. 169.

same yardstick as priests—augurs all, who for thousands of years have been betraying the trust of the people and exploiting them to further their own personal interests and ambitions.

Among the encouraging signs of the time the most important is that legislatures, with their statutes and laws, are continually falling into greater contempt with the people. The sentiment is steadily growing in larger circles that the legal machinery is perfectly useless for the necessary social and economic improvement of the masses. The struggle of the toilers for better conditions takes place outside the halls of legislation. Wherever the workers have gained comparatively better living conditions, they did so not because of any laws or politicians, but exclusively as a result of their own efforts, courage, and solidarity.

This experience impresses itself daily with greater force upon the observation of the thinking proletarian. Step by step he is led to the conclusion that the final emancipation of labor can never come through any political Providence, but that on the contrary it must be the work of this initiative and determination.

He learns still more. He grows to understand that government and legislation are not only useless for the proletarian, but that they are positively harmful, the conscious enemies of labor, against whose emancipation they systematically rear new obstacles. Their purpose is to work for the greater development and glory of capitalism. They divide the spoils among its sycophants, and cover every injustice and brutality with the cloak of legal authority.

It is of utmost importance that the workers thoroughly realize all this. For only clarity of understanding can save them from again and again becoming the prey of politicians, which signifies the crippling and paralysis of the labor movement.

In the House of Commons Oliver Cromwell[16] once said: "There is one general grievance, and that is the law." A splendid motto for the revolutionary workers of today.

It is easy to understand why politicians of all parties look askance at the enlightenment of the masses in this direction. They feel themselves in danger of becoming superfluous; their inflated dignity and blustering importance is going to the devil. The more intelligent among them may occasionally even catch a glimpse of the day when the doors of the law factories will be closed, and the people will regulate their own affairs through free cooperative associations.

'Tis no promising outlook for the politicians, and they must therefore seek new ways and means to justify their existence.

One of these means, to which Socialist politicians resort to in particular, consist in playing the tail end on the occasion of the larger strikes. From that safe background they make a great noise, in order to impress the people with their importance as the "leaders of the vanguard" of the movement. The smallest factory boy knows that strikes can be fought and won only by the workers, but these superfluous politicians put on a very wise look, as though they were about to perform a great miracle for the strike, and then solemnly shout—legislative investigation!

That's just their line. Conferences with professional politicians, bureaucrats and would-be statesmen, exchange of conventional phrases, committee sessions, great waste of good paper and—much ado about nothing. The main thing is that the newspapers should herald the

---

16   Oliver Cromwell (1599–1658) was an English general, politician and statesman. After leading the Parliamentarian forces to victory in the English Civil War and arranging for the execution of Charles I, Cromwell was established as Lord Protector. His regime would collapse under his son, Richard Cromwell, leading to the restoration of Charles II.

tireless activity of the Messrs. politicians. They are off—they have departed for the strike regions—ah, how they sacrifice themselves for the people, at the same timekeeping a shark eye for a chance to increase their own political prestige among the ignorant.

If the workers accept as leader one of the intellectuals of self-appointed reformers in place of a man risen from their ranks, they are as badly off as ever. The intellectual has his own definite set of interests, and though they man coincide with those of the proletariat in calm and sunny weather, they are bound to separate in time of storm and stress. Artists, scientists, thinkers, in a word of the intellectuals, do not have an ingrained class consciousness. They have interests which labor has not yet had the leisure to cultivate; they have possessions, material and spiritual, which they dare not run the risk of losing. They are the neutrals, as it were, in the conflict between the capitalists and the workers. If they favor the proletariat they can render valuable aid. Labor should never disdain their aid but it should never deliver to them its independence.

Workers should be less sheep and more like men. Then if their leaders deserted them their onward movement would not cease. Each mans should learn to think for himself, to arrive at opinions independently of his fellows. If each man reached a certain conclusion in his mind played upon by the logic of events, and all these individual conclusions happened to shape themselves toward a common end, there would arise in their collective action, a strength and power that no amount of money and no force of government could defy.

It is not surprising that investigating the conditions in strike districts becomes ever more popular with politicians of all shades. Investigations are well calculated to cover up the rottenness of our social conditions. The people indeed feel that something is wrong; they notice the fearful stench coming from somewhere. But the politicians are immediately at hand to perfume the obnoxious spot with the investigation disinfectant. And the good citizen thanks them, "Ah, after all, something is being done to purify the air." To be sure, something is being done: the good people are being hoodwinked by the politicians. If anything of vital importance is to be emasculated of its significance, all that is necessary is to order a legislative investigation, and the matter will quickly be demagogically distorted beyond all recognition. Investigations are the cheapest trick of the masters to get around the pressing social and economic problems.[17]

* * *

The masters argue that because we cannot have equality in a silk factory we cannot have it anywhere. Because we cannot have good-fellowship in business we cannot have it at all. They argue that society cannot do without "labor," meaning servitude—without the bossing and the firing and the too old at forty and all the rest of their filth. If society cannot do without masters and wage slaves, so much the worse for society. For we are prepared to sacrifice our machines, our wheels and tunnels and wires and systems and slave lines for one hour of happiness.

Do not be led astray by the towering materialism which dominates the mind of the wage earners today which rests upon the false assumption that because a few generations go on doing the same thing over and over again, we all live in a system of clock-work evolution. Do not let fear prevent you from leading a free life. Live up to your own ideal and to the standard inscribed on the banner—No Gods, No Masters.[18]

---

17 The twelve paragraphs beginning with "Among the encouraging signs" and ending with "economic problems" are taken from Anonymous, "Blustering Politicians," *Mother Earth* 8, no. 4 (1913): pp. 97–99.

18 The two paragraphs beginning with "The masters argue" and

The development of consciously intelligent units among the working class is the only factor toward genuine progress. To make labor conscious of itself, of its tremendous inherent strength and of its limitations, to foster its sense of critical judgment, its examination into the cogs of things, to impress upon it the secret of the vast power of concerted action, to do these things is to emancipate labor from the bondage, not only of society, but also of itself.

The leaders usually desert the rank and file in an issue of emergency. They become better educated, adopt a higher standard of living, and get out of touch with their fellow workmen; they rise in the social scale, they go into politics, hobnob with the capitalists and compromise the interests of labor.

Powerful as the master class is depicted to be, owing to the apparent acquiescence and ignorance of its victims, it is inherently in a weak and dangerous position. For its very life it now depends upon the division and delusions which sway the working class. And these divisions and delusions are fostered and maintained by paid union officials, writers, and politicians, aided by a venal press.

* * *

Perhaps the most popular and enervating idea accepted by the majority of workers today, is the doctrine of economic evolution, a doctrine which was formulated by the 'sociologists' and which asserts that the capitalist system of production for profit cannot be broken by any conscious effort on the part of the workers; that we must have masters and recognize the authority of masters until the dawn of some 'ism. The one thing the sociologists like to talk about is "Evolution," i.e., expansion and development.

---

ending with "No Gods, No Masters" is taken from Margaret Sanger, "No Masters," *The Woman Rebel* 1, no. 6 (1914): p. 47.

The evolutionist, like the madman, is in a prison—the prison of one idea. These people seem to think it singularly surprising if the worker suddenly flings to the wind all social theories and raises the banner "No Masters." They system must go on, they say. The time is not yet "ripe" for a change. The "machinery of government" and the "machinery of production" must be captured and so on.

To tell the workers that they must wait for the accumulation of capital and for the "economic development" of the capitalist regime is like telling a prisoner in the penitentiary that he would be glad to hear that the jail now covers the state of New York. The jailer would have nothing to show the prisoner except more and more long corridors of stones lit by ghastly lights and empty of all that is human. So these expanders and evolutionists have nothing to show us except more and more infinite multitudes of wage slavery empty of all individuality, courage, idealism, humanity and spirit, and hopelessly submissive to the demigods of Capital.

No one doubts that the ordinary worker can get on with the capitalist system as it is—at a price. The demand of the class-conscious worker however, is not strength enough to get along with it, but to destroy it.[19]

Under Anarchist Communism work will not be for profit but for use. The products of free cooperative labor will not be steadily handed over to speculation, but would be directly at the disposal of the consumer. Production and consumption would go hand in hand, eliminating the parasitism for the middle-man and trader. There would be neither room nor desire for "cold storage", to create artificial scarcity of necessaries, to advance prices for the enrichment of the speculator. Shoes, clothing, and other necessary articles will then not be manufactured for the

---

19 The five paragraphs beginning with "Powerful as the master class…" and ending with "but to destroy it" are edited and paraphrased from Sanger, "No Masters" (see footnote 18 above).

trade, but for the needs of the community, for the men, women and children requiring those articles. Agriculture and cattle raising will not be for the purpose of giving some speculator a corner of the products at the cost of human misery and want, but for the sake of human well-being, to satisfy the physical needs of the people. Under such a social arrangement men would no longer be the miserable products of material conditions; they would possess the power and intelligence to order society in harmony with individual independence, and cease to be the helpless subjects of environment.

On the basis of assured existence individual liberty will flourish. For now man need no more prostitute his labor and ability, each free to follow his inclination and enjoy life to his full capacity.

Labor, science, love will no more be degraded by being sold to the highest bidder. They are freed form servitude. The place of the institutions of force and of the whip of hunger is now taken by the production-associations of free men and women.

We call ourselves Anarchists Communists because we consider the economics of Communism as the indispensable fundamental condition for social harmony and of the liberty and independence of the individual.[20]

The hopes of the Anarchists for a grand future are based upon the exercise of the feeling of solidarity of free individuals. We do not wish to catechize people. The business of making man uniform we leave to military drillers. Anarchism recognizes the diversity of life, the differentiation of individuality in its fullest sense. It finds in voluntary communism—free enjoyment of commodities— the safest material basis for the highest development of

20 The four paragraphs beginning with "Under Anarchist Communism" and ending with "the independence of the individual" are taken from Baginski, "Communism the Basis of Liberty (see footnote 14 above).

diversity, which after all is the only creative source of life. Social institutions can have but one reason for existence, to lift man out of his bondage; but in the name of various deities, man had ever been subjugated, he was ever to lose himself for the sake of something foreign to his real nature. In Anarchism, however, the individual is to refine himself, and to become a conscious molder of the conditions of life.[21]

* * *

Leave men free and the needs of the moment will enforce cordial unison. Man is a social being and in the absence of coercive interference his own interests would lead him to closer unison with his fellows, to a kinder regard for their necessities, to a warmer interest in their welfare and a clearer conception that their distress relieved would be his own social advancement. This is not the view of a sect, but founded upon the fundamental principles of human nature. Remove restrictions and the incentive to greed and selfishness disappears. Proclaim liberty and the better nature of man will assume control and in the genial warmth of an emancipated race a closer social feeling would be engendered, in which disputes relative to the different merits of deeds and needs would sink into insignificance and deserved derision.

The most oft-quoted objection with by the anarchist is that pertaining to violence. It would seem, were one to take this objection seriously, that any form of government, no matter how despotic, is preferable to no government at all. To the casual observer this reason is sufficient to preclude any further investigation of the subject. And yet,

---

21 The paragraph beginning with "The hopes of the anarchists" and ending with "conditions of life" are taken from Anonymous (probably Max Baginski), "Observations and Comments," *Mother Earth* 1, no. 9 (1906): pp. 4–5.

if even the superficially inclined would give but passing thought to the question they would be bound to admit that all government either in theory or practice depends finally upon physical force; upon violence for its continuance. The law of a nation is in itself nothing but a paper threat depending entirely upon coercion and violence to enforce it.

To say that without authority or the fear of authority, all sorts of crimes would continually be indulged in is not entirely true. This is provable, not by mere theory, but by practical observations of facts.

The per capita protection of urban communities in the person of police is much less on the whole than that of the large cities. Nevertheless the number of crimes committed in the thickly populated districts far exceeds those committees in the rural communities. Not only is the excess actual, but it is also proportional. There are extenuating circumstances and contributing causes, no doubt, which make for this abnormal lawlessness in the cities as compared to the villages, but the fact remains that fewer crimes are committed where fewer minions of force and brutality patrol the by-ways in their continual hunt for trouble.

Not even the lowest slum proletarian can vie in corruption with the most successful policeman. The very nature of his calling deprives him of all sense of justice. Modern society has no competitor with the policeman and detective in viciousness unless it is the politician—the master and maker of both. The individual police officer is necessarily different from any other member of society when he first assumes the role of public guardian. But the close and continual association with all that is base inhumanity produces an environment that even educated men would eventually succumb to, let alone the policeman who is seldom ever over-intelligent.

If the average quality of what is considered good citizenship were of no finer degree than the personnel of the forces of law and order we would each and every one have to be officers to protect ourselves from our friends. The truth is apparent that all peoples are naturally peaceful or it would not be possible for a comparatively handful of policemen to control multitudes of the people and hold them in check.

* * *

Sincerity of purpose always expresses itself in action. Such sincerity never fails to compel attention. So long as you merely talk about your ideals, they will remain mere ideals. But if your talk is no mere lip-service, if you feel your convictions, if they permeated your being, they will inevitably express themselves in your daily life, in your attitude toward things, in your every action. They will then shape your life; they will make you different from other people, in proportion as your ideal is different from theirs. Then your ideal will cease to be merely an ideal. It will have become a part of yourself; and to that extent, materialized. Thus, and thus only, are ideals propagated and transmitted into life.

Anarchy is such an ideal. It expresses the highest conception of individual liberty and social solidarity. It is not a mere theory to be realized in some distant future. It is a mode of living, to be practiced right *here* and *now*.

FAREWELL TO SASHA (1936)[1]

It is very difficult to write of the demise of a comrade and friend with whom you were intimately connected for so many years. Innermost feelings seem cold on printed pages.

Only those who worked and lived side by side with Alexander Berkman felt and esteemed the fine spiritual qualities of our departed comrade. Anarchists are not made of different clay than the rest of humanity. Human as they are, they also have their differences and misunderstandings, but I dare say that Sasha never had a bitter antagonist in our movement.

Berkman was a fine combination of an active rebel and a clear intellectual thinker. His work among us has been appreciated, and will be appreciated, as years pass by—as long as Anarchism is propagated. To the last hours of his life he worked for the Ideal, to which he had consecrated his life.

Berkman's *Prison Memoirs of an Anarchist*, *The Bolshevik Myth*, and *The A.B.C. of Anarchism* will remain standard works in our movement.

Although deported from our country, he belonged to the last hour in his journey on this planet to the Anarchist Movement in America. His death closes one of the heroic periods of our movement in this country.

And what a coincidence! Alexander Berkman dies at the hour when the struggle against the Steel Barons breaks

---

1   This tribute appeared in the pamphlet *Alexander Berkman: Rebel and Anarchist*, published by the Alexander Berkman Memorial Committee and the Jewish Anarchist Federation (New York) in July 1936. Berkman died on June 28, 1936 in Nice, France from complications from a self-inflicted gunshot wound.

out anew.[2] It was at the seat of the mighty in Pittsburgh that he struck at the oligarchy and it was here that he suffered so many years of martyrdom.

Facing today a new ordeal, the Steel Workers ought to keep the name of Alexander Berkman as a symbol in their hearts and an ensign of victory.

---

2   Havel is most likely referring to the Steel Workers Organizing Committee, a CIO union founded in Pittsburgh on June 17, 1936. The SWOC made dramatic breakthroughs in organizing steelworkers before disbanding in 1942 to assist in the formation of the United Steel Workers of America.

THE GREAT HERITAGE (1940)[1]

In joining the great line of martyrs for freedom Francisco Ferrer y Guardia left us a great heritage: the ideal of the Modern School.

The shots before the fortress of Montjuich in Barcelona ended the life of an individual, but gave life to education through self-development. Inspired by the work of the Spanish martyr some comrades to the idea in New York organized the Francisco Ferrer Association: the result was the Modern School in Stelton, celebrating this month the twenty-fifth year of its existence.

Twenty-five years of heartrending struggle to keep the school alive... and so very few realize the importance of the institution. We hear nowadays many effusions about democracy... the only path toward democracy is the education of the child through self-development as practiced in the Modern School. Many of us are only too eager to criticize some phases in the development of the School, but taking the general situation in consideration we find how picayune our objections and criticisms prove to be.

Observing the children of the Modern School at play and at work we notice only the true path toward freedom: development of free individuals through self-expression.

The great forerunners and pathfinders in libertarian education, a Rousseau, a Tolstoi, a Froebel, a Montessori, a Pestalozzi, great nonconformists like Whitman and Thoreau... all would feel themselves at home in the

---

1 This essay appeared in a pamphlet entitled *The Modern School of Stelton Twenty-Fifth Anniversary*, published in May 1940 by the Modern School.

Modern School. [2] They would rejoice in observing the children in activity at play and at work.

And no less a person than the grandson of two presidents of the United States has left us a remarkable testament on education: *The Education of Henry Adams.*

Declaring that education has never been stated and cannot be stated in terms of dollars and cents, Adams declares:

> "A teacher must either treat education as a catalogue, a record, a romance, or as an evolution; whether he affirms or denies evolution he falls into the burning fagots of the pit. He makes of his scholars either priests or atheists, plutocrats or socialists, judges or anarchists, almost in spite of himself. The chief wonder of education is that it does not ruin everybody concerned in it, teachers and taught."[3]

The Modern School did not fall into such a pit. Free development through self-expression is the goal and no free society is possible without free individuals.

The Modern School is in need of a greater support from individuals and organizations striving for a free

---

2   In addition to previously cited (or famous) individuals, Havel is referring, respectively, to Friedrich Froebel (1782–1852), a German educator and reformer who originated the idea of the kindergarten; Maria Montessori (1870–1952), Italian educator and physician who developed the Montessori method of education; and Johann Heinrich Pestalozzi (1746–1827), a Swiss educator and theorist who integrated the ideas of organized education systems with the Romantic movement. All three were great innovators in primary education.

3   *The Education of Henry Adams* (New York: Houghton Mifflin Company, 1918), pp. 300–301.

society. It is kept alive through sacrifice on the part of the Principal and Teaching Staff and the comrades of the Board of Management. In neglecting to support the school libertarians commit a great error and a great crime against their own ideals.

SUGGESTIONS
FOR FURTHER READING

Alexander, Doris. *Eugene O'Neill's Last Plays: Separating Art from Autobiography*. Athens: University of Georgia Press, 2005.

Antliff, Allan. *Anarchist Modernism: Art, Politics, and the First American Avant-Garde*. Chicago: University of Chicago Press, 2007.

Avrich, Paul. *Anarchist Voices: An Oral History of Anarchism in America*. Oakland, Calif.: AK Press, 2005.

Avrich, Paul. *Sasha and Emma: The Anarchist Odyssey of Alexander Berkman and Emma Goldman*. Cambridge, Mass.: Harvard University Press, 2012.

Avrich, Paul. *The Modern School Movement: Anarchism and Education in the United States*. Princeton: Princeton University Press, 1980.

Ben-Zvi, Linda. *Susan Glaspell: Her Life and Times*. Oxford: Oxford University Press, 2005.

Bruns, Roger. *The Damnedest Radical: The Life and World of Ben Reitman, Chicago's Celebrated Social Reformer, Hobo King, and Whorehouse Physician*. Chicago: University of Illinois Press, 2001.

Buchan, Perdita. *Utopia, New Jersey: Travels in the Nearest Eden*. New Brunswick, N.J.: Rutgers University Press, 2007.

Cornell, Andy. *Unruly Equality: U.S. Anarchism in the Twentieth Century*. Berkeley: University of California Press, 2016.

Dowling, Robert. *Eugene O'Neill: A Life in Four Acts*. New Haven, Conn.: Yale University Press, 2014.

Falk, Candace. *Love, Anarchy, and Emma Goldman*. New

York: Holt, Rinehart, and Winston, 1984.

Falk, Candace, Barry Pateman, and Jessica Moran, eds. *Emma Goldman: A Documentary History of the American Years, Volume One: Made for America, 1890–1901*. Berkeley: University of California Press, 2008.

Falk, Candace, Barry Pateman, and Jessica Moran, eds. *Emma Goldman: A Documentary History of the American Years, Volume Two: Making Speech Free, 1902–1909*. Berkeley: University of California Press, 2008.

Falk, Candace, Barry Pateman, and Jessica Moran, eds. *Emma Goldman: A Documentary History of the American Years, Volume Three: Light and Shadows, 1910–1916*. Stanford, Calif.: Stanford University Press, 2012.

Freilicher, Mel. *The Encyclopedia of Rebels*. San Diego: San Diego City Works Press, 2014.

Goyens, Tom. *Radical Gotham: Anarchism in New York from Schwab's Saloon to Occupy Wall Street*. Chicago: University of Illinois Press, 2017.

McFarland, Gerald. *Inside Greenwich Village: A New York City Neighborhood, 1898–1918*. Boston: University of Massachusetts Press, 2005.

Reichert, William O. *Partisans of Freedom: A Study in American Anarchism*. Bowling Green, Oh.: Bowling Green University Popular Press, 1976.

Watson, Steve. *Strange Bedfellows: The First American Avant-Garde*. New York: Abbeville Press, 1991.

Zimmer, Kenyon. *Immigrants Against the State: Yiddish and Italian Anarchism in America*. Chicago: University of Illinois Press, 2015.

INDEX

N